3-14

E. WILDER SPAULDING · THE QUIET INVADERS

E. WILDER SPAULDING

THE QUIET INVADERS

THE STORY OF THE AUSTRIAN IMPACT UPON AMERICA

With a Foreword by

JOSEF STUMMVOLL

VIENNA

ÖSTERREICHISCHER BUNDESVERLAG
FÜR UNTERRICHT, WISSENSCHAFT UND KUNST

1968

Distributed in the United States by
Frederick Ungar Publishing Co.,
10003 New York

Cover design: Franz Röckel, A 1014 Vienna

Printed in Austria

Printed by E. Becvar, A 1130 Vienna

To my many Austrian friends who came to the United States in 1938
and to the even greater number
who had to endure Nazism at home.

CONTENTS

FOREWORD

At the invitation of the Library of Congress I was able to spend much of the winter of 1948—1949 in visiting that great American national library as well as some other significant libraries in the United States. Just before I returned to Austria the Director of the Library of Congress and later General Director of Unesco, Dr. Luther H. Evans, introduced me to Dr. E. Wilder Spaulding of the Department of State. Spaulding was about to depart for Austria as his government's Cultural Attaché in Vienna.

Some weeks later we met in Vienna. There, between Dr. Spaulding and me, began the kind of rare friendship that doesn't end with the exchange of a few Christmas and New Year's cards. Certainly Dr. Spaulding's interest, as a Harvard-trained historian, in the cultural bases of early and recent history and thus in Austria's past that has so often been cultural (Austria's theater and music and literature have especially appealed to him), provided us with many common interests.

In the fall of 1949 when the Austro-American Institute of Education — which has helped so many Americans to make themselves at home in Austria and so many Austrians to understand a bit of America — when that Institute was facing a crisis, Dr. Spaulding, as Cultural Attaché, asked me whether I could not take the chairmanship of its Board of Directors. I did accept that chairmanship, the crisis was overcome, and the Institute has continued until this time to serve as common ground where Americans and Austrians meet and enjoy one another.

This success sealed our friendship. It naturally involved even our families. And when Dr. Spaulding was transferred to Bonn, to be Cultural Attaché there in Germany, I regretted it very much.

Two years later when Spaulding returned to the United States he found that he could not forget Austria. He had become very fond of our little country. He had read much of its history and literature. But he found that although American historians had written scores of books about, for instance, the Irish, the Poles, the Czechs, the Hungarians, and many other nationalities in the United States, the German-speaking subjects of the old Habsburg monarchy were generally subsumed under the label "Germany".

Dr. Spaulding realized this gap in America's history and resolved to close it. The author of the standard work, "New York in the Critical Period, 1783—1789" (1932), was well qualified for the task. He spent several years in exhausting American sources and the Austrian sources available to him in the United States and wrote the present book. All his friends and acquaintances who have known of his project have applauded it.

The completed manuscript has been read by me, with the assistance of Dr. Walter G. Wieser of my staff, and by numerous Austrian and American friends of Dr. Spaulding. In 1964 there appeared the possibility that the work could be published in the Museion Series of the Austrian National Library.

That possibility Dr. Spaulding at first rejected. That was characteristic of his wish to avoid any indication of influence from the Austrian side. His spirit of fairness led him to believe that it would be more proper to have the book edited and printed in the United States in order that its intellectual independence might be ensured.

He communicated with several American publishers who were either not at all interested in the book or who wanted to change the manuscript to suit their wishes. Meanwhile Dr. Spaulding came twice to Austria and talked over his problems with me. The idea of cultural pluralism – that America was welcoming other cultures without insisting that they be submerged in some old concept of one-hundred percent Americanism – seemed important to both of us. I felt I should repeat my offer that our National Library cooperate in the publication of such a competent account of Austria's influence upon America. It was a great pleasure to me that the author then agreed to have his study published with the cooperation of our National Library.

The Library of Congress may eventually be in a position to promote a counterpart to this book – a book on America's influence upon Austria. Whether the author should be American or Austrian, I should be proud to have him realize that in the publication of this book it never occurred to me to try to influence the author to include the favorable or to eliminate the unfavorable. I can state here in all candor that Spaulding has been under no pressure whatsoever from the Austrian side to make substantive changes in his book. That does not mean, on the other hand, that my assistant, Dr. Wieser, and I are in agreement with all the views and nuances expressed by the author.

This book, the work of an American diplomat and historian (recently referred to as a "classic scholar of New York History") is now ready. I hope that it will find many understanding and friendly readers in America, Austria, and elsewhere; and that its appearance will provide inspiration for many similar studies.

Vienna

JOSEF STUMMVOLL
Ph. D., Sc. D., M. Sc.
Former Director General of the Austrian National Library

ACKNOWLEDGMENTS

The author owes his interest in Austria and the Austrians primarily to the hundreds of friendly Austrians who did so much to introduce him to their country while he lived in Vienna from the sad days of 1949 to the far more hopeful ones of 1955. Their insistent pessimism, combined with his growing realization that many fine things were still stirring in the little Alpine land, led him to wonder whether the Austrian impact upon the western world, and especially upon the United States, had not been much greater than the modest Austrians and the too-distant Americans had been willing to admit. The result was the present study.

The author owes much to Dr. Wilhelm Schlag, director of the Austrian Institute in New York. Not only did Dr. Schlag's fine essay on Austrian emigration to the United States – the only competent study ever published on the subject – serve as a sturdy foundation for the present work, but Dr. Schlag's personal advice and assistance were of great value. DDr. Josef Stummvoll, Director General of the Austrian National Library, not only reviewed the manuscript and allowed his very helpful assistant, Dr. Walter G. Wieser, to check innumerable facts, but he also provided invaluable encouragement.

The author is also greatly indebted to Professor Robert A. Kann of Rutgers University who helped clarify many of the nationality problems of the old monarchy, to Angelo Eagon of the United States Information Agency whose suggestions for revising the chapters on music were indispensable, and to Dr. Frederick Ungar of New York whose comments were invaluable.

Among those who helped with the revision of chapters in fields where the author was far from being at home were Professor Stefan Horn of Georgetown University, Professor Eduard F. Sekler, architect of Harvard, and the philosophers Professor Alfred Stern of the California Institute of Technology, Dr. William Gerber of Washington and Professor Boyd Graves of the University of Virginia (the latter one of the dozens of competent Americans who helped Austria to get on its feet at the end of World War II).

Dr. Oscar Karbach gave genereously of his knowledge of Jewry in Austria and the United States. Professor Felix F. Strauss in science, Dr. Joseph Wilder in medicine and Dr. Emilio von Hofmannsthal were all of genuine assistance.

The bibliographical publications of the United States Committee to Promote Studies of the Habsburg Monarchy have been useful. Many librarians should be mentioned with appreciation and gratitude. Miss Georgia Cowen of the Washington Public

Library and several of her colleagues were most helpful. The librarians of the Austrian Institute in New York, of the Carl Schurz Memorial Foundation Library at Philadelphia, of the National Science Foundation Library and of the American Institute of Architects in Washington, not to speak of Dr. J. Mayerhöfer of the Austrian National Library, have all been most cooperative.

At the Library of Congress, where the gaps in its Austrian titles would doubtless distress the Vienna-born architect of its main building, Mr. David J. H. Cole, the author's erudite friend James B. Childs, and the Austrian-born Dr. J. L. Dewton were all interested in my project as well as helpful. And at home the author's son John Spaulding caught some serious errors, questioned the inclusion of some names and the omission of others, and, all in all, contributed much to the completion of the manuscript.

Washington, D. C. *E. WILDER SPAULDING*

CHAPTER I

THE QUIET MIGRATION

To learn that a few years ago, at mid-century, only four foreign lands had furnished more distinguished Americans for listing in "Who's Who in America" than little Austria would surprise most Americans.[1] They would doubtless be even more surprised to discover from the 1962–63 edition of the "Who's Who of American Women" that Austria ranked third, after only Germany and Canada, in supplying distinguished foreign-born women for inclusion in the volume.[2] For a foreign-speaking land, lying farther east than any of the countries which colonized the American continent in our formative years, small as the state of Maine and less populous than the city of New York, to take its place as a major contributor to American life and culture is indeed surprising.[3]

Most of us would think first of a dozen other nationalities whose immigrants have helped to make American history – of Italy, Poland, Sweden, the Netherlands, Hungary, France, and Ireland, as well as the four peoples who came first in the "Who's Who" for 1952: the Canadians, British, Russians, and Germans. For the Austrians were the quiet immigrants. From the very start they were content to be counted with the Germans and, in later years, to rush for their first papers for American citizenship without stopping to wave the flag of the often unpopular Habsburgs or the little-known Austrian Republic. An amazing number of distinguished Austro-Americans have been playing a part in American life for over a century without beating any drums for their native land. Indeed, they constituted – quite unlike so many other peoples who came here to shout the achievements of their homelands and of their compatriots from the housetop – the quiet migration.

Most of the Austrians have come so quietly and with so little to say about the glories of the old monarchy or the charm of the young republic that Americans are surprised to learn that they were ever anything but American. That is true of film greats like Billy Wilder, Jed Harris, Otto Preminger and Sam Spiegel, of lawyers like Justice Felix Frankfurter, of actors like Paul Muni, Paul Henreid, Oscar Homolka, Luise Rainer, Erich von Stroheim, Walter Slezak, and Lotte Lenya, of many fine figures in the world of opera like Rudolf Bing, and Maria Jeritza, of composers like Schönberg, Korngold, and Frederick Loewe, of dozens of impressarios and orchestra conductors like Fritz Stiedry and Erich Leinsdorf, and of notable virtuosos like Fritz Kreisler. It has also been true of Nobel Prize winners like the physicists Pauli and

Hess, of other scientists including Frederic de Hoffmann who helped to create the hydrogen bomb, of many physicians like Manfred Sakel who gave us shock therapy, of important figures in the arts such as the architect Neutra, of some significant names in business like Brentano who founded the famous bookstores, Kohler of plumbing fame, Hattie Carnegie, and Drive-Yourself Hertz. Others like Franz Werfel, Max Reinhardt, and the Trapp family singers were more often recognized as Austrians. In any event, the sum total of the distinguished Austrians who came here to live or work is amazingly large.

And the Austrians have not only come here as immigrants but they have contributed much from their Alpine and Danubian strongholds to American life. Austrians like Mozart and Haydn and Mesmer and Freud and Adler and Hitler and the dozen or more Austrian Nobel Prize winners in medicine and the other sciences may or may not have come to the United States but they have shaken our world. The Hitler, whom Austrians despise as heartily as he despised them, was Austrian by birth and education. And the great figures like Beethoven and Brahms and Prince Eugene of Savoy and Metternich, who were born elsewhere but found their life work in Austria, made history that Americans cannot disregard. No one could maintain that the impact of such triflers with human history as Metternich and Freud and Hitler was a quiet one. But the understanding that momentous things like the Monroe Doctrine and psychoanalysis with all its breathtaking accompaniments and the evil genius of Nazism had roots in little Austria is given little attention in this country. In this study we shall mention some Austrians, native or adopted, whose impact upon America was notable even though they themselves never came here.

An English historian has written of Austria's Habsburg dynasty that "No other family has endured so long or left so deep a mark upon Europe: the Habsburgs were the greatest dynasty of modern history, and the history of central Europe revolves round them, not they round it."[4] They ruled Austria as dukes and archdukes after 1282, Hungary and Bohemia as kings after 1526, Austria as emperors after 1804, Spain as its royalty from 1516 to 1700 before Spain's decline, and they were German emperors, with some significant breaks, from 1273 to the abolition of the Holy Roman Empire in 1806. Yet the Habsburgs are doubtless almost unknown, by comparison with, for instance, the ruling family of Monaco, in the United States.

And the great role of the Austrians in Central Europe as a barrier, so significant in world history, is relatively unknown here: that the Romans established on the Danube near Vienna their frontier against the barbarians to the northward; that the eastern tribes that always threatened to overwhelm western Europe were so often stopped on the Austrian frontier as the Turks were stopped in the sixteenth and seventeenth centuries at Vienna's own gates; that German nationalism ran into Austrian opposition in the nineteenth century and discovered that it could establish itself only by the defeat of Austria (1866) so that it could create a far more nationalistic

Reich than the cosmopolitan, melting-pot Austrians would have agreed to; and that Soviet aggression after World War II yielded to Austria's complete rejection of communist wiles and propaganda, the only part of the old monarchy that rejected communism so firmly that it never went behind the iron curtain. Austria's liberation in 1955 was the first triumph of the West – the only retreat that communism had made since the end of the war. Austria was still playing its ancient role of barrier against the East.

Our failure to understand the significance of the Austrians was illustrated by a book written by the author's own German teacher, Francis E. Clark, whose "Old Homes of New Americans: the Country and the People of the Austro-Hungarian Monarchy and their Contribution to the New World" (Boston and New York 1913), is concerned with all the Austro-Hungarians except the core-Austrians. Professor Clark, a German teacher, was interested in all the nationalities of the monarchy that were non-German. That is, an American writing a half century ago could assume that his American readers could interest themselves in the Hungarians and Czechs, Croats and Poles, and most of the people of the Habsburg monarchy, excepting only the core-Austrians.

It is interesting, but perhaps not surprising, to note that, while there are dozens of books in American libraries on the contributions that virtually every people in Europe have made to American life, there is no full-length study of the Austrian contribution. There are reasons for that.

Austria has always, up to 1918, been submerged, to the American mind, in its empire. Back in 1784, for instance, Secretary of State Thomas Jefferson, in instructing his ministers to negotiate commercial treaties, referred to Russia, Prussia, Denmark, and so forth, but to "the Court of Vienna."[5] Secretary of State Seward wrote in 1861 that the Austrian Empire "is largely ... destitute of the element of nationality." He added that we find Italians and Hungarians in the United States, "but no one has ever seen a confessed Austrian among us."[6] And much later, in 1910, the United States Immigration Commission reported that Austrian was "not a race name and not used by the Bureau of Immigration and Naturalization. It has no significance as to the physical race or language ... The term 'Austrian' simply means an inhabitant or native of Austria." The Commission added, it is interesting to notice, that the Swiss also did not constitute a race, and that the Belgians likewise not constituting a race were not recognized by the Bureau of Immigration.[7] Such findings may sound as unconvincing as quibbling about the right of the United States to have a place in international statistics on the ground that it is racially only a transplant from Europe.

Indeed, our immigration, naturalization, and census officials found so few "confessed Austrians" in the long years before the creation of the Austrian Republic in 1919, and they were so confused by the multitude of nationalities that came to us from the Habsburg monarchy, that our statistics for Austrian immigrants and Austrian-born are almost useless.[8] They are so scrambled, not only to 1919 but for later years when immigrants showed no consistency in reporting their native places, that they will never be unscrambled. "Germans" born in Prague, for instance, might report that they were born before 1918 in Austria-Hungary, Austria, Bohemia, or Czechoslovakia. And a Transylvanian could state that he had been born in Austria or Hungary or Austria-Hungary or Rumania or Transylvania.

Thus, the immigration and census statistics used in this volume are for the most part mere approximations of the facts. Figures for what the Census Bureau calls Austria-Hungary (which existed only from 1867 to 1918) were first reported as of 1861. Then, since 1905, Austria and Hungary were separately reported. The Austrian Republic has been separately reported since World War I except for 1938–1945 when it was included with Germany. Meanwhile, despite the division of Poland in the eighteenth century between Austria, Prussia, and Russia, Poland was reported separately from 1820 to 1898 but the Polish-speaking immigrants were later and until 1918 assigned to either Austria, Germany, or Russia. Bohemia, including Moravia as well as Bohemia proper, with all their ethnic Germans, was also listed separately.

There were other statistical practices that served to confuse the record: only steerage passengers were included in the first immigration statistics, temporary visitors were included in the statistics up to 1867, a logical division between immigrants and non-immigrants (those already resident here or not intending to live here) was arrived at only in 1906, and in that year also immigrants were assigned to the countries of last permanent residence instead of to the countries from which they came. Much of the very considerable European immigration that came by way of Canada, and the lesser amount that came via Mexico, was uncontrolled and uncounted. And the fact that thousands of immigrants who came as Austrians, especially the Burgenlanders, returned home after a few years of work in America had supplied them with nest eggs, was not taken into consideration. Little wonder that historians and statisticians alike have shied away from the problem of Austrian immigration. We have never been quite certain what an Austrian was.[9]

The Director General of the great Austrian National Library, Dr. Josef Stummvoll, and his assistant Dr. Walter G. Wieser, have described for us the Austrians of the period with which we are especially concerned as follows:

1. In the sense of nation, i. e., the inhabitants of a particular territorial state, "Austrians" would be all those born within the borders of the Austrian Empire (1804/1866) and, for the period from 1867 to 1918, those born in the *Königreiche und Länder* represented in the *Reichsrat*. The latter definition would apply only to the Cis-Leithanian, i. e. the Austrian half of the Empire. The other half, Trans-Leithanian, was the Hungarian half. In the Austrian half one would have to distinguish, during the period from 1867 to 1918, the Czechs and other Slavs and the German Austrians.

2. By "Austrians" one could understand also that branch of the German people which inhabited the various parts of the monarchy and developed its own particular traits (and went its own way).

3. Those can be called Austrians who embraced, or embrace, the "Idea of Austria" and acknowledged their ties to their country.

For the purposes of this study we shall disregard the legalistic concepts set forth in the first of the above categories. Here we shall be concerned in that legalistic sense only with all the peoples of the Austria of the years since 1918. For the earlier years we shall confine ourselves primarily to the German Austrians as defined in categories (2) and (3), who were Germanic in language and culture and who looked to Vienna or to the other Germanic cultural centers of the old monarchy as their spiritual homes. We shall interest ourselves only occasionally in Austrian subjects of other nationalities when they came to Vienna, imbibed some of their training there, or contributed there something that has, directly or indirectly, had its impact upon American life.

This usage of the term Austrian, after centuries of historic confusion, would seem to be logical and useful. Austrians have for too long been confused with all their neighbors. Historical developments have given us an Austria distinct from Germany and from the succession states of the old monarchy and it has thus become increasingly easier to distinguish Austrians from their neighbors.

Austrians have always been confused with Germans. Indeed, the core-Austrians plus tens of thousands of German-speaking folk all over the old monarchy were, and are, ethnic Germans. Their sovereign was during much of the period after 1273 the Roman Emperor. They have long been called Germans and until recently have been ready to call themselves Germans.

Indeed, until 1804 when Kaiser Franz II of the Empire became Kaiser Franz I of Austria and 1806 when the Holy Roman Empire was abolished, there was no Austria in the later sense of the word. And it was only in 1866, after Prussia's defeat of Austria in the Seven Weeks' War, that Austria ceased to be merely one of the German states. Even then the Austrian empire had its *Gross-Deutsche* — German nationalists who believed that the political union of all German speaking peoples was more desirable than the preservation of the multinational Habsburg monarchy. There was a goodly number of those German nationalists left to welcome the *Anschluss* in 1938. And such people never objected to being called Germans.

In the following chapters we shall anticipate the use of the term Austrian, or use the term German Austrian, to designate the Germanic peoples of the Habsburg monarchy who were generally called Germans, within the monarchy and even in America. We shall generally reserve the word German for Germans who did not live in the Austrian Empire or in Austria-Hungary or in the Austrian Republic, despite the knowledge that such usage is unhistorical.

We shall, on the other hand, be concerned here only with what were once called Germans: the people of the present Austrian Republic (irrespective of their racial origins, and parts of little Austria itself have been genuine melting pots) and, earlier, their Germanic colonists in the other lands of the Austrian empire. For the old monarchy, all the way from northern Italy to Ruthenia and from Bohemia to Carniola, had planted Germanic colonies: merchants, imperial garrisons, religious dissenters and loyal churchmen, hosts of civil servants, noble families with vast estates throughout the old monarchy and sometimes peasants to work them – such folk had infiltrated the entire empire, reenforcing the German settlements of pre-Habsburg days and carrying with them the German language and Germanic culture. If they remained so conspicuously Germanic and contributed so little to the local non-Germanic cultures of the lands where they settled that the nationalistic historians of those areas have not claimed them, they must, it seems to us, properly be thought of as Austrians. If they looked to Vienna or Innsbruck or Graz as their cultural homes, they were doubtless Austrian. Such minorities in Europe have often had a legal and cultural status, totally unlike our American minorities, that has preserved the character of their compact enclaves in the midst of utterly different and even hostile cultures. The historian of Central Europe, therefore, does no injustice to the majority peoples when he ascribes the accomplishments of recognized minorities to their parent peoples.[10]

It will also be necessary in this study to mention some of the many who, because relationships were so close in Central Europe, were forever crossing the cultural and political lines – especially those between Austria and Germany. Hitler is mentioned because he was Austrian-born before he made a career for himself in Germany, and Beethoven is included because, German-born as he was, he made his career in Vienna.

The Austrians are not only confused with the Germans: they are also confused with other nationalities of the multinational empire. Our American Census of 1930, for instance, reported that some 31,000 immigrants from Czechoslovakia gave German as their mother tongue as did some 48,000 Hungarian-born, nearly 32,000 from Poland, and over 23,000 from Jugoslavia.[11] No practicable standard will be found to determine how many of these people were really German Austrian in origin and how many were ethnically Czech, Slovak, Hungarian, and such. The monarchy had been too much of a melting pot for that. We shall include in this study those who appear to have been Germanic by race or culture, who were so "Austrian" that they have not been claimed by the historians of the monarchy's succession states, and, in the case of immigrants, those who in America have chosen to call themselves Austrian and who cannot logically be called anything else.

But the relationships and antagonisms between the German Austrians and the other peoples of the old monarchy are, fortunately and unfortunately, very significant in any story of Austrian impact upon the United States. American heroes have not only been the William Tells, the Frederick the Greats, Bismarcks, and Napoleons whose causes seemed always to triumph over the villainous Austrians, but they have been, in even greater number, the heroes within the old monarchy who allegedly fought against it for the independence of their peoples. The list is a very long one: Huss, Kosciuszko, Kossuth, Deák, Mazzini, Paderewski, Beneš, and Masaryk to mention only a few. Some have had parades in American streets, accolades from whole segments of our population, and even millions of postage stamps issued in their honor. Young Americans used to read anti-Austrian hero stories like Jane Porter's "Thaddeus of Warsaw" and college students were fascinated, for instance, by William Roscoe Thayer's biography of Cavour and how he freed Italy from the Austrians. The hyphenated Americans from the outer monarchy worked adeptly with promises of votes to swing American politicians to their causes – and with such success that almost the entire American people cheered when President Wilson persuaded the Paris Peace Conference of 1919 to liberate the Czechs, Poles, Hungarians, and Jugoslavs from their Austrian oppressors. It is strange that the Austrians at the heart of the empire never nurtured a single hero who could win American sympathies or win Americans to any Austrian cause. The Austrians were never nationalists who could produce heroes to intrigue the outer world.

Certainly no persistant phase of Austro-American relations has been, at least until 1919, so entangled in the otherwise straightforward story. The core-Austrians seemed always to be involved with these other peoples, ethnically and politically – as indeed they were.

Ethnically the most significant ties were with the Czechs. Their area was one of the historic crownlands of the monarchy. Its nineteenth century historians and patriots could crusade against the "Germans" in their midst and in Vienna with stirring tales of the Bohemian past and Hussite Protestantism in the years before the Battle of White Mountain (1620) when Bohemia lost its independence to the Habsburgs and its Protestantism was stamped out by the Counter Reformation. American schoolbooks, like "Samuel Putnam's Reader," were in the nineteenth century reflecting the new nationalism in the non-Germanic lands of the empire by, for instance, describing John Huss to Protestant America as a "zealous reformer from Popery" who was burned at the stake after "trusting himself to deceitful Catholics" – meaning Austrians.[12]

But much of Bohemia and more of Moravia became Germanic in culture. That region was part of the *Deutscher Kultur-Kreis*, a German cultural outpost, with a population that was two-fifths Germanic and that, often living in the major towns and cities with a majority of sophistication and learning and wealth in its ranks, dominated the area culturally. In 1961, after almost half a century of independence, there were still some 140,000 Germans in Czechoslovakia. Of all the Germans of that area contemporary Americans have heard most of the dense German population on the German border comprising what we called by the generic term *Sudetendeutsche* and whose protection Hitler used as his excuse for taking over the entire country in 1938. Many of them had come originally from the north and many looked to Germany as their cultural homeland. Properly used, the term *Sudetendeutsche* means, not just the Germanic peoples on Hitler's German frontier in 1938, but all the Germanic peoples in Bohemia and Moravia. Southward, especially in Prague and Brünn, we find the homeland of many of the greatest of the German Austrians: Mendel and Freud and Werfel and Kafka and scores of others who were in no sense Slavic and who were often described as Germans. Those who remained there, without coming to Vienna, were called Germans by their own fellow-countrymen, Czech or Austrian.[13]

The Czech lands were a battleground between the Slavs and the Germans. The Slavs were often loyal to Vienna when they feared the growing power of Russia. It was a Czech, the well-known Palacký, who told the Frankfurt Parliament in 1848 that if the Austrian state did not exist it would be necessary, for protection against Asiatic elements, to create it. But they resented the contention that Bohemia was an ancient German land with enclaves of Slavs. They thought of it as a Slavic land with enclaves of Germans.

The impact of Czech nationalism upon the United States was a potent one and contributed generously to America's conception of the Austrian monarchy as a *Völkerkerker*, a prison of peoples. Charles Sealsfield, a native of the area who was proud to call himself both Austrian and American, denounced in 1828 "the Austrian monarchs (who), since the Revolution, in 1618, did everything in their power to extirpate the national spirit of this people."[14] Germans, Austrians, and Bohemians might all read German-language papers in the United States but they mixed as little as oil and water.[15] And the eloquent propaganda of Masaryk and Beneš before and during the first World War helped to convince President Wilson that the Czechs should be freed from the Austrian *Völkerkerker*. Their triumph was a triumph for the cause of elimination of Germanic culture from the new Czechoslovakia. It left German Austrians like Franz Kafka holding strange new non-Austrian passports and it made it clear that the land wished to be rid of all Austrianism. We have, consequently, included in this study the German Austrians of the present Czechoslovakia who, if they cannot be called Austrian, would be men without a country.

Although the complexities of the Bohemian-Moravian melting pot were, in the history of the immigration of Austrians and of things Austrian to America, the most perplexing of all, the same situation existed, to a lesser degree, in other parts of the old monarchy. The historian of "Americans from Hungary" (Philadelphia and N. Y., 1948), Emil Lengyel, writes that "Distrust of the Germans is in Hungarian bones, as is to be expected. The German, mostly in the form of the German-speaking Austrian Habsburgs, represented oppression."

The Magyars of Hungary constituted another of the historic nationalities of the empire. Hungary had a host of heroes, a long history, a mixed population (Germanic tribes, Huns, Avars, Magyars, and more Germans), and a proud culture. The land had fallen on bad times in the sixteenth century. Its subjection by the Turks (at the Battle of Mohács in 1526) brought it to look to the archdukes of Austria for support — who also needed all the help they could obtain to stem the ever-threatening Turks. The result, even after the final defeat of the Turks in 1683 and up to 1918, was an uneasy Austro-Hungarian partnership with the Habsburgs generally wearing the Hungarian crown and the Hungarians resenting any and all disregard of Hungarian interests and prestige in favor of Vienna and the empire. They even clung to Latin as an official tongue rather than speak German.

That the Hungarians were one of the "historic peoples" of the empire — a people with its own history and culture and often a passionate pride in its primitive backgrounds — was the Austrian tragedy that led, more than anything else, to the fall of the old monarchy. The softer, more-yielding Austrians were almost always more prepared to make concessions to the numerous Slavic elements of the empire. It was time after time the Hungarians, unwilling to contribute to Slav nationalism in their parts of the empire, who blocked the way to any imperial federation that would recognize the Habsburg Slavs as equal partners with the Magyars and the German Austrians. When the Hungarians achieved the great compromise of 1867, that made the Austrian empire into the Austro-Hungarian Dual Monarchy, the Habsburgs were doomed. Only a tripartite monarchy, with the Slavs as equal partners, could have saved them.

The epoch-making revolutions of 1848 that lighted the torch of nationalism in so many parts of Europe and most especially in the Habsburg dominions, stirred the Hungarians with chauvinistic fervor.

Those revolutions, despite their failure, led to the decline of the Austrian empire. They aroused some of the non-Germanic peoples of the empire who had forgotten their never-vigorous nationalism for decades or centuries — and they gave new life to the Prussian nationalism that Napoleon had stirred to fever heat in 1814. They even awakened Austria's Poles who were happier under the Habsburgs than they were to be decades later as satellites of Soviet communism.

Kossuth's crusade for Hungarian independence attracted American sympathies as no other foreign movement for independence has ever stirred this country. Americans did not realize that Magyar supremacy would have been anathema to most of the monarchy's Slavs, the pro-Vienna Croats especially, whom the Austrians had had to throw to the Hungarians, to the same extent that Austrian supremacy was distasteful to the Hungarians, and for more convincing reasons. And, despite the great Austro-Hungarian compromise of 1867, which recognized the equal partnership of the Hungarians in the Habsburg monarchy, the independence movement bore fruit in the peace settlement of 1918. The division of the monarchy in 1867 into an Austrian half and a Hungarian half transferred more than a full share of the clamor of the lesser peoples for autonomy or independence to the Hungarian doorstep, but in America it was all thought of as "the Austrian problem" and the inevitable result was the dissolution of the empire in 1918.

A quarter of Hungary before World War I was Protestant. Some of its leaders, like Admiral Horthy and Count Tisza, well known in the United States, were Protestant. And that, as in the case of Protestantism in Bohemia and Moravia, was doubtless a factor in American interest in seeing Hungary achieve its independence. Indeed, the entire story of Austro-American relations, from the time when the Habsburgs ruled Mexico and much of South America, through the days when the Protestant Frederick the Great worsted the Catholic Empress Maria Theresia, to the nineteenth century when the Leopoldinen-Stiftung worked for Catholicism in the American West, may well have been colored by the fact that Protestants have, for the most part, written history for Americans. That circumstance is doubtless as important as the fact that Americans outside the universities have read almost no Austrian history written by Austrians. The University of Chicago's great series of world histories, for instance, includes "The Dissolution of the Habsburg Monarchy" (Chicago 1929) written, not by an American or by an Austrian, but by the Hungarian Oscar Jaszi. And the fault is partly that of the Austrian historians who have come to this country to write French or some other European or American history without regard for their own Austrian past.[16] The quiet Austrians have never been adept at publicizing their own cause.

Also significant to this study is the fact that Hungary's early history and the much more recent era of Hungary's inclusion in the Habsburg empire gave it a very considerable German population. From Siebenbürgen in the east to Budapest and Burgenland in the west, there were large enclaves of Germanic folk who looked to Vienna rather than to Budapest. And there were many of mixed race, Austrian and Hungarian, like the great musician Franz Liszt or the distinguished American journalist Joseph Pulitzer or the fine writer of our own day, Arthur Koestler, whose culture was Germanic and whose roots went deep on both sides of the border.

If we seem, in the following chapters, to concern ourselves unduly with the background of such hyphenated Austrians, it is because it seems necessary to make clear why they are included in the story of Austrian impacts upon the United States. The settlements of 1918 and the failure of the Hitler *Anschluss* of 1938 have changed the face of Central Europe and historians will have to change some of their labels and terminology. We cannot simply assume, in an area where minorities were so long recognized, that the German Austrians of the long years before 1918 have simply become historically non-existent. We must doubtless assign the non-Slav and the non-Magyar peoples — the German Austrians scattered about the empire — to Austria.

There were German Austrians, in vigorous little cultural, and often political, enclaves over most of the old monarchy. A great deal of the best of Austria's literature, for instance, which has unfortunately been inadequately translated and published here, is the story of these Germanic folk who lived far from the core of Germanic Austria. Musil's novel "Young Torless" is one of the few known here.

In general the "subject peoples" realized vaguely that Austrian domination was not as ruthless as that of others. Sealsfield wrote in 1828 that the Poles of Austrian Poland realized that the easy-going Austrians made their lot easier than that of the Russian and Prussian Poles. But Thomas Campbell had written that "Freedom shriek'd as Kosciuszko fell," Jefferson agreed, and, despite the feeling of some Americans that Polish nationalism, anti-Austrian as it was anti-German and anti-Russian, had been overrated and given more support in America than it warranted, Americans were attracted to the Polish cause.[17] Just as they had always been attracted to revolutionary causes, from the early decades of the nineteenth century when Latin America broke away from Iberia with our blessings, to the twentieth century when empires broke on every side into surprising revolutionary fragments. It did not matter that Poland's Pilsudski was loyal to Austria and fearful of Russia in the early days of World War I: the American government finally resolved upon the dissolution of the monarchy and the Poles were naturally agreeable. The Polish-Americans, like the Hungarian-Americans, the Czech-Americans and the other South-Slav Americans, were well organized politically in the United States and the Austrians were never a political force. The quiet Austrians, ineffectively organized here and there, never brought their few votes to bear upon such matters as the peace settlement of 1919.

One interesting outpost of the old Austria was the Ukraine. There, far from Vienna, was an Austrian nobility that had not always been benevolent: it had, for instance, opposed emigration to America through its clergy and its officialdom. Only a decade before 1914 had it removed its restrictions upon emigration. But, despite Ukrainian restlessness under the old monarchy, the Ukrainians who were given to Russia after the first World War now recall that the Austro-Ukrainians always enjoyed far more liberties than the Russo-Ukrainians.[18]

It is impossible in a modest study to comment upon all of Vienna's significant relationships with the other peoples of the monarchy. It is important to point out, however, that so many of the minorities in those other lands were so Germanic in culture and language and in loyalty to the Habsburg regime, *kaisertreu* is the proper German term, that they are included in this study as Austrians. And it is also important to understand the relationships of the various non-Germanic peoples of the monarchy to the core-Austrians — the long history of association and rivalry that was so often reflected when they came to America as immigrants.

Austria's history has been responsible in large part for its neglect by American historians. As we have seen, there was no Austria in any national sense until the establishment of the Austrian Empire in 1804. And the peoples of the empire, although they might be *kaisertreu*, loyal to the emperor and his regime, seemed to lack patriotism. Indeed, the old Holy Roman Empire of which the Austrian lands were for centuries such an essential part, was in no sense nationalistic. It was based, both politically and religiously, upon the idea of universality. ". . . the Austrian has not the least national pride," Charles Sealsfield wrote in 1828.[19] And in 1843 a Hamburg volume declared: "Austria is a purely imaginary name, which means neither a distinct people nor a land or nation . . . no Austrian nationality. . . . National feeling, national pride, a vigorous, exalted consciousness of its own strength is strange to the Austrian . . ."[20]

Too typical was the great Austrian poet Rilke who denied being a German and could not endure being called an Austrian. He was devoted to French letters, loved Switzerland, thought his Czech friends miserable nonentities. Incidentally, he failed to distinguish between the English and the Americans. He wanted only to think of himself as a homeless cosmopolitan — a European and no Austrian.[21] And too many other Austrians, unhappy in their native land, have supported the thesis that there is no patriotism in the land on the Danube. They may love its mountains and its lakes, its wine and its good eating, but they assume that its politics and its men and women are as impossible as those that brought about all the tragedies in its national history.

The Austrian, especially the Viennese, was always supranational, cosmopolitan rather than nationalistic. That was natural, perhaps, in core-Austria that was so small in relation to the entire German and Habsburg area that Austrians were always spilling over, culturally, ethnically and even politically, into the surrounding lands. A recent book on German literature, as an example, leaves almost all of the great Austrian writers out of its chapter on "Post-War Austrian Writers" on the ground that they were so markedly international and had had such profound influence upon German letters as a whole that they have been scattered through the volume among the outstanding Germans and Swiss.[22]

This trait of cosmopolitanism, combined with the natural dislike of many emigrés for their former homeland where many were so willing to welcome the Nazis in 1938 — has marked the Austrians who have come to America and has contributed to our lack of understanding as to the magnitude of the Austrian impact here. It has been a commonplace for such distinguished ones as Max Reinhardt or the singer Lotte Lenya or the composer of "My Fair Lady," Frederick Loewe, to appear in the United States as Germans. They have had no patriotic impulses to sing Austria's praises. Utterly unlike the enthusiastic Irish- or Hungarian- or Italian-Americans, they have been quite ready to let Americans ignore their Austrian origins. The contrast between a President John Kennedy who loved the Ireland of his grandfathers and a Mayor La Guardia in New York who was so ready to remember his Italian birth, and an Austrian-born Justice Felix Frankfurter of the U. S. Supreme Court who gave his biographers virtually no hint of his Austrian homeland is striking. Austrians have been cosmopolitan but not patriotic.

Americans have, as a consequence, seldom been convinced of the significance of the Habsburg monarchy on the Blue Danube. Indeed, their knowledge generally ends with the generalization that the Danube is by no means blue. Typical was the point of view of the very significant (to American historians) "Manual of Historical Literature" by the president of Cornell University, Charles Kendall Adams (New York 1882), which not only listed many more historical works about Prussia and Germany than about Austria, but was able to list not one single volume about Austria published in the United States. Books about Austria in English all came from London. Professor Adams even listed the memoirs of Prince Metternich, the Austrian statesman who has had the greatest impact of all Austrian diplomats upon the United States, in his section on "Histories of Germany." Thus, since Austria until recently has remained a great unknown in America, Austro-Americans have had no incentive to boast of their Austrianism.

Indeed, some of the Austrian-born have changed their names in order to forget their past. Johann Schmitmeyer, the architect of the Library of Congress, became John L. Smithmeyer; Jacob Horowitz, the film producer, became Jed Harris; Smylla Brind became the film star Vanessa Brown; and Paul Weisenfreund became actor Paul Muni. Some, like Judge Henry Ellenbogen, formerly a Congressman from Pittsburgh, have left their places of birth out of "Who's Who in America." The craving for assimilation in the new home is a common trait among immigrants: among the cosmopolitan Austrians it has been so strong as, in many instances, to deprive the homeland of considerable prestige.

As early as 1799, however, Schiller could write in his "Wallensteins Tod" that the Austrian has a fatherland and loves it and has reason to love it:

„*Der Österreicher hat ein Vaterland*
Und liebt's und hat auch Ursach', es zu lieben."

His patriotism was seldom political. He loved his mountains and his rivers, his music and his art, his town and his province. By mid-century Austrians were beginning to feel themselves Austrian as never before: Hans Kudlich, the famous Forty-eighter, called himself *einen wahrhaften Österreicher* and Grillparzer wrote: "I am not a German, but an Austrian, of Lower Austria; and above all I am a Viennese."[23]

Austria became more and more aware of itself without becoming nationalistic. Its great achievements in music, medicine, and art gave it cause for pride. Austrians like Stefan Zweig began to write of their love of country. It became less and less a mere part of Germany. Gustav Pollak called it in 1907 "a land which from time immemorial has cultivated German poetry and song, but which in the march of centuries had become completely estranged from the progress of German thought."[24]

Outsiders came to realize that the heart and soul of Austria were things quite different from the spirit of Prussia which, since Bismarck violently ejected Austria from the Germanies in 1866, had been the fulcrum of the new Germany.[25] The Austrians were in general softer, more *gemütlich* or friendly, more international in their outlook, even more devoted to culture and the amenities of life, than the North Germans.

Sealsfield noted some of the Austrian traits more than a century ago: they were thrifty, kind-hearted, passionately fond of music, loved their wine but seldom drank too much.[26] They have always been easygoing. Robert Musil, the fine Austrian novelist, included this passage in his "Man Without Qualities:"[27] "Do you know what you're saying?' he exclaimed. 'Muddling through! You're simply an Austrian. You're preaching the Austrian national philosophy of muddling through!' 'That may not be such a bad thing as you think,' Ulrich replied."

Austrians, with their famous *Schlamperei*, have too often muddled through. Too many of the easy-going ones joined their nationalistic compatriots who were crusading for the *Anschluss* with Germany in accepting Hitler and all he stood for because they hoped that a desperately impoverished country could somehow muddle through under some new regime that had a record of accomplishment in the land of their closest neighbor. And Austrians have made for themselves a reputation of being romantically devoted to the past. When Freud's biographer, Ernest Jones, remarked to his friend that it must have been inspiring to have lived in Vienna, the great man replied, "I have lived here for fifty years and have never come across a new idea . . ."[28]

Freud's reply is typical of the eternal pessimism of the Austrians. Vienna in his day was teeming with revolutionary ideas, in science and architecture and music and the arts, even in literature and in community housing, but Freud, the typical Viennese, had closed his eyes to it all. That same trait, so typical of Austrians in Austria and of Austrian immigrants in America, leads them so often to disparage the remarkable achievements of their land that has played such a remarkable role in world history. It was obviously a surprise to the easy-going Austrians themselves when, in 1950 to 1960, their first complete decade after the sad years of Nazism, they found that no other country in Europe except the German Federal Republic had made such a record of economic progress for itself.[29] This was a magnificent achievement, which few Americans have understood.

Robert Musil, Austria's fine novelist, summed up the problem of Austrian achievement when he wrote: "Yes, in spite of much that seems to point the other way, Kakania (his term for Austria-Hungary) was perhaps a home of genius after all; and that, probably, was the ruin of it."[30] The stresses and strains within the old monarchy and the outbursts of talent even after its demise in 1918 profited Austria but little. But they have left a legacy of inestimable worth in the outside world, and especially in America. We can only hope that despite Austria's loss of so much talent through emigration and Nazism, it will continue to produce great minds and talents and remain a breeding place of great names — in such numbers that it can continue to share them with America without loss to itself.

The founding of the republic in 1918 and 1919 has introduced a period of friendly Austro-American relations. The Hitlerian conquest of Austria in 1938 was happily recognized by Washington as aggression and Austria was thus, at the end of the war, no ex-enemy but a liberated country. The occupation of parts of Austria by the American forces from 1945 to 1955 introduced thousands of Americans to a land that had been previously a kind of *terra incognita*. Americans interested themselves in Vienna's Austro-American Institute, founded by Dr. Paul Dengler whose interest in cementing Austro-American relations led him to teach and lecture at dozens of American universities from Harvard and Columbia to Evansville, and the Austro-American Society with its fine summer school for Americans and programs in Vienna and the provinces; and they returned home, in many cases, to join American-Austrian societies and federations in the United States. They welcomed the establishment in 1963 in New York of the Austrian Institute which was to interpret Austria to America much as our *Amerika-Häuser* had interpreted America to Austria. They set up their American International School in Vienna and they flocked to the University of Vienna's Institute for European Studies and to the various summer schools that Austrians and Americans were sponsoring for them, especially in and around Salzburg. They acquired Reinhardt's old Schloss Leopoldskron for their Salzburg Seminar in American Studies, doubtless the finest American cultural outpost in Central Europe. Only the fact that comparatively few American tourists went to Austria when it became, by 1963, Europe's third greatest tourist attraction, underscored the distance between the two lands.

But that distance between Austria and America, so formidable in the days of Metternich and the Leopoldinen-Stiftung's missionary period, has fortunately shrunk. With two disastrous world wars behind us, with the coming of the great Thirty-eighter migration, with the appearance of skiing as a sport of interest in both lands, and with the discovery of so many other common Austro-American interests on the Iron Curtain frontier after the second World War, little Austria and the United States forgetful as we may be of our friends in Central Europe, must find that they have more and more in common. Indeed, the prophets who suggest that America's future lies not so much in Asia or Africa as in "our" Europe, must realize that western oriented Austria, with borders on three communist lands, is a strategic spot in which America must continue its interest.

[1] *Who's Who in America*, 1952—53. Canada, Great Britain, Russia, and Germany provided more names than Austria. Only those who were apparently German-Austrian were counted omitting peoples of the former Austro-Hungarian monarchy who could more properly be counted as Hungarians, Czechs, Croatians, Poles, etc. The various issues of *Who's Who in America* will generally be cited below as *Who's Who*.

[2] Only Germany and Canada provided more names than Austria.

[3] According to the *Statistical Abstract of the United States*, 1958, Austria's area is 32,373 sq. miles (that of the United States 3,022,387 sq. miles) with a population in 1951 of 6,934,000 that was almost static with a growth rate of only 1%.

[4] A. J. P. Taylor, *The Habsburg Monarchy*, London 1948, p. 10.

[5] Saul K. Padover, ed., *The Complete Jefferson*, N. Y. 1943, p. 177.

[6] M. C. Lynch, *Diplomatic Mission of John Lothrop Motley*, Washington 1944, p. 50.

[7] *Reports*, X, p. 219. Cf. V, p. 21 for the statement on Belgium.

[8] We make no effort in this study to cover second-generation Austrians in America. Census figures for such a study are as misleading as they are for the first generation.

[9] U. S. Census Bureau, *Historical Statistics of the United States, Colonial Times to 1957*, Washington 1957, pp. 48—50; Wilhelm Schlag, "A Survey of Austrian Emigration to the United States," *Österreich und die angelsächsische Welt*, Wien 1961, pp. 139—196. The inquiry on the country of birth of the foreign-born was first made in the 1850 Census and information concerning the birthplace of parents first obtained in 1880 and first published as of 1890.

We shall indicate on the following pages some of the norms that we have observed throughout this volume in identifying Austrians as such. We have doubtless erred in certain cases through defective judgement or because of insufficient information.

Since we include many present-day figures, it is of interest to note the definition of Austrian adopted by the editors of *Österreicher der Gegenwart* (Wien 1951): The concept of Austrian is a broad one, including first all born in contemporary Austria, then those originating in the old monarchy who live in our country or devote to it a substantial part of their activity, even though they have meanwhile assumed some other citizenship. Foreigners are included only when they have become Austrian citizens, or are working in Austria, or, in special cases, when they have found here the high point of their career of achievement.

[10] An excellent account of the establishment of military outposts on the borders of the monarchy is to be found in G. E. Rothenberg, *The Austrian Military Border in Croatia, 1522—1747*, Urbana 1960. It is of interest to note that American, as well as Austrian historians are now using the term "Austrian" for the period before 1804.

[11] *Abstract of the 15th Census*, p. 153.

[12] Carleton Beals, *Brass-Knuckle Crusade*, N. Y. 1960, p. 75.

[13] Oskar Jellinek's *Novelle*, for instance, and the more recent Austrian poet Urzidil, both born in the area, use the term "German" consistently to distinguish what we should like to call "Austrians" from the Slavic peoples. Important for any study of the nationalities within the monarchy are Robert A. Kann, *Multinational Empire*, 2 vols., N. Y. 1950; Hans Kohn, *The Habsburg Empire*, 1916; Elizabeth Wiskemann, *Czechs and Germans*, 1938; and for the anti-Austrian point of view: Oscar Jaszi, *Dissolution of the Habsburg Monarchy*, Chicago 1929; and Thomas Čapek, *The Cechs in America*, Boston and N. Y. 1920.

[14] Charles Sealsfield, *Austria As It Is*, London 1828, p. 53.

[15] E. G. Balch, *Our Slavic Fellow Citizen*, 1910, p. 410, mentions the antagonisms in Texas. Čapek, *op. cit.*, pp. 124 ff., describes the nineteenth-century German-language Czech paper in Milwaukee, *Flug-Blätter*, that was anti-clerical and anti-Austrian. He describes also the Czech priests who gave up their priesthood rather than work with Austrian-born priests.

[16] There are a few seeming exceptions to this generalization such as Robert A. Kann's fine *Multinational Empire* but that work is not narrative history in the usual sense of the word.

[17] L. L. Gerson, *Wilson and the Rebirth of Poland*, Yale 1953, pp. 2–22.

[18] Wasyl Halich, *Ukranians in the United States*, University of Chicago Press 1937, pp. 6–19.

[19] *Austria as It Is*, p. 100.

[20] Victor von Andrian-Werburg, *Österreich und dessen Zukunft* (Hamburg 1843), quoted by Kann, *op. cit.*, I, p. 8.

[21] Endo C. Mason, *Rilke, Europe, and the English Speaking World*, Cambridge U. Press, 1961, 2ff.

[22] Jethro Bithell, *Modern German Literature*, London 1946.

[23] Quoted from Gustav Pollak, *Franz Grillparzer and the Austrian Drama*, N.Y. 1907, p. 34.

[24] *Ibid.*, p. 30.

[25] R. L. Sedgwick, "The German Character," *Blackwood's Magazine*, June 1962, p. 538.

[26] *Op. cit.*, *passim.*

[27] London 1953, I. p. 255.

[28] *Arts* magazine, Oct. 1960, p. 46.

[29] From 1953 to early 1960 Austria's gross national product shot up 46%, only one percent less than that of West Germany. *Austrian Information*, 29 Oct. 1960, p. 4. Employment had reached such a high point by the end of the decade that Austria was importing labor from southern Europe. Its gold reserves were so plentiful that it was to make deposits with the United States Federal Reserve System to help bolster America's gold reserves. The periodical *Austrian Information*, published by the Austrian Information Service in New York, will be cited in the following chapters without further reference to its publisher or place of publication.

[30] *Man Without Qualities*, N.Y. 1953, I, p. 35.

CHAPTER II

WHEN AUSTRIA WAS A GERMAN LAND

The "historic mission" of Austria for centuries was to defend the West against the East. That was the mission of the early tribes in the Danube valley where they turned back the invaders from the East — Huns, Avars, Magyars, and Turks. It was the mission of the Danube outposts of the Romans when they built the garrison town now called Vienna. And, best known, it was the Austrian historic mission when in 1529 and 1683 they stopped the Turks at the gates of Vienna and kept Europe Christian. The French had supported the Turks because their arch-enemies were the Habsburgs of Spain and of the Holy Roman Empire, and the ultimate victory of the Turks and their French allies would have Balkanized Europe far west of Budapest and Vienna. The Europe that settled America would have been a far different Europe if the Austrians and their allies had yielded to Suleiman the Magnificent and his successors.

Even in the nineteenth century when nationalism began to erupt among the various peoples of the Austrian monarchy, most of those peoples wanted only more autonomy. They still wanted protection against the East, specifically against the Russians. They still wanted Austria to perform its "historic mission." They believed that if Austria did not exist it would be necessary to create it. And if a British historian could write that up to the end of the Habsburg era "every nationality in Austria, except the Italians and a minority of the Germans, preferred the Habsburg monarchy to any conceivable alternative," that was because they still had confidence in the validity of the concept of the Austrian "historic mission." Indeed, not long after Austria had in 1918 been rendered too small to carry on that mission, every segment of the old monarchy except core-Austria itself fell a victim to the East — to Moscow's communism. The Czech who over a century ago invented that famous remark about the necessity of creating Austria had she not existed, might feel well justified by a glance today at the map of the Iron Curtain.

Indeed, the Central Europe that has through the last century contributed so much to the building of America would have been a far different place, racially, culturally and religiously, had the peoples of the middle Danube not held their borders against the East.

American and Austrian paths crossed in the sixteenth century when the Habsburg Charles V, Emperor of the Holy Roman Empire, with an empire on which the sun never set, ruled all of Spanish America up to the borderlands of British North America.

But he was one of the less Austrian of the Habsburgs and Americans have always thought of him, quite properly, as a Spaniard. Those who followed him on the Spanish side usually had much more influence in the New World than the Austrian Habsburgs who were the poor cousins until the Austrian side forged ahead in the late 17th and early 18th centuries. Other early points of contact between North America and the Habsburg lands were less significant and, like so much in the history of Austro-American relations, never thought of by Americans in terms of Austria or the Austrians.

There was, for instance, the famous Captain John Smith of Jamestown in Virginia who fought for the Habsburgs against the Turks. He was an adventurer from Lincolnshire in old England (b. 1579/80) who went to Graz, Styria, in the days when Archduke Ferdinand of Habsburg was recruiting forces at Graz to fight the Turks. Assigned as a Protestant to a Hungarian regiment he experimented with weird fireworks and explosives that didn't prevent his capture by the Turks and a whole series of adventures that he doubtless exaggerated in the accounts that he prepared for posterity.[1] It was a fascinating story — significant here as an indication that our early Austrian backgrounds are remote, of minor significance, and generally unknown. The Austrian lands have simply been outside the American orbit.

Other examples can be cited. Neglected even by American tourists in Austria is Hallstatt in deepest Austria which was important from 900 to 500 B. C. as a center of the new Iron Age. About 500 B. C. the Celtic wave swept up the Danube carrying Hallstatt's culture into Germany and on into France.[2] Marcus Aurelius wrote the third of his well-known "Meditations" near Vienna in Roman days; St. Virgilius, the Irish-born Bishop of St. Peter's in Salzburg, allegedly discovered way back in 748 that the world was round (this was denied in 1924 by Franz Betten, a German-born scholar writing in the "Catholic Historical Review"); Walther von der Vogelweide (born c. 1170 — died c. 1228), the greatest of the Minnesingers and "the greatest lyric poet of Germany before Goethe" was probably Lower Austrian or Tyrolese by birth (some accounts indicate he was Franconian) and learned his craft in Vienna during the last decade of the twelfth century. The great Hugo von Hofmannsthal found him a great German-Austrian whose writings ennobled the wonderful mountain country from which he came.[3]

And also, in literature, the "Nibelungenlied," so well known to those tracing the history of the most famous of Scandinavian sagas and loving the Wagner operas based upon them, may well have come in the 12th century out of the Austrian Danube region where its mighty heroes, according to some unknown man of song and of letters, acted out a drama of murder and revenge.[4] And almost every American schoolboy knows that the Duke of Austria captured Richard the Lion Hearted on his return from the crusades and held him cruelly in the castle at Dürnstein (some miles above Vienna where tourists who depart from the beaten path love now to go and sip the good Dürnstein wine) until he was ransomed. Sir Walter Scott's reference in the seventh chapter of "Ivanhoe" to "the perfidious and cruel Duke of Austria" is one of those unhappy, but too frequently unflattering, references to Austria that gave nineteenth century Americans anything but a favorable picture of that land on the Danube.

And Austria's eighteenth century heroes, Empress Maria Theresia and her generals, were forgotten here in our enthusiasm for Maria Theresia's victorious Prussian opponent, Frederick the Great. One could cite dozens of hero-worshipping accounts of the despoiler of Austria, Frederick the Prussian, from Macaulay to our own day that millions of Americans have found fascinating, and virtually no readable account in English of the valiant Austrian empress who was despoiled by Frederick. Maria Theresia's complete failure to find responsive chords on the American continent is indicated in one volume of sixty-five years ago on German literature in America that granted that during the entire eighteenth century the most celebrated person of foreign birth in America's estimation was the great Austrian empress's arch-enemy, Frederick the Great.[5] The reforms of her forward-looking son, Joseph II, that might possibly have made Austria a focal point of hope in despotic Europe, entitled Joseph only to a brief mention in our textbooks as one of the benevolent despots of his time. And Andreas Hofer, the martyred "Austrian Tell" who fought the Bavarians and Napoleon I for the freedom of the Tyrol, is an unknown in the United States. The best-known name here from all Austrian political history is, rather unfortunately, that of Metternich. But even Metternich is far less well-known than the German von Steuben, aide to Frederick the Great, who came in 1777 to help Washington drill the Continental Army.

Indeed, even Americans who are thoroughly familiar with the Washingtons of Sulgrave Manor, would be surprised to know that George Washington died in Pöls, south of Graz, in 1930. He was a descendant of the English Washingtons whose ancestor had fled England to Holland in Stuart times. The family made a distinguished career for itself in Bavaria before, in 1855, one Maximilian Washington married a noble lady with a castle at Pöls. He served in the Austrian army and in the parliament at Vienna. His son George, who met Theodore Roosevelt on the latter's visit to Vienna, was an Austrian country gentleman of the old Franz-Joseph school. He was proud of his relationship to his great American namesake but he never came to the United States.[6]

The fact that the name Austria is almost non-existent in early American writing is due largely to the fact that, until Kaiser Franz I created the Austrian Empire just before Napoleon abolished the Holy Roman Empire, there was no Austria in the modern sense of the term.

It was not only the little-known name, Austria, that was responsible. German Austrians did not come to America in numbers until later. And then they came on the coattails of the North Germans and became identified with them. German Austrian traditions were too generally swallowed up in the larger community or group in which the emigrants from Austria found themselves.

Place names are indicative. America is dotted with French and German and Dutch and Swedish place names, to mention only a few of the well represented lands. The most unlikely Polish or Russian or Hungarian towns, for instance, have given names to American cities and villages. But the name Austria and most of the other Austrian place names like Salzburg, Innsbruck, Bregenz, and Graz, Tyrol, Styria, and Carinthia, are almost unknown here. Vienna alone has been privileged to give its name to some nineteen small American communities.[7] And of these Vienna, Maryland, is said to be a corruption of an Indian name, "Vinnacokasimmon."[8] The largest of America's Viennas in the 1950's, with a first-class post office and a population of some 12,000 (1966), was Vienna, Virginia, a suburb of Washington.

The hot dog has, however, introduced the word *Wiener*, German for Viennese, into every American home. According to the great grandson of Johann Georg Lahner the hot dog was invented in the first years of the last century by Lahner, a butcher from Frankfurt, Germany, who had settled in Vienna in 1798. The inventor called it a Frankfurter after his earlier home but, since it emerged from Vienna, millions of Germans called it a Wiener and Americans have used both terms with little or no distinction between them. The land of its birth, so fond of the sausage in all its forms, has generally called it simply *Würstel*. Few Americans would ever think of it as Viennese.[9] We are, fortunately for Austria's culinary reputation, inclined to credit the Alpine land with the choicer products of its restaurants and cafés — with the Wiener Schnitzel, that fine breaded veal cutlet that the Austrians discovered in Italy and adapted without the Italian's tomato sauce, and with all the rich cakes and pastries that tourists enjoy in Vienna's Café Demel and in Bad Ischl's Café Zauner and elsewhere. Austria's time-honored reputation for good food has stimulated the use of the name Vienna in the United States. We have for generations had scores of Vienna Bakeries and restaurants with names such as the The Little Vienna or Habsburg House and we have been offered "Vienna bread" or "Vienna rolls" that would, for the most part, never be recognized in Vienna. The Wienerwald restaurant chain has recently established its outposts in New York.

The noble Danube has provided a name for one American town with a post office, Danube, Minnesota, and also for the village of Danube in New York. Mozart gave his name to a village of twelve dwellings in Bucks County, Pennsylvania.[10] And Mittersill in Land Salzburg is represented by the name of an inn in Franconia, New Hampshire. Even the Wachovia tract in North Carolina, named for the estates in the Wachau of a nobleman who had long since become a Saxon, has had its name absorbed by modern terms unrelated to the Moravian Brethren who first settled there. No immigrant group as significant as the Austrians have been for the last century is so poorly represented by American place names. The fact that the Austrians came so late is the obvious, but not the only, reason.

The omission of the word Austria from English-language accounts of Central European history up until the 20th century was due, not only to our late introduction to the Austrians, but also to the fact that nationality and race were so confused in the old Habsburg lands. This confusion is an earmark of almost every early contribution to American history by men or institutions that we may choose now to call "Austrian."

Father Eusebius Franz Kühn, known to Americans as Eusebio Francesco Kino (b. Segno, c. 1645 – d. New Mexico, 1711), the great seventeenth century explorer and civilizer of the American southwest, for instance, was not certain whether his birth in the South Tyrol made him Italian or German.[11] Augustin Herrman (probably born Prague, 1621), one of the most noted of Maryland's early settlers, is claimed both by the Czechs and the Germans. The facts that he reached New Amsterdam by way of Germany and Holland, wrote only in English and Dutch in the New World, appeared to have German and no Czech acquaintances are all introduced in the argument over his nationality. Professor Faust called him a German; the Library of Congress in an exhibit of 1962 stated that he was believed to have been the first Czech settler in America. In any event he came from the Empire, spent some fifteen years in New Amsterdam, fell out with Governor Stuyvesant, and became a power in settling Northern Maryland, mapping it so competently that his maps have come down in history, acquiring his great Bohemian Manor from Lord Baltimore, and representing Baltimore in the General Assembly.[12] Cornelius Commegys was, according to Faust, a German from Vienna and a contemporary of Herrman who helped settle Cecil County, Maryland, somewhat before 1660.[13]

Whether John Lederer (b. c. 1644) was an Austrian has also been a subject for debate. He could have been one of the Jewish Lederers of Austria or a Franciscan friar or a learned geographer who published a volume on the Alps at Innsbruck. It is certain only that he lived his youth in Hamburg, came to Virginia as a young man, and went west under Governor Berkeley's commission to seek the Northwest Passage. The charts and descriptions that he made of western Virginia and the Carolinas ensured his fame – he was the first ever to map that territory. And he involved himself later in Maryland's early history. He was more than notable in America's pioneer days.[14]

Years later, in 1742, there arrived Friedrich Post, a German missionary from Moravia. He was one of the few Habsburg-empire emigrants who came in those years when the Palatines were beginning to come in shiploads.[15]

One of the most intriguing of the racial snarls in the old Habsburg lands was that of the Moravian sect that has become so well-known in the United States. These "Protestants," who called themselves *Unitas Fratrum,* or United Brethren, dated back to the followers of John Hus in the fifteenth century. They suffered near extermination during the Counter Reformation. Some of them emigrated about 1724 to Count Zinzendorf's vast Saxon estate (Zinzendorf came of a noble family in the Austrian Wachau but had himself been born in Dresden in Saxony), and emigrated again in 1735 to Georgia which wanted settlers to defend the British colonies against the Papist Spaniards in Florida. They were generally called *Herrnhuters* in German from the name of their settlement on the Zinzendorf estate.

The Moravian story – how they pushed north into North Carolina (where their settlement was named Wachovia after Count Zinzendorf's homeland, the Wachau) and in greater numbers into Pennsylvania where Bethlehem became their best-known center and where they enjoyed their European musical traditions and contributed much to the rise of good music in America – that story is a long and fascinating one. Our concern is only with its Austrian aspects.

Professor Faust, champion of the German-Americans, argues that the Moravians were Germans and not Slavic Moravians. He maintains that most of them never saw Moravia. They were Saxons, he implied. He admits that some of them originated "in Moravia (Austria)." Thomas Čapek, historian of the Czechs in America, states that the so-called Moravians had Germanic names and came from towns where German was spoken. He, however, pleads that many were Czech by birth and ancestry – that German names in the Moravian melting-pot did not always signify German blood.

But the Moravians, who spoke German, have always been thought of as Germans. They had a German culture – which in America they made part of the fine heritage of the so-called Pennsylvania Dutch. They doubtless acquired converts on Zinzendorf's Herrnhut estate who were Saxons and were thus Germans of the non-Austrian variety. But the few Moravians (and we assume, pending further research, that it was few) who had come to America from Moravia, speaking German and showing themselves to be Germanic in culture, were, if they were not Slavic Moravians as Čapek would have us believe, what we now call Austrians.

The very names were German and not Slavic: Neiser, Franke, Leibisch, Münster. As late as 1749 there were more "Moravians" arriving in Pennsylvania from Europe and four of the twelve married men in one particular group were from Moravia and Bohemia. The proportion in 1753 was much smaller.[16] In brief, there may have been a core of Austro-Germans among the Moravians even in the eighteenth century. How much Slavic blood there was in their veins and to what extent they had intermarried with north Germans will probably never be known. But it does seem likely that the old monarchy contributed substantially, through the Moravian Brotherhood, to the Germanic influences that the Pennsylvania Dutch helped so effectively to spread in 19th century America.

The Georgia Salzburgers were always referred to as Germans – never as Austrians. They were, if the Moravians are excluded, the only significant group of Protestants (Lutherans) that ever came out of Austria to settle in America. Some may have had forbears among the persecuted Waldensians of the southern Alps but their immediate ancestors came from the isolated mountain villages of the Archbishopric of Salzburg and its neighbor *Länder*. Isolation had not protected them from the scourge of that champion of the Counter Reformation, Archbishop Leopold Anton Graf von Firmian, whose renewed efforts to purge Salzburg of heresy in 1731 involved the cruel, almost immediate exile of some thirty thousand Protestants. The story of their enforced odyssey into Protestant Germany and the further trek of some of them on to Holland and then to Georgia is a fascinating one that is all too little known.

One small group of Salzburgers was fortunate. For the charitable General James Oglethorpe (1696–1785), who had fought in 1717 against the Turks under Prince Eugene of Savoy, one of Austria's greatest military heroes,[17] had received a charter from George II to settle Georgia in America. The project would give asylum, Oglethorpe believed, to the Salzburgers and other refugee Protestants and it would also provide a bulwark against the Spanish in near-by Florida.[18]

Some fifty Salzburg families, with pastors Bolzius and Gronau of Halle who had taken charge of them in Germany, and with the blessings of the London Society for Promoting Christian Knowledge that helped with funds, left Holland in 1734 for Charleston and Savannah and settled at what they called, in Biblical terms, Ebenezer, some 25 miles from Savannah. It was the southernmost "German" settlement in colonial America. It was not exactly paradise – many died prematurely, the soil was indifferent and crops were bad, the prohibition of slavery produced long debates until the prohibition was abandoned in 1749, and the first group of Salzburgers lacked the mechanical skills that a new colony needed. So they moved to New Ebenezer, a better site not far away, which survived for a time even though it never prospered. Incidentally, the orphanage that they built in New Ebenezer may have been the first ever built in America. The trust fund built up from early contributions from Europe for the benefit of the Salzburgers has survived to our own time.

Father Bolzius seems to have been a gifted leader of the Salzburgers, in secular as well as spiritual matters. He pleaded for help from Europe and received it. Ebenezer vineyards might never produce good wine or its fields profitable indigo, but under Bolzius the settlers found they could grow good crops of corn, grains and garden vegetables and even of rice. Silk culture prospered. Some of the labor was provided by the redemptioners, men like Frederick Helfenstein who was, according to Faust, probably a descendant of Maximilian I, who signed away three to seven years of their lives for meeting the cost of transportation over the sea.[19] By the time of the Revolution Ebenezer was such a model village that we wonder why, after its destruction, the Salzburgers chose to leave it in ruins. It had contributed its pastor and a few of its citizens to the Tory cause and a far larger number to the patriotic side. It also contributed the first elected governor of Georgia, John Adam Treutlen.

More Salzburgers came after that first voyage and some eighty came in the winter of 1735–36 with a couple of dozen of Moravians. The Georgia Moravians, who were pacifists, soon moved north to avoid the obligation of having to fight the Spaniards to the southward. It was perhaps more significant that John Wesley with his brother Charles came with the Salzburgers and the Moravians. John Wesley learned German during all the delays before the ship actually got to sea and that was perhaps important for the history of Methodism and Evangelicalism in American Protestantism. For he could pray with the Germans. And when, during a frightening storm, he could say to himself, "How is it that thou hast no faith? being still unwilling to die," and a bit later: "A terrible screaming began among the English. The Germans... calmly sang on. I asked one of them afterwards, 'Was you not afraid?' He answered, 'I thank God no'," then Wesley felt that his religious convictions were sadly inferior to those of his German companions. He gave himself up to prayer and found a new approach to religion that was to have a genuine influence upon America's Great Awakening – the kind of pietism that gave us revivalism and emotionalism in American Protestantism. John Wesley's own journals give generous credit for his "awakening" to the Germans with whom he crossed the Atlantic on the way to infant Georgia in 1736. It is barely possible that the effect of Salzburger and Moravian piety upon the Wesley brothers was more significant in American history than the building of short-lived Ebenezer in the Georgia wilderness. It is also significant to note that another great Methodist preacher, George Whitefield, spent four months in Georgia in 1738 and came to accept "the essential principles of pietistic religion as professed and portrayed by the Georgia Salzburgers."[20] It is interesting that Catholic Austria should have contributed to the growth of American Protestant pietism!

In general there were very, very few immigrants from the Habsburg lands in the eighteenth century. German Protestants, and even Swiss, were coming in greater numbers than in the seventeenth century. The Germans were generally identified as from the Palatinate. But Catholics were few and far between. America was still generally unknown in the Austrian area; Catholics were unwelcome in America especially during the French and Indian Wars, and, in addition, the Vienna government frowned upon emigration. Joseph II's decree of July 7, 1768 made emigration virtually impossible from the entire Holy Roman Empire and the more liberal emigration policies of the regime of Kaiser Franz made emigration possible but not easy.[21] The Napoleonic wars put a complete stop to emigration in any event. It was indeed not until the second half of the nineteenth century that Austrian emigration to the United States became more than sporadic.

[1] *Dictionary of American Biography*; Bradford Smith, *Captain John Smith*, Phila. and N. Y. 1953.

[2] Fay-Cooper Cole, *The Long Road*, Baltimore 1933, pp. 78–81.

[3] C. D. Warner, ed., *Library of the World's Best Literature*, N. Y. 1897, XXVI. H. A. Pochmann, *German Culture in America*, Madison 1957, p. 344, indicates that Walther ranks 18th among German authors in translation in the U. S. 1830–1899. M. B. Quincy, *Critical Bibliography of German Literature in English 1481–1927*, Stanford 1938, pp. 577–578, ranks him 14th among all German poets translated into English. He lived in Vienna from 1190 to 1198.; H. v. Hofmannsthal, *Gesammelte Werke, Prosa*, vol. III, Frankfurt/Main 1952, p. 322.

[4] W. T. H. Jackson, *Literature of the Middle Ages*, Columbia U. Press 1960, pp. 198–209; *Cassell's Encyclopedia of World Literature*, vol. I, N. Y. 1954, p. 280.

[5] F. H. Wilkens, *Early Influence of German Literature in America*, N. Y., Berlin, London, 1900, p. 280.

[6] See Gary C. Grassl, "The German Washingtons," *The American-German Review*, Oct-Nov. 1963 and Dec. 1963-Jan. 1964.

[7] Henry Ganett, *American Names*, Washington 1947, p. 310. Ganett found 37 post offices under the name Berlin and 22 under Rome. Cf., U. S. Post Office Dept., *Dictionary of Post Offices*.

[8] Dieter Cunz, *Maryland Germans*, Princeton 1948, p. 390.

[9] *Neues Österreich*, Wien, 14 July 1963, p. 14.

[10] *American-German Review*, Dec.-Jan. 1956–57, p. 35.

[11] For Kino see our next chapter.

[12] A. B. Faust, *German Element in the United States*, 2 vols., Boston and New York 1909, I, p. 163; Dieter Cunz, *Maryland Germans*, Princeton 1948, pp. 12–14, 431–32.

[13] Faust, *op. cit.*, p. 161.

[14] D. L. Rights and W. P. Cumming, *Discoveries of John Lederer with Unpublished Letters*, U. Va. Press 1958; Cunz, *op. cit.*, pp. 30–37; Faust, *op. cit.*, II, pp. 342–43.

[15] I. D. Rupp, *A Collection of Thirty Thousand Names of German, Swiss, Dutch, French, . . . Immigrants in Pennsylvania 1727–76*, Harrisburg 1856, p. 91.

[16] A. L. Fries, *Road to Salem*, Chapel Hill, 1944; I. Daniel Rupp, *A Collection of Upwards of Thirty Thousand Names . . . Immigrants in Pennsylvania 1727 to 1776*, Phila. 1876, pp. 421–23; A. L. Fries, *Records of Moravians in North Carolina*, 6 vols., 1922, I, p. 62; Faust, *op. cit.*, see index to both vols.; *Dictionary of American Biography* for Zinzendorf. American historical literature is full of references to the Moravians.

[17] *Dictionary of American Biography.*

[18] The best brief account of the Georgia Salzburgers is in the article, "A Survey of Austrian Emigration to the United States," by Wilhelm Schlag in *Österreich und die angelsächsische Welt*, Wien 1961. Faust, *op. cit.*, I, has a good account. There are too many brief, indifferent accounts to mention here and there is also a wealth of source material like the *Journals of Mr. Commissary von Reck* (London 1734) and Bolzius's diaries. P. A. Strobel, *The Salzburgers*, Baltimore 1855, and C. F. Arnold, *Die Vertreibung der Salzburger Protestanten*, Leipzig 1900, should be mentioned. It is interesting to note that in George Bancroft's classic *History of the United States*, vol. III, Boston 1854, the Salzburgers are completely confused with the Moravians.

[19] Faust, *op. cit.*, I, pp. 66–67.

[20] H. A. Pochmann, *German Culture in America . . . 1600–1900*, Madison 1957, pp. 37–38. Pochmann points out that Wesley worked with both Jonathan Edwards and George Whitefield. See also P. A. Strobel, *The Salzburgers*, Baltimore 1855, pp. 75–80, and the *Journal of the Rev. John Wesley, A. M.*, N. Curnock ed., 4 vols., London 1938, I, pp. 110ff., especially pp. 142–51.

[21] Leo Goldhammer, "Jewish Emigration," *YIVO Annual 1954*, p. 350; A. B. Faust, *Guide to the Materials . . . Austrian Archives*, Washington 1916, p. 188. "Staats-Rath Index," 1784, no. 375.

CHAPTER III

DEFENDERS OF THE FAITH

The Austrian lands, from the times of the East Mark to the fall of the Iron Curtain, have not only defended the West from the East because the invaders were barbarians but, often far more important to the subjects of the Habsburgs, because they were infidels. Although Popes and Emperors might fall out, Roman Catholicism had no more faithful defenders than the Habsburgs. They gave the Hussite heresy no quarter, and they saw to it that the Counter Reformation triumphed, more completely than in any other important area in Central Europe, over Lutheranism and Calvinism. Catholicism has remained, in today's Austrian republic, the only religion of any size.

Austria's loyal Catholics, like so many religious denominations in America, have often felt the missionary urge. Their priests and monastic orders have carried the faith pretty much to all quarters of the world – including North America.

Proselyting for souls was in the early days of American history an essential part of the discovery and settlement of the continent. It was here, especially on the "old frontier," proselyting the Indians and maintaining the faith of the German-speaking pioneers, where the Austrians made their contributions. Some of the Austrians worked back on the east coast in German parishes where the faithful yearned for a priesthood that could speak more German than the Irish and native Americans. But those that helped make American frontier history went west to Ohio, Michigan, Illinois, Missouri and Wisconsin.

The most interesting of all was the Jesuit Father Eusebius Franz Kühn, known here as Eusebio Francesco Kino (b. Segno near Trent, South Tyrol, 1645 – d. St. Magdalene, 1711), who discovered the mouth of the Rio Grande for Spain and explored, civilized and Christianized so much of southern Arizona and Sonora. His most significant biographer, Professor Herbert E. Bolton of the University of California, is inclined to give him to the Italians on the ground that they have been most vociferous in claiming him. But Bolton recognizes that his real name was Eusebius Franz Kühn, that he was born under the aegis of the Holy Roman Empire, and that he was educated in lands where his own language was spoken, at Hall in Tyrol and Bavaria. Father Kino, in the proper Habsburg-monarchy way, was not certain whether he was Italian or German. The famous map that he made of Lower California nine years before his assassination by difficult natives bore the notation that he was a German. That meant that he was, in modern terms, Austrian.

Father Kühn's work in the New World was momentous. He baptized tens of thousands in Mexico where he went in 1687, made an historic map of Pimeria Alta (now North Sonora and South Arizona), worked his way up the Gila and Colorado Rivers (too late to be the genuine discoverer), and was the first to prove that Lower California was not an island. His bringing cattle and sheep and seed grain to the Indians and the whites of New Spain was doubtless far more important than his founding of some famous missions in the Arizona-Sonora country. He was one of the great figures of the American frontier.[1]

Another martyr to the Indians – in this case from poison in 1688 in New Mexico where he was working with the Tarahumara Indians – was the Styrian Jesuit Father John Ratkay (b. Pettau). Eighty years later the Moravian Martin Steffl made a dictionary for the same Indians who had poisoned Ratkay.[2]

The Habsburg regime might in the eighteenth century frown upon emigration – and emigration to America was no great problem in those early days when the New World was almost unknown – but there was an occasional man of courage, like Friedrich Post, "an unassuming, honest German, a Moravian," who came to America in 1742 to preach the Gospel among the Indians. He married an Indian squaw, was persecuted and imprisoned in Albany, returned to Europe, but came back later to work in the Pennsylvania country. He was only one of those Habsburg-monarchy clerical immigrants whose life history, could it be known, would be a fascinating story.[3]

And the Jesuit Francis Inama (b. Vienna, 1719 – d. Vienna) was sent to Mexico in the middle of the eighteenth century, worked his way converting Indians up into California, and after the suppression of the Jesuit order in 1773, returned home.[4]

Many years later, in 1796, an Austrian priest named Joseph Goetz came from his professional chair at the Wiener Neustädter academy to Philadelphia. There he found, before he disappeared from history, a common situation in the America of the time: the German Catholics unhappy in a world of Irish Catholic priests and Americans with little or no interest in the newly arrived Germans and Austrians who could speak nothing but German.[5]

The nineteenth century was the period when the Austrian missionaries and immigrant clergy made their greatest contribution to American Catholicism. After the Congress of Vienna in 1815 all of Catholic Europe turned to the business of winning converts abroad and especially in the Americas. The Society for the Propagation of the Faith in France and the Bavarian Missionsverein were only two of the many groups that found a warm welcome in their early years from America's confident, but still small and poor, Catholic parishes. And prominent among the European groups was Austria's Leopoldinen-Stiftung.

That foundation was established in 1829 upon the appeal of the German-born Father Rese who had been working, trying to make bricks without straw, with

Cincinnati's German-speaking Catholics. Kaiser Franz in Vienna and the Pope in Rome gave the plan their blessing. The Prince Archbishop of Vienna was its president. The Stiftung was named in memory of the Kaiser's daughter, Empress of Brazil, whose abuse by Pedro I may have been a contributing cause of his downfall two years after the establishment of the Stiftung that was, for almost a century, to donate Austrian money and clergy to the support of the American Church.

The Leopoldinen-Stiftung started out bravely enough, collecting the "weekly Kreutzers" from the lowest parish levels in dozens of quarters throughout the monarchy – all for North America. Some forty thousand dollars' worth of assistance was provided in its first two active years, 1830–1832. Aid during the next decade, according to one historian of the Foundation, totaled over $ 157,000, and the grand total, to 1921, was over $ 700,000. The useful "Berichte," or reports, of the Foundation, that constitute a major source of information on the Catholic Church in the United States, showed, in 1876 for instance, that the imperial family as well as the parishes of Vienna and of the distant provinces were all contributing to help bring the faith to America.

The funds were devoted to travel for missionaries, altar appurtenances and vestments and books for the churches, the building of over four hundred churches on the east coast as well as in the Middle West and in the Indian country, translations into Indian languages, and a thousand and one minor needs to help the cause. Sometimes the aid went to the East as when Bishop John England of Charleston visited Vienna and found help there from the Stiftung, and when in 1853 the first bishop of Newark, James Roosevelt Bailey, appealed for help on the ground that his German and Irish parishioners were too poor to support the new diocese. Much of it went to the Middle West. And some, as in the last decade of its charities, to 1913, went to Indian country – that included in those years Little Rock, Galveston, Santa Fé and Boise. The concept of the Leopoldinen-Stiftung was fine and generous. It was only unfortunate that such "foreign aid" was appreciated only by those who shared the Catholic faith, and they were relatively few in the America of the Stiftung's early years.[6]

Most important were the men and women who came – with or without the Kreutzers of the Stiftung. The bolder ones worked with the Indians. The others remained behind to do what proved the more significant task of helping to build vibrant Catholicism in the dioceses on the civilized side of the frontier. Some like Father Clemens Hammer, who came in 1838 to spend thirty years at the Marienkirche in Cincinnati, ultimately returned to die at home.[7]

There were really not very many German Austrians here. Blied's interesting book on Austrian and American Catholics shows that only about a quarter of the 98 "Austrian" priests that he discovered in the United States in 1869 and an even smaller proportion of the 121 Austrians of 1882 were from the area of the Austria of today.[8]

But there was a fairly large group, born perhaps outside the borders of 20th century Austria, who came because they were German in speech and culture, and because Vienna sent them, whom we cannot very well ignore in this account.

The Leopoldinen-Stiftung sent Catholics of all orders. The Jesuits, restored to grace by the Pope in 1814 after the abolition of their order in the eighteenth century, were, perhaps unfortunately for some Americans who thought the order "too Jesuitical" for the free New World, active here, especially in Cincinnati and St. Louis. It had some three dozen priests and monks here at mid-century. Fathers like the poet Christoph Genelli (b. Berlin, 1800 – d. 1850), who came here in 1848 to work in St. Louis and who died of cholera in Cincinnati on his way back to Austria, are relatively unknown. There were Jesuits as far east as Boston, playing a minor but important part.[9]

But the Jesuit Francis Xavier Weninger (b. Marburg, Styria, 1805 – d. Cincinnati, 1888) was a striking figure. He was a Forty-eighter who was no Forty-eighter in spirit: he distrusted even Catholic revolutionaries of 1848 and found Jews "the ruination of the body and soul of the German nation." But he was willing to preach to Negro slaves in New Orleans (1852) and spread the Gospel in the central states in German, French, and even in English. His boxes of holy books in German and English he carried with him and used for spreading the faith wherever he went. Weninger was one of those conservatives who should have been better known to the Americans who criticized the radicalism of the Forty-eighters. He was notable as a champion of the preservation of the German language and culture among the immigrants. "Language Saves Faith" was the slogan of Weninger and of many other German-speaking clergy in America.[10]

More effective were the little-known Redemptorists who worked from the Northeast out to Wisconsin. They had helped Father Rese when he came to Vienna in 1828 to find aid for American missions and they had promptly sent a group of three priests and three lay brethren to work in the New World. Others followed and the Redemptorists counted their converts by the tens of thousands.[11]

There were a few Benedictines like Father Nikolaus Balleis of St. Peter's in Salzburg.[12] And the Franciscans, who included Father Alexander Martin in Boston and Father William Unterthiner in New York and Cincinnati, both from the Tyrol, established a *Mutterhaus* in 1844 near Cincinnati.[13] Another Tyrolese, Father Inama, in Roxburg, Wisconsin, received for his church from the King of Bavaria a fine Madonna and Child by the famous painter Kaulbach. Indeed, the austerity of the frontier, and of some eastern communities, was often tempered by the occasional art objects, as well as by the music, that the German-speaking clergy brought with them.[14]

The church also sent a few Sisters. One group of Franciscans who left Vienna in 1850 established its first cloister in the German community of Oldenburg in Indiana.[15]

But the Sisters like the male clergy were usually so mingled with Germans that it is difficult to assess the impact of the relatively few Austrians as such. Even Austrians thought of themselves as one kind of German.

By comparison with Germany, Catholic Austria may well have furnished more than its quota of German-speaking priests and brethren. The Leopoldinen-Stiftung encouraged dozens of fine personalities to emigrate.[16] And a number of the twelve bishops of the American hierarchy whom Blied's book credits to Austria came with the Stiftung's assistance.[17] The bishops worked chiefly in the Middle West; other clergy there and in the east. Almost none went south and virtually none worked with the Negroes. A well-known Austrian Chargé in Washington in mid-century called the Negroes "scum." The "Wegweiser" or guides for immigrants warned them out of the South where opportunities for immigrants were few, and so the Austrians seldom went south of Baltimore and St. Louis.

The mid-century idealization of the Indian by Austrian writers like Lenau and Sealsfield, on the other hand, interested the missionaries in the poor Reds who had been born free and trampled on by white pioneers. Most of the early Austrian missionaries, from Kino to Baraga, were more concerned with the souls of the Indians than with those of the German-speaking immigrants who were soon to claim more and more attention.

Bishop Frederic Baraga (b. Treffen, Carniola, 1797 – d. Marquette, 1868) was perhaps the greatest of the Austrian missionaries to the Indians. Born near Laibach, educated in law at Vienna and in theology in Laibach, he was sent by the Leopoldinen-Stiftung in 1830 to bring salvation to the Indians. His career led him from Cincinnati to Upper Michigan. He learned the languages of the Ottawas and the Chippewas, used them in the translation of the holy books, a life of Jesus, and some poetry of his own, won the Indians with kindness and tobacco and protection against alcohol, and learned to know, by canoe and snowshoe, every community in Northern Michigan. They made him bishop of Northern Michigan in 1853 and later, in 1865, bishop of a new diocese at Marquette. The $ 160 which the Leopoldinen-Stiftung had invested in Baraga in 1830 had yielded a great harvest.[18]

It was perhaps his influence that brought others from the Laibach area to America. The Leopoldinen-Stiftung helped him send us Father Franz Pierz (probably from Pirče in Carniola where he was born in 1785) who helped with the religious work among the Michigan Indians, set up Indian schools, recruited others like the renowned Bishop Katzer of Green Bay and Milwaukee from the Austrian homeland, and became bishop of the St. Paul diocese.[19] Ignatius Mrak (b. Laibach – d. Marquette, 1901) who came to America in 1840 not only assisted Pierz at Abre Croche and took over his Indian mission there but he succeeded Baraga as Marquette's second bishop. Mrak was in turn succeeded by John Vertin (b. Carniola, 1844 – d. Marquette, 1899) who came here as a boy of nineteen to study with Baraga at St. Francis in Wisconsin and receive his consecration as bishop in 1879.[20]

The second American and the first of his sex to achieve beatification by the Pope, in 1963, the final step before sainthood, was John Nepomuk Neumann (b. Prachatitz, Bohemia, 1811 – d. Philadelphia, 1860), a saintly, charitable Redemptorist, whom Baraga persuaded to immigrate.[21] Neumann, who established dozens of parochial schools and several sisterhoods when he was bishop of Philadelphia and gave most of his worldly goods to the poor, was another of the proponents of the retention of the German language and culture who were so obnoxious to the American nativists at mid-century.[22] The Benedictine Father Stephen Raffeiner (b. Mais, Vintschgau, 1785 – d. Williamsburg, 1861), an addict to goat's milk from the Tyrol, started for Cincinnati in 1883 but was intrigued by the opportunities in New York and Boston, built the St. Nicholas Church in New York, and never did go west.[23] The Linzer priest, Joseph Salzmann (b. Münzbach, Upper Austria, 1819 – d. Milwaukee, 1874), on the other hand, reached Wisconsin to found the St. Francis Seminary in 1856 and some other useful church schools and societies that reflected his concern with better training for priests. He was another of the conservatives who did battle with the free-thinkers of '48 among his fellow-countrymen.[24]

There were others who came before the Forty-eighters. Father Andrew Viscoczkry, for instance, a Hungarian who had studied in Vienna, helped Father Raffeiner with his New York Germans before he went on to Ohio and Michigan where the devil had introduced immorality and indifference to the church and love of luxury among the German-speaking immigrants.[25] There was the fanatical Andreas Bernadus Smolnikar (b. Stein, Carniola, 1795) of Klagenfurt whom the Lord himself sent to Boston where he found a parish of 143 Germans to support his work. The Bostonians and Professor Karl Follen of Harvard refused to accept his credentials from the Almighty, and Smolnikar moved on to greener pastures.[26] Canon Joseph Salzbacher (b. St. Pölten, Lower Austria, 1790 – d. Baden bei Wien, 1867) of Vienna came to investigate the tensions between the Germans and their Irish and American priests and to justify the ways of the Leopoldinen-Stiftung.[27] And Joseph Melcher (b. Vienna, 1807 – d. Green Bay, 1873) became in 1868 bishop of Green Bay with sixteen priests and a Catholic population of some 50,000 souls.[28]

Such Austrians were pioneers who contributed much to the building of America. But, unfortunately and entirely unintentionally, they provided tinder for the flames of nativism – that ugly manifestation of American nationalism that swept too much of the country in the late 1830's and the decades that followed.

Distrust of Catholic Europe as personified by the French in Canada and the Spanish on our southern borderlands had been ever-present in eighteenth century America which had inherited so much of the religious and nationalistic intolerance of the Protestant Reformation. The intellectual and political radicalism of the Enlightenment and of the French Revolution had disturbed Puritan-Anglican America. And European concern for maintaining colonies in this hemisphere during the Age of Metternich and the Holy Alliance had done more to arouse our sensitive nationalists even before the immigrant tides of the middle and late nineteenth century began to threaten our Puritan traditions. The consequences, nativism and, a bit later, Know-Nothingism, were of tremendous significance in American life.

Unfortunately the Austrians contributed to all of the nineteenth century elements of nativism. Metternich was the master builder of the Holy Alliance, the Vienna revolution of Forty-eight helped dispatch a group of radical intellectuals to spread their doctrines here, the New Immigration of the 1880's that so changed the cultural pattern of the United States came in large part from Austria's empire, the way of life of the music-loving, wine-drinking Austrian immigrants was often alien to ours, and, most important of all in the earlier years, their faith was Catholicism.

"A national faith . . . thrives best, as Emerson remarked, when its prophets have a fallacy to expose, a blunder to pillory . . . What the capitalist was to Lenin in 1917 and the Jew to Hitler in 1935, the Catholic was to the American democrat in the middle of the nineteenth century . . ."[29]

The Leopoldinen-Stiftung was chiefly responsible for throwing the nativist floodlight upon Vienna. A Heidelberg student named Lewis Clausing told us in the 1830's how the Leopoldinen-Stiftung was bringing over hundreds of Jesuits expert in espionage to work for the Holy Alliance.[30] And the electors of Washington County, New York, for instance, memorialized Congress for stricter immigration laws back in 1838 on the ground that there was "a plan in operation, powerful and dangerous, under the management of the Leopold Foundation for the subversion of our civil and religious liberties, to be effected by the emigration of Roman Catholics from Europe."[31]

Although Lyman Beecher's Boston was far more concerned with Irish Catholics than with Austrians, Beecher thought of Vienna after a nativist riot: "Has it come to this? — that the capital of New England has been thrown into consternation by the threats of a Catholic mob, and that her temples and mansions stand only through the forbearance of a Catholic bishop? . . . dependent on the Catholic powers of Europe and the bayonets of Austria?"[32] Beecher's "Plea for the West" (1835) was a plea to save the Mississippi Valley from Papist Austria! He was doubtless encouraged in his fears by the British traveler, Captain Marryat, who had encountered the Leopoldinen-Stiftung in the United States and had predicted, in his "Diary in America," that the continent west of the Alleghanies would become Catholic.[33] That must have sounded like a compliment to the work of Austrian, German, and French missionaries! And one of the famous Peabody sisters, Elizabeth, sister-in-law of Nathaniel Hawthorne and Horace Mann, published in 1852 her dull but angry little book, "The Crimes of the House of Austria against Mankind."

Another native of New England, Samuel F. B. Morse, the inventor of the telegraph, was the real Don Quixote of the war on the Austrian Catholics. Morse "endeavored to rouse Protestants to a renewed and more vigorous use of their religious weapons in their moral war with Popery."[34] And he pointed out that Austria had commenced the attack upon our liberties through the "St. Leopold Foundation." The Mississippi Valley was in danger! "*Austria is now acting in this country*. She has devised a grand scheme ... She has her Jesuit missionaries traveling through the land; she has supplied them with money, ... She had expended a year ago more than *seventy-four thousand dollars* in furtherance of her design! These are not surmises. They are facts ... The society is called St. Leopold Foundation ... Prince Metternich has it under his watchful care. The Pope has given it his apostolic benediction ... It is high time that we awake to the apprehension of danger."

Morse and Elizabeth Peabody and Beecher were only a few of the notable enemies of the dangerous Austrians! James Fenimore Cooper, whose scouts and Indians the Austrians have long loved, warned against foreigners. And Thomas R. Whitney of the Order of United Americans launched an attack on the Leopoldinen-Stiftung in his journal "The Republic." The Stiftung was "set up by Metternich ... to convert the United States from heretical Protestantism to the parental sheepfold of Papal Hierarchy ... whose path is stained with blood, whose chariot is drawn fiercely onward ages after ages, amid groans and tears ..."[35] And Austria, which occupied much of the north of Italy that had never pulled itself together since the fall of Rome, was the culprit on occasions like that of a Papal legate's visit to Baltimore in 1854 when the unfortunate legate was burned in effigy for the ostensible reason that he was opposed to ejecting the Austrians from Italy. In Baltimore with all its Germans and Irish, Know-Nothingism was strong. Its watchword, "Put none but Americans on guard tonight," quoted from Washington, was doubtless aimed at a few Austrian new-comers as well as at thousands of German and other Catholic immigrants.[36] It made life unhappy for thousands of new Americans all over the land. It contributed to the tendency that was all too common among the newcomers, to live apart in foreign colonies with their own language, customs, and churches.

Difficult as it is to distinguish the Austro-American Catholics from their German-born cousins, we find evidence here and there after the Civil War that the Austrians continued to come. Some of the earlier ones came as missionaries to the Indians. Father Pierz visited Vienna in 1864 to recruit missionaries for work among the Minnesota Indians and brought back with him the famous Frederic Xavier Katzer (b. Ebensee, Upper Austria, 1844 – d. Fond du Lac, 1903). Katzer found his work in Wisconsin, fought against legislation making it compulsory to use English in the schools, and was accused in the "Review of Reviews" (August 1892) of being one of the agents of the Catholic powers of Europe that were trying to infiltrate America – which Katzer indignantly denied. He was then bishop of Milwaukee.[37] Father Pierz brought some sixteen Austrian priests to the United States in 1864 including Father Buh as well as the young Katzer. James Trobec (b. Carniola, 1838), one of the recruits of 1864, studied in Minnesota and achieved some fame there as missionary, parish priest, and bishop of St. Cloud.[38] Joseph Rainer (b. Kattern, Tyrol, 1845) who came in 1867 was for years rector of the St. Francis Seminar for priests.[39] Father Weninger was a Tyroler Benedictine who found in Newark, New Jersey, a German settlement which welcomed his ministrations.[40]

The later arrivals came chiefly to work among the German-speaking Catholics. For the church feared that it was losing them. New American ways of life, materialism, godless public schools, the isolation of the frontier, and lack of a sympathetic clergy resulted, the secretary of the St. Raphaelsverein at Vienna estimated in 1907, in the loss of a half or more of the Catholic immigrants.[41]

That St. Raphaelsverein, the controversial child of a certain Peter Paul Cahensly who was notorious to American nativists, had as its mission the assistance of migrants of the Catholic faith and aid in keeping them within the fold. Cahensly attended the 1889 *Katholikentag* in Vienna to plead for help. Interested in preserving the faith of Austrian emigrants, Emperor Franz Joseph and other dignitaries gave generously to the fund and Prince Schwarzenberg became chairman of the Austrian branch. Suspicious nativists found it, like the Leopoldinen-Stiftung, evidence of the Austro-Papist conspiracy in America.[42]

As intolerance waned and Catholicism took an honored place in the American world, the Austrian-born Catholics found it easier to fit into the American scene. Their roles were less dramatic than those of Father Kühn and Father Baraga. Mother Mary Agnes (1870—1962), for instance, came here in 1921. She was a distant relative of the Habsburgs and had taught Franz Joseph's grandchildren. She became the founder of the order in America of the Franciscan Nuns of the Most Blessed Sacrament and of the St. Paul Shrine of Perpetual Adoration in Cleveland.[43] The order called *Die Söhne des heiligsten Herzens Jesu* came in 1956 to work with Negroes.[44] But there were almost none in the later years who came to maintain their Austrian identity.

The pleasant receptions that Chancellor Seipel, the most Catholic of all Austrian chancellors, received when he came to the World Eucharistic Congress in Chicago in 1926 were perhaps significant as the first glorified social affairs since World War I where the German-speaking had dared show themselves.[45] The Austrians were always a little less German than the Germans and were thus always a useful entering wedge when Germans, in the broader sense, were not entirely in favor.

American aid to Austrian Catholics after the World Wars may have come chiefly through the efforts of American Catholics of Austrian blood. And the gratitude of the Austrians was expressed in such ways as the presentation in 1962 of some $ 40,000 for American-Catholic relief work in Senegal in deepest Africa.[46]

It was doubtless significant that hundreds of American Catholic clergymen have, in recent years, studied at Austrian Catholic Seminars and especially at the one in Innsbruck which seems to have had a special attraction for Americans. That was perhaps because Father Noldin, of the professorial chair there of theology, had written some of the textbooks most widely used in America's theological schools. One of the most distinguished American students at Innsbruck, John La Farge, who joined the Jesuit order there, found in 1901 an Innsbruck American colony of some thirty student theologians.[47] That Innsbruck colony grew a bit through the years and had, by the middle 1960's, more than doubled its numbers. It was only natural that Indiana's Notre Dame University should in 1964 have inaugurated a European studies program in Innsbruck which had been a cultural home for so many American Catholics. And on this side of the water the Catholic schools and universities like, for instance, The Catholic University of America in Washington, have welcomed dozens upon dozens of Austrian-born, especially the refugees of 1938, to teach in theology and many other more secular fields. Nondenominational and even Protestant colleges and universities have taken Austrian Catholics to contribute to the solution of the refugee problem of 1938 and to strengthen their faculties. The scores of able Austrians who have been teaching within recent years in the American colleges and universities have doubtless had even more of an impact in this hemisphere than Father Kühn with all the livestock that he introduced to the Indians of the Southwest.

[1] W. Böhm, *Universitas Vindobonensis*, Wien 1952, p. 217, calls him Kühn. See authoritative biographies by Herbert E. Bolton published in 1932 and 1936 and Bolton's *Kino's Historical Memoir*, 2 vols., 1919. See also Lambert Schrott, *Pioneer German Catholics*, U. S. Cath. Hist. Assc. monographs, 1933, p. 6–7, and *Österreicher als Erforscher der Erde*, Notring, Wien 1956.

[2] Schrott, *op. cit.*, p. 5. Wilhelm Schlag's study of "Österreichische Pioniere und Forscher in Nordamerika," available at the Austrian Institute in New York, mentions Steffl, Georg Brandt who worked in Mexico 1648–1690, Marcus Anton Knapp who died 1717 as Superior of the Sonora Mission, Ferdinand Komschak a Visitator of Missions in California, and Wenzel Linck, explorer in 1766 of the Colorado River valley, who was deported with the other Austrian Jesuit priests from New Spain in 1767.

[3] I. D. Rupp, *A Collection of Thirty Thousand Names of German, Swiss, French, ... and other Immigrants in Pennsylvania, 1727–76*, Hamburg 1856, p. 91. The title of this volume indicates that in 1856 the Austrians were, unlike the Swiss, included with the Germans.

[4] *Appleton's Cyclopaedia of American Biography*, vol. II, N. Y. 1888.

[5] B. J. Blied, *Austrian Aid to American Catholics 1830–1860*, Milwaukee 1944, p. 58.

[6] For the Leopoldinen-Stiftung the *Berichte* are a major source. There are many secondary accounts such as Johannes Thauren, *Ein Gnadenstrom zur Neuen Welt*, Wien 1940; Theodore Roemer, *Ten Decades of Alms*, St. Louis and London 1942; and Benj. J. Blied, *op. cit.* See also the *Catholic Encyclopaedia*, vol. XVI, N. Y. 1907, and *Austrian Information*, 26 Nov. 1960, p. 2, which states that the total expen-

ditures of the Stiftung were 4,257,614 gold crowns. Founder Friedrich Rese published a book on American missions in Vienna in 1828–29.

[7] *Das Buch der Deutschen in Amerika*, Philadelphia 1909, p. 371.

[8] Blied, *op. cit.*, p. 149.

[9] Blied, *op. cit.*, pp. 162–65.

[10] Georg von Bosse, *Das deutsche Element in den Vereinigten Staaten*, Stuttgart 1908, p. 468; Gilbert J. Garraghan, *The Jesuits in the Middle United States*, 3 vols., N. Y. 1938, II, pp. 53–65. Weninger contributed to the Baltimore *Katholische Volkszeitung*, a conservative sheet; Dieter Cunz, *Maryland Germans*, Princeton 1948, p. 359.

[11] Blied, *op. cit.*, pp. 150–59; *Catholic Encyclopaedia*, XII, pp. 683–84.

[12] Georg Timpe, *Katholisches Deutschtum in ... Amerika*, Freiburg 1937, pp. 85–87.

[13] Blied, *op. cit.*, p. 169; *Das Buch der Deutschen*, p. 253.

[14] I. L. U. Lacher, *German Element in Wisconsin*, Steuben Soc. 1925, p. 24.

[15] *Das Buch der Deutschen*, p. 254.

[16] The *Catholic Encyclopaedia*, 1907, p. 52, found over two dozen worthy of mention.

[17] Pp. 115–18.

[18] *Dictionary of American Biography*; G. G. Govorchin, *Americans from Yugoslavia*; C. von Wurzbach, *Biographisches Lexikon des Kaiserthums Österreich*, 60 parts, Wien 1856–91, I, pp. 148–49; A. B. Faust, *German Element in the United States*, 2 vols., Boston and New York 1909, I, p. 463; *Der deutsche Pionier*, I, p. 291. Many accounts mention the close cooperation between Catholics and Protestants: Protestants attending Catholic services and priests like Baraga ministering to Protestants when they had no Protestant clergy.

[19] *Dictionary of American Biography*; Blied, *Austrian Aid*, p. 114.

[20] *Catholic Encyclopaedia*, 1912 ed.

[21] *Ibid.* and *Das Buch der Deutschen*. The press announced his beatification 14. Oct. 1963.

[22] *Ibid.*, p. 252; C. J. Barry, *Catholic Church and German Catholics*, Milwaukee 1953, p. 11; *Dictionary of American Biography*.

[23] *Dictionary of American Biography*; Wurzbach, *op. cit.*, XXIV, pp. 223f.

[24] Timpe, *op. cit.*, pp. 11, 151; Faust, *op. cit.*, I, p. 471; *Catholic Encyclopaedia*, 1912 ed., XIII, p. 415.

[25] Roemer, *op. cit.*, p. 201.

[26] *Mitteilungen des deutschen Pionier-Vereins von Philadelphia*, vol. XVI, 1910, pp. 27–36.

[27] Barry, *op. cit.*, p. 15; Wurzbach, *op. cit.*, XXVIII, pp. 162–64.

[28] *National Cyclopaedia of American Biography*, XII; *Das Buch der Deutschen*, p. 252.

[29] Quoted from R. H. Gabriel, *The Course of American Democratic Thought*, N. Y. 1956, p. 54. See also John Higham, *Strangers in the Land*, Rutgers 1955, for an excellent discussion of nativism.

[30] Blied, *op. cit.*, p. 42.

[31] U. S. House of Reps., Exec. Docs., 25th Congress, 2nd Sess., no. 154.

[32] Carleton Beals, *Brass-Knuckle Crusade*, N. Y. 1960, p. 37.

[33] Blied, *op. cit.*, pp. 43–44. Blied cites Robert Baird, *Religion in America*, 1844, that mentions the "large sums" available to the Leopoldinen-Stiftung.

[34] Quoted, as is much of what follows, from Morse, *Foreign Conspiracy against the Liberties of the United States*, N. Y. 1835. It is interesting to note that Americans seemed utterly oblivious to the fact that the Leopoldinen-Stiftung was named from a martyred empress in their own hemisphere.

[35] Beals, *op. cit.*, pp. 117–19; Thomas R. Whitney, *A Defense of the American Policy*, N. Y. 1956, pp. 71–72.

[36] L. F. Schmeckebier, *History of the Know Nothing Party in Maryland*, Baltimore 1899, pp. 11–49. Schmeckebier maintains that the Germans aggravated the situation by trying to Germanize America, making no effort to Americanize themselves.

[37] *Dictionary of American Biography*; Barry, *op. cit.*, p. 211.

[38] *Who's Who*, 1899–1900; *Catholic Encyclopaedia*, 1912 ed.

[39] *Buch der Deutschen in Amerika*, p. 391.

[40] Berichte der Leopoldinen-Stiftung, 1880, pp. 7–8.

[41] Barry, *op. cit.*, p. 132.

[42] *Ibid.*

[43] Obit. in *New York Times* and *Washington Post*, 4 Nov. 1962.

[44] J. Fried, *Österreichische Priester . . . in aller Welt*, Wien 1957, p. 33.

[45] Timpe, *op. cit.*, p. 144.

[46] *Austrian Information*, 28 July 1962, p. 6; Timpe, *op. cit.*, pp. 62 and 132, refers to American Catholic help to Austrians, especially to Caritas, after World War I.

[47] *Austrian Information*, 31 Oct. 1962, p. 6; John La Farge, *The Manner is Ordinary*, N. Y. 1954, p. 81.

CHAPTER IV

YEARS OF MISUNDERSTANDING 1800–1870

Benjamin Franklin told an anecdote of Kaiser Joseph II which throws a light upon the great void between distant Austria and young America in the last years of the eighteenth century. Joseph, incognito in Paris under the title Count Falkenstein, was asked, "How happens it M. le Comte . . . that while we all feel so much interest in the cause of the Americans, you say nothing for them?" To which the Kaiser replied, "I am a king by trade."[1] Ex-President Jefferson illustrated in 1810 the American attitude by declaring that the "king of Austria" was an idiot like so many of Europe's rulers.

In all the years when monarchy ruled "Austria" there were, to generalize, no cordial official relations between the Americans and the Austrians. The Habsburg monarchy was always, to America, a remote despotism, and the American states were too long, to the Habsburgs, an upstart, often troublesome, democracy. That we were distantly allied with Austria during the War of the Austrian Succession when Vienna and London became allies against Frederick II seems to have made no impression upon the American colonies. In any event the European system of alliances was reversed before the Seven Years' War leaving the British allied to Maria Theresia's arch-enemy Frederick of Prussia.

During our early revolutionary and republican years when we sent diplomatic agents all over western Europe to make treaties with the Netherlanders, Swedes, Prussians, Norwegians, and even with the Barbary pirates, we made no treaty with Austria. We did indeed, in 1777, commission one of our least successful diplomats to visit the Court of Vienna but Kaiser Joseph, who had no love for American rebels and saw no reason for antagonizing Britain, refused to receive him.

After American independence was assured, in 1782, Vienna indicated that it would like to negotiate a treaty; Benjamin Franklin, our Minister to France, was provided with full powers; but negotiations were delayed and, when Jefferson took Franklin's place, he let the whole matter lapse on the ground that Austria's trade was for us "no object." His indifference may well have been connected with Austria's role as one of the mediators of the peace of 1783 – a role that Americans did not appreciate because it seemed likely to involve the American settlement with Great Britain as a mere pawn in the European settlement. But, despite Jefferson's indifference, there were further negotiations for a treaty that ended only when America was more concerned with setting up its government under its new Constitution and

Austria with the revolt of the Austrian Netherlands.[2] The paucity of trade between the two lands must have contributed to the lack of zeal in the negotiation of a treaty.

The Vienna Court, however, convinced either that Austria as a great power needed an observer in the new-born republic or that Austria's potential trade with America was worth a bit of encouragement, sent its first agent to Philadelphia in 1783. That was a certain Baron de Beelen-Bertholff. His efforts between 1783 and 1790 led to no treaty but Vienna found him useful in representing the Empire's commercial interests and he sent home volumes of comprehensive reports that must have thrown more light upon the United States than the Austrians were to receive for at least two generations to come.[3]

It was not until the late 1820's, long after the Congress of Vienna in which Americans showed so little interest, that any significant steps were taken to bring Americans and Austrians more closely together. Austria sent a consul to New York and on August 27, 1829, he and Secretary of State Van Buren signed a Treaty of Commerce and Navigation — a late edition of the treaty that Joseph II and William Lee had failed to arrive at more than fifty years earlier.[4]

Finally, in 1837, the United States sent Nathaniel Niles to Vienna as a special diplomatic agent to try to persuade Austria to lower tariff barriers against American imports and to welcome American tobacco. Our first normal diplomatic representative in Vienna, however, was Minister Henry A. Muhlenberg of Pennsylvania who was not appointed until February 8, 1838, long years after we had sent diplomatic representatives to such small "powers" as Central America and Denmark.[5] We then sent another minister, Daniel Jenifer of Maryland, followed from 1845 to 1854 by five lower-ranking chiefs of mission, chargés d'affaires. That was an indication that our sympathies, during the mid-century, revolutionary years, lay not with the Vienna government but with the non-German nationalities of the old monarchy which were already working successfully upon America's inclination to side with any revolutionary cause. Of the next four American diplomatic representatives in Vienna John Lothrop Motley, one of three ministers who represented us from 1858 to 1867, and John Hay, a chargé d'affaires, were the two most distinguished Americans that were ever sent to the Vienna mission. Those that followed during the next hundred years were, with the occasional exception of a competent person like Llewellyn Thompson, ambassador from 1952 to 1957, relatively unknown — political appointees or, at best, good career men on their way to greener pastures or to retirement. All in all, American representation in Vienna has been less distinguished than in any other great European capital.

At the Congress of Vienna which ushered in a century of comparative peace the United States was not represented. Our State Department was allergic to European questions and American books on foreign policy long treated that significant Congress with scarcely a word of comment.[6] That "the Congress danced" generally sufficed for its characterization in the books that Americans read.

Indifference turned to distrust during the long years to 1848 when Prince Metternich dominated the Ballhausplatz and European great-power politics in general. Metternich, born a Rhinelander, was always to Americans a reactionary Austrian, a self-seeking tool of the Pope at Rome and of a frightened group of European powers whose design was only to crush democracy and liberty in the New World. We ignored the generally accepted interpretation of Metternich as a genius of conservatism, perhaps "the most important diplomat of modern times," an inveterate enemy of the kind of revolution that had unsettled the Western World since 1789, who tried to make of Austria a cornerstone of the *status quo* and, most important, of the peace of Europe. We thought of him chiefly as the author of the Holy Alliance.

That Alliance was indeed committed to the denial of the right of revolution and to the support of legitimacy. That it was ready to intervene to rescue legitimacy from revolution, as when it commissioned Austria to put down democratic movements in Naples and Piedmont, seemed to Americans to indicate that it was eager to return to Bourbon Spain its rebel American colonies. Spain's appeal to the Holy Alliance for help and the possibility that Spain might receive help from France seemed to Secretary of State John Quincy Adams, as well as to George Canning at London, to point to danger. And the result was the famous Monroe Doctrine that declared in 1823 any effort of a European power to interfere with the political system of the Americas an unfriendly act.

It was then, in a very real sense, Prince Metternich and his system that gave us the Monroe Doctrine. Thomas Jefferson, in discussing the proposed Doctrine with President Monroe, doubtless reflected American thinking: "Nor is the occasion to be slighted which this proposition offers, of declaring our protest against the atrocious violations of the rights of nations, by the interference of anyone in the internal affairs of another, so flagitiously begun by Bonaparte, and now continued by the equally lawless Alliance, calling itself Holy."[8] And Americans ever since have believed that the Monroe Doctrine saved the Americas from subjection to Europe even though our historians have recently pointed out that these continents were never actually threatened by the Holy Alliance. Metternich himself thought that Spain would gain nothing by trying to recover her lost colonies.[9]

The lack of understanding between Vienna and the New World was appalling. Metternich wrote to Nesselrode in 1824, probably right after reading Monroe's new Doctrine: "These United States of America, which we have seen arise and grow, and which during their too short youth already meditated projects which they dared not then avow, have suddenly left a sphere too narrow for their ambition, and have astonished Europe by a new act of revolt, more unprovoked, fully as audacious, and no less dangerous than the former. They have distinctly and clearly announced their intention to set not only power against power, but, to express it more exactly, altar against altar ... In permitting themselves to these unprovoked attacks, in fostering revolutions wherever they show themselves, in regretting those which have failed, in extending a helping hand to those which seem to prosper, they lend new strength to the apostles of sedition, and reanimate the courage of every conspirator."[10] It was clearly unfortunate that the United States had no diplomatic representation at Vienna in those times.

America reciprocated Metternich's distrust. Samuel F. B. Morse, the inventor of the telegraph who was so perturbed by the Catholic missionary activities of Vienna's Leopoldinen-Stiftung in America, called Metternich "the arch contriver of the plans for stifling liberty in Europe and throughout the world." He blamed him for helping to crush the liberties of Greece, Spain, Sicily, Naples, and Genoa. He quoted Dwight as saying that the liberals of Europe regarded Metternich as "the greatest enemy of the human race who has lived for ages." And Morse maintained that the Holy Alliance was aimed at "the destruction of liberty everywhere." The Pope, the Jesuits, and Kaiser Franz were, of course, all involved in the great Metternich plot to subvert America.[11]

And Charles Sealsfield, the well-known Austrian author whose most fervent wish was to be known as an American citizen, revisited his homeland and wrote in a book he published in London in 1828 that "Never has there been a man more detested and dreaded than Metternich ... the author and mainspring of the Holy Alliance ... The consequences are, universal detestation of Austria among the nations of Europe ..."[12]

It was unfortunate that Austria itself shared Prince Metternich's unpopularity. The secret police, the censorship, the poverty of peasant and worker, the army of spies to enforce the Metternich system – all these were cited to prove that Austria was Europe's outpost of reaction. The American chargé d'affaires in Austria in 1848 wrote in his unflattering volume on Austria[13] that he had seen a Vienna crowd dragging a poor devil through the streets to a lamp-post and was told that the fellow had been caught merely talking with a friend about the republican form of government. Samuel F. B. Morse's books proclaiming that the American "democratic system is vitally felt by Austria. She confesses it. It is proscribed by the Austrian Cabinet. This country is designated ... as the great *plague spot* of the world, the poisoned fountain ..." – his books were well-read because he himself was a well-known figure. Elizabeth Peabody of a noted New England family helped to denounce what she called the crimes of Austria and the House of Habsburg.[14] And, a bit later, in the sixties, our Minister to Austria, the historian John Lothrop Motley who had studied in Germany, finding Austria absolutist in both politics and industry, concluded that he prefered Bismarck and Protestant Europe to Franz Joseph and his empire.[15]

American prejudices against Austria must have been confirmed when Charles Sealsfield wrote: "The tide runs in Vienna towards gross sensuality in the people; — mute obedience in the public officers; — gloom or dissoluteness among the high nobility, and towards the most complete despotism in the government . . . Should an Austrian author dare to write contrary to the views of the government, his writings would be not only mutilated, but he himself regarded as a contagious person . . ." He found the land teeming with official spies and censors.[16]

Unlike Sealsfield, most Americans disliked Austria, not only because of Metternich, the Holy Alliance and the Catholicism which its Jesuits and Leopoldinen-Stiftung were promoting here, but because they knew almost nothing about it and because what they did know seemed to indicate that Austrians and Americans had very little in common. Frances Trollope, the English critic with the sharp pen, was writing for both England and America when she explained in 1838:[17] "Austria is a *terra incognita* to England . . . it is to be regretted . . . for a million of English visiting Paris, for one who visits Vienna. The loss is wholly ours." She would doubtless have regretted that in the 1960's when Austria had become Europe's third most popular tourist country, so few Americans visited and understood it. She mentioned the "thousands who have been taught to hate the name of this (essentially) unknown country." And she pointed up the temperamental differences between Americans and Austrians: "I have never known when the gayest of (America's) painstaking citizens would have turned for a moment from their undying labours of electioneering for the merriest amusement . . . nor on the other hand, have I ever known Austria when her populace would have preferred (politics) to a waltz . . ., or a chorus in a vineyard." She found the voteless Austrian peasants far happier than the Americans who took their universal suffrage so seriously. The Englishwoman doubtless understood the differences between the two peoples much better than they themselves did.

The Revolutions of 1848 in the Habsburg Empire contributed much on both the positive and the negative sides to Austro-American relations. On the positive side was the arrival in America, along with thousands of Germans, of a small but distinguished group of Austrian emigrants whom we shall deal with in succeeding chapters. On the negative side was America's sudden, but very badly documented, realization of the nationality problems that were, beginning with 1848, coming to plague the old monarchy, and the difficult diplomatic problems that they spawned. The United States thought of the revolutions of '48, not as centering as they did in Vienna and as involving the liberal German Austrians themselves, but as revolts of unhappy, oppressed, subject peoples against the Austrians. Even the fall of Metternich in the first phase of the revolution and the valiant resistance of Vienna's Academic Legion attracted little attention here. There were a few American contributions to the Legion and that was all.

The diplomatic story centered in Washington. There the able Austrian chargé d'affaires, Chevalier Johann Hülsemann, who had back in 1823 written a book proclaiming that America was anti-monarchical and irreligious and hence hostile to Austria,[18] was an unfortunate proponent of the Austrian cause. He often warned his government against American spread-eagleism as exemplified by the Mexican War, our alleged designs upon Canada and Cuba, and the democratic license that he found here. He could scarcely have helped to interpret monarchical Austria to democratic America. Our chargé in Vienna to 1849 was the pro-Hungarian William H. Stiles.

Since the American electorate sympathized with any revolutionary group opposing monarchy, and especially with the Hungarians, the Taylor administration was inclined to yield to anti-Austrian pressures and send a diplomatic mission to Hungary. Such a mission might hopefully recommend American recognition of Hungarian independence. The plan was good politics whether or not anyone knew whether the majority of Hungarians really wanted independence. So, in June 1849, Secretary of State Clayton instructed attaché A. Dudley Mann of our Paris legation to go to Hungary, investigate, and recognize its government if conditions warranted it.[19]

The anti-Austrian sentiment throughout the United States led to much unfortunate demagoguery. An Illinois Congressman named Abraham Lincoln, for instance,was in 1849 supporting the Hungarians "in their present glorious struggle for liberty."[20] The administration snubbed Hülsemann by letting him learn of the Mann Mission from the press. Senator Cass of Michigan offered a resolution suggesting the breaking of diplomatic relations with Vienna. The President expressed sympathy for Hungary in his annual message. And when, next year, in 1850, President Taylor died and President Fillmore made Daniel Webster his Secretary of State, Webster jumped onto the anti-Austrian bandwagon.

Austria's protests on the score of the Mann Mission were for the most part informal with pleas for the continuance of good relations to water down their franker expressions of protest. Yet Webster's famous reply to Hülsemann denied in vigorous and demagogic terms that the sending of the Mann Mission was an unfriendly act. There was nothing conciliatory in Webster's language. "The power of this republic at the present moment," he declared, "is spread over a region one of the richest and most fertile on the globe, and of an extent in comparison with which the possessions of the house of Habsburg are but as a patch on the earth's surface. Its population, already twenty-five millions, will exceed that of the Austrian Empire within the period during which it may be hoped that Mr. Hülsemann may yet remain in the honorable discharge of his duties to his government . . . Certainly the United States may be pardoned, even by those who profess adherence to the principles of absolute government, if they entertain an ardent affection for those popular forms of political organization which have so rapidly advanced their own prosperity and happiness, and enabled them, in so short a period, to bring their country, and the hemisphere to which it belongs, to the notice and respectful regard, not to say admiration, of the civilized world."[21] Webster had obviously no desire to weaken his chauvinism by admitting that the Revolution of 1848 against the Metternich system had been fought behind barricades in Vienna by German Austrians as well as by the empire's Hungarians, Bohemians, and Italians.[22]

A few sane minds like that of the editor of the "Washington Express" realized that Webster's reply was political bombast. But the "New York Herald" was able to "question if any document that ever emanated from the State Department gave more general satisfaction than the reply . . . to the insolent and supercilious letter of the Austrian minister."[23] American foreign policy was otherwise quiescent and Webster, ambitious to be President, had provided the flag-wavers with an appealing issue to shout about. The nativists found it much to their liking. It was, of course, an anti-climax when Dudley Mann found the Hungarian situation so far from meriting a serious investigation that he never even visited Budapest.

Louis Kossuth's visit to America only muddied the waters a bit more. For Kossuth was a far more eloquent, convincing, special pleader than German Austria has in all its history ever sent to the United States. To prevent the Hungarian peasants, intellectuals, gentry, and nobility from making revolutions among themselves, Kossuth directed the Budapest revolution against the Habsburgs, the Austrians, and the other non-Hungarian nationalities.[25] He was an amazingly great popular leader. And, fortunately for his cause in America, he was a Protestant.

It was more than ironical when Secretary of State Webster assured Chevalier Hülsemann that Kossuth's visit in the United States (he was arriving on the U. S. S. *Mississippi* whose captain had found him a difficult passenger) was to be strictly non-political and unofficial. When he arrived in New York on December 5, 1851, he was greeted by salutes from the harbor forts' cannons and Webster's celebrated speech at the Congressional banquet for Kossuth early in January was hardly non-political. Webster told the Chevalier that he had spoken only in his private capacity. And Hülsemann, at Prince Schwarzenberg's instructions, left his post and the country in protest.

Kossuth, "Noble Magyar! Illustrious Kossuth!", to quote the health officer who boarded his ship in New York harbor,[26] received a tremendous reception. Typical was a Baptist clergyman's comparison of Kossuth's arrival with that of the second coming of Christ. "He spoke to us," Senator Chauncey M. Depew recalled in 1894, "in our own majestic tongue of which he was a master." Dr. Henry Ward Beecher's church contributed mightily to the Hungarian cause. Ralph Waldo Emerson called him "the angel of freedom" and Charles Sumner underscored New England's special devotion to Kossuth and his cause.[27] New England liberalism seems always to have had a special affinity with Central European liberals, who were always anti-slavery, in the pre-Civil War years. Kossuth hats and Kossuth beards swept the country. Kossuth became the symbol of liberty. Women wept for the cause of Hungary and sold their jewelry to support it. The Catholic Bishop Hughes of New York was criticized by the nativists because he believed Kossuth to be a humbug. The nativists thought that showed that American Catholics were always dominated by the Pope at Rome. Even the German element in this country welcomed the great Kossuth[28] doubtless because many of those Germans had emigrated as refugees from German, or perhaps Austrian, oppression, in '48 or earlier. The Hungarians were not the only revolutionaries in Central Europe.

There was, of course, an anti-climax when the great Hungarian showed his hand by pleading for too much – for American intervention to establish an independent Hungary. Americans liked revolutionaries of any brand so long as they did not have to pull their chestnuts out of the fire. They hesitated, at least, until 1918, before their admiration for the anti-Habsburg elements in Hungary brought them to pull the final Hungarian chestnuts out of the fires of the Paris Peace Conference. Certainly the attitudes that brought President Wilson to help to destroy the Habsburg empire in 1918–1919 were being created in mid-century America in the era of Hülsemann and Kossuth. There were Kossuth parades in New York even in 1894 when the great Hungarian died.[29]

The Italian patriot Garibaldi was for a time in New York after his unsuccessful war against the Austrians and the French – a phase of the revolution of 1848 that was to bear fruit sooner than those at the core of the Austrian monarchy. But, unlike the famous Kossuth, Garibaldi was then a relatively unsung hero who made candles on Staten Island for a few months at mid-century before he returned home. His shop on Staten Island was later to become a shrine for those who fought for liberty against the Habsburgs.[30] Indeed, the reverence in which Italian-Americans have long held the Italian heroes who fought the Austrians in those times has contributed to anti-Austrianism in the United States. At a labor meeting in 1925, for instance, an Italian-American brushed off the death of one of his colleagues with: "Sure, he's dead . . . So are Mazzini and Garibaldi, and we are still for them too."[31]

When Daniel Webster died in October 1852, the Ballhausplatz announced that the Hülsemann reply and the Webster banquet speech would then be buried in the grave of the great New Englander. It was a noble gesture. But then came the case of another Hungarian, Martin Koszta, who was to find a protector in another American Secretary of State who wanted to be President, Secretary Marcy. Koszta was an associate of Kossuth's and a refugee in the United States where he had taken out his first papers for citizenship. Then, returning to Turkey on business in 1853, he was kidnapped and turned over to an Austrian warship. The American consul demanded his release; the Austrian captain proposed yielding him to the French, as a compromise; whereupon the American naval sloop *St. Louis* entered Smyrna harbor, threatened immediate "action" if Koszta were not turned over to him; and carried off the prize with the complete approval of the Washington government. The international law situation may have been questionable, but America's response was not. "Had Captain Ingraham sunk the Austrian vessel, he would have become the next President of the United States," wrote Horace Greeley in the "Tribune." President Pierce and Secretary Marcy achieved immediate popularity at Austria's expense.[32]

Napoleon III's efforts to save Mexico for its many creditors and from possible Yankee imperialism, involved us again with Austria. Franz Joseph and the Ballhausplatz were never enthusiastic about placing the Archduke Maximilian upon an imperial throne in Mexico, as the puppet of the French forces that fought the patriot Juárez and occupied Mexico City in 1863. Austria's ambassador in Paris, Prince Metternich, had warned: "What a lot of cannon-shots it will take to set up an emperor in Mexico, and what a lot to maintain him there."[33] That was in 1861, and by 1863, when the American Civil War was beginning to go sour on the South and the North was beginning to grow indignant over the French violation of the Monroe Doctrine on our own American continent, the outlook was even less propitious.

Maximilian and Carlotta were, however, a fine-looking couple. They were fond of their new Mexican subjects. There was an air of romance about this great adventure of European royalty in a backward American country. And Mexico's new Emperor Maximilian was inclined to admit United States supremacy on the North American continent provided that Brazil had the upper hand south of Panama.[34] Maximilian was reasonable but he had magnificent dreams; the idea of creating a great American empire was overpowering and he ignored all the warnings. He tried to influence the United States with agents whom he sent here and he even tried to buy an American newspaper from James Gordon Bennett that would justify his cause.

Public opinion in the United States was almost unanimously anti-Maximilian. We resurrected the Monroe Doctrine. The press, as it became less concerned with the War of the Rebellion, picked up the issue. The House of Representatives, in the very month when Maximilian mounted his rickety throne, resolved unanimously that "it does not accord with the policy of the United States to acknowledge any monarchical Government erected on the ruins of any republican Government in America under the auspices of any European Power."[35]

France was primarily responsible for the whole Mexican affair and American ire was directed primarily at France. Only occasionally, as in April 1866, was Washinton concerned that Vienna might try to rescue its Archduke. Austria had sent no troops to support its Archduke but it had not objected to the emigration of six thousand Austrians, who had already satisfied their military obligations to their own country, to give Maximilian a voluntary Austrian Legion. By 1866 the Legion needed replacements. About 800 of them had been gathered at Laibach on their way to shipping at Trieste. It was then that Secretary of State Seward instructed Minister Motley to ask in protest for his passport just as soon as the first Austrian troopship should sail for Mexico. But that troopship never sailed.[36]

Minister Motley, the fine historian of the Dutch republic, found it more than difficult to threaten the Austrian foreign minister with American resentment should Austrian volunteers sail for Vera Cruz. Motley was convinced that the foreign office had informed him correctly throughout the crisis: that the Kaiser never wanted his brother to take the Mexican throne and that the *K. u. K. Regime* (the Imperial and Royal government) had never promised Napoleon III to support Maximilian. Motley was more than a bit unhappy when Secretary Seward in Washington told him that our minister in Paris had informed Washington that thousands of Austrian volunteers were shipping for Mexico. Motley knew that only some 750 volunteers were in Laibach and they might not all reach Trieste. But Washington did not know the entire story.

In any event the end of the Civil War freed Federal troops for an invasion of Mexico and Napoleon III soon decided to give up the entire project. He left the gallant Maximilian with his beloved but disloyal Mexican subjects to face the Mexican firing squad, that failed to appreciate his love of Mexico, on June 19, 1867. Professor Bailey very properly quotes at this point in his story of the Mexican episode from the "Portland Transcript" (June 8, 1867): "If anybody deserves to be shot it is Louis Napoleon."

The Maximilian affair was very significant in the history of the Monroe Doctrine. Metternich had contributed much to the creation of the Doctrine; Maximilian of Habsburg contributed to the solution of its greatest challenge. It was perhaps because of the charm of the beautiful Empress Carlotta and the sympathetic if gullible Maximilian that the entire episode was blamed so much on Paris and so little on Vienna. It was, after all, Napoleon's project.

The Maximilian episode helped, however, to sustain American dislike of the Habsburg regime. It seemed to our nativists to confirm their suspicions that the Ballhausplatz was committed to the entrenchment of Catholicism on this continent as well as to the establishment here of monarchy based on European absolutism. It confirmed our preference for Prussia over Austria in German-speaking Europe, even when American liberals were somewhat fearful of Bismarck with his policies of *Blut und Eisen*.

The Maximilian episode doubtless helped also to confirm Austria's suspicions of America's motives. The Austrian Baron Hübner declared in 1873 that the children of Europe could see in America only "the born antagonist of Europe . . . All the world admires you. But all the world does not love you. Those among us who judge you from an exclusively European point of view see in you nothing but enemies of the fundamental principles of society . . . They dread your success as a dangerous example to Europe, and as far as they can they try to stop the spread of your ideas."[37] It would be three-quarters of a century later before Austrians would really understand Americans.

On this side of the Atlantic, even the German-American press, still edited by the liberals of Forty-eight who had no love for Bismarck's conservatism, showed no sympathy for Vienna's reactionary regime when Bismarck's blitz of 1866, the Seven Weeks' War, resulted in Austria's humiliation and ejection from the German Confederation. And even such Austria-born editors as Ottendorfer of the "New Yorker Staats-Zeitung" and Kudlich, the *Bauernbefreier*, who was to denounce Bismarck some years later, greeted with enthusiasm the Iron Statesman's greatest achievement, the unification of Germany.[38] On the American side there were very many who regretted Bismarck's victory of 1870 over France but few who were concerned with his relegating Austria to the position of a second-class power.

[1] Saul K. Padover, ed., *The Complete Jefferson*, N. Y. 1943, p. 893.

[2] E. C. Burnett, "Negotiations with Austria," *American Historical Review*, XVI (1911), pp. 567.

[3] Hanns Schlitter, "Die Berichte des ersten Agenten Österreichs in den Vereinigten Staaten von Amerika," *Fontes Rerum Austriacarum*, sect. II, vol. XLV., Vienna 1891.

[4] Baron de Lederer, Austria's consul, was later appointed consul general. It is not clear whether he had been recognized as consul general before he signed the treaty. He was not the only Austrian consul in the later 1820's.

[5] U. S. Department of State, *Biographic Register 1957*, pp. 723—26.

[6] Paul Sweet, "Erich Bollmann at Vienna in 1815," *American Historical Review*, Apr. 1941, p. 580.

[7] The quotation is from Constantin de Grunwald, *Metternich*, London 1953, p. 5. See also P. W. Schroeder, "Metternich Studies Since 1925," *Journal of Modern History*, Sept. 1961.

[8] Padover, *op. cit.*, p. 175.

[9] Dexter Perkins, *Monroe Doctrine*, 1955, *passim.*

[10] *Ibid.*, p. 27.

[11] Brutus (S. F. B. Morse), *Foreign Conspiracies Against the Liberties of the United States*, N. Y. 1835, pp. 27f.; Morse, *Imminent Dangers . . .*, N. Y. 1835, p. 7.

[12] Charles Sealsfield, *Austria As It Is*, London 1828, pp. 144—56.

[13] William H. Stiles, *Austria* in *1848—49*, N. Y. 1852, p. 132.

[14] *Crimes of the House of Austria against Mankind*, N. Y. 1852.

[15] M. C. Lynch, *Diplomatic Mission of John Lothrop Motley*, Washington 1944, pp. vii, 2, 49, 64, etc.

[16] His anonymous volume, *Austria As It Is*, London 1828, is one long tirade against the regime.

[17] *Vienna and the Austrians*, 2 vols., Paris 1838. It may be significant that authors like Sealsfield and Trollope did not publish their books on Austria in the United States which would doubtless have provided a poor market for them.

[18] *Geschichte der Democratie in den Vereinigten Staaten von Nord Amerika*, Göttingen 1823. Hülsemann was in Washington as secretary of legation 1838—41, chargé 1841—55, and minister resident 1855—63.

[19] See Merle E. Curti, "Austria and the United States 1848–1852," *Smith College Studies in History*, April 1926, for a careful study of the Mann Mission.

[20] Emil Lengyel, *Americans from Hungary*, Philadelphia and N. Y. 1948, pp. 37–38.

[21] *Works of Webster*, 6 vols., Boston 1851, VI, p. 496. This volume contains the Webster-Hülsemann correspondence.

[22] This point-of-view has been perpetuated in books like Emil Lengyel's generally excellent *Americans from Hungary*.

[23] Quoted from Thomas A. Bailey, *Diplomatic History of the American People*, N. Y. 1946, p. 286.

[24] A. L. P. Taylor, *The Habsburg Monarchy*, London 1948, p. 59.

[25] See Curti, *op. cit.*, pp. 169ff., for a well-balanced account of the entire Kossuth affair. Ray Allen Billington, *Protestant Crusade*, N. Y. 1938, pp. 330ff., is also useful and objective. For the Hungarian side, see Lengyel, *op. cit.* Biographies of Webster are generally unsympathetic toward Austria.

[26] Bailey, *op. cit.*, p. 286.

[27] Lengyel, *op. cit.*, p. 39. Lengyel and almost all other accounts state that no foreigner since Lafayette had had such a reception.

[28] *Mitteilungen des Deutschen Pionier-Vereins von Philadelphia*, vol. 18, 1910, pp. 19–21.

[29] Carl Wittke, *We Who Built America*, N. Y. 1945, p. 432.

[30] Carl Wittke, *Refugees of Revolution*, Philadelphia 1952, p. 79.

[31] Benjamin Stolberg, *Tailor's Progress*, N. Y. 1944, p. 131.

[32] Curti, *op. cit.* and most other accounts of American foreign policy have commented on the notable Koszta case. Lengyel, *op. cit.*, pp. 59–60, gives the Hungarian point-of-view.

[33] As quoted by Thomas A. Bailey under the head to his chapter on "France and Maximilian's Mexican Empire," *op. cit.*, p. 377.

[34] Egon Caesar Conte Corti, *Maximilian and Charlotte of Mexico*, 2 vols., N. Y. 1929, II, p. 400.

[35] *Congressional Globe*, 38th Congress, 1st sess., p. 1408.

[36] Corti, *op. cit.*, II, p. 619.

[37] Quoted from Oscar Handlin, *This Was America*, in Emily Davie, *Profile of America*, N. Y. 1954, p. 386.

[38] Wilhelm Schlag, "A Survey of Austrian Emigration to the United States," *Österreich und die angelsächsische Welt*, Wien 1961, pp. 161–62.

CHAPTER V

THE EARLY NINETEENTH CENTURY AND THE FORTY-EIGHTERS

Immigration from the Habsburg lands was so inconsequential during most of the nineteenth century that American officialdom reported no figures for the Austrian-born until 1850 when the Census discovered just 946 of them living in the United States. The figures for the decades that followed (25,061 Austrian-born in 1860; 70,797 in 1870; 124,024 in 1880; 241,377 in 1890; and 432,798 in 1900) are far from being precise because of the Census Bureau's very vague ideas about what an Austrian was, but they serve to indicate the trend: an enormous increase in the number of "Austrians" who came in the later years of the century.[1] That trend is also apparent in the otherwise meaningless (for German Austrians) statistics on the arrivals at United States ports of aliens and immigrants from the establishment of the Dual Monarchy in 1867 and into the twentieth century: a few thousand in the 1860's, some 73,000 in the 1870's, almost 354,000 in the 1880's![2] The German Austrians thought of in the earlier years simply as Germans, had been a part of that great flood of Germans which in the 1850's went ahead of the tremendous Irish immigration and was never again, until World War I, overtaken by the Irish.

The few who did come in the early decades of the nineteenth century never called themselves Austrian. They signed as from the "Empire of Germany" and towns like Linz, Horn, Zell, Feldkirchen, Braunau, or Wien. They were clerks or smiths or such – people who looked for opportunities in cities and towns[3] and not, like their German cousins, on the farms. They were greatly outnumbered even in Pennsylvania by their German cousins and even by the Swiss and the Bohemians who may or may not have been more on the German Austrian side than on what we now call Czech.

These few early Austrians, often finding permanent homes in New York and seldom pushing farther south than Baltimore, found themselves at home in the substantial towns of the Middle West. But always in small numbers. An historian of Milwaukee points out that the Austrians had a sizable colony in that Germanic center after 1848 but ranks that colony in size under those of the Germans, Irish, Bohemians (many of them doubtless Germanic), British-Americans, and Hollanders.[4] Away from the civilization of the towns one finds an occasional Austrian settlement as in Korntal near Anna in southern Illinois,[5] in Forestville, Michigan, in Alpenburg, Virginia, where there were settlements of Tyrolese, and in New Wien, Iowa. Catholic missionaries, priests and religious orders were more adventurous than most of their fellow countrymen in pushing out to the Indian frontier and into raw, new communities that needed religious guidance. A few Austrians helped swell the population of the lurid, goldrush town of Columbia, California.[6] But many more Czechs than German Austrians responded to the appeal of California gold in the tempting times of 1849. Even though a goodly number of German Austrians were confused with Germans and Bohemians, there were clearly few of them.

The Vienna government, which had virtually forbidden emigration in the last years of the eighteenth century, yielded a few concessions during the reign of Kaiser Franz, but continued to frown on the exodus of its peoples. Travel papers were so difficult to obtain that would-be emigrants to the New World had often to escape over the borders into Germany and make their travel plans there. Even at mid-century the authorities were warning the restless of the difficulties of travel without sufficient funds and preparations and were making it clear that those absconders who returned would be unwelcome and devoid of their Austrian citizenship.[7]

There were other reasons why emigration from the core of the Habsburg lands came so late. One was remoteness from the seaports. Not until Trieste had been developed well into the century as Austria's own outlet to the sea did the people of the monarchy have a port of their own closer than Bremen, Hamburg, and the harbor cities of the Low Countries. And not until the coming of the railroad and the development by the Austrians of the world's first Alpine line, over the Semmering pass, and on to Trieste, was it easy for the emigrants from eastern Austria to reach the sea. Even so Trieste never handled more than a small proportion of Austria's emigrants. Many of the peasants wanted to migrate precisely because times were bad and living difficult – and it was such poor folk who found it more than difficult to work their way to the far distant ports of Northern Europe. They waited for the building of better roads and railroads and the later coming of the agents of the grasping steamship companies who would help them finance their ventures.

Another negative factor was the adequacy of fertile land in the old monarchy. The revolution of 1848 freed the peasants from the land. But only in Bohemia was there, in those early days, a desperate shortage of land. There was therefore a far earlier exodus of peasants from Bohemia than from the other parts of the monarchy.[8]

After Bohemia, the Tyrol supplied the largest group of mid-nineteenth century emigrants. Good agricultural land had never been plentiful in the Alpine country and the peasants were ripe for emigration. It was, furthermore, a devout land, *das heilige Land Tirol*, that had sent early missionaries to America whose letters encouraged their friends and relatives to cross the sea. The Innsbruck archives still treasure old newspapers and letters with reports from the New World – warning the gold seekers that all that glittered in California was not gold but reporting, even from Alaska at the end of the century, the alluring prospects that awaited the immigrant. One late Innsbruck item that helps to put the emigration story into its perspective is a report that in 1886 only 167 emigrants from Trent went to North America as contrasted with 547 who had sailed for South America. A critical report of the same year on Florida, *das amerikanische Eden*, shows why Austrians seldom went south on the North American continent.[9]

Such records of a century ago show how important letters from the New World and newspaper accounts in the Old were in the encouragement of emigration. Newspaper publicity was often suppressed by the police but it persisted and brought results.[10]

The bulk of the migrants of the early nineteenth century were peasants — folk who were generally too poor to buy themselves the American farms that they wanted and who had arrived too early to be welcomed as the answer to America's need for cheap labor during her greatest period of industrialization. It was fortunate for the Austrian peasants that they came in no great numbers.

But they were not all peasants. Typical of the intellectuals who came was "Fackel-Ludvigh," Dr. Samuel Ludvigh (born Ludwig in Günz, Styria, 1801 — died Cincinnati, 1869) an anti-clerical free-thinker who seems to have been several degrees more advanced in his thinking than most of the "grays" — the name that the fiery Forty-eighters were later to give to the more moderate refugees of 1830. He criticized the Vienna government, had his troubles with the censorship, and was forced to escape, penniless, for America in 1837. Here he published a surprising number of German-language periodicals all the way from Philadelphia to Minnesota including Baltimore's well-known "Die Fackel" (1846—1869) and a Van Buren campaign sheet. He was one of the many radical immigrants who were Democratic in their politics until the anti-slavery issue weaned them away.[11]

The educated, more sophisticated immigrants came, like Ludvigh, chiefly as refugees from the persecutions and revolutions of the Era of Metternich. There was in Germany and Austria the period of censorship and repression of liberal ideas, the *Demagogenverfolgung*, which sent many of its victims to America to escape, especially in the 1830's. The Metternich regime had not only the laudable objective of giving Europe a period of stability and peace but, less happily, it intended to rid the continent of the advanced ideas of the French Revolution and even of the American Revolution. Its victims, those who were well enough educated in liberal ideas to seem dangerous to the regime, were charmed by the reports of liberty in the New World. All of the teachings of the Enlightenment seemed to them to have their play in America. The United States was the land of escape from autocratic despotism, the land of freedom. It was the land of the noble savage where men could revert to nature. It was the land that Franz Schubert had recalled on his deathbed when he had asked his friend Schober to bring him Cooper's "Leatherstocking Tales."[12] "*Amerika! Welcher Name hat einen Inhalt gleich diesem Namen!*" wrote an Austrian describing the American fever of the thirties and forties. "*Amerika! heilige Erstarrung ergreift mich bei deinem Anblick ...*

Asien die Wurzel, Europa der Stamm, Amerika Laub- und Blüthenkrone."[13] All of the ideas of Rousseau seemed to be exemplified in America.

The young Austrian dramatist, Franz Grillparzer, told his famous friend Beethoven in the 1820's that "One has to emigrate to North America if he wants to give free expression to his thoughts."[14] The wellknown Austrian poet, Nikolaus Lenau, was at first enchanted by the American idea. His visit here in 1832–1833 was a search for the poetic inspiration that was eluding him in Central Europe. He wanted to see the noble Indian and the primeval forests with his own eyes. But he found only dross. People were selfish, grasping, pushing, without taste. Lenau arrived at Baltimore during a cholera epidemic, he was ill in Pennsylvania, he fell out of his sleigh and injured himself in Ohio, and had a sorry venture trying to turn farmer. Americans, he found, were sad fellows, burned-out, without animation or spirit. The country he called *die verschweinten Staaten*. He thought that the love of the immigrant for his native land was too quickly lost and turned into hate.[15]

Lenau is not only significant as typifying those who found only disillusionment in America. He was doubtless also significant as a deterrent to emigration. Indeed, more than two decades after his eager return to Europe another Austrian, Ferdinand Kürnberger (b. Vienna, 1823 – d. Munich, 1879) based a notable novel, "Der Amerikamüde," upon Lenau's American experiences. It was designed to be an answer to those who were weary of Europe, *europamüde*, and anxious to escape to America. And, although its author had never crossed the seas, it remains a notable account of what sophisticated Europeans found lacking in the raw young land. The hero Moorfeld found Americans boorish, money-grabbing, vulgar in their eating habits, ridiculously primitive in their religion, disgustingly Puritanical, and hostile to the immigrant. His thesis that shoddy American culture should be replaced with a superior Germanic culture suggested a thesis that helped to make German immigrants unpopular for decades to come. It may have been fortunate that "Der Amerikamüde" was never translated into English.[16]

It was only too true that the early decades of migration from the Old World were, except for the few fortunate ones whose friends had prepared the way for them, a sorry time. Transportation was so primitive that thousands died on the Atlantic. The immigration business was a new, completely unregulated "racket" that was concerned with profits and not with human beings. And America itself had not yet discovered that it needed the immigrant. When Canon Joseph Salzbacher visited here from Vienna in 1842 in response to appeals for more Catholic priests to minister to the new parishes, he found the German-speaking colonists poor in spirit and in body.[17] They were called in derision "Dutchmen." They had come to make their fortunes, "*ihr Glück zu machen,*" but remained poor in the land that had seemed so entracing from afar. They had little money, big families, and all kinds of difficulties in finding work. They were losing the battle to retain their former cultural interests.

We read, for instance, of the determination of an unnamed Captain L— and family who, by about 1835, still had their grand piano brought from Vienna in their cheerless log cabin.[18] They were generally unpopular. Although Salzbacher made no mention of Viennese, Bohemians, or Tyrolese, there were doubtless a few from the old monarchy among the Germans whom he visited.

The nativist movement, to which we refer in other chapters, was both a cause and a result of the unpopularity of these early immigrants. It had its roots in the thirties when Samuel F. B. Morse, inventor of the telegraph, denounced the Habsburg papists who had, in 1829, established the Leopoldinen-Stiftung in Vienna to aid and abet Catholicism in Protestant America. It produced Know-Nothingism and the American Party in the fifties, and it marched on into the next century. Although the Irish Catholics were often the principal objects of hate, the Germans came in for their share, even in Boston.

Boston's preachers denounced the "dirty, ignorant Irish and German immigrants... guzzlers of beer and whisky . . ." Even the famous preacher Lyman Beecher of Boston's elite Hanover Street Congregational Church, in warning against "the whoredom of Babylon," proclaimed that the "Immigrants were blind agents of two great autocratic forces: the Church of Rome aud the Austrian despotism, in its turn an obedient vassal of Rome. The immigrants bowed down 'to a foreign power, bedizened with the trappings of royalty and tyranny.'"[19]

Specifically the champions of Americanism against what they called Austrian despotism and other alien cults wanted to exclude as many would-be immigrants as possible and deprive the few whom they would admit of all rights to citizenship and to the ballot until they should be well Americanized. The American Party platform of 1856 demanded the exclusion from our shores of all paupers and persons who had ever been convicted of a crime and the denial of citizenship to all who could not prove twenty-one years of continuous residence. The platform also paid its respects to the threat of Roman Catholic interference in our institutions by declaring opposition to any union of church and state.[20] That intelligent Europeans came to our shores in the face of such discouragements is evidence of their dire need to escape from things far less charming than the Vienna Woods and the Blue Danube.

The two finest groups of immigrants from Austria were the Forty-eighters and the Thirty-eighters — those who came after the failure of the Revolution of 1848 and those who came as refugees from Hitler. Both groups contained far more than the usual percentage of capable, trained minds and both groups were comprised largely of men and women of liberal ideals. They were for the most part people who possessed the time-honored traits of the immigrant to America: courage of their convictions, a yearning for new freedoms and new economic opportunities, and the ardent desire to build a future that should be free of the authoritarian aspects of their European past. That many came because life in the old homeland had become untenable does not detract from the fact that America was fortunate to receive such highly talented groups of new citizens.

It was fortunate, both for the United States and for the Forty-eighters themselves, that, by the time of the collapse of the revolution, the disappointed revolutionaries had learned so much of America from the emigrants of the thirties and forties that the country loomed large as a haven. The warnings of disillusioned travelers like Lenau were quickly forgotten and hundreds of veterans of the Vienna barricades joined thousands of Germans in their escape to the idealized New World. Many who came suffered disappointments but the majority remained. One fine Forty-eighter, Joseph Goldmark, expressed the optimism of this group: "The man of European culture who has fled from the old world in its ossification and decay is alienated by the still unformed, uncultivated conditions of the new. Only in its new principles, in the brilliant promise of its vigorous youth, does he find hope of a new and better organization of society."[21]

But more often quoted is a letter to Goldmark from his friend Anton Füster, showing why so many of the finest of the revolutionaries of 1848 came to America and stayed:[22] "Only a year ago we were reverently singing the German national anthem. Now it sounds different. What is the German fatherland? Is it Austria? No, I was forced to flee from there. Is it Prussia? No. There I was arrested. Is it Saxony? No. There the warrants were issued against me. Is it the free city of Hamburg? No. There I was driven out by the police. Where is the German fatherland? In England and America! Only in those lands is there a safe and honorable refuge for Germans whose love of liberty and honor has not been silenced by Russo-Prussian-Austrian bayonets." Men who could write like that were grist for the American mill! They could accept the worst of American spread-eagleism; they could understand the young America that was just feeling its oats; and they could dream of reforming the world from St. Louis or Cincinnati instead of from Vienna.

They were, however, quite un-American in many other ways. They not only spoke differently and lived differently — with the strange cut of their clothes and their beer and wine and passion for music and unfamiliar ways of worship — or their indifference to all worship. They were intellectuals in an age when America was practical. They had tried to fight the revolution of 1848 more with arguments than with barricades. After all, the core of the revolution in Vienna, which was in turn the core of the entire revolutionary movement in the Habsburg empire, was the Academic Legion — the university's revolutionaries. America was by no means academic in 1848. And the Austrian Forty-eighters knew little or nothing of the nationalism that was uniting America. The Jacobins had been nationalistic enough to unify France in 1789 — the revolutionaries against the Habsburgs in 1848 had developed only regional "nationalisms" that were in time to destroy the empire. The most vocal of those was the Hungarian movement that was so well directed that most Americans have believed ever since that 1848 was a revolt of oppressed, democratic Hungarians against arrogant Austrians who were unanimously supporting the reactionary system of Metternich and Kaiser Ferdinand. And the concept of regional or racial "nationality," rather than that of national unity, led the German Forty-eighters, at least, into grandiose schemes for developing German communities in Texas and the West. American nativism had helped to revitalize Germanism, and the Germans then became more interested than before in creating, exactly what the nativists were objecting to, German cultural islands on the American continent. The Austrian-born shared with the Germans the blame for the American renaissance of Germanism.[23] The process of Americanization might be long and sometimes painful but it was a natural, essential part of the building of modern America.

On the whole the Forty-eighters were very welcome. The United States had been happy about the revolutions of 1848 and their victims were greeted here as heroes. Only a few conservatives in the North (the propertied classes as well as the nativists) and the slavery interests in the South—who wanted to hear as little as possible about liberty—frowned upon the Forty-eighters. New England was generally on the side of revolution because it had been a breeding place of revolution against England only some sixty years earlier and because its anti-slavery convictions of the more recent period had led it into anti-Habsburg paths. And the American West was naturally opposed to all despots like the Habsburgs.[24]

Dozens of American communities celebrated the European uprisings of '48. They rejoiced that European democrats were beginning to follow in the footsteps of their American friends. And they subscribed money to the cause. The "New Yorker Staats-Zeitung" sold caricatures of Kaiser Ferdinand and of Prince Metternich. And there was a plethora of meetings to commemorate the brutal execution by the Habsburgs of Robert Blum, a German-born leader of the left in the Frankfurt Parliament, who had helped defend Vienna from reaction in 1848. High Hill in Texas was originally called Blum Hill in honor of that victim of the Habsburgs.[25]

The Forty-eighters were significant here, despite the fact that they were not as numerous as all the attention they have received would indicate, because such a high proportion of them were intellectuals.[26] They were generally young men, often without families. They came chiefly from southwestern Germany. Relatively few were Austrian. But there were some dozens of really distinguished German Austrians who came direct from the Vienna barricades and there were other empire Austrians who had come via Vienna although their homes had been in other parts of the monarchy.

Letters to the folks back home have always been a primary cause of emigration to the United States. Many of those who came in and around 1848 had friends and relatives already here who persuaded them to come and prepared the way for them. The Moravian Jew, Isaac M. Wise, for instance, was invited almost immediately after his arrival in 1846 to an Albany synagogue and Karl Taussig of Prague, father of Harvard's famed economist of later years, went at once in 1848 to the grocery business in St. Louis—which indicated that they had been in touch with friends here who had made arrangements for them. Kuranda's "Die Grenzboten" had been for several years urging emigration to America upon Austro-Hungarian Jews and had in 1843 even appealed, in vain, to the Vienna Rothschilds for money to help colonize the Jews in the New World.[27]

There was a surprisingly large contingent of Jews among the Austro-Hungarian Forty-eighters.[28] The Jews in the monarchy still labored under some of the cruel disabilities with which they had been cursed since medieval times, and thus the failure of liberalism in Central Europe in 1848 was an even more serious setback to them than to the Christians. Two American Jews visited Vienna in the year of revolution with a gift of 8000 florins for the Academic Legion. And as the revolution approached failure, Jewish leaders renewed their advice to emigrate to America. Kompert's appeal in the "Österreichisches Central-Organ," "Up and to America!," was the most famous of the attempts to stimulate emigration. Other Jewish journals like the "Allgemeine Zeitung des Judentums" published correspondence to encourage Jewish emigration while the less adventurous Jews advised remaining in Austria to continue the fight at home. Emigration associations were established to help finance the emigration of revolutionaries who were threatened with persecution.

Isidor Bush, spelled Busch before emigration, editor of the Jewish "Central-Organ" in Vienna, was the leading spirit of the Vienna Committee for Emigration Problems which helped emigrants to arrange their escape to America. In 1849 Bush himself came to New York to publish the first Jewish weekly in the United States, discover that his readers found him too academic and literary for American taste, and go on to St. Louis to make a career for himself in store-keeping, viticulture, and public service. He was as advanced in his abolitionism as in his politics.[29] He was one of the radicals of '48 whose coming disturbed so many conservative Americans.

The nativist Know-Nothings of the 1850's were, indeed, as much concerned over the German infidels as over the arrival of more Catholics. The Latin Farmers—the Germans who went farming—were laughed at for their learning, their books and their music and their foreign tongue—but the radical intellectuals were feared as a menace to the American way of life. Some of them were radicals in a Marxian sense before the name of Karl Marx had become famous. Others were radical in their plans to reform America itself, abolishing clericalism and slavery and rewriting its revered consitution. They founded German societies, which met together at Cleveland in 1854 to form a Central Union of Free Germans, that hoped to spread about the entire world the ideals of revolution and liberty that had been struck down in Europe in '48. Typical of the American response to such schemes was J. B. Angell's article in the "North American Review" of 1856,[30] which warned against free-thinkers from the German universities who were disregarding America's "most hallowed customs and beliefs."

Of the Austrian Forty-eighters, the conservative Catholics like Father Franz Joseph Pabisch (b. Zlabings, Moravia) who gave up the law in Vienna for theology and came to America in 1851 to teach church history at a Catholic Seminary in Cincinnati,[31] and like several dozen other well-known clerics who distinguished themselves in the Catholic hierarchy here, took no part in the radical movements. There were, however, Austrian agnostics, liberal Catholics, and a few Jews who worked with the extremists.

Isidor Bush, mentioned above, was one of the extremists. Others we will mention in later chapters, especially that on Austro-American journalists. Friedrich Hassaurek (b. Vienna, 1831 – d. Paris, 1885) was one of them: twice wounded fighting with the Academic Legion on the Vienna barricades he edited the radical "Hochwächter" in Cincinnati, supported the young Republican Party and was rewarded by appointment to be Lincoln's minister to Ecuador. Father Anton Füster (b. Radmannsdorf, Carniola, 1808 – d. Vienna, 1881) was interesting as a theologian who had worked with the extreme left wing in the Academic Legion and in the Austrian parliament and who worked for free, non-sectarian schools in this country.[32]

Typical of the radical ideas that disturbed conservative America was Heinrich Börnstein's (b. Hamburg, 1805 – d. Vienna, 1892) little campaign in his "St. Louis Anzeiger" in 1850 to celebrate July Fourth on July fourth despite the fact that it fell that year on the Sabbath. Even the Jesuits fought him on the issue but his *Freien-Männer-Vereine* (typical of the many German-liberal groups) supported him and the St. Louis Germans did their celebrating on Sunday.[33]

Börnstein is a fascinating example of the Vienna refugees of '48 because he had been born of Catholic and Protestant parents in northern Germany, brought up in Poland, educated in medicine in Vienna, tempted into dramatic criticism there, and urged to come to America by Horace Greeley.[34] His two volumes of memoirs contain a unique account of his adventures here. After two months and four days on the seas from Le Havre to New Orleans, he found Louisiana pork and bacon and corn bread and molasses repulsive, coffee undistinguishable from tea, table service from common dishes detestable, and conversation confined to the asking of the same questions that everyone asks a foreigner. "Ginger-Pop" he found no substitute for the seldom-to-be-found beer. So he went on to St. Louis, made the same complaints about American food and American boarding houses (their refinements did not impress him), found the city a big, dirty town with cholera rampant, and so turned to medicine. Later, before he returned to Vienna to direct the *Theater in der Josefstadt,* he established a city library and a community theater while he acquired and improved the journalism of the "St. Louis Anzeiger."

Some of the Forty-eighters came like Börnstein separately with personal funds that sufficed until they found their places in the New World. Others came in groups with help from back home. For instance, one of the groups that Isidor Bush and his Vienna committee assisted was composed of 25 men and two women, all from Vienna (although born elsewhere), that included Herz Emanuel Bondi, or Bondy, and young August Bondi who was soon to fight for John Brown in Bleeding Kansas, and the Brandeis family that was later to become famous through Supreme Court Justice Louis D. Brandeis. Another group of 41 came, led by Bush himself, which included Karl Taussig. The father-in-law of Justice Louis D. Brandeis, Dr. Joseph Goldmark (b. Keresztur, Hungary, 1818) who had learned in Vienna the medicine that he practiced in Brooklyn, came with the Jewish refugee groups, and Dr. Adolf Wiesner (b. Prague, 1807 – d. New York, 1867), born Wiener and a convert from Judaism to Catholicism, "among the noblest Austrian representatives in the German pre-Parliament in Frankfurt," came to New York and Baltimore, distinguished himself in letters and aid to the Civil War wounded, and died, homesick, on his way back to Europe.[35]

Where the Austrians of 1848 settled in the United States may remain a mystery. Official American census and immigration statistics are of course almost worthless because the Austrians were either confused in the middle of the nineteenth century with the Germans or with the non-Germanic peoples of the Habsburg empire. Here and there we find evidence of the presence of Austrians as in Iowa where there was the German-Catholic town of New Wien.[36] In general we conclude that the more notable ones settled in the cities from New York to Cincinnati and St. Louis and Milwaukee.[37] Those with notable names certainly did not settle in rural areas.

Some more of the better known Forty-eighters from the Austrian area should be mentioned. And those would include a few names in medicine like that of the dentist Joseph Deshauer who had studied in Vienna and helped defend it against the valiant General Windischgrätz in 1848 before Deshauer reached Chicago to practise there.[38] The medical category would include the Vienna-born Dr. Julius Hausen who became surgeon general in Lincoln's Army of the Potomac[39] and Dr. Ernst Krackowitzer (b. Upper Austria, 1821 – d. Sing Sing, N. Y., 1875) who was reputed to have been the first Viennese to submit to the use of chloroform as an anesthetic. He was a friend of Dr. Joseph Goldmark who helped cure the wounds of the Academic Legion before he came to practice in New York. Krackowitzer was a radical free-thinker, a kind of universal genius, and he remained a New Yorker for all his American years. He was a president of the Pathological Society of New York and, thanks to a friend back in Vienna, the introducer of the laryngoscope to the United States.[40] The Dr. Kratochwill who was one of three first-class passengers to New Orleans in 1849 on Kratochwill's way to California was described by his fellow-passenger as an Austrian and "*Arzt aus Prag.*"[41]

Austria's *Bauernbefreier*, Dr. Hans Kudlich (b. Lobenstein, Silesia, 1823 – d. Hoboken, New Jersey, 1917), was one of the most notable figures of '48. He called himself "*einen wahrhaften Österreicher*," a true Austrian. He gloried in the greatness of the old monarchy, regretted Austria's racial mixture (he was certain that it was the union of the non-German elements of the Habsburg monarchy that caused the collapse of the Vienna revolution of 1848), was nevertheless an admirer of the Silesian Slavs and one of the radical reformers of '48. In the Austrian Parliament he achieved the final steps in the liberation of the peasants, especially the abolition of the *Robot* or work tax, found himself facing death for treason, and fled by way of Germany and Switzerland to Hoboken across the river from New York to practice medicine. Here he was of course an ardent abolitionist and liberal while he delighted in his treasured portrait of the allies of 1814, Frederick William of Prussia on one side, Alexander of Russia on the other, and his beloved Kaiser Franz in the middle. Kudlich was one of those few champions of progress who, back in the middle of the nineteenth century, was a confessed, patriotic Austrian.[42]

Far more important than the men of medicine in American life were the musicians and the lovers of music. America was ripe by 1848 for more good music. And the Germans and Austrians who came were, for the most part, men and women whose music was a part of their lives. Whether or not the influx of foreign musicians was an important deterrent to native American musicians, is debatable.[43] Certainly the mid-European immigrants provided an appreciation of good music and a market for it that had not existed before.

As far as Austria was concerned, it was more significant that the Forty-eighters brought with them a fondness for Haydn and Mozart and Schubert and all the other composers who had worked in Vienna, than it was important that there were, among the Forty-eighters, a few fine musicians.

One of those was Frederick Brandeis (b. Vienna, 1835 – d. New York, 1899), a very young Forty-eighter who settled in New York to achieve fame both as composer and as virtuoso: on piano and organ in several Catholic churches and one synagogue.[44] The most famous name among those of the Austrian musical refugees of mid-century was that of Hans Balatka (b. Hoffnungsthal, Moravia, 1827 – d. Chicago, 1899), often called a German Bohemian,[45] who brought good music to the Middle West especially, after no great success as a "Latin farmer," in Wisconsin, in Milwaukee and Chicago (where he was eventually overshadowed only by the great German Theodore Thomas). It was immigrants like this who sponsored here the great music of Austria and Germany. And it is interesting that an offshoot of the European controversy over the merits of Richard Wagner was the cause of Balatka's move from Milwaukee to Chicago.[46]

Not to be overlooked is the almost completely unknown violinist, Misha (Michael) Hauser (b. Pressburg, 1822 – d. Vienna, 1887), who learned both music and revolution in Vienna and sought out America in 1850 as one of the earlier seekers after American gold, on concert tours and, literally, in California. He had dreamed of the golden rewards that virtuosos received in far-off America. Yet his American story was only partly a success story.[47]

Hauser's first American tours, from 1850 to 1853, taught him that there were Americans who wanted good music despite the agents who squeezed blood out of the concert trade. He eluded his agents, went to California, found a thousand Germans and five Hungarians in San Francisco, plus filth and vice and gambling and brutality and inflation which were offset only by the high prices paid to visiting artists. His is a fascinating story of the West Coast's first waves of culture. He paid fifty cents to have a shirt laundered! But he earned thirty dollars a day and his farewell concert, including Beethoven's overture to *Leonore*, brought him $2500. It is significant that Hauser, having done well in California, returned to his European homeland. Rather few of the Forty-eighters ever returned.

There was, for instance, E. F. Fähtz (b. Linz, 1823 – d. Washington, 1882) who had to flee the revolution of 1848, arrived here in 1850, taught in Elkton, Maryland, and fought in the Civil War with the rank of Lieutenant Colonel in the Union Army.[48] There was John L. Smithmeyer (b. Vienna, 1832 – d. Washington, 1908), the architect who designed the Library of Congress.[49] There were Jews like Rabbi Benjamin Szold (b. Nemiskert, Hungary, near Pressburg, 1829 – d. Berkeley Springs, W. Va., 1902), a scholarly champion of Negro education in Baltimore, whose daughter Henrietta was to be one of the great protagonists of Zionism and Hadassah in America and an unselfish worker in the cause of the Americanization of immigrants.[50]

There were of course dozens of less distinguished Forty-eighters: Anton Brookman, for instance, a veteran of what Professor Wittke calls the Vienna National Guard, came here to conduct a jewelry business in Newark, Saginaw, and Chicago.[51] Joseph Rudolph, a Vienna revolutionary well trained in the Latin classics, lived for three dollars a month with two others in an attic room, made shoe polish and cigars, and retired in prosperity from his Chicago furniture store.[52] And more intriguing was the Vienna revolutionist Franz Wutschel (b. Brünn, 1815) whose Vienna Academic Legion experiences in '48 inspired him to call his New York restaurant the Vienna Legionair Restaurant. He was one of those who were sentenced to death by the Austrian regime for his revolutionary activities. Not content with revolution in Austria he enlisted in the Union Army in 1861, fought at Bull Run, achieved the rank of Colonel, and remained for some years in the military services of his adopted land.[53]

Most of the *Turner* enthusiasts, those who made gymnastics a focal point for neighborhood institutions that sometimes championed reform and progressive politics as well as physical culture in America's schools, were Germans. The best-known Austrian *Turner* was Ernst Voiland (b. Lower Austria, 1821), a radical member of the

Kremsier Reichstag, a refugee of 1849 who eked out a meager living in America by making cigars, and an enthusiastic *Turner* in the United States.[54] And among the artists of '48 was the Breslau-born Heinrich Berger, who studied the arts in Vienna and found a career as sculptor in New York City.[55]

Most of the Forty-eighters, devoted to the cause of freedom at home, became abolitionists in America. Despite the fact that the Democratic Party had traditionally shown more friendliness to immigrants than its opposition, the many intellectuals among the Forty-eighters turned in the late 1850's to the new Republican Party. There might be among them an occasional Democrat like the great editor of the "New Yorker Staats-Zeitung," Oswald Ottendorfer, but even he deserted the Democratic candidate in 1860 and came out for the Union. The German and Austrian Forty-eighters were not discouraged by the adherence of Know-Nothings, Sunday-observance Puritans, and temperance people to the young Republican Party. Schurz and Hassaurek, among others, represented them at the Chicago Convention of 1860 that nominated Abraham Lincoln for the presidency.[56]

John Brown's supporter, August (originally Anshel) Bondi (b. Vienna, 1833 – d. St. Louis, 1907), was one of the most interesting of the dedicated abolitionists. He had fought as a boy in Vienna's Academic Legion. He came as a refugee with his family to St. Louis, planned to help free Cuba from Spain, and joined a Jewish merchant in Bleeding Kansas in time to meet John Brown and join his little abolitionist force. He carried a flintlock in the Lilliput battle of Black Jack when on June 2, 1856, the free state men won over the Border Ruffians and he fought again with John Brown at Osawatomie. Even after Brown had left Kansas Bondi stayed on to fight for a free-state constitution. And his Kansas home was later burned by the slavery faction while he was fighting with the Union Army.[57]

The German-speaking immigrants may have thrown the election of 1860 to Abraham Lincoln – a contribution, if true, of no small importance.[58]

Many fought in the Northern army. The Austrians were often placed in units with other German-speaking recruits. None achieved great fame. Bondi was a first sergeant, Isidor Bush a captain, Hausen was brigade physician, the journalist Heinrich Ramming was a colonel in a Missouri regiment, and Franz Wutschel, already mentioned as the proprietor of the Vienna Legionair Restaurant in New York, who has been called the only Forty-eighter to be dismissed during the Civil War for incompetence, was colonel of New York's Eighth Regiment.[59]

There were many in the ranks and many others who fought as officers. It is probable that these veterans of the cause of freedom on the Vienna barricades were more eager to fight for the cause of liberty in their adopted country than many native Americans. The Germanic contribution to abolitionism and to the Civil War was one notable exception to the fact that the foreign-born in America generally contributed more to intellectual and scientific life than to political and military.[60]

Certainly the Austro-Americans have generally made their contributions on the cultural, rather than on the political, side.

The whole sad episode of the revolutions of 1848 was mitigated only by the tremendous advantages that accrued to America when so many able émigrés came to its shores. Politically the revolutions of '48 produced little that contributed favorably to American historical development. They aroused prominent patriotic Americans like Clay and Fillmore to revive Washington's Farewell Address and all the doctrines of non-interference with European affairs that it involved. Kossuth's indifference to the cause of anti-slavery confused the issues of European liberalism and American abolitionism. American reaction to the revolutionaries of 1848 helped unfortunately to produce here that most reactionary of all 19th Century conservative movements, Know-Nothingism. And American Catholics, never certain that they wanted Central European revolutionary movements to go completely liberal, often complicated the American political scene by opposing American intervention on the side of the revolutionary darlings in Europe of the American liberals.[61] All in all, the era of 1848 contributed confusion as well as construction, to American life.

[1] *Fifteenth Census of the United States, 1930, Population*, vol. II, p. 233. Figures for those born in Austria-Hungary were first given for the decade 1861–70 but the term was so broad and poorly defined that the statistics have only general interest for our study. The German Austrians among them were so few that virtually none of our historians of immigration have attempted to separate them out.

[2] Statistics prepared by the Bureau of Statistics in 1893 and published in F. F. Schrader, *Germans in the Making of America*, Boston 1924, p. 29.

[3] *Pennsylvania Archives*, 2nd series, vol. 17, Harrisburg 1892, "Names of Foreigners ... Pennsylvania;" R. B. Strassburger, *Pennsylvania German Pioneers*, 3 vols., Norristown 1934, II, *passim.*

[4] Bayrd Still, *Milwaukee*, Madison 1948, p. 131.

[5] *American-German Review*, Apr. 1947, p. 34.

[6] *Ibid.*, Aug.-Sept. 1963, p. 9. There were 256 Germans, 17 Swiss and only 8 Austrians.

[7] A. B. Faust, *Guide to the Materials for American History in Swiss and Austrian Archives*, Washington 1916, p. 256.

[8] Thomas Čapek, *The Čechs (Bohemians) in America*, Boston and N. Y., 1920, pp. 25–28 emphasizes the importance of the discovery of gold in California and states that, between 1850 and 1868, 43,645 of the 57,736 emigrants from "Austria" came from Bohemia – chiefly from its rural, southern districts. Before that period crop failures had been chiefly responsible for emigration.

[9] Faust, *op. cit.*, pp. 266–67.

[10] Čapek, *op. cit.*, p. 31.

[11] Dieter Cunz, *Maryland Germans*, Princeton 1948, pp. 261–62; *Der Deutsche Pionier*, Feb. 1870, pp. 354–60; *Das Buch der Deutschen in Amerika*, Philadelphia 1909, p. 514.

[12] Wilhelm Schlag, "A Survey of Austrian Emigration to the United States," *Österreich und die angelsächsische Welt*, Wien 1961, p. 157.

[13] Ferdinand Kürnberger, *Der Amerika-Müde*, Frankfurt/Main, 1855.

[14] Gustav Pollak, *Franz Grillparzer and the Austrian Drama*, N. Y. 1907, p. 426.

[15] Karl Knortz, *Deutsch in Amerika*, Leipzig 1906, p. 11; T. S. Baker, *Lenau and Young Germany in America*, Philadelphia 1907; Schlag, *op. cit.*, pp. 153–57.

[16] Baker, *op. cit.*, was written and published in 1907 as a warning against the Germanization of America.

[17] Joseph Salzbacher, *Meine Reise nach Nord-Amerika im Jahre 1842*, Wien 1845, pp. 366–67. Salzbacher found that the German colonies in the United States contained Swiss, Danes, Hollanders, Bavarians, in addition to the North Germans, but he makes no reference to migrants from the Habsburg area. See C. J. Barry, *The Catholic Church and German Americans*, Milwaukee 1953, p. 13, for Salzbacher's mission.

[18] Edwin C. Guitlet, *The Great Migration*, N. Y. 1937, p. 223.

[19] Carleton Beals, *Brass-Knuckle Crusade*, N. Y. 1960, pp. 23–25.

[20] Thomas R. Whitney, *A Defense of the American Policy*, N. Y. 1856, p. 368.

[21] Josephine Goldmark, *Pilgrims of '48*, New Haven 1930, p. 171.

[22] *Ibid.*, pp. 165–66.

[23] Cf. Marcus Lee Hansen, *The Immigrant in American History*, Harvard 1942, pp. 135–36.

[24] Arthur J. May, *Contemporary Opinion of Mid-Century Revolutions in Central Europe*, Phila. 1927, *passim*.

[25] A. B. Faust, *German Element in the United States*, 2 vols., Boston and New York 1909, I, p. 499, note 1. See also p. 312 for the proposal that Schiller's death be celebrated in New York with the anniversary of Blum's death. See also R. J. Rath, *Vienna Revolution of 1848*, Austin, Texas, 1957, p. 391.

[26] It is estimated that there were less than 4,000 Forty-eighters. A. E. Zucker, ed., *The Forty-eighters*, N. Y. 1950, pp. 184–85.

[27] Leo Goldhammer, "Jewish Emigration from Austria-Hungary in 1848–1849," *Yivo Annual*, vol. IX, N. Y. 1954, pp. 332–62.

[28] *Ibid.*, *passim*. This Goldhammer article is exellent for the entire Forty-eighter emigration, Gentile or Jewish. He estimates that up to 300 Jews came to America from "Austria" and that more came from Bohemia.

[29] Harry Simonhoff, *Jewish Notables in America*, N. Y. 1956, pp. 340–42.

[30] Vol. 82, p. 259. For radicalism among the Forty-eighters see Ray Allen Billington, *Protestant Crusade 1800–1860*, N. Y. 1938, pp. 328–29; Ernest Bruncken, *German Political Refugees*, 1904, *passim*; Wilhelm Schlag, *op. cit.*, pp. 157ff.

[31] Wilhelm Schlag, *op. cit.*, p. 160.

[32] Rath, *op. cit.*, p. 395; Carl Wittke, *Refugees of Revolution*, Philadelphia 1952, pp. 129 and 316.

[33] Heinrich Börnstein, *Fünfundsiebzig Jahre in der Alten und Neuen Welt*, 2 vols., Leipzig 1884.

[34] E. W. Dobert, *Deutsche Demokraten in Amerika*, Göttingen 1958, p. 39.

[35] Goldhammer, *op. cit.*, pp. 353–54; C. v. Wurzbach, *Biographisches Lexikon des Kaisersthums Österreich*, 60 parts, Wien 1856–91, LVI, pp. 78–82.

[36] A. B. Faust, *op. cit.*, II, p. 461.

[37] The Germans did settle in rural areas and some Austrians doubtless followed suite. But in general Austrians have preferred the cities. The contention of Moses Rischin in a paper read before the American Historical Assc., Dec. 1960, that German Jews did not concentrate in American cities is, we believe, far less true of Austrian Jews. A useful check-list is to be found in Zucker, *op. cit.*, pp. 270ff., where brief biographies of a number of the Austrian Forty-eighters may be found.

[38] Wittke, *op. cit.*, 330.

[39] Zucker, *op. cit.*, p. 301.

[40] H. A. Kelly, *American Medical Biographies*, Baltimore 1920, pp. 673–74, which describes his career states that Krackowitzer sometimes wrote in German and sometimes in English. See also Wittke, *op. cit.*, p. 334.

[41] Börnstein, *op. cit.*, II, p. 7.

[42] Hans Kudlich, *Rückblicke*, 3 vols., Wien 1873, is an important source that deserves translation into English. There is very little about Kudlich in English although he is mentioned in Wittke, *op. cit.*, Rath, *op. cit.*, and Schlag, *op. cit.*, etc. See also Bruno Gebhardt, *Handbuch der Deutschen Geschichte*, vol. III, Stuttgart 1960, p. 323 and *Meyers Lexikon*, vol. VI, Leipzig 1939.

[43] John Tasker Howard, *Our American Music*, N. Y. 1946, p. 211, concludes that the net result was advantageous for our native music.

[44] *Who's Who in America*, 1899–1900; *International Cyclopedia of Music* for date of death.

[45] Josef Nadler, *Literaturgeschichte des Deutschen Volkes*, vol. IV, Berlin 1941, p. 120. Balatka will be found in almost all accounts of the refugees of 1848. See our first chapter on music, below. Čapek's *Čechs in America* calls him German and not Czech.

[46] Wittke, *op. cit.*, p. 295.

[47] Told in his *Aus dem Wanderbuche eines österreichischen Virtuosen*, Leipzig 1859. The title is significant in that Pressburg where Hauser was born was always in either Slovakia or Hungary. The title is evidence that the "Germans" who came from there, of which there were many, often considered themselves to be Austrian.

[48] Cunz, *op. cit.*, p. 272.

[49] See our chapter on architects.

[50] Wittke, *op. cit.*, p. 87; Cunz, *op. cit.*, p. 331.

[51] *Ibid.*, p. 340.

[52] *Ibid.*, p. 65.

[53] Wurzbach, *op. cit.*, LIX, pp. 36–37; Wittke, *op. cit.*, p. 64.

[54] Schlag, *op. cit.*, p. 161.

[55] Zucker, *op. cit.*, p. 277.

[56] F. J. Brown and J. S. Roucek, *One America*, 1957 ed., p. 110.

[57] *Publications of the American Jewish Historical Soc.*, No. 23, 1915, pp. 63–76; Harry Simonhoff, *Jewish Notables in America*, N. Y. 1956, pp. 344–45. Of interest is the recent book for children, *Border Hawk: August Bondi*, N. Y. 1958, by Lloyd Alexander. It is based on Bondi's autobiography.

[58] M. A. Jones, *American Immigration*, Chicago 1960, p. 333, cites authorities pro and con.

[59] See Ella Lonn, "The Forty-eighters in the Civil War," in A. E. Zucker ed., *The Forty-eighters*, N. Y. 1950. The Wutschel biography is on p. 356.

[60] Dumas Malone cited in Wittke, *We Who Built America*, N. Y. 1945, p. 345.

[61] May, *op. cit.*, pp. 124ff.

CHAPTER VI

THE IMMIGRATION EXPLOSION AND WORLD WAR I

The decade of the 1880's marks the most phenomenal of all turning points in the entire history of American immigration. Immigrants came then in greater numbers than ever before and they came in vast numbers from eastern and southern Europe by contrast with the earlier predominance of the western Europeans. Some 2,812,000 came in the 1870's; 5,246,000 in the 1880's. The all-time peak was reached in the first decade of the twentieth century with some 8,795,000 newcomers. And the contribution from southern and eastern Europe, which was just beginning to pick up momentum in 1882 with thirteen percent of the total, reached about eighty-one percent in 1907.[1]

The German Austrians, who had previously come in inconsequential numbers, were caught up in the flood and began, for the first time, to play a role quantitatively in the immigration story. Utterly neglected in the statistics until after World War I, they may have constituted, as one expert estimated, only about 30,000 souls in our foreign-born census of 1870. They were then greatly outnumbered even by the Swiss Germans.[2] And if our expert was correct, and his estimate can be projected on the basis of subsequent census figures, the 30,000 Austrian-born of 1870 may have become some 180,000 by 1900 and twice that ten years later. Professor Faust believed that in 1900 there might be some 439,912 Americans who were born of Austrian parents. The official statistics that showed 946 Austrian-born in the United States in 1850 and 275,907 in 1900 were doubtless grossly inadequate for 1850 and far more than adequate for 1900 (many of the non-Germanic peoples of the monarchy were still reporting themselves to the census takers as Austrians). But they show in a general way how great had been the increase in immigration from the monarchy.[3]

Germanic or non-Germanic, it was also significant to a study of Austro-American relations that the entire Austro-Hungarian monarchy made such a tremendous contribution in those years of America's immigration explosion. It poured so many immigrants into the United States in those three decades that when the books were balanced later in 1945 it was found that Austria-Hungary, in the 125 years since 1820, had furnished more immigrants (4,144,000) than any countries except Germany (six million), Italy (4,700,000), Ireland (4,500,000) and Great Britain (4,200,000). Russia (3,000,000) and Sweden (1,200,000) were well behind Austria-Hungary.[4] The peak year of Austro-Hungarian immigration was 1907. In the decade 1881–1890

Austria-Hungary sent us 353,719 immigrants; 592,707 in the 1890's; and a magnificent 2,145,261 during the decade to 1910. That is significant to our story because, despite the fact that comparatively few of the new-comers were Germanic, they were generally known as Austrians.[5]

It is interesting to notice that the great influx began in the 1880's, well after the American economic panic of 1873. Immigrants generally avoided American bad times. And the timing is significant because after 1873 American industry came to realize that it needed the immigrant for building and manning its factories, operating its mines, building its cities, and even, but to a lesser extent, for cultivating its farms.[6]

The effect of bad times in America was also apparent after the depression of 1903 when the German Austrians, according to one authority, sent only 7,883 emigrants to the United States in 1904–05 after having sent 11,256 in the previous year and 11,798 in 1902–03.[7] The emigrant agents and the steamship companies that wanted customers tried to suppress the news of America's bad times but it inevitably spread, by letter and word-of-mouth, and had a very definite effect upon migration.

Here the Austrians settled, as they had always done, chiefly in the North Atlantic States. An Austrian vice consul who served in Chicago wrote that in 1900 of the Austro-Hungarians without the Bohemians and Hungarians, whom he listed separately, 62% settled in the Northeast, 25.5% in the North Central, States, 7.4% in the West, 3.7% in the South Central, and only 1.4% in the South Atlantic States.[8] Rural America was predominently Protestant and hostile to foreign intruders. It disliked all that Austria had to offer: Catholics, free-thinkers, Jews, sophisticates. So the Austrians avoided the small towns, both in the South where the economic system seemed like *Lohnsklaverei* (a kind of tenant bondage) to them and northward where they disliked our Evangelical forms of worship and the indifference to new-comers that was born of the decline of farming areas and the decreasing need for labor. The city bosses of the Northeast, even though they never realized that there was such a thing as an "Austrian vote," were more attractive to the Austrian immigrants than the austere Puritans of rural America.[9]

Although the Austrian half of Austria-Hungary was by no means all German Austrian when, in 1905, it was separated in our statistics from the Hungarian half of the monarchy, it is interesting to note that the 1910 Census[10] reported 190,237 "Austrian-born" in New York City, 251,773 in the state of Pennsylvania, 163,020 in Illinois (132,059 in Chicago alone), 72,887 in Ohio, 38,691 in Wisconsin, 20,566 in Texas, 17,163 in California, and only 2,413 in Boston. The totals for the South Atlantic States, below Maryland (8,251), were insignificant.

Vice Consul Schwegel's statistics for 1902–1903 showing the origins of the Austro-Hungarian immigrants to the United States are important because Schwegel, as an Austrian official, had an insight into all the Austro-Hungarian conflicts of race and nationality that American census and immigration officials lacked:[11]

German Austrians	23,597
Poles	37,499
Slovaks	34,412
Croats and Slovenes	32,892
Magyars	27,113
Jews	18,759
Ruthenians	9,819
Czechs	9,577
Bulgars, Serbs, Montenegrins	4,227
Rumanians	4,173
Italians	2,170
Dalmatians, Bosnians, Herzegovinians	1,723

The German Austrians were, indeed, such a minority of the whole that it is not difficult to understand why they were so often forgotten. An expert on American immigration has estimated that of the total of 4,132,351 Austro-Hungarians who came to America during the entire period from 1820 to 1930, the German Austrians supplied fewer than the Poles, Hungarians, Slovaks and Czechs, but more than the Jews, Croats, Ruthenians, Rumanians, Serbs, and Dalmatians. Just before the first World War the German Austrians constituted a bit less than a third of the population of the Austrian portion of the monarchy.[12]

During the half century after 1867 the terms of the *Ausgleich* permitted emigration but the Austrian government never looked upon it with favor. The only encouragement the emigrants received was the prevailing laxity in the enforcement of such regulations as those requiring passports. Only where military service was concerned was the Vienna regime greatly concerned. The obligation of the emigrant subject to the draft could be cancelled only after a year of foreign residence and demonstrated intention to remain abroad.[13]

During that half century some Austrians emigrated to escape from the conservative regime's persecution of radicals. The Social Democratic movement, of socialists and laborites, was struggling to achieve recognition and it often encountered vigorous resistance as in 1884 when martial law was proclaimed in Vienna and civil rights were suspended. There were thousands of political convictions. It was then that socialists and radicals like Johann Most, the German anarchist who operated for years in Austria, came to the United States.[14]

The primary reason for emigration was, however, economic: The McKinley tariff or the competition of Italian wines in the southern provinces or the prevalance of destructive phylloxera in the vineyards were typical of the special economic problems that plagued the monarchy. Industrial establishments were still too small and too backward to absorb the peasants who wanted to find jobs in the cities. Wages were ridiculously low. The Austrian annual income per person in dollars has been estimated at $ 79 in 1870, $ 169 in 1890, and $ 262 in 1910.[15] Agricultural wages in Lower Austria just before the turn of the century ranged from fourteen to thirty-six cents a day and they were somewhat lower in Salzburg and the Tyrol.[16] But fundamental was the long period of distress that followed the breakup of Austria's feudal economy. The revolution of 1848 had freed the peasants from the last of the more onerous feudal restrictions but they still found the remaining great estates unhappy places to work and the newly divided lands inadequate, in many corners of the country, to supply crops enough to support life. In brief, the maladjustments of Austria's late agricultural and industrial revolutions encouraged emigration.[17] And it has been estimated that 83 percent of all "Austrian" emigrants chose the United States as their refuge.[18]

The United States Immigration Commission found that the solicitation by agents of emigrants in Austria around 1900 was illegal but was common practice. American industry began looking for labor after the Civil War. Some American companies came to depend largely upon the European labor market. Agents of lines like Hamburg-American and Cunard had neglected Austria until the 1880's when they began to swarm there, advertising their wares with lurid and irresponsible promises of immediate jobs and high wages in America. The ships that they represented were far superior to the tiny, filthy vessels of the years before mid-century, but they were more expensive and still primitive in the steerage. As early as 1869 the Hamburg-American Line was advertising ten ships of 2400 to 3000 tons on the New York—Hamburg run with eastbound fares of $ 36 in steerage.[19] Even as new luxury vessels were built the contrast between first class and steerage remained striking.

Most of the Austrian emigrants used the ports in northern Europe: 72,502 left in 1905 from Hamburg and Bremen, 14,398 from Antwerp, 7,167 from Le Havre, 6,105 from Rotterdam and only 7,481 and 1,112 respectively from Trieste with Austro-American and Cunard. Most of the departures from Austria's own port of Trieste were of Galicians and South Slavs.[20]

The German and Swiss had for decades many dozens of periodicals retailing advice for prospective emigrants. Austria, with a government unfriendly to emigration, had almost none.[21] Some of the German sheets, like Röding's "Columbus: Amerikanische Miscellen" (Hamburg 1825—32), were probably distributed in Austria as well as in Germany.[22] Travelers' accounts of the charms of America, like Gottfried Duden's idealistic "Bericht von einer Reise nach den westlichen Staaten" (1829) which went through several editions, were read in Austria as well as in Germany and Switzerland. And the many fascinating immigrant guides or *Wegweiser* that were published in Germany doubtless found their way all over German-speaking Austria. Few were published, like Jünemann's "Ratgeber und Wegweiser für Auswanderer nach . . . Nordamerika" (1849) in Vienna. On the other hand, some Austrians published their *Wegweiser* in Germany. One of the finest was Francis J. Grund's "Handbuch und Wegweiser" (Stuttgart 1846). He was a learned Viennese who knew America well. His advice was generally sound: remember that riches come in America, as in Europe, only with industry and frugality; take with you plenty of courage and determination and not too much sentimentality; apply for citizenship as soon as possible. He recommended settlement in the Middle West, especially in Wisconsin and Iowa, and he favored farming and settlement in small communities where one could know his neighbors. It would be interesting to know how many Austrians read his common-sense advice before they emigrated.

Letters in the press, correspondence from emigrant friends, and the high-pressure of the omnipresent steamship agents were, however, the principal reasons why the restless Austrians of the later years of the nineteenth century chose to go to America.

When they arrived in America in the late years of the last century the German Austrians found themselves suspect because they were confused with the Hunkies, Polacks, Bohunks, and all the other too-often unpopular immigrants from Austria-Hungary. America needed these people to man its new mines and heavy industries, to replace the Irish in building its railroads and never-ending roads, and, in general, to do the hard and disagreeable work of America's industrial revolution. America needed those people of the old monarchy but because they seemed unskilled and difficult to understand and strange in their ways, America looked down upon them. "The enemy forces are not American," explained the "Chicago Tribune," but "Hussite desperados with such names as Wazinski, Hitt, and other Cossack and Teutonic appelations . . . rag-tag and bobtail cutthroats of Beilzebub from the Rhine, the Danube, the Vistula and the Elbe."[23] The immigration explosion of the 1880's brought these non-German Austro-Hungarians to America by the hundreds of thousands and it frightened the nativists as they had never before been frightened in those earlier years when only the Irish potato famine and the Metternich despotism were bringing difficult-to-assimilate immigrants to America. Representative Henry Cabot Lodge, the champion of Nordic America, compared two eight-year periods in the 1870's and the 1880's – before and after the New Immigration – and found that while French immigration had decreased almost 20% and that of Great Britain and Ireland had increased by only 67.8%, the immigration from what he called Austria had increased 136.5%, from Poland 166%, from Italy 286%, Russia 297% and from Hungary by 476.4%.[24] Millions of Americans agreed with Representative Lodge that America was being contaminated by the infusion of central and southern European blood. And Lodge quoted our consul general in Vienna on the score of Austrian emigrants:

"The young men who want to escape military service, the ultra-socialist, the anarchist, the man who has lost all social and business footing here, the bankrupt, embezzler, and swindler, stop not to obtain permission of the government, and naturally the authorities have no sort of record here either as to the number or place of destination of this class of emigrants ... The government ... feels no regret to get rid of the ultra-socialists and anarchists, and that it is quite willing the bankrupt and swindler should depart for foreign countries and that the paupers should find support away from home." The consul, who was of course not speaking primarily of German Austrians, added that the Bohemians were "illiterate and ignorant in the extreme." And Lodge concluded that the immigration "is making its greatest relative increase from races most alien to the body of the American people and from the lowest and most illiterate classes among those races." And he quoted from Jacob Riis' book, "How the Other Half Lives," to show how such immigrants were degrading American life. They were "unskilled labor of the lowest kind."[25]

The nativists out in rural, Protestant America could agree with Lodge. The folk in Tremperlean County in Wisconsin, for instance, liked the honest, frugal Germans but they disliked the quarrelsome, Sunday-breaking, Catholic Poles and they somehow confused those other poor farmers, the Bohemians, with the Poles.[26] And in New York City the Reverend H. A. Brannon of St. Agnes declared in 1892: "We want no foreign bishops here, with the stamp of Kaiser Wilhelm or of Franz Joseph ... We say to faultfinders from Austria, purify the corrupt capital of your half-infidel empire ..."[27]

The American nativists made capital of the "unassimilable" immigrant who was lowering the American standard of living. The American Protective Association provided fuel for the flames and even Samuel Gompers and the labor movement pleaded for protection against the cheap immigrant labor that remained so long outside the fold of organized labor. The Ku Klux Klan, founded later in 1915, campaigned against foreigners, Catholics and Jews, as it campaigned to keep the Negro in his place.[28] Virtually all the enemies of the New Immigration thought of all Austrians, Germanic or non-Germanic, as belonging to the undesirable element. Those that they came to know and respect for their achievements on this side of the ocean they called Germans, and the German Austrians were only too ready to accept that designation.

The clamor for restrictive legislation was to produce a sheaf of laws that would have no special impact upon Austrian immigration: the Chinese exclusion laws of 1882 and the laws excluding the physically defective, the insane, the criminals, public charges, anarchists, and such, the alien-labor-contract laws that made it impossible to import labor already under contract to American employers, the law of 1903 increasing the immigrant head tax to two dollars, and the illiteracy law which, after vetoes by three Presidents, was finally enacted in 1917 to exclude illiterate immigrants over sixteen years of age.

According to an Austrian authority the United States government rejected over 13,000 immigrants in one year, 1906–1907, principally under the liable-to-become-a-public-charge (6,866 cases) and contagious diseases (3,822 cases) laws.[29] The Austrian government, generally indifferent to its emigrants if they were not subject to military duty, left it to the Germans to prevent obviously ineligible Austrians from shipping to America from German ports, and at Trieste, where the Hungarian government had built a useful emigrant station, left it to the American consuls. Austrian officials in the United States also seem to have been altogether too ready to leave their Austrian constituents to the protection of the far more enterprising and helpful German consular officers.[30]

But the immigration quota laws of 1924 and 1952, based upon the proportions of the number of people born in a given country who were residing in the United States in 1890 and 1920 respectively, were to reduce the Austrian quotas to 1,413 in 1929 and 1,405 in 1952.[31] Such a quota proved to be unfortunately small during Nazi and post-Nazi days when so many Austrians wanted to escape. The men who made the quotas were doubtless as confused as most of their fellow-countrymen as to the definition of an Austrian.

America's unsympathetic reception of immigrants helped to compound the difficulties. Editor Ottendorfer, an Austro-Moravian, highlighted in his "New Yorker Staats-Zeitung" all the brutalities that the immigrant faced: the delays, harshnesses, uncertainties, heart-breaking deportations, the Ellis Island inquisition, the division of families, the arbitrary medical inspection. Ottendorfer could observe for himself since most of the immigrants arrived in New York, ten times as many as at the second port of Boston.[32]

Alien efforts to help the bewildered immigrants often complicated the situation. The Austrian Society of New York, founded in 1898 to help Austrians at Ellis Island and supported by an annual grant of $ 5000 from the Austrian government as well as by dues,[33] was Catholic-oriented and hence anathema to the nativists. And the St. Raphaelsverein, created by the German Cahensly in the 1860's at an Innsbruck *Katholikentag* to help improve the lot of the German emigrant, became an American issue in the 1890's when it came out for the cultural individuality of emigrants: maintenance of their native tongues and churches and clergy. Even the Irish Catholics joined in the attack. And the fact that the Archbishop of Vienna and "the princes of the Austrian aristocracy" were involved did not help the Austrian cause.[34] Americans did not realize that the German Austrians were generally far easier to assimilate than most of the new comers. They did not settle in their own colonies like the *Reichsdeutschen* and celebrate their own national holidays like even such small groups as the Swiss and the Hollanders.[35] Vienna might be concerned with the welfare and the faith of its emigrants but it exhibited none of the "cultural imperialism" that was prevalent in Berlin.

The Austrians who came here during the generation before the first World War were on the whole good substantial people, with better backgrounds than those of most of the immigrants of eastern Europe but not outstanding by comparison with the new-comers from western Europe. The distinguished professionals among them were few. The first issue of "Who's Who in America" (1899–1900) listed 32 "Austrians" and that entitled them to seventh place among the foreign-born Americans in the volume, just behind Scotland and France and well ahead of Italy, Russia, and Sweden with 15 each.[36] Some of the most notable of that period were, like Gustav Mahler and Leo Slezak, scarcely more than visitors in the United States and many were, like Mahler, natives of present-day Czechoslovakia who had found their careers in Vienna. That first issue of "Who's Who" found the largest Austrian group in music – Gericke, Paur, Schalk, Kneisel, Fanny Zeisler, Grau, and Frederick Brandeis – followed by the church with bishops Katzer, Trobec and Vertin. The United States Immigration Commission's findings for 1900 also found relatively few "Austrian-born" in the professions (2357) but pointed out that musicians came first (475) followed by the clergy and the teachers. The figures were based upon the Census of 1900.[37]

The "Austrians" were still among the least agricultural of all the new Americans, with a mere eight percent. And the percentage of genuine German Austrians in agriculture was doubtless still lower. But for what the Census called Austrians, excluding self-confessed Bohemians, Poles, and Hungarians, domestic service ranked first, miners and quarrymen second, laborers third, trade and transportation fourth, agriculture fifth with its eight percent, tailors next (which leads one to believe that a goodly number of good Czech tailors called themselves Austrians), and merchants seventh, just before iron workers and the professionals (1.5%). Bartenders ranked a notch lower.[38] One American expert on immigration puts the tailors at the top of the "Austrian" list followed by miners, hucksters and peddlers, and iron workers, in that order. Although he lists Bohemia, Hungary, and Poland separately, his statistics seem to represent the entire monarchy rather than core-Austria. He tells us also that in the second generation the Austrians were better represented in the professions.[39]

The Austro-Hungarian immigrants were not supermen. Although Professor Handlin[40] finds its conclusions inaccurate, the United States Immigration Commission was able, in 1907, to state that Austro-Hungarian immigrants were responsible in New York for more assault cases than any other nationality except the Italians. Professor Handlin also doubts the validity of the Commission's reports that Austro-Hungarian immigrants ranked eight in feeblemindedness, ninth in insanity, seventh in crime, sixth in epilepsy, and third in tuberculosis – with the anticipated conclusion by the Commission that these central Europeans did not make good citizens.

The Austro-Hungarian immigrants of the turn of the century were by no means so anxious to take American citizenship as those of forty years later. Slightly over half of those resident in the United States in 1900 (53.4%) had taken citizenship which was decidedly better than the Hungarian record, far better than the record of the Austrian Poles, but not by any means so good as that of the eager Bohemians.[41]

It is as impossible to find valid illiteracy figures for the German Austrians as it is to separate out their naturalization statistics. The clothing industry in the United States might in 1900 report that its German, Bohemian, and Moravian workers were about 99% literate while the more critical experts were concluding that the immigrants from the more backward regions of the monarchy were 29% illiterate.[42] The core Austrians, many of them from Vienna and its good schools, were among the most literate.

American critics of our immigration policy often pointed to the tremendous sums that immigrants sent out of this country to the folks at home. The exact amounts will never be known. From 1893 to 1903 the so-called Austrian immigrants are said to have sent home an average of about 34,000,000 Kronen a year – almost seven million dollars.[43] On the other hand an Austrian authority, Schwegel, estimates that Austria-Hungary lost $ 28,000,000 in the five years 1895–99, when a quarter of a million emigrants took $ 3,000,000 *Bargeld* (in hard money) with them to America after having paid $ 25,000,000 (about $ 100 per capita) for travel costs. The Immigration Commission estimated a few years later that the average immigrant brought about $ 30 with him to this country.[44] Whatever the balance of accounts, the United States Post Office was busy for many years sending immigrants' dollars back to their native lands.

It was estimated that migrants that came only to return to their homeland in the monarchy after working a few years in America brought home with them in the one year 1907 some 100,000,000 Kronen, about $ 20,000,000. The returnees were especially numerous among the young immigrant men, chiefly non-Germanic, who went into the dreary Pennsylvania coal mines to stay six or seven years and accumulate enough capital to buy a small farm or shop when they returned home. How many did return home is uncertain. Figures differ radically. But the returnee percentage was certainly a substantial one: 32% of the number admitted from 1908 to 1910 are said to have left the United States, including 19% of the German total, 11% of the Bohemians and Moravians, 30% of the Poles, 56% of the Croats and Slovenes, and 64% of the Hungarians.[45] Caro, who admits that there were no reliable figures available to him, states that the number of Austrian returnees in 1906–1907 was more than a third of the number who entered the United States during that year. And it is significant that an unusually large number returned as a result of our Panic of 1907.[46] Caro also found that from 17% to 27% of the returnees emigrated a second time.

The German Austrians seem, in general, to have come to stay. Only 7,058 of them returned in the year of bad times, 1907–1908, in a total of 130,197 steerage passengers returning to Austria-Hungary.[47] But the fact that so many from the monarchy did return served to reinforce the arguments of the critics who maintained that the "Austrian" immigrants were undesirable.

World War I marked the end of an era in American immigration history as well as in Austria's history. It first shut off migration at the European source, in 1914, and it brought closer, with all its furor about disloyal and hyphenated Americans, the restriction of immigration to numbers that were infinitesimal as compared with the totals before 1914. The country that had welcomed over five million immigrants in the one decade of the 1880's was to fix the annual quota in the 1920's at about 150,000. The Austrian republic was to send us scarcely more than three thousand emigrants a year in the 1920's.

The war itself was, of course, one more unhappy milestone in Austro-American relations. The consensus of the American historical profession, after the era of wartime propaganda, was that Austria had aided and abetted the Germans in bringing on the war.[48]

Austria-Hungary, as the principal ally of Germany, shared in America's indignant reaction to all the real or alleged atrocities of the Germans, the image of German militarism, and of Prussian autocracy. Austrian music and opera, musicians and actors, came under the ban along with everything Germanic. And Austrian diplomats were condemned with their German allies for trying to propagandize America, spying upon its military installations, and sabotaging aid to the Western Powers. Internment camps were set up for enemy aliens and the recently naturalized lost their citizenship. The times were sad.

At Washington Austria's Ambassador Dumba complained years later that his government never kept him properly informed when, for instance, it sent the world-shattering ultimatum to Serbia in the tragic and critical days of 1914. He was a victim of the eternal Austrian indifference to public relations. Uninformed he could scarcely justify the Austrian position to the United States. And so, when he was caught subsidizing an American journalist in his effort to prevent the American steel industry from helping the other side to win the war, he was ignominiously sent home to Vienna. He was caught redhanded, and he could only forget all his pleasant relationships with the British Ambassador and with General Leonard Wood and with those friendly American assistant secretaries of state, William Phillips and John Bassett Moore, and retreat to Vienna. He took with him only the friendliest recollections of pre-war America. He had doubtless overstepped the line of diplomatic privilege when, in indignation at the work of the American steel industry in supplying his enemies, he not only encouraged strikes in American steel plants but allowed the German press to threaten imprisonment or worse to Austro-Hungarian subjects who worked in plants with Allied munitions contracts.[49]

It was reported that the "mailed fist of Austria-Hungary in America" was reaching out to control and manipulate its subjects and even its former subjects here. One

Croat newspaper in Duluth, for instance, warned in 1916 that Austro-Hungarians serving in American munitions factories faced penalties, if they ever returned home, of from ten years to death; and a Hungarian paper in Cleveland in 1917 after America had entered the war threatened any Austro-Hungarians who should aid in the recruitment of Rumanian legions to fight against Hungary. [50] The pro-Austrian and pro-German "Svoboda," America's largest Ukranian paper, was said to have harbored a staff member who was in the employ of the Vienna government. But such papers generally turned pro-American after the United States entered the war. Some of the radical papers published for groups from the old monarchy were bold enough to invite criticism by supporting the Bolshevik revolution and the cause of class war in general. [51] The other Austro-Hungarian papers that devoted their efforts to pleading for independence from Vienna for "oppressed nationalities" attracted only sympathy.

Of the foreign-language press which played such an important role during the war in presenting all kinds of foreign and American, rational and crackpot, points of view, the German-language papers were still in the lead. They had indeed fallen from contributing almost four-fifths of the entire foreign-language-press output in 1885 to 46 percent in 1914, and they were to boast only 26 percent of the total after the war in 1920. But of the thousand or more foreign-language papers listed in the "American Newspaper Annual" for 1920 the German papers led with 276 and, to mention only those concerned with the peoples of the old monarchy, the Poles had 76, the Bohemians 51, the Slovaks 28, the Hungarians 27, the Ukranians 10, and the Croats 9. These papers produced a babel of demands and pleas and points of view that, on the whole, contributed but little to the Austrian cause.

Indeed, the foreign-language press represented the battles of the old world that were being fought out in the new world. Hungarian, Czech, Polish, and South Slav patriotic movements that had operated from the American base ever since 1848 gained momentum during World War I and, building upon wartime prejudices, millions of hyphenated Americans with tremendous voting power, and American idealism, triumphantly overturned the ancient Habsburg empire. It seemed appropriate to President Wilson and to many Americans that the great War for Democracy should destroy what they had long thought of as the ramshackle monarchy on the Danube, the *Völkerkerker* that had so long oppressed its aspiring subject peoples.

Organizations like the Ukranian Federation, the American Committee for the Liberation of the Czech People, the National Croatian Society, and the Polish Central Relief Committee propagandized the American people and their government. They appealed to Catholics and also, in the cases of Hungary and Czechoslovakia, to Protestants. They appealed to America's traditional sympathy for oppressed peoples and to Woodrow Wilson's desire to recast Europe according to his political philosophy.

The Poles reminded America of the services of Pulaski in the American revolution and of Kosciuszko whose fall had caused freedom to shriek. Paderewski worked in the United States to round up the Polish-American vote for Wilson in 1916 and Pilsudski, loyal to Austria in 1914, finally jumped on the independence bandwagon.[52] The Hungarians, with their old proverb "Trust not the German," reminded Americans of Kossuth and Deák and skilfully led them to forget that Austro-Hungarian "oppression" had emanated from Budapest at least as often as from Vienna. The South Slavs scarcely had to remind us of the Habsburg regime's blustering ultimatum to Serbia in 1914. And the Czechs, doubtless the most successful of all in creating a useful democratic image in the American mind, discovered towers of strength in Masaryk and Beneš, perhaps the greatest propagandists of their age. Masaryk sent the Czech "Declaration of Independence" to President Wilson late in 1918 with the explanation that the National Council was compelled to issue it by "Austrian moves for peace and towards a mock-federation calculated to deceive the world."[53] What could have made a greater appeal to Americans than a Czech pronouncement named after our own historic Declaration! Congressman Adolph Sabath, who was born in what is now Czechoslovakia in 1866 and who represented an Illinois district in the American Congress for several decades, has been given credit for prevailing upon Wilson to champion Czechoslovak independence. Czechoslovakia, to the confusion of its many German-Austrian residents like Franz Kafka who had in 1919 to take Czech citizenship,[54] achieved independence to become the favorite in America of all the succession states. It was quite clearly "made in America."

Typical of the anti-Austrian campaign was the mass meeting of September 1918 in New York's Carnegie Hall, with Paderewski representing the Poles, where all the "oppressed peoples" of Austria-Hungary met to denounce the Austrians and demand self-determination. The peace treaties were to bring success for most of them. There would, however, be the Ukranians (known in the monarchy as Ruthenians) who would be thrown to Russia and Poland.[55] And, probably unrepresented at the Carnegie Hall meeting, were Austria's South Tyrolese who would also do violence to the rule of self-determination when the treaties should hand them over, for strategic reasons, to Italy.

As a matter of fact, President Wilson's final decision to break up the monarchy came only in 1918. That decision was based, not primarily upon the political pressures of the minority groups, not upon the appeals of Masaryk or Sabath, but upon American strategy for winning the war. President Wilson had played for a separate peace with Vienna. But when in April 1918 Clemenceau of France injudiciously revealed the secret negotiations with Czernin of Austria, the monarchy saw no recourse but to reaffirm its loyalty to Germany. And if Austria could not be detached from its German allies, and if the war was still far from being won, Wilson felt he must yield to Secretary of State Lansing and the pressure groups and promise independence to the Czechs and the South Slavs. That would weaken the morale of the Czech and and Slav contingents in the Austro-Hungarian armies. It would encourage disloyalty within the monarchy. In any event, Wilson accepted the policy of dissolution and it helped, not only to win the war but to winnow votes for the Wilson administration in the November elections. Long before he went to the Paris Peace Conference, Wilson was committed to the destruction of Austria-Hungary.[56]

Whether the Wilsonian policies of 1919 were valid and whether the survival of the monarchy would have prevented, after World War II, the absorption of all of the old empire except core-Austria by communism, can never be proven. It is, however, significant to our study that the young Austrian republic of 1919, freed of all the cares of empire, is no longer, in the American mind, the ogre that the Habsburg monarchy so long seemed to us to be. The Austro-American antagonisms of 1815 to 1918 fortunately disappeared with the Treaty of St. Germain. To that extent the end of the first World War was a happy turning point.

[1] *Statistical Abstract of the United States 1961*, p. 92; M. A. Jones, *American Immigration*, Chicago 1960, p. 179.

[2] Theodor Poesche, "Anzahl der Deutschen in den Vereinigten Staaten," *Der Deutsche Pionier*, July 1873, p. 174.

[3] A. B. Faust, *German Element in the United States*, 2 vols., Boston and N. Y. 1909, II, p. 9. Faust counted only a fraction for those with only one Austrian-born parent. The figures for 1850 and 1900 are used in the *Reports of the U. S. Immigration Commission*, 1910, I, p. 134.

[4] U. S. DP Commission, *The DP Story*, Washington 1952, p. 1. There were doubtless very few "Austrians" among the 7.4% of the population that, according to the Census, was German-born in 1790.

[5] Henry Cabot Lodge, "Restriction of Immigration," *North American Review*, Jan. 1891, for instance, indicates that there were 215,101 Austrian immigrants 1880–1889 which is obviously too large a proportion of the Austro-Hungarian total for 1881–1890 as indicated above (353,719).

[6] Charlotte Erickson, *American Industry and the European Immigrant*, Harvard 1957, p. 67; F. J. Brown and J. S. Roucek, eds., *Our Racial and National Minorities*, N. Y. 1937, p. 13.

[7] Leopold Caro, *Auswanderung in Österreich*, Leipzig 1909, pp. 70–71.

[8] Hans Schwegel, "Die Einwanderung in die Vereinigten Staaten: Mit besonderer Rücksicht auf die österreichisch-ungarische Auswanderung," *Zeitschrift für Volkswirtschaft, Sozialpolitik und Verwaltung*, vol. XIII, Wien und Leipzig 1903, p. 178.

[9] Oscar Handlin, *Adventure in Freedom*, N. Y. 1954; Adolf v. Noe in *Österreichische Rundschau*, 15. Juli 1909, p. 70.

[10] Vols. II and III.

[11] Schwegel, *op. cit.*, p. 170.

[12] Maurice R. Davie, *World Immigration*, N. Y. 1936, pp. 116f.

[13] Caro, *op. cit.*

[14] Thomas Čapek, *Čechs (Bohemians) in America*, Boston and N. Y. 1920, pp. 140–42.

[15] Wilhelm Winkler, *Der Geburtenrückgang in Österreich*, Wien 1935, p. 36.

[16] *Reports of the U. S. Immigration Commission*, 1910, IV, pp. 361–63. Also useful is M. A. Jones, *op. cit.*, pp. 196–99.

[17] *Ibid.*, p. 198.

[18] Davie, *op.* cit., p. 120. Here the term "Austrian" doubtless refers to the entire Austrian half of the monarchy. According to G. G. Govorchin, *Americans from Yugoslavia*, Gainsville 1961, p. 9, six-sevenths of the three and a half million people who left Austria-Hungary from about 1875 to 1910 came to the United States.

[19] *Der Deutsche Pionier*, I, March 1869.

[20] Caro, *op. cit.*, pp. 23–26.

[21] Marcus Lee Hanson, *Immigrant in American History*, Harvard 1942, contains a long list of German and Swiss titles but mentions for Austria only the *Berichte* of the Leopoldinen-Stiftung of Vienna, p. 216.

[22] H. A. Pochmann, *German Culture in America*, Madison 1957, p. 66.

[23] Quoted from Carl Wittke, *We Who Built America*, N. Y. 1945, p. 408.

[24] Lodge, *op. cit.*, pp. 27–28.

[25] *Ibid.*, pp. 28, 31–33.

[26] According to the Census of 1850 Wisconsin had 365 churches of which 64 were Roman Catholic, a relatively large proportion in comparison with that in states like Illinois and Missouri. See Merle Curti, *The Making of an American Community*, Stanford 1959, pp. 95ff., for Tremperlean County.

[27] Quoted from *Catholic World* by C. J. Barry, *Catholic Church and German Americans*, Milwaukee 1953, p. 201.

[28] Oscar Handlin, *Race and Nationality in American Life*, Boston 1957, pp. 172–75, has an excellent account of this era.

[29] Caro, *op. cit.*, p. 23.

[30] Noe, *op. cit.*, p. 71.

[31] *Statistical Abstract of the United States, 1961*, pp. 89–91. The quotas of 1929 gave Ireland 17,853, Sweden 3,314, Poland 6,524 and Czechoslovakia 2,874. Hungary, on the other hand, received a quota of only 869.

[32] Schwegel, *op. cit.*, p. 185.

[33] "Emigrant Aid Societies," *Catholic Encyclopedia*, V, p. 404.

[34] *Ibid.*, p. 403; Barry, *op. cit.*, pp. 26–27, 136–52.

[35] Noe, *op. cit.*, pp. 70–71.

[36] There was in this count by *Who's Who* editors the usual confusion about the definition of "Austrian" but, since names we would not include are roughly compensated for by names attributed to other lands by *Who's Who*, the count is fairly accurate. *Who's Who* had separate listings for Hungarians (7), Bohemians (6), Poles (4), and Moravians (1).

[37] *Reports of the Immigration Commission*, 61st Cong., 2nd Sess., Senate Doc. 282, pp. 216ff.

[38] *Ibid.*, I, p. 821.

[39] E. P. Hutchinson, *Immigrants and their Children*, N. Y. and London 1956, p. 172.

[40] Handlin, *op. cit.*, pp. 128–32.

[41] Schwegel, *op. cit.*, p. 184.

[42] Schwegel, *op. cit.*, p. 174. Cf. *U. S. Immigration Commission Reports*, XI, p. 330.

[43] Caro, *op. cit.*, p. 48, gives the figures for Austria and Hungary.

[44] Schwegel, *op. cit.*, p. 193; *Reports of the Immigration Commission*, 1910, IV, p. 36.

[45] *Ibid.*, p. 41.

[46] *Op. cit.*, pp. 44–46; Austria's last Ambassador to Washington before our involvement in World War I, Konstantin Dumba, frowned upon a liberal Austrian emigration policy and disapproved of Austrian subsidies to the Cunard Line which was carrying only third-class, and no between-the-decks passengers from Fiume to New York. Dumba stated that only about a third of the Austrian Poles

and Ruthenians ever returned to the monarchy with their savings and he thought that another third perished in America from underpaid work in the mines and from malnutrition. Dumba quoted Count Tisza as hoping that the radical Slavs of the monarchy would, unlike the radical Magyars who so often came back, never return home: Konstantin Dumba, *Memoirs of a Diplomat*, Boston 1932, pp. 158—59.

[47] Caro, *op. cit.*, citing U. S. statistics.

[48] The temporarily significant revisionist group headed by Harry Elmer Barnes attempted to prove that Berlin and Vienna had not been primarily responsible for originating the war but the conclusions of the other school, headed by Bernadotte E. Schmitt, came to be generally accepted. Sydney B. Fay's *Origins of the World War*, N. Y. 1928, was a significant middle-of-the-road interpretation.

[49] Dumba, *op. cit.*, pp. 157ff; C. J. Child, *German-Americans in Politics 1914—1917*, Madison 1939, p. 44.

[50] R. E. Park, *The Immigrant Press and its Control*, N. Y. and London, 1922, pp. 200—01.

[51] *Ibid., passim.*

[52] L. L. Gerson, *Wilson and the Rebirth of Poland*, Yale 1953, treats of the thesis that Polish nationalism was overated and Poland achieved independence only through American aid.

[53] Quoted from the caption on the Declaration as exhibited at the Library of Congress, August 1962. For the Czech campaign for independence see Čapek, *op. cit.*

[54] For Kafka's confusion over his change of citizenship see the *Germanic Review*, Oct. 1957, p. 163.

[55] Wasyl Halich, *Ukrainians in the United States*, U. Chicago 1937, pp. 6—18, is a useful, objective account that indicates that 19th century Ukrainians under Austrian rule fared much better than those under Russian rule.

[56] See Victor S. Mamatey, "The United States and the Dissolution of Austria-Hungary," *Journal of Central European Affairs*, Oct. 1950. Mamatey states that Professor Guido Kisch maintained in 1917 that Representative Sabath converted Wilson to the policy of the dissolution of Austria-Hungary but that that interpretation was erroneous. Louis L. Gerson, *The Hyphenate in Recent American Politics and Diplomacy*, U. Kans. 1964, pp. 77—78, describes the indignation of certain of the nationalities of the old monarchy when Wilson's Fourteen Points offered them (except for Poland that was offered freedom) only opportunity for autonomous development instead of independence. Nationalist discontent was, however, stirred up and by June 1918 Wilson decided on dismemberment. The military advantages of such a move were obvious.

CHAPTER VII

THE THIRTY-EIGHTERS AND BEFORE AND AFTER

Following World War I and until Hitler pounced upon the first Austrian Republic in 1938 the new American immigration statistics for Austria seemed to tell, for the first time, the story of the core-Austrian immigrant and only that: 32,868 immigrants from Austria in the decade after 1920 and 3,563 for the early years of the next decade.[1] But the 1920 estimate that there were in the United States over two million Austrian-born (575,627) or second generation Austrians was surely exaggerated by the old statistics of the days of the monarchy and even the figure of 954,648 for the Austro-Americans of 1930 (including the second generation) was doubtless swollen by old monarchy Austrians who had lived outside the bounds of the republic.[2] Yet, compared with 1850 when the official figures showed 946 Austrian-born in the United States, there was clearly a multitude of them here during the period between the two great wars. Austria ranked in eleventh place in 1930 for its contribution to America's foreign-born population, following immediately after sixth-place England, Ireland, Mexico, Sweden, and tenth-place Czechoslovakia.[3] But the largest group of Austro-Americans of 1930 (38.1%; 141,306 immigrants) had come to this country when the term Austrian still meant all things to all people: which means that even the Census of 1930 remained unreliable for our purposes.

More than a third of the Austrians, first and second generation, were in 1930 in New York State.[4] Five-sixths of the totals for the entire country were urban dwellers and two-thirds of the countrymen among those of that final sixth were not farmers but small-town folk. Austro-Americans had always avoided our farms. Indeed, the people that the Census of 1930 called Austrian were to be found in the greatest numbers (216,000) in the Middle Atlantic States, then in the East North Central States (82,600 with Illinois in the lead followed by Ohio, Michigan, and Wisconsin in that order), and in the West North Central States in almost equal number in Missouri and Minnesota. California alone had attracted about as many Austrians as New England and more than all the South Atlantic States.[5] In general they preferred the northeastern and the well-populated areas.

There were in 1930 still more Austrian-born men than women in the American population totals.[6] The number of middle-aged Austrian-born was about the average for all immigrant groups while, in the lower and the higher age groups, the Austrian count was less than average.[7] Five percent of New York City's Austrians could not speak English (6,301 out of 126,659). That was better than the Italians' 18%, the Poles' 9.2% and the Czechs' 7.4%. But it was, strangely enough, not so good as the Hungarians' 4.2% and the Germans' 3.8%. It was the older immigrants who spoke the least English[8] – probably the veterans from the old monarchy.

All in all the Austrian immigrants were coming to feel more and more at home in the United States. By 1930, for instance, the proportion that had taken American citizenship was far greater than it had been ten years earlier: some 63% in the later year contrasted with a mere 37.7% in 1920.[9] And dozens of notable Austrians came definitely to stay as evidenced by their promptness in taking out citizenship papers.

During the period between the two wars more of the Austrian-born were distinguishing themselves here. By the time Hitler took Austria, "Who's Who in America" (1938–39) listed sixty-four of them, giving the Austrian-born eighth place after five much more populous countries – Great Britain, Canada, Germany, Russia, and Italy, and two smaller ones: Sweden and Ireland. And dozens of them like writer Ludwig Bemelmans, producer Jed Harris, Nobel prize-winner Karl Landsteiner, actors Paul Muni, Luise Rainer and Erich von Stroheim, and conductor Hugo Reisenfeld, were widely known. Most of them were, indeed, so well known and so completely assimilated into American life that no one thought of them as foreign-born. Sophisticated Austro-Americans, no matter how Austrian they may have seemed when they occasionally got together for some nostalgic affair in honor of the homeland, were generally able to appear more American that the Americans. That was especially true of the first generation. Whether or not it was a fortunate trait, it has served to make them much more welcome here than their predecessors of, for instance, 1848.

The greatest unsung saga of Austrian emigration between the wars was the story of the Burgenlanders. Seventy percent of all the Austrians who came in the period between the two wars came from Austria's little province on the Hungarian border that was so rural in character that its largest city, Eisenstadt, boasted a population of only some 7,000 persons. In 1923, for instance, some 6,683 emigrants, 72% of the Austrian total, came from Burgenland.

Austria's birthrate, almost the lowest in Europe, was an incentive to emigration only in the Burgenland where birthrates that would have appeared sub-normal in America, combined with an acute shortage of farm land and opportunity for younger sons, and the backwardness of industrialization, produced an emigration of almost 14,000 back in the 1880's (mostly to America after the first Burgenlander came here in 1884) and of nearly 40,000, its peak, in this century's first decade. And Burgenland lost thousands more (18,400 from 1923 to 1934) after the first World War.[10] From 1870 to 1951 Burgenland's population increased only from 254,300 to 276,100 but it had led all Austrian lands in supplying emigrants for America: Chicago with 34,000 has the largest number of them, New York with 8,000 comes next, and Allentown in Pennsylvania is said to be, in 1963, the third largest settlement of Burgenlanders in the world – not in the United States only but in the world.[11] The Burgenlanders themselves estimated in 1964 that America had 180,000 of their fellow-countrymen.

The Burgenlanders were peasants at home but in America they seldom found places on the farms. They settled in sad industrial towns where their friends and relatives had already settled and lined up jobs for them. They made what money they could where they could – more than half of them were men, who probably wanted only to make money to send home and to take home with them when they returned – and a quarter of them did return. There in the Burgenland the American dollar became so well known that prices were often quoted (before Hitler) in dollars and cents. And later, in the 1960's, Austrian friends who introduced American friends to Burgenland would point out to them the "American villas" that the successful returnees had built in the prosperous Burgenland countryside. Even an American tourist who spoke a few words of German was suspected in the optimistic Burgenland of having some connection with America's Burgenland colony. The genuine Burgenlanders who came back to find a wife or a farm often went to Styria where land was more easily come by.

The high point of all Austrian immigration, a most significant part of the great twentieth century epic of the unrooted, was the coming of the Thirty-eighters, the fugitives from Hitler. Austria in the thirties was a sorry land of maladjustment, unemployed, beggars, and frustration. Too many despondent Austrians, hoping for better things, welcomed the advent of the Austrian-born dictator who was bringing some kind of order out of the German chaos. There had always been German nationalists in Austria who found it difficult to forget that Vienna had long been the capital of the "German Empire," the Holy Roman Empire. But, aside from those who quickly became disillusioned with the Hitler who showed so little compassion for his native land, there were hundreds of thousands who knew from the beginning that they would have no place in a Nazi Reich.

There were the Social Democrats, the socialists and laborites, whose party had already been declared illegal in 1934 by the Dollfuss–Schuschnigg Catholic conservatives who were too Austrian to accept Hitlerism, and who, the Social Democrats, could expect nothing but exile or concentration camps from the Berlin regime. There were the Jews who were culturally far more important in Austrian life than their numbers would indicate. These groups, if times had not been so appallingly bad, should have fought Nazism tooth and nail. As it was, bad times weakened their resistance and some of them helped cheer Adolf in Vienna's streets before they realized that they must seek asylum in Britain or America. When they came, America received one of the finest immigrant contributions of its entire history.

As in 1848 it was largely a migration of intellectuals from Vienna. And that dispersion of the best of Viennese culture has been compared, in a narrower sense, with the dispersion of Athenian culture centuries before.[12] It is difficult to realize what Vienna lost during those years of crisis: Freud, in psychoanalysis,Schönberg, Oscar Straus, Korngold, Bruno Walter, Fritz Stiedry, and scores of other great names in music, von Mises in economics, Nobel prize winners including Schrödinger, Otto Loewi and Viktor Hess, actors Luise Rainer, Karlweis and Schildkraut, Max Reinhardt of theatrical fame, doctors like Manfred Sakel, the famed philosophers of the Vienna Circle, writers as renowned as Franz Werfel, Otto Preminger in motion pictures, and dozens of others. It was an amazing collection of genius and talent – a tremendous loss for the Third Reich and an inestimable gain for the West.

One should not forget the tragedy that lay behind it. Koestler, the well-known Austro-Hungarian writer who found refuge in England, tells his story: "... the stimuli to which I reacted were first the financial, then the physical destruction of the cultural stratum from which I came. At a conservative estimate, three out of every four people whom I knew before I was thirty, were subsequently killed in Spain, or hounded to death at Dachau, or gassed at Belsen, or deported to Russia, or liquidated in Russia; some jumped from windows in Vienna or Budapest, others were wrecked by the misery and aimlessness of permanent exile."[13] Most Americans have never realized what men and women suffered in those tragic days.

A relatively small number reached America. Hundreds of thousands died. Chancellor Schuschnigg reached America after years in concentration camps. Some, like the postwar Austrian Chancellor Leopold Figl who spent years in the Dachau and Mauthausen concentration camps and the later Chancellor Alfons Gorbach who spent almost seven years in Dachau (both conservative Catholics) never escaped but managed to survive. A goodly number of refugees, like Freud who was released by the Gestapo at the behest of President Roosevelt, reached England before the coming of the war closed that asylum to them and deprived the British of much talent that they could have made good use of. A study of refugee men-of-letters from both Germany and Austria indicates that five-sixths as many of them found refuge in Britain as in America, that almost an equal number died in distress or by their own hands, and that a few settled in Switzerland, in France for a few months, and in Palestine.[14] Britain was, like France, sometimes a way station to the United States, often far more than that.

The American Congress, still dominated by the restrictionists who believed fervently in the national origins law of 1924, failed at first to rise to the occasion. It was not until 1948 that the Displaced Persons Act for admitting displaced persons and refugees without regard to quota, showed Congress' good will. And the Refugee Relief Act of 1953, designed primarily to provide asylum for the victims of communism, was of less importance to the Austrian immigration.[15] In the meanwhile, during the war and immediately thereafter, Presidents Roosevelt and Truman used all their administrative authority to liberalize the old system and use the quotas, and all the non-quota loopholes, for the admission of fugitives from Germany and Austria. Over half of all the European immigrants of 1939 were, as a consequence, from those two lands.

And the United States played a major role in setting up international groups, such as UNRRA and the Intergovernmental Committee for Refugees and, much later, the International Refugee Organization, which did so much to relieve Austria of many of the hundreds of thousands of refugees she had sheltered at the end of the war.

In the private orbit America gave generously. The Jews, always conscious of the pressing needs because of the plight of so many European Jews, set up the American Jewish Joint Distribution Committee that fed some half million unhappy European Jews. The Quakers' American Friends Service Committee set aside in 1946 some $ 600,000 for Austrian relief. The Rockefeller Foundation and CARE made their contributions and the American Red Cross in 1946 set aside a special fund of two million dollars for Austrian aid. And there were others who, first conscious perhaps of the existence of an Austria that had been Hitler's first victim, sent help in one form or another to help the Austrians on their amazingly rapid road to recovery.

In the peak year of relief, 1948, when Americans were giving some $ 300,000,000 for Central European relief, American Jews were responsible for almost half of the total, and Protestants led the Catholics by more than three to one.[16] There was also a nonsectarian block of givers that was responsible for perhaps a fifth of the whole. All in all, it was a golden age of American benevolence that did much to make the United States comprehend its role as a world power in the finest sense of that term. And it helped to produce a post-war Austria, utterly unlike that of 1919, that was in less than a decade to find itself on the way to well-being. America, despite the shilly-shallying of Congress, played a major role in the relief of the uprooted of Nazi times.

Since the United States immigration statistics for Germans and Austrians were combined for the years of the *Anschluss*, and since Austrians often came on non-Austrian quotas, it is difficult to tell how many Austrians came during the most tragic years. Statistics show that some 115,000 Germans came on the quota during the decade ending in 1945. During the five years after 1945, 11,460 Austrians came as quota immigrants.[17] It is estimated that 7,622, or 7.3 percent, of the 104,098 Germans who came between 1933 and 1941 and Austrians who came in 1939 through 1941, chiefly Jews, were professional people. That was more than twice the normal percentage among immigrants.[18] But the character and ability of the refugees was, in any event, far more significant than their numbers.

Almost half (48 %) of the German and Austrian intellectuals who contributed to one post-war study of the Thirty-eighters, found their American careers in education, fourteen percent in law, ten percent in medicine, seven in journalism, five in music, and three percent in each of engineering and art.[19] The medical immigrants might resent having to qualify once again, under all the demanding American requirements, to practice their profession but the younger ones persisted and achieved a remarkable degree of success. The jurists, including some notable names like Hans Kelsen who had written Austria's first republican constitution, more often turned away from their former profession – in their case it was generally to teaching.[20] Many musicians also turned to teaching.

American colleges and universities rose to the occasion and welcomed dozens of the refugee scholars to their faculties. The New School of Social Research in New York created in 1934 a Graduate Faculty of Political and Social Science which rescued scores of immigrants and their families and prepared them for useful work in American universities. There were special committees, service agencies, and newly created institutions to help almost all of the new-comers.[21] Almost three-quarters of the professional group mentioned in the last paragraph had been able to return in America to the same profession that they had practiced in Europe.

The refugee scientists contributed to the American defense effort. The Austrian Frederic de Hoffmann, for instance, made the mathematical calculation which proved the feasibility of the hydrogen bomb. He was then working as the deputy of the Hungarian Eduard Teller, "the father of the hydrogen bomb." And earlier, during the war, Dr. Otto Halpern developed a counter-radar device for which the United States government finally paid him $ 340,000.[22]

It is interesting to note that over half of the professional refugee immigrants were married. And among the Austrian newcomers as a whole, the women began, for the first time, to outnumber the men. By 1950 there were among the Austrian-born in the United States scarcely 97 men to every one hundred women.[23] And the Austrian expert, Wilhelm Winkler, found that by 1952 some 63 % of all Austrian-born living in the United States were females.[24]

Since so many of the Austrians were city-dwellers from Vienna, it was not surprising that a very large proportion of them settled first in New York. There they may or may not have avoided the Yorkville area that achieved a Nazi reputation, but they found compatriots, German and Austrian food and wine and beer, and a bit of continental atmosphere. They worked their way later westward – the professionals among them still preferring large cities by wide margins.[25] By 1953 the Austrian consul general at Los Angeles reported some 22,000 former Austrians and one thousand Austrian citizens in his jurisdiction. Cleveland, on the other hand, reported only a few hundred while, from the South, came consular reports that there were about 1500 former Austrians in the Atlanta, Georgia, district and 4500 in the consular district of Dallas, Texas.[26] A few of the Austrian-born were finally penetrating the South.

Even the Austrians, non-joiners at heart, organized and propagandized among themselves in New York during the war. They had there the only tolerably vigorous

Austrian newspapers that ever appeared in this country, *Freiheit für Österreich* and its successors, plus a small press for labor and youth. The Jewish element read *Aufbau* which has had a long and honorable career. And the Austrians began to organize: there was the Austrian Committee, Austrian Action, *Die Arbeitsgemeinschaft für eine demokratische Republik Österreich*, and the Austrian Social Club which united to form the Austro-American Association, and a few others. They all boasted some well-known names among their memberships, names like that of Ferdinand Czernin (d. N.Y., 1965) who was the Hitler-hating chairman of the group called Austrian Action. Almost all of them, from the Marxist Social Democrats to the monarchists, wanted an independent Austria and acclaimed the opinion of the United States Attorney General that Austrians were not Germans and not enemy aliens. They were victims of Hitler and not confederates. "Niemals sollte 'Austria' mit 'Australia' oder 'Österreich' mit 'Deutschland' verwechselt werden können" (no more confusion of Austria with Australia or with Germany!) was the objective of Hans Rott, a former cabinet minister who fled the Nazis to reach America in 1940 and to work here for the re-establishment of a free Austria.[27] They were all happy about the American government's decision that Austria was no enemy but a victim of the Nazi regime.

The Austrian refugees found friends among the Germans but hated the Nazi regime. "*Die Österreicher hassen die Deutschen*," editorialized the "Austro-American Tribune" in August, 1943, in a sense that was by no means entirely true. The Austrian press in America reported Nazi executions in Austria and starvation in the homeland, happy desertions by Austrians from the *Nazi Wehrmacht*, and suicides in American prisoner-of-war camps when Austrians were threatened by their Nazi fellow prisoners. It brought the war home to the Austrians who had found refuge in peaceful New York.

Otto von Habsburg who was spending the war years in America complicated the Austrian situation. He wanted, not only a return to the monarchy, but an Austrian Battalion in the American army that might help to rescue his country in the cause of monarchy. He had access to White House and State Department, and the Defence Department agreed with his plans for an Austrian legion until it discovered that most Austro-Americans were republicans and not monarchists, and the battalion soon disappeared from history. The Austrians never succeeded in setting up any government-in-exile. Austrians have always been too individualistic, too much divided ideologically, to present a united front. That is not entirely true since the Austrians' almost-united front of 1938–1945 was for the restoration of the republic – which was achieved at the end of the war.

The great Austrian immigration of World War II and the starvation years that followed were over by 1952 when Winkler estimated that there were about 104,000 Austrian-born in the United States.[28] That was a small percentage of our foreign-born. But "Who's Who in America" now listed twice as many Austrian-born as it had fourteen years earlier and that entitled the Austrians to fifth place among the foreign-born, after Canada, Great Britain, Russia, and Germany, all having tremendous advantages in proximity or language or population over little Austria. Less well represented were Italy, Poland, Sweden, The Netherlands, Hungary, France and Ireland which followed in that order.[29]

Among these distinguished Austrian-born Americans there were dozens of teachers in our colleges and universities – and principally in the best of those universities. After the professors the largest group was that of scientists, many of whom were teaching or working in university and industrial laboratories. Then came the musicians. The medical immigrants, who came next in number, were chiefly psychiatrists in mental health and many of those also found places in teaching. Austria's contributions to American business came next (although the contributors were more often on the professional side than on the commercial – Vienna's great commercial academy, *Die Hochschule für Welthandel* is scarcely represented), art followed, with law and politics, economics, and the films, well represented. It was an interesting group, more typically Austrian in its interests than American. Only music and the theater seemed, by comparison with earlier years, to be underrepresented – music because "Who's Who" leaves the musical people to other reference books and the theater because needy Austria was calling its theater people back home very soon after the end of the war. The prestige of the Austrian stage and language differences brought many of them back to Austria. What Austria lost when its other fine emigrants found permanent places in America is difficult to estimate.

Of the entire Austrian-born group, non-professionals as well as professionals, relatively few, by comparison with other foreign-born groups, were to be found at mid-century as private household workers and as farm or industrial laborers. The Austrian group ranked higher in the professions and in management. Statistics show them far above average in banking, manufacturing, building management, management of personal services, medicine, and artistic and literary pursuits. Their women also ranked relatively low in the categories of household workers and laborers and higher in specialities in the other areas.[30]

Concentration in this study upon success stories will too often ignore all the frustrations, disappointments, and failures that these people faced in trying to find new lives for themselves in a strange, new land. Relatively few, except for professionals like the actors and musicians and men of letters and some who could look forward to pensions back in the homeland, did actually return. But thousands had to adjust themselves to temporary, or even to permanent jobs that they found degrading and to the equally disagreeable alternative of depending upon the work their wives could pick up. One study a few years after the end of the war found 7.3% of the professionals still not self-supporting. While those that were fortunate prospered, the majority lived on meager incomes – the median was found to be from $ 65 to $ 75 a week. Little wonder that most of them felt insecure and longed for Austria's social security system.[31] An Austrian-born businessman of Philadelphia, writing in 1947 for his compatriots in Austria, advised Austrians not to think of America as "the golden land." He had faced scrounging employers who had given him twelve dollars a week for hard labor; he had found prejudices against foreigners, and language difficulties, and disillusionment in the discovery that Americans worked to live but not to enjoy life. He advised his Austrian friends to come if they had specialties like barbering or mechanics, earn some money, and then plan to return.[32] There were doubtless many other Austrians who were equally unenthusiastic about their adopted country who nevertheless stayed on.

There were, on the other hand, the amazing successes and the "alrightnicks" among them. The "alrightnicks" were new-comers who were ready to give up all of their heritage from the homeland in order to assimilate as rapidly as possible in the new. These, among the Austrians, were generally the Jews and others whose fearful past in Nazi Europe made them eager to forget. They often adjusted emotionally to the new country with remarkable rapidity. They applied immediately for citizenship, made a tremendous effort to find friends outside the émigré circle, worked hard to improve their English, and sometimes even changed their names and their religion. Most Jews went over to Reform-Judaism or to liberal Protestant churches like the Unitarian. In politics they usually voted Democratic in gratitude for Roosevelt's anti-totalitarian policies in Europe.

The professional group already mentioned was remarkably proficient in English: a quarter of them had already spoken English well when they immigrated and only six percent had known no English.[33] Three years allegedly solved the language problem of the vast majority – an indication that assimilation was progressing at a rate far better than that of the nineteenth century when Germans and Austrians had clung to their German-speaking colonies. Three-quarters of the same professional group indicated that they had had no trouble making friends outside the immigrant circle although the Austrians were slightly less successful in this regard than the Germans.[34]

The Thirty-eighters broke all records for the rapidity of naturalization. They showed far more eagerness than any other immigrant group and far more than their predecessors from Germanic Europe had ever shown. And the educated among them led the way: about 64% of the Austrians in the already-mentioned professional group took citizenship in the general minimum of five years. And only about one in twenty showed no interest in taking American citizenship.[35] The number of Austrian-born naturalized in recent years has often been more than the Austrian immigration quota![36]

The number of the distinguished in this recent Austrian-born group was amazing. "Who's Who in America" for 1962 to 1963 listed almost twice as many of them as it had listed ten years earlier.[37] And the count of distinguished American women of Austrian birth, as listed in the "Who's Who of American Women" for 1961–1962, was also most impressive: the Austrian-born women ranked in third place among all the foreign-born women, after only the German and Canadian women and before the English, Russian, Polish, French, Hungarian, Italian, Swiss, and Czech ladies.[38] It is difficult to understand how so many of these people who came as refugees from a small and distant land speaking a foreign tongue, managed in the first generation to acquire distinction over here.

It was, of course, the fine group of Thirty-eighters who for the first time in all American history brought the Austrian-born into such prominence. Just before the great tide of Thirty-eight, in 1937, the reliable "Dictionary of American Biography" counted its long lists of notable Americans (mostly 18th and 19th century personalities) and found only 24 Austrian-born.[39] They had been outnumbered during the long course of American history even by the Swedes (26), and by greater margins by the Russians (42), Swiss (48), West Indians, Dutch, Canadians, French, Scots, Irish, Germans, and English. They had been virtually tied by the Welsh, Belgians, and Poles. In brief, when the Austrians lived at the heart of one of the world's great monarchies they contributed little to the American elite, but when their little republic could boast of only some seven millions, they made contributions of major importance.

And it is interesting to note that the distinguished Austrian-born Americans of 1962–1963 followed in the footsteps of their forerunners: the scientists and musicians came first. Then, a bit surprisingly, came the men of business, followed closely by the doctors, university professors, and men of art. Those university professors were often scientists, doctors, and lawyers who taught to supplement their laboratory work or the legal knowledge that could seldom be fully utilized in the United States. There were some good names in public service, the law, motion pictures, and engineering. The renown of the Vienna school of economics enabled some nine Austrian economists to find recognition in "Who's Who," and writers like Vicki Baum provided another substantial category that only just outnumbered the really notable group of historians and the somewhat less notable journalists. Of the professions where one might have expected to find a lot of fine Austrian names, only the theatrical one was disappointing. Austria itself needed its men and women of the theater that it might train them and lend them from time to time to the American stage. Or rich Germany was weaning them away to its well-paid stages.

Among the distinguished Austrian-born American women of the same period, dozens of physicians found their way into the "Who's Who of American Women" and almost half of them were psychiatrists and psychoanalysts. The artists, greatly outnumbered by the physicians, came next, and then came the musicians, scientists, teachers, and designers. The Austrian-born women naturally fall far behind the men in business and surprisingly far behind them in the motion pictures. Hedy Lamarr had not been forgotten but new stars like Romy Schneider and Maria Schell were too foreign for inclusion. Most of the fine stars of the theater who had come here as refugees had returned home – in any event, the theater was almost completely unrepresented by the Austrian-born women.[40]

The contributions of able men and women that Austria has made to America in recent years has been an impressive one. If Austria continues to send so many of its best now that Hitlerism is only a horrible spectre of the past, America will be grateful. But if the renaissance of republican Austria since the second great war is to provide the opportunities that will help Austrians at home, the little land of the Danube and the Alps, to continue to be the breeding place of fine names and great achievements, America will not begrudge the loss of magnificent immigrations like that of the Thirty-eighters.

[1] The figures for the 1920's were doubtless swollen by the registrations of immigrants from the old monarchy who still called themselves Austrian. Most of them came before the law of 1924 became effective.

[2] E. P. Hutchinson, *Immigrants and their Children*, N. Y. and London 1956, analyses some of these statistics, e. g. on p. 5. The figure for 1920 is from the 15th Census.

[3] *Fifteenth Census 1930, Population*, II, p. 228.

[4] *Ibid.*, p. 269.

[5] *Ibid.*, pp. 232–35.

[6] *Ibid.*, p. 807: 193,636 males to 177,278 females.

[7] *Ibid.*, p. 806.

[8] *Ibid.*, pp. 1315ff.

[9] Brown and Roucek, *One America*, 1957, p. 679. The Census of 1930 showed an increase in New York City from 45.4% to 72.5%. *Ibid.*, p. 472.

[10] Wilhelm Schlag's article "A Survey of Austrian Emigration to the United States," *Österreich und die angelsächsische Welt*, Wien 1961, and the article in the supplement to the *Wiener Zeitung*, 30 Aug. 1959, p. viii, are based upon official Austrian sources. The *Burgenländische Gemeinschaft*, March 1964, a periodical for emigrants from Burgenland, has a useful article on Burgenlanders abroad and especially in America.

[11] *Austrian Information*, 12 Jan. 1963, p. 5.

[12] M. W. Fodor, "What Happened to Vienna," *Survey Graphic*, Feb. 1939, p. 69.

[13] Arthur Koestler, *Arrow in the Blue*, N. Y. 1961, p. 107.

[14] N. D. Bentwich, *The Rescue and Achievement of Refugee Scholars*, The Hague 1953; Rudolf Felmayer, *Dein Herz ist deine Heimat*, Wien 1955, p. 367.

[15] 8,954 and 5,243 Austrian-born immigrated in 1948–55 and 1954–60 respectively under authority of these two laws. *Statistical Abstract, 1961*, p. 95.

[16] Robert A. Divine, *American Immigration Policy, 1924–1952*, Yale 1957, pp. 104–41; U. S. Displaced Persons Commission, *The DP Story*, Washington 1952, pp. 5–9; Merle Curti, *American Philanthropy Abroad*, Rutgers U. Press, 1963, contains an excellent account.

[17] *Statistical Abstract of the United States*, 1961, p. 92.

[18] D. P. Kent, *The Refugee Intellectual*, N. Y. 1953, pp. 4–14. This very useful study of German and Austrian intellectuals among the Thirty-eighters has been drawn upon often in the present study.

[19] Kent, *op. cit.*, p. 15.

[20] Schlag, *op. cit.*

[21] Bentwich, *op. cit.*, p. 48, calls the Graduate Faculty the most useful and successful American enterprise for displaced scholars. M. R. Davie, *Refugees in America*, N. Y. and London 1947, mentions the refugee artists as being generally successful in making places for themselves without assistance.

[22] Schlag, *op.* cit., p. 189.

[23] Hutchinson, *op. cit.*, pp. 18–19; Kent, *op. cit.*, p. 13.

[24] Wilhelm Winkler, *Die Österreicher im Ausland*, Wien 1955, p. 15.

[25] Kent, *op. cit.*, pp. 20–21; Davie, *op. cit.*, p. 343. According to Emil Lengyel, *Americans from Hungary*, Philadelphia and N. Y. 1948, p. 226, the Hungarians lived in this same Yorkville area but were no longer rubbing elbows with the Austrians, Czechs, and Germans a few blocks away.

[26] Winkler, *op. cit.*, p. 16.

[27] *Österreichische Nachrichten*, N. Y., Jan. 1963. Rott helped in 1957 to found the Austrian American Federation in New York. He died in Vienna 30 Dec. 1962.

[28] Winkler, *op. cit.*, p. 15, finds the U. S. Census figures far too high because they were still including many names from the old monarchy. He therefore reduced the Census figure of 409,795 to 104,000.

[29] *Who's Who in America*, 1952–53. Our count was based on the first thousand pages. The entire volume contains some 127 names listed as born in Austria after eliminating some who were not clearly German Austrians and adding a few like Bemelmans who seem clearly to have been Austrian in origin.

[30] Hutchinson, *op. cit.*, pp. 224–25, 250, has an excellent analysis of the occupations of the Austrian-born in 1950. Cf. Schlag, *op. cit.*, whose conclusions were based upon wide personal acquaintance.

[31] Kent, *op. cit.*, p. 91.

[32] Karl H. Kneisel in M. F. Gat, *Erfolgreiche Österreicher im Ausland*, Wien 1947, pp. 104–07.

[33] Kent, *op. cit.*, pp. 42–46.

[34] *Ibid.*, p. 59.

[35] *Ibid.*, pp. 25–31.

[36] Some had come in earlier years, some had come outside the quota from Canada, for instance, or as spouses of American citizens.

[37] 225 in 1962–63 compared with 127 in 1952–53.

[38] This 2nd edition lists (according to our adjusted count) 141 German-born, 126 Canadian-born, 108 Austrian-born, 88 English-born, 78 Russian-born, 35 Polish-born, 33 French, 26 Hungarian, 19 Italian, 15 Swiss, and 13 Czech.

[39] The *Dictionary's* count omitted names like Sealsfield and Father Kino who may properly be claimed by the Austrians and included some that we would omit.

[40] Based upon *Who's Who of American Women*, 2nd ed., 1961.

CHAPTER VIII

THE JEWS

Almost all of the notables among the Thirty-eighters were Jewish by religion or by race. The High Commissioner for Refugees, an American, estimated, perhaps too conservatively, that some eighty percent of the total of German and Austrian refugees from Nazism were Jewish and an Austrian scholar writing more recently places the number of Austrians who fled for racial reasons at almost 130,000.[1] Since these Jews represented a very important segment of Austrian cultural and intellectual life, their arrival in the United States was an event of epoch-making significance. No other immigration in American history has given us such a tremendous proportion of talent as the German-Austrian immigration of 1938.

Almost all of the Jewish Thirty-eighters came from Vienna. That was partly because the Nazis after the *Anschluss* had ordered all Austrian Jews to move to Vienna. And it was also because most of Austria's Jewish population of 192,000 (1934), 2.8 percent of the total, was Viennese. There were in the 1930's only some 15,500 Jews outside Vienna, a mere .33 percent of the total Austrian population and a bit over 8 percent of the total Jewish population of the country. Graz, Austria's second city, was the only significant center of Judaism outside of Vienna and the Jewish colony of Graz was tiny.[2]

Earlier migrations of "Austrian" Jews had come from all over the monarchy. Some distinguished ones came in 1848, not only for the reasons that brought so many fine Gentiles across the seas, but because of the medieval restrictions upon Jews in most parts of the monarchy. Austrian Jews had been emancipated in the late eighteenth century but some of the old disabilities and too many of the old prejudices had lingered on. Typical was the Metternich regime's ban on Jewish ownership of real property that compelled even such a prince as Baron Solomon Rothschild to live in Vienna in a hotel.[3] There were heavy taxes upon the Jews. Many came to Vienna from Galicia, Hungary, Bohemia, and Moravia to help fight on the barricades in 1848 and, after the failure of the revolution, did their best to reach America. Some of those who came were too able and too talented to be swallowed up in the flood of lower or middle-class German Jews that was America's principal injection of Jewry in the middle nineteenth century. And their professional talents helped keep them out of New York's Jewish Ghetto. Typical was the Austro-Hungarian Myers family of Newport whose son, Mordecai Myers (b. 1776), became a Richmond merchant and a mayor of Schenectady.[4]

The lot of Austrian Jews was greatly improved by 1867, the year of the inauguration of the dual monarchy. Although Austria-Hungary was far less bitter towards its Jews after 1867 and in the late years of the nineteenth century than, for instance, Russia with its notorious pogroms, the exodus of Jews from the old monarchy assumed tremendous proportions. Bad economic conditions were doubtless the most important cause of the Jewish exodus. Jews were going from outlying regions like Bohemia to Vienna where opportunities were more favorable. But there was economic distress enough, combined with some anti-Semitism, to drive many Jews out of the empire. Professor Carl Wittke estimates that eighteen percent of the Jewish immigration of the three decades from 1881 to 1910 came from Austria-Hungary. And during the early years of the present century an average of some 16,000 Jews came each year from Austria-Hungary to the United States, a fraction of the number that came from Russia during those years. Most of them came from the fringes of the monarchy, far from Vienna. A few came from the monarchy's cultural centers and from Vienna. It was this latter group that was generally highly cultivated and with a profusion of trained workers.[5] They were almost never peasants and seldom professionals — chiefly from industry and trade in the larger towns of the monarchy.

The Jews were blamed for the economic crises of 1873 and 1893 and for a multitude of other economic evils. Austria-Hungary went off silver in 1892 and blamed the Rothschilds and the other Jewish bankers, and here in America the Jews were accused of having been concerned in some financial conspiracy connected with William Jennings Bryan's cross of gold and the evils denounced by the Populist movement.

And then came Zionism. The anti-Semites in both America and Austria discovered a Jewish conspiracy in the Zionist movement of the late nineties.[6] Austria had produced both the arch-anti-Semite, Georg von Schönerer, and the father of Zionism, Theodor Herzl. Von Schönerer was the first to discover the enormous political possibilities in Jew-baiting.

Von Schönerer, who found the Bible a disquieting Jew book and Catholic priests more than a bit obnoxious, was pan-Germanist enough to hope for the absorption of Austria in the German empire. He found the American Chinese exclusion act of 1882 to his taste and would have applied similar restrictions to Jewish émigrés from Russia. He wanted to restore all of the anti-Semitic laws of the past (restoring Ghettos, prohibitions upon Jewish employment of Christian women, special taxes upon Jews, prohibitions upon Jewish acquisition of real property, etc.).[7] And he chose to be buried in Germany near to his hero, Bismarck. This prince of anti-Semitism in Vienna was of significance to the United States not only because he made Vienna uncomfortable enough to Jews that hundreds of the best were ready to yield to America's opportunities, but because the young beatnik from Upper Austria, Adolf Hitler, learned in his Vienna days so much anti-Semitism from von Schönerer and his press and his pan-German following. The entire Hitler story might have been quite a different one if there had been no anti-Semite of von Schönerer's caliber in Vienna in the years when the hateful Adolf lived there prone to absorb all of the worst that the Austrian capital had to offer. Hitler managed to blame most of the indignities that he had suffered in the flop-houses of Vienna, when no purchasers came for his third-rate paintings and sketches, and he cursed everything Viennese, upon the Jews.[8] And Adolf Eichmann, the German-born executioner of so many Jews, was brought as a boy to Upper Austria, Hitler's native land, where he doubtless absorbed some of the venom of the Schönerer era before he moved on to Vienna. There he became so objectionable that in 1933 the authorities sent him back to Germany.

The anti-Semitic movement unhappily included more than von Schönerer at the top and a few malcontents like Hitler at the bottom. It was active and obnoxious enough to bring many Jews to think about emigration. The great conductor and composer, Gustav Mahler, who suffered from Vienna's anti-Jewish press, spent some years in America. And those that remained there suffered from the clamor in sheets like the "Volksblatt" about Jewish parasites corrupting Vienna's cultural life.

Vienna was not a Jewish city. It was probably less than ten percent Jewish from the early years of the century to the Nazi purge.[9] And for the entire monarchy in 1910 only 3.9 percent was Jewish compared with 77.2 percent Catholic, 8.9 percent Protestant, and 8.7 percent Greek Orthodox.[10] But the great immigration of "Austrian" Jews from the entire monarchy, confused in the American mind with the migration of vast numbers of Polish and Russian Jews and known collectively as Eastern European Jews, had prejudiced Americans against what so many of them called Austrian Jews. Social opportunities in America, clubs, hotels, and employment opportunities were closed to Jews. The professions, especially medicine, found them unwelcome. We denounced the conspiracy of the Jewish international bankers, and the Vienna Rothschilds were included. Even our western agrarians were especially concerned about the "money power" of the Jews. Socialism was considered a Jewish plot. The Ku Klux Klan tried to save the nation from Jewish magnates as well as from Negroes and Catholics. Henry Ford and his "Dearborn Independent" thought that the Jews were conspiring to enslave the entire United States of America.

The "Dearborn Independent" capitalized upon the forged "Protocols of the Elders of Zion," allegedly from the secret police of Russian Czardom, that told of a Jewish conspiracy in Prague to use the gold standard to capture the world for international Jewry.[12] Those Jews in Prague were obviously Austrian Jews!

Many of those who immigrated to America to minister to Jewish congregations came from the non-Germanic parts of the monarchy and were generally known here as German Jews. Indeed, so many of the gifted Jews and Gentiles born in Moravia and Bohemia contributed mightily to Vienna's finest culture that the wits invented the slogan, "All Viennese hail from Prague, with the exception of those who come from Brünn."[13] Rabbi Alois Kaiser (b. 1840 – d. Baltimore, 1908), for instance, who studied in Prague and Vienna and spent most of his life in Baltimore, was a native of Hungary.[14] The famous Zionist and reform Rabbi of New York, Stephen S. Wise (1874 – d. New York, 1949), was born in Budapest and lived in Moravia before he emigrated.[15] But Louis Grossmann (b. 1863 – d. Detroit, 1926) who came here to Brooklyn with his rabbi father in 1873 and settled later in Ohio to minister and to teach was Vienna-born.[16] An unusual pair were the father and son, Leopold and Joseph H. Cohn (b. Austria-Hungary, 1886), who came here to work in the Williamsburg Mission to the Jews – an effort to convert Jews to Christianity.

Most of these notable Jewish immigrants belonged to, or soon turned to, reform Judaism. Some of their more liberal followers even joined the less orthodox Christian denominations like the Unitarian Church; some simply turned away from all forms of worship. The number who professed Judaism was a small proportion of the Jews who came.

Many of the Jewish immigrants of the half century before Hitler were scholars of distinction who helped to maintain Hebrew scholarship in their adopted country. There were men like the editor of America's "Jewish Encyclopaedia," Isidor Singer (b. Weißkirchen, Moravia, 1859 – d. New York, 1939), who was educated in Vienna and Berlin and served in the French Foreign Office before he came to New York in 1895.[17] His assistant on the "Encyclopaedia," Gotthard Deutsch (b. Austria, 1859), with a doctorate from Vienna, has been called America's leading Jewish historian.[18] And a generation later there were Jewish theologians and historians here like President Abraham A. Neuman (b. Austria, 1890; immigrated 1898) of Dropsie College for Hebrew Learning,[19] Professor Salo W. Baron (b. Tarnow, Austrian Galicia) of Columbia University who had studied and taught in Vienna before he came to New York in the 1920's,[20] and the Austro-American Judaic scholar Philip Friedman (b. Lemberg, 1901 – d. New York, 1961) who took his doctorate in Vienna, taught in Poland, and came to New York in 1948.[21] Nathan Ausubel, a world traveler who served under Allenby in Palestine, edited a "Treasury of Jewish Folklore" and a "Treasury of Jewish Humor" (1951). Some of the scholars found their way into less Judaic fields like Emanuel Hertz (b. Austria, 1870 – d. New York, 1940), a lawyer whose hobby was writing on Abraham Lincoln.[22] We shall encounter in our later chapters others of the dozens of Austro-American Jews who taught and wrote in various disciplines in American universities, who worked in scientific laboratories, and, perhaps even more important, who practiced and taught medicine in their adopted country.

Zionism was born in Vienna. The founder of this movement to find a national home for Jews was Theodor Herzl (b. Budapest, 1860 – d. Edlach, Lower Austria, 1904), whose father had left the family home in Croatia to settle in Budapest four years before Theodor's birth. He was a "German Jew" and not a Hungarian by language, culture, or inclination. That was why his family moved to Vienna in 1877. There the young Theodor studied law at the university and developed a passion for writing plays and for journalism. He was a failure with the pen, it is said, until one of his plays, "Tabarin," caught the fancy in 1885 of New York audiences. But his writing career had its ups and downs and by 1895, back in Vienna after a period as correspondent of Vienna's "Neue Freie Presse" in Paris, he was distressed by the *Kaiserstadt's* growing anti-Semitism and he turned to the Jewish question.

The idea of Zionism, developed by Herzl in the middle and later 1890's, caught on in a few months. Zionist headquarters in Vienna's *Türkenstrasse* found enthusiasm for the cause in all Europe. Herzl visited over the entire continent and organized the First Zionist Congress at Basel in 1897. The very next year Rabbi Stephen S. Wise from the United States attended the second Congress and America founded a Zionist Federation under Herzl's central authority. In two years it had 135 branches in the United States. And forty Americans attended the Zionist Congress of 1913 in Vienna.

Its first years in America were, however, years of slow growth. It was an "import," "America is our Zion," United States Jews had no great desire to mix in with the projects of Europe from which so many of them had happily escaped. But enthusiasts like Henrietta Szold, Cyrus L. Sulzberger, and Louis D. Brandeis, as well as Rabbi Wise, were fired by the cause and, despite the opposition of some Jewish groups, it became well established by 1917.

Theodor Herzl worked himself into the grave in 1904, still a young man, and was buried with honors in Vienna. Years later, after his work had resulted in the creation of a Zion that was named Israel, his remains were removed to Jerusalem and placed on the hill now called Mount Herzl.[23]

The change that Nazism brought about in Austrian emigration from the numerical predominance of the Burgenlanders between the two wars to the predominance of the Jews among the Thirty-eighters was a momentous one. The Jews represented much of what was superlative in Austrian culture and learning. Six of Austria's Nobel prize winners have been Jews.[24] Over half of Vienna's doctors and lawyers, most of its journalists, and some of its most notable men of letters were Jews before the purge. Although Austria's Jewish population was estimated at only some 200,000 in a total of 7,000,000, with a vast majority of the Jews in Vienna, it had played a role in Austrian intellectual life that was out of all proportion to its size. Similarly, the Jewish refugees who came to the United States were significant to us to an extent far beyond their numbers. The "miserable spittoon," as Mussolini had called Austria in deference to its Jews, seemed to Hitler to require aryanization not because of the numbers but because of the importance of its Jews. The immediate consequence was America's gain. Who can say whether America as well as Austria might not eventually have profited more if that fruitful Jewish element in Viennese life had not been so savagely uprooted!

Not all of them came to America. Sigmund Freud found safety in England and Stefan Zweig an unsatisfying asylum in South America. Many who emigrated under the displeasure of the Gestapo went first to France and then to Spain and Portugal, or, like Baron Louis Rothschild who later settled in Vermont's hills, to Switzerland. Some came to Canada and Cuba to wait before they reached the United States. Rothschild, like many of his co-religionists in the earlier months of the *Anschluss*, was able to buy his way out. Later on, the Nazis refused to be satisfied even with the confiscation of Jewish properties and the payment of the heavy Jewish émigré taxes that they had prescribed. Then the process of escape became more difficult and painful.[25]

Whether or not the Austrian Jewish refugees left Vienna with America as the goal (and some of them had relatives and friends here who were encouraging them to come), the fear that Europe might become a single, horrifying, Nazi citadel eventually persuaded them that the United States was the only safe place of asylum.

Some of the Jewish refugees retained their love of Austria and, like Oscar Straus, returned as soon as possible after the war. Many of them, embittered by what they and their friends had suffered at the hands of the Nazis in Austria, never wanted to return. Refugees in New York could read in the "Jewish Morning Journal" in 1940 that in one year after the *Anschluss* and as a result of Jewish persecution there had been 3,741 suicides, 11,000 imprisoned, 87,000 emigrated, and 7,856 enterprises aryanized.[27] "As a Jew compelled to leave my homeland, I have no reason to be predisposed toward Austrians in recent years," wrote the economist and publisher, Walter Federn. But, he added, "I, too, love Austria, her countryside, and her artistic and charming people . . ."[28] There were doubtless many with such mixed emotions.

Such people generally made good American citizens because they had come to stay. They took citizenship as promptly as they could. Their friends and relatives and the Jewish Refugee Committee, with a few other Jewish and academic and, perhaps, Quaker, welfare organizations, in New York helped them to get rooted. The less sophisticated ones among them found jobs in shops or as artisans. Most of them knew some English and worked to improve it. Some of them changed, more often than the Catholic immigrants, their religion. They found American Puritanism a bit forbidding, as had most of the Austrian immigrants for over a century, and they missed the coffee houses and wine and music, the theater and carnivals and constant anniversaries of birthdays and name days that they had enjoyed at home. They found American virtues of work for work's sake and thrift's sake unrewarding. They missed Austria's social benefits when they realized that there was nothing comparable in America. Some remained among their compatriots in areas like New York's

Yorkville, despite its Nazi coloration during too much of the critical period, but most of them eagerly welcomed assimilation.

The desire to be assimilated was indeed one of the chief reasons why so many of them changed their names. Many Cohns, Levis, Solomons, Friedlaenders, Goldsteins, and Israels, to mention some of the names most frequently changed, who had lost some of the traditional Jewish desire to remain separate from the Gentile world, wanted new names that harmonized with the American pattern. They were weary of being looked upon and ridiculed as strange non-conformists who would never at the best be more than tolerated. Besides those who wanted finally to escape from the burden of Jewishness, there were a few who wanted, by a change of name, to protect themselves and their relatives back home, from discovery by the Nazis. There were some who wanted to shed the Germanic names that linked them with a part of Europe that had been so cruel to them and theirs. And there were some, Gentile as well as Jewish, who simply wanted names that older Americans could understand. Hence, one Zenon Zakowski, to the confusion of all future historians of immigration and racial origins, chose to become Robert Lind! A few, like the pioneer Samuel Ludwig who became Samuel Ludvigh, changed the spelling of their names simply to preserve the original pronunciation. Some, like the many Josefs who became Josephs, changed only to Americanize the spelling. It was all quite understandable. It is said that some fifteen percent of the intellectuals among the Austrian and German refugees (so largely Jewish) changed their names while only about a quarter as many among the unsophisticated took that step.[29] Whatever the reason for name changing it will doubtless be regretted by future generations with fewer prejudices than ours.

Yet, despite the new values to which they had to adjust themselves here, most of them stayed on. Indeed, the experience of such a fine Jew as Professor Siegfried Altmann (b. Nikolsburg, Moravia, 1887 – d. New York, 1963), who had worked long for the cause of the blind in Vienna and who had in New York helped to organize the older Austrian Institute there and become its second president,[30] might demonstrate that Austrian Jews and Austrian Gentiles had found a harmony in the New World that was lacking in the Old. Jews were active elsewhere in the Austro-American community, as in the American Austrian Society in the nation's capital or in providing generous audiences for Austria's good Institute in New York. But more significant was the fact that the distinction of many of the best of them, musicians, scientists, doctors, film producers, and such, drew them out into all corners of the country where they contributed, as we shall see in our later chapters, to American life.

American Jews were, very naturally, most receptive to the allegation, so often repeated in Germany, that Austrian anti-Semitism was more virulent than the German variety. And the allegation was doubtless very injurious to Austrian prestige in post-war America. On the other hand the horrible Nazi Mauthausen concentration camp near Linz has happily not become a center for American crusaders against Hitlerism.

Whether Simon Wiesenthal's Jewish Documentation Center in Vienna, that has recently received a tremendous amount of publicity in the United States, has contributed to America's conviction that there have been too many Nazis in Austria, or that an Austria that will permit a Wiesenthal to help run down Nazis like the notorious Jew-killer Eichmann shows that Austria never had its heart in the shot-gun marriage with Hitler, is questionable. Wiesenthal's Vienna Center has collected the records of tens of thousands of former Nazis – chiefly German – which he passes on to any authorithies that may be inclined to prosecute. He suspects that Austria does not appreciate his efforts, but he stays on.[31]

It is almost too much to hope that the Jews that fled from the Austria of the *Anschluss* will ever forget Mauthausen. But we may hope that they, and every American who visits Vienna, may go to the banks of the Danube Canal and read the inscription there on the stone on the ground which the Nazis once occupied:

"Here was the house of the Gestapo. It was the way, for many, to death. Now the house of the Gestapo is gone. The Republic of Austria has been reconstructed and its citizens will never forget the Austrians who suffered and died in the war against the Nazis."[32]

[1] D. P. Kent, *The Refugee Intellectual*, N.Y. 1953, cites J. G. McDonald on p. 17. Dr. Oscar Karbach's estimate of 128,700 who emigrated for racial reasons may be too conservative since many immigrated via third countries or on non-Austrian quotas.

[2] Figures furnished by Dr. Oscar Karbach of New York City.

[3] Egon Caesar Conte Corti, *Reign of the House of Rothschild*, N.Y. 1928.

[4] H. L. Golden, *Jews in American History*, Charlotte 1950, p. 106.

[5] Carl Wittke, *We Who Built America*, N.Y. 1945, p. 333; Leopold Caro, *Auswanderung und Auswanderunspolitik in Österreich, Schriften ... für Sozialpolitik*, vol. 131, Leipzig 1909, pp. 16–20. Joseph Samuel, *Jewish Immigration*, N.Y. 1914, pp. 21–22, states that of the three countries from which the United States received its Jewish immigrants (Russia, Austro-Hungary, and Rumania) Russia had about five million Jews and Austria-Hungary two million.

[6] Oscar Handlin, *Adventure in Freedom*, N.Y. 1954, pp. 184–88.

[7] Oscar Karbach, "The Founder of Modern Political Antisemitism: Georg von Schoenerer," *Jewish Social Studies*, Jan. 1945.

[8] William A. Jenks, *Vienna and the Young Hitler*, Columbia 1960, gives an excellent account of the Hitler story in Vienna.

[9] *Catholic Historical Review*, Jan. 1961, p. 498.

[10] Robert A. Kann, *Werden und Zerfall des Habsburgerreiches*, Graz 1962, p. 59.

[11] Oscar Handlin, *Race and Nationality in American Life*, Boston 1957, pp. 173–74.

[12] Handlin, *Adventure in Freedom*, pp. 200–03.

[13] E. H. Buschbeck, *Austria*, London 1949, p. 39.

[14] Dieter Cunz, *The Maryland Germans*, Princeton 1948, pp. 331–32. He was long president of the Society of American Cantors.

[15] Emil Lengyel, *Americans from Hungary*, Philadelphia and N.Y. 1948, pp. 191f.

[16] *Dictionary of American Biography*.

[17] *Das Buch der Deutschen im America*, Philadelphia 1909, p. 271.

[18] Rufus Learsi, *Jews in America*, Cleveland and N.Y. 1954, p. 185; *Who's Who*, 1899–1900.

[19] *Who's Who*, 1962–63.

[20] *Ibid.*

[21] *Directory of American Scholars*, 3rd ed.

[22] *Universal Jewish Encyclopedia*, 1948 printing.

[23] Oscar B. Frankl, *Theodor Herzl*, N.Y. and London 1949; Israel Cohen, *Theodor Herzl*, N.Y. and London 1959; and other biographies and numerous useful commentaries, especially Handlin, *Adventure in Freedom*, pp. 168–72, and Max Grunwald, *Jews of Vienna*, Philadelphia 1936, pp. 448–50.

[24] *Österreichs Nobelpreisträger*, Wien 1961, p. 23.

[25] Wilhelm Schlag, "A Survey of Austrian Emigration to the United States," *Österreich und die angelsächsische Welt*, Wien 1961.

[26] *Ibid.*, p. 178.

[27] *Universal Jewish Encyclopedia*, 1948, I, p. 630.

[28] Charles A. Gulick, *Austria from Habsburg to Hitler*, 2 vols., U. California Press, 1948, I, p. XII. As to Austrian Nazis, Federn wrote: "There is no doubt that only too many Austrians, I am sure not the majority, went willingly into Hitler's camp."

[29] Ernest Maass, "Integration and Name-Changing among Jewish Refugees from Central Europe in the United States," *Names*, Sept. 1958.

[30] *Austrian Information*, 30 Sept. 1963, p. 6.

[31] Wiesenthal's visit to America in 1967 brought him much publicity. See for instance, the *Saturday Evening Post*, 25 Feb. 1967, and the *Washington Post*, 12 April 1967, p. A3.

[32] A very loose translation.

CHAPTER IX

THE DISCOVERY OF AUSTRIAN MUSIC

An Englishman has written that the three greatest eras in the history of the arts were the Age of Pericles, the Elizabethan Age, and, the years before and after 1800, Vienna's age of greatness.[1] Whether the learned Englishman was correct or not, it cannot be denied that the genius of Vienna which brought her greatness was chiefly musical. In the late 18th century and much of the 19th, Vienna was the musical center of the world. Much of the classical music that has been at the heart of our greatest music ever since developed there.

Vienna, international in its music as in almost all phases of its cultural life, borrowed from its neighbors. "Many musical styles were mingled in the music of the Viennese school: English keyboard music, French comic opera, and German *Singspiel* all found their way there, uniting French *sensibilité*, Italian *dolcezza*, and Austrian *Gemütlichkeit*." Bohemian folk music and Hungarian gypsy tunes were at home in Vienna as in Prague or Budapest. And the popular music of Vienna's own wine gardens added freshness and charm to it all.[2] No one society in human history has been so devoted to music as Vienna's.

Relatively few of the greatest musicians were born there like Schubert and Johann Strauss and Schönberg. But dozens of the great ones came to visit and remain, to compose and to perform. Haydn and Mozart and Bruckner came from the Austrian provinces, Liszt from the Hungarian border, Lehár from Hungary, the genius Gluck came from Bavaria, Chopin from Poland, and Brahms and Beethoven came from Germany to live for months or years on the musical banks of the Danube. Some who came to America, like Frederick Loewe who composed for the tremendous Broadway success "My Fair Lady," were Vienna-born. Still others came from the less Germanic corners of the old monarchy to study and work in Vienna, like Korngold of Brünn and Rodzinski of Dalmatia, before they came to America.

Music has been, by almost any norm, Austria's most important export to the New World.

The young America of the 17th century had no music and the America of the next century had so little that it escaped all association (for a couple of centuries) with the Austrian baroque period. The Quakers had no interest in music. The Puritans might be interested in hymns but secular music was, through most of America, the devil's own creation. Indeed, the godly Protestants of the new republic were to resist secular music well into the 19th century. The Episcopalians were a bit more liberal;

the Catholics, with their European tolerance for music, were an insignificant part of the population; and the music-loving German sectarians, of Pennsylvania and the first West, were too much isolated to interest their English-speaking compatriots in anything but the hymnal. Most famous of all American colonial music was that of the Moravian Brethren whose settlement of 1741 at Bethlehem in Pennsylvania began at once to create a musical life worthy of the Old World. For they soon developed orchestras and chamber music groups, vocal and instrumental music, and they played the great classical Austrian composers Haydn and Mozart. The Moravians, who were by no means confined to Bethlehem, had had, when they migrated, a small hard core of German Austrian Protestants.[3]

Nearby Philadelphia was a pioneer in music. Its Francis Hopkinson (1737–1791) is generally recognized as America's first composer. It borrowed music and musicians from the Moravians and it welcomed the foreign born musicians and composers who, in the period after the American Revolution, threatened for a few years the very existence of native American music. "... the most gifted and the most distinguished of the professional musicians who emigrated to this country before 1800" was, according to Gilbert Chase, Alexander Reinagle (b. England, 1756 – d. Baltimore, 1809), son of Austrian parents, who came to New York in 1786 and soon moved on to Philadelphia. There he helped develop the theater but his greatest achievements were on the musical side – establishing Philadelphia's early musical supremacy.[4] Incidentally he taught music to Washington's stepdaughter, Nelly Custis. Even Puritan Boston felt the new urge. The concert became an American institution on a very modest scale, before the turn of the century. And in 1815 Boston established its Handel and Haydn Society – a landmark in American musical history.

America's early folk music and its later popular music came chiefly from the grass roots. The folk music had some British and Celtic origins and the popular music of the late 19th century owed a debt to such foreign sources as Gilbert and Sullivan in England and the Strauss group in Vienna. America's concert music has owed infinitely more to Europe: much to the Italians, some to the French, a great deal to the Germans and Austrians, and, even in the mid-20th century, we find native American composers and virtuosos relying for encouragement upon able foreign-born figures like the Vienna-born Julius Rudel of the New York City Center. As late as the 1960's the profession of operatic impresario in the United States was very largely in the hands of Austrians like Rudolf Bing, Herbert Adler, and Julius Rudel;[5] many of our finest orchestras were conducted by Austrians like Leinsdorf, Krips, Szell and Rosbaud; Austrian artists such as the singer Elisabeth Schwarzkopf, the pianists Demus and Badura-Skoda, and the folksinger Theodore Bikel were providing much superb vocal and instrumental music; and Austrian composers of the past (from Haydn and Schubert to Mahler and Schönberg) or present (Frederick Loewe of

"My Fair Lady," for instance, and Jacques de Menasce) were still outstanding in our concert and theater world.

The impact of Austrian and German music began on a significant scale late in the 18th century when the music of Haydn and Handel and, to a lesser degree, of Mozart and Gluck and Beethoven began to reach the American shores by way of England.[6] Some of it was anglicized beyond recognition. And the yeast worked slowly. Yet as early as 1815 the Boston Handel and Haydn Society played Haydn's great oratorio, "The Creation," to a delighted audience of nearly a thousand people and six years later Philadelphia's significant Musical Fund Society introduced Beethoven's first symphony to the United States. It was about this time that the Boston group asked the aging Beethoven in Vienna to compose an oratorio for its use and there is evidence that Beethoven hoped to comply with the request. It is said that Mozart's "Figaro" reached our shores in 1823, his "Magic Flute" in 1832, and Beethoven's "Fidelio" later in the same decade – all via England and in English. Opera made little progress, however, so long as there were no Germanic musicians to interpret and perform it and so long as the vast majority of Americans treated music only as the handmaiden of religion. As late as 1874 the "New Yorker Staats-Zeitung"[7] carried a notice of a "Sacred Concert" at the Germania Theater consisting of the comic opera "Czar und Zimmermann!"

By the middle of the 19th century, thanks to the abortive revolutions of 1830 and 1848 in Central Europe, the German musicians began to fill one of these gaps. Italians had occasionally come to America to introduce a bit of Italian music and then return home. The Germans and Austrians ensured the permanency of American interest in the music that they brought with them by remaining and becoming a part of American life.[8] The Germania Society of the 1840's, for instance, which has been called the most important European group of musicians to come to America, was an orchestra of some two dozen professionals which managed to survive here for six years (adequately appreciated only in Boston) before it broke up. Howard, a historian of American music, informs us that the Germania favored Beethoven and Mozart but had to appease public taste with the more popular waltzes and polkas. Somehow the charming light music of the Strauss family was more attractive than that of their more serious compatriot Haydn.[9]

The triumphs of Austrian, and German, music were striking around mid-century. Baltimore's Liederkranz Society, a real landmark in a state where the Germans played no tremendous role, gave what may have been the first Beethoven symphony in Baltimore at its first public concert in 1837.[10] It intrigued its members with Haydn's "Four Seasons" and "The Creation" and it discovered that its audiences could enjoy Mozart's "Don Juan" and his "Magic Flute." Uriah Hill who had studied in Germany founded the New York Philharmonic Society in the early forties and saw to it that Germans and Austrians were imported to ensure its success. Milwaukee's Beethoven

Society was organized in the same decade.[11] Niblo's Theater in New York was playing German opera by 1855.[12] "Dwight's Journal of Music" which appeared at mid-century with the support of the Harvard Musical Association took the position "that the composers of the 'classical' school from Mozart through Beethoven had carried the art to the apex of its development, . . ."[13] As late as the 1880's Theodore Thomas, the German-born conductor of the New York Philharmonic Society, found less interest in the new composers than in the "instrumental compositions of Haydn, Mozart, Beethoven, Schubert, Mendelssohn, Schumann"[14] – Austrian and German music.

The importation of the music of the great Austrian classical and early romantic composers was important to American musical development in the early 19th century. Of lesser interest, for instance, was the mid-century introduction of the male quartet – the secular foursome that the Salzburg Cathedral organist Michael Haydn had "invented" in 1788 and which was one of the significant musical innovations which the Germans brought with them to this country.[15] And "Good King Wenceslas," a carol that originated in German-Austrian Prague (from the old student song in the German language, "Bin der Doktor Eisenbart") and came to America as an English carol,[16] was superseded in popularity by "Silent Night, Holy Night," which the Catholic schoolmaster and organist Franz Gruber composed in a tiny Salzburg village in 1818. It came to America only after the Germans had discovered it, loved it, and passed it on to Britain and America.

One of Austria's most intriguing exports was the fugitive from his native Venice, Lorenzo da Ponte, a gifted ne'er-do-well, friend of Casanova, who had written libretti for Mozart's operas in Vienna. After the death of his patron, Emperor Joseph II, the brilliant Jew had tried England, reached New York in 1805, attempted everything from running a grocery store and teaching Italian at Columbia College to operating an Italian opera. The fame of his fine Mozart libretti meant nothing in America and he died a pauper remembered chiefly because Samuel F. B. Morse had painted his portrait in his bitter old age.[17] Da Ponte's career serves to remind us of the constant rivalry between Germans and Italians in music, from the era of Joseph II who invited to Vienna all the Italians he could get until the great setback for Germanic music during World War I.

Far more successful was Fanny Elssler, the Viennese queen of the dance who came on tour to America with her sister in 1841. Not since Lafayette had the New York crowds taken the horses out of a foreign visitor's carriage to draw it themselves as they did during Fanny Elssler's tumultuous welcome. In Washington the Congress adjourned so that it would not miss her performance. Her triumph and the demand for tickets for her performances which led in New Orleans to their being auctioned off, so impressed our circus king, P. T. Barnum that he was encouraged to sponsor Jenny Lind years later with the auction technique included.[18] The Elssler was an amazingly successful missionary of the dance in a land that had been allergic to the art. And, with her romantic charm, she doubtless helped create America's stereotype of musical Austria.

About the same time the Rainer family from the Tyrol's lovely Zillertal brought the family-singers idea to America. Little ensembles of vocalists were roaming the Alps, yodeling and singing and fiddling the folk songs of their native villages. The Rainers became near-professionals with their tours in central Europe and Britain. So, in 1839, three Rainer brothers and a sister set off on a tour of the United States and Canada. Here they were all the rage. They might be neglected by their French sponsor in New Orleans but they swept Boston by storm and were by no means deterred by minor discouragements, such as the desertion of the sister and the change-of-voice of the Irish boy they recruited to sing her soprano parts. The Rainers left dozens of imitators, like the Hutchinsons of New Hampshire, behind them when they returned to reconquer Europe.[19]

Those Rainers were to be followed a century later by the Trapp family that left its Salzburg home to escape the Nazis, came to America, and became famous. George von Trapp (d. Vermont, 1945), a native of Zara, Dalmatia, back in 1880 and an Austrian submarine hero of World War I, brought his baroness and his ten children to indifferent New York, survived poverty and discouragement, and soon achieved such success that they were able to send relief money after the war back to their less fortunate friends in Austria. The Trapp group toured the country spreading Austrian folk songs with concert after concert. Mother Trapp's book, "The Story of the Trapp Family Singers," did more than ordinarily well while the Trapp-family film, "The Sound of Music," was a great box-office success. Its music was carried all over the country by radio. And the Broadway musical, "The Sound of Music" (1959), was a major Broadway hit by Rodgers and Hammerstein that actually threatened to break the Street's cherished records. By the time the Trapps built their gift and coffee house on the hills of Stowe, Vermont, near their Austrian-type home, they were doubtless the most famous musical family in America. And the Trapps, with the Austrian ski masters who settled at Stowe, helped to make the town a curious Austrian enclave in Puritan Vermont.[20]

Europeans of 1866 were reading a book called "Mes Voyages en Amérique" by Henri Herz (b. 1803 – d. Paris, 1888). The author, born in Vienna and long a resident of Paris, toured America for six years. He was a pianist and the father of the "florid runs and trills that permeated 19th century piano music." He dazzled his American audiences of the mid-century and aroused their interest in music before he retired into oblivion.[21]

Of the Forty-eighters, the refugees from the ill-fated revolution of 1848, there were relatively few Austrian musicians. Yet 1848 was a notable year in American musical history: the hundreds of Germans and Austrians who did find a haven in

America came with a Continental love of good music and they encouraged the later influx of European men of music who were to dominate American music for some generations, and, secondly, the few who did come around mid-century so dominated the musical scene here that American composers and virtuosos suffered, as they had in the years after the American Revolution, a period of eclipse. Some believe, John Tasker Howard wrote in his history of American music, that "American composers were forced to give way to Germans and Austrians, and that American music would be a more vital thing today if it has not been shoved aside by foreigners. In many ways the experience of the latter 18th century was repeated. This mid-century immigration was the second of the foreign invasions." Yet, Howard maintains: "It is obvious that the immigrants did not kill American music."[22] They made it more difficult for the Americans to compete but they introduced a new musical world that America desperately needed to become acquainted with.

The Forty-eighters included men like Frederick Brandeis (b. Vienna, 1835 – d. New York, 1899) who had not been too young to study in a Vienna gymnasium, to work under Czerny, that greatest of all musical instructors, get involved in the revolution of '48, and reach the United States in 1849. Here, in New York, he played the organ both in Roman Catholic churches and in a synagogue; he taught music, made music on the piano, and composed it – instrumental, chamber, and vocal. His name indicates the close relation between the Austrian and the Bohemian parts of the Habsburg empire which gave America the family of the American jurist Louis D. Brandeis.

We have already mentioned the Forty-eighter Hans Balatka (b. Moravia, 1827 – d. Chicago, 1899) whose *Musikverein* in Milwaukee was producing operas and oratorios and symphonies as early as 1850. He considered himself a "German,"[23] studied music in Vienna, avoided the consequences of the Revolution of 1848 by escaping to a Wisconsin farm, and then moved on to Milwaukee to help bring good music to his adopted country. So successful was he that he was made conductor of the young Chicago Philharmonic Society in 1860, kept his hand upon Milwaukee music, and finally settled permanently in Chicago to found there the Mozart Club, to introduce the first complete performances of Beethoven and Schubert symphonies, to import stars from central Europe, and to go on occasional tours to Cleveland where over 5,000 people listened to his "Magic Flute." His was a tremendous cultural influence in the life of the Middle West.[24] Vienna's court pianist, Sigismond Thalberg (b. Geneva, 1812 – d. Naples, 1871) toured America in the 1850's.[25]

The musical immigrants from Austria and Germany were for the most part less important to music-starved America than the music of the giants which the immigrants brought America to know and love. And a goodly share of those musical giants were either natives of Austria or neighbors who were fascinated by the magnetism of Vienna's musical greatness.

Some of the great names sound so German to us that it is a surprise to know that they lived and worked so long in Vienna. The German-born Christoph Willibald Gluck (1714–1787), for instance, composer of some of the finest 18th century operas, not only spent six years as a boy in Bohemia on the estate of his father's employer, Prince Lobkowitz, but he became a member of the Lobkowitz household in Vienna in his twenties, he married there, returned inevitably from his Italian or Parisian travels to Vienna, became Empress Maria Theresia's *Kapellmeister*, and died in his adopted home. The French influence that he brought to Vienna helped to internationalize Austrian music and to replace some of the Italian impacts with French.[26] After two centuries Gluck is still well represented in America on concert programs and in record catalogs.[27]

A bit later came Joseph Haydn (1732–1809) whose fine religious music, and especially his great oratorios, did more than that of any other Austrian to break down America's resistance to the often godless music of decadent Europe! He was the first of the three towering figures of the Vienna classical period – Haydn, Mozart and, in his earlier years, Beethoven. No one of them was Vienna born: Haydn's native place was a tiny village in nearby Lower-Austria, Mozart's was Salzburg, and the German Beethoven a native of Bonn who spent most of his life in and around Vienna.

The patronage of the great Esterházy family gave Haydn a home, an audience, an orchestra, and opportunity to compose in the Esterházy palace at Eisenstadt and in the Esterházy circle in Vienna. His career was thus less tragic than that of so many of the great names of Vienna's musical history who encountered poverty and indifference and whose fame came only after death.

America's musical history is studded with Haydn's name. The Moravians at Bethlehem, Pennsylvania, brought his music to America long before the end of the 18th century and were perhaps the first to play his "Creation" and "Seasons" in this country. His works were stock-in-trade in the 1790's in Philadelphia where Alexander Reinagle,[28] the composer son of Austrian parents living in England, played them frequently at the City Concerts which he conducted and managed. And, beginning with the Boston and New York Handel and Haydn Societies, there grew up a whole crop of musical groups that stressed the Haydn name. The Musical Fund Society of Philadelphia wanted to play the "Creation" in 1820 at its first concert but couldn't obtain the music. There was a famous *Haydn Collection of Church Music* a century ago which drew upon the works of other Austrians and Germans as well as Haydn's.[29] There was, for instance, a Haydn Society in Cincinnati in 1819, one in Baltimore in 1860, and there was still an active Haydn Society in the mid-20th century which, despite bankruptcies and reorganizations, delighted the Haydn devotees with its great successes in recording the works of the master or, with American funds and Austrian collaboration, collecting, publishing, and researching in everything connected with "the father of the symphony."[30]

"Stop that noise; give us 'Bonyparte Crossing the Rhine,' 'Washington's March,' or 'Yankee Doodle.'" That, according to A. B. Faust, was the audience reaction to a New York attempt in 1838 to play a Haydn symphony.[31] America learned very slowly to accept Europe's classical composers. But "Papa" Haydn's spiritual and religious qualities, his simplicity and humor combined with dignity soon endeared him to American music lovers.

Wolfgang Amadeus Mozart (1756–1791), "greatest musico-dramatic genius of all time," was doubtless less important to the early story of Austria's musical infiltration into America than his countryman from eastern Austria, Haydn. Mozart's, a far greater name today, was less appealing to America in the years of America's musical apprenticeship. The child prodigy from Salzburg, with the persistent, ambitious father who knew a genius when he saw one, was more sophisticated and so less readily accepted in the pious New World. The Moravians might have copies of three of his symphonies dated 1785 but one can surmise that they were seldom played until years later. The Mozart Society of Chicago, one of the few early music groups bearing his name, was not founded until 1847. Now, in the 1960's, even Miami has its Mozart Society, and Mozart's operas and other compositions are represented on the programs of every American orchestra and opera society.

Mozart's recognition here came slowly just as it had in Austria. Because of the Habsburg court's concentration upon Italian artists and Italian music, Mozart never received the patronage of the great that 18th century artists required. In Vienna he lived on the verge of poverty. He died there in misery at the early age of thirty-five. Today his symphonies and chamber music, his fine masses, and great operas are the pride of Austria. And in the United States, in the middle of the 20th century, his popularity is amazing.[32] One may say with some confidence that America is more interested in Mozart's works than in the works of any other composer, whatever the nationality or era!

Mozart's competitor in greatness, Ludwig van Beethoven (1770–1827), often called the last of the classicists and the first of the romantics, has left dozens of shrines in and around the Vienna that he loved. For he deserted his native Bonn in his early twenties to pursue his friend Haydn and to meet and admire Mozart among the Vienna vineyards. It was the brother of Kaiser Joseph II, Elector Maximilian Franz of Cologne, who sent the young Beethoven to visit Vienna and who, after Ludwig had decided to remain there, tried in vain to get him to return to the Rhineland where he had achieved fame as a boy prodigy. Father Beethoven, like father Mozart, had thrust the boy out into the musical world long before he reached his teens – even concealing his true age to make him seem even more of a prodigy than he really was.[33] Beethoven's entire career was, indeed, similar to Mozart's in that both men were pursued by tragedy, unhappiness, and constant frustration in the midst of all of the musical glories of the Vienna they loved too well to leave.[34]

Yet no amount of isolation and drab living could deprive the master of his basic intellectual sanity. The "Ninth Symphony" and the "Missa Solemnis" which came from his crabbed old age are as beloved in America as the earlier works such as the so-called "Moonlight" and "Kreutzer" sonatas and the immortal "Eroica Symphony." His great influence upon the development of the orchestra, which Haydn and Mozart had brought far from its "string quartet era," was a contribution from which America has profited as well as Europe.[35] And, in general, he was a creative power in a revolutionary age. Some of his music was so revolutionary in its tonality that his critics "charitably" blamed it on his deafness!

Beethoven's name has been ubiquitous in American music. Even the strong Italian influences of the early 19th century failed to discourage his admirers. Boston's Handel and Haydn Society played him in its earliest days as did Philadelphia's Musical Fund Society. The latter has long disputed the claim of Lexington, Kentucky, for the honor of having first presented his first symphony.[38] And when the German Graupner founded his Philharmonic Society in Boston in 1810, his enthusiastic group of pioneer musicians played Beethoven as well as Haydn. The attention that he received in Boston is perhaps responsible for his sympathetic consideration to the request of the Handel and Haydn Society there for an oratorio. One of his biographers declares that he, who wrote only the one opera "Fidelio," had planned half a dozen years before his death to do one on an American theme: "Die Begründung von Pensilany oder die Ankunft des Pen in Amerika."[37] It was apparently in 1853 that the Boston Handel and Haydn Society provided the chorus for the Germania Society's American premiere of the fine Beethoven "Ninth Symphony."[38] Americans had discovered a spiritual enobling character in Beethoven's symphonies, as they had discovered something similar earlier in Haydn's oratorios, that made him acceptable even in the era of nativism. The Austro-German immigrants of 1848 brought their Beethoven with them and, despite reaction against foreign composers and reaction against so-called German music during the world war, Beethoven's has remained in America until this day one of the names to conjure with and to love.

Franz Schubert (1797–1828) was another of the great Austrians who never came to America and who nevertheless are known here as few native composers are known and loved. He was the romantic representative of classical Vienna. Many an American who never sat through a serious concert came to know him in the music of the operetta "Blossom Time" (1924) by Sigmund Romberg who was born in the Hungarian half of Franz Joseph's Austria-Hungary. Others came to love the more than six hundred *Lieder* that Franz Schubert wrote. He reveled in the pleasant life of Vienna, its Biedermeier wine gardens and its comfortable coffee houses. He was at home in the little inns and footpaths of Hungary and of Austria's Styria and its Salzkammergut, paradise of lakes and sweet mountains.

Like Mozart and Beethoven he wanted to live nowhere but in Vienna. Yet, like Mozart, he composed for posterity and failed to reap a decent living for himself. He lived on the generosity of his friends and died, like Mozart, young, impecunious, and destined to immortality. His compositions, that his native city loved, but took lightly, were a century and a half later to crowd dozens of better-known Viennese out of American concert programs and record catalogs. One standard American catalog of recordings at mid-century was to show Schubert in better standing than Beethoven and Brahms and Puccini and only slightly behind Chopin, Wagner, and Verdi.[39] Schubert is largely responsible for the charm that the word *Lieder* has in America. "Truly he has the divine spark," said Beethoven.

A few years later there appeared upon the Vienna scene Karl Czerny (1791–1857), the great pianoforte teacher, whose fame brought Franz Liszt (1811–1886) to the music capital at the tender age of ten. Czerny might have been too timid to appear in public but his fame as Austria's finest instructor brought him the best of the young hopefuls trying to break into the music world – and he took only a few of the best.[40] He came close to making a Viennese out of young Franz Liszt who was born in Esterházy country in the present Burgenland and only six miles from today's Hungarian frontier. His father was of Hungarian descent, his mother an Austrian from Krems on the Danube. Franz himself was as international as the old monarchy.

Another child prodigy with an ambitious father, Liszt studied in Paris as well as in Vienna. He gave his second Vienna concert with the aging Beethoven in his audience when he was eleven and soon became the finest of Europe's roving piano virtuosos. He contributed to Weimar's fame in the mid-century and divided his later years between Rome, Weimar and Budapest. Often in Vienna, his love for Hungary, his work at the academy in Budapest, and the famous Hungarian rhapsodies that he composed led him to think of himself as a Hungarian rather than an Austrian.[41]

The long list of musicians who made in Vienna music that has become so well known in America should include at least one other non-Austrian of the romantic period, Johannes Brahms (1833–1897). Brahms, a native Hamburger, settled in Vienna in 1862 and made it his home for the remaining thirty-five years of his life. Hamburg had disappointed him by failing to recognize his greatness, his many Vienna friends had beckoned, and he had become as Viennese as the Viennese: conductor of the *Singakademie*, director of the *Gesellschaft der Musikfreunde* (the Society of the Friends of Music which still sits at the top of the Viennese music world), a friend of the great surgeon Billroth, symphonist second only to Beethoven, and worthy of burial in the central cemetery with Beethoven and Schubert.[42] On Thanksgiving Day in 1895 the young American composer Daniel Gregory Mason wrote, "Thank God Wagner is dead and Brahms is alive."[43]

Like Brahms, the Austrian-born Hugo Wolf (1860–1903) produced some of the finest *Lieder* of the late 19th century, and like Mozart his life was sad and he died young. He was one of the great composers of his time[44] and his popularity in America has rivaled some of the greatest even though his output was primarily *Lieder*. Born in Windischgrätz in Styria, that charming southern Austrian *Land* that has produced more men of science than men of music, he studied at the Vienna Conservatory, abused Brahms and admired Wagner when he tried his hand at criticism, and composed feverishly in his later years. This genius of the song, who died in a Vienna insane asylum, did all his finest work in a few years in his thirties. The International Hugo Wolf Society in New York, which busies itself in presenting both serious and popular types of Austrian music, finds the name of Hugo Wolf so well known in America that its programs have a universal appeal.

Less universal was the appeal of "the Viennese twins," Anton Bruckner (1824–1896) and Gustav Mahler (1860–1911). Bruckner was a simple, modest countryman from Upper Austria whose name is reverenced at the fine monastery of St. Florian and in nearby Linz where he played the organ and, to a lesser degree, on the Vienna Schottenring where he passed his later years. He combined the pleasant melodies of Vienna with the seriousness of a schoolteacher family and of devout spiritual Catholicism. His battle for recognition in Vienna was an uphill one. Only since World War II has he become an Austrian favorite. And in America critics have argued over the tedious and the brilliant portions of his nine symphonies ever since Walter Damrosch, Anton Seidl, and Theodore Thomas began "the American battle for Bruckner" in the 1880's. His "Seventh Symphony" emptied Boston's Symphony Hall when Conductor Gericke tried it on a startled audience in 1887. A generation later his Eighth filled the hall and critic Philip Hale called it "one of the greatest symphonies of the world." Bruno Walter and George Szell, Bruckner devotees, did much in later years to establish the master's reputation.[45]

Far less conservative was Professor Bruckner's young Jewish friend Gustav Mahler, the last of Vienna's great romantic composers and, as a conductor, one of the first to become a part of the American musical world. He was born in Kalischt in Bohemia,[46] schooled in the humanities at the University of Vienna and in music at the Vienna Conservatory. Bruckner's apartment in Vienna was his second home. A great conductor, vigorous, sensitive, "relentlessly pursuing the problems of life and death," he moved from one Austro-Hungarian or German city to another until he settled down in Vienna in 1897 to hammer the *Hofoper*, Court Opera, into its peak of greatness. In 1907 he yielded the baton there to Felix von Weingartner whose fine recordings of Beethoven have been acclaimed for years in the United States.[47] Then Mahler's American career began as principal conductor at the Metropolitan in New York in 1908 with a performance of "Tristan and Isolde" that aroused superlative praise. Two years later he began a stormy career as conductor of the New York Philharmonic Society. Many critics like Arthur Foote recognized him as "one of the greatest conductors of all time."[48] But his intensity and uncompromising intransigence brought him into conflict with the Philharmonic trustees and he left New York broken in spirit and body to die at his Vienna home. He and his wife Alma had been only hotel transients in New York, living with other foreign-born – like their close friend Enrico Caruso – and looking forward to retirement in their new house on the banks of the Danube.

Mahler's symphonies may not be universally admired but he is an influence to be reckoned with in America. The Bruckner Society of America has promoted Mahler's music along with Bruckner's. Bruno Walter called him "the greatest musician I have ever known."[49]

Austria means light music to a multitude of Americans – not Jazz, for in that field exportation was all in the opposite direction,[5] but in operetta and the waltz. American student songs that came from Austria are scarcely recognized as Austrian. The well-known Yale song, "Old Eli's Sons May Proudly Boast," said to have been composed by someone named Smith, is actually from a beloved Vienna song, the "Fiakerlied." "My Love hath now Left Me," sung by American students, is a version of the sentimental Carinthian "Verlassen, verlassen bin ich." Amherst's "Fairer far than poet vision" was set to Mozart music, and Haydn's old Austrian national anthem, "Gott erhalte Franz, den Kaiser," became not only "Deutschland über alles" but also a beloved American hymn and the alma mater of a middle-western university as "Hail to thee, O Alma Mater."[51]

We have, however, no doubt that Strauss was Viennese. We may not recall that there were several composers of that name and we may attribute to Johann Strauss, without distinction as to whether he was father or son, the "Rosenkavalier" of the German Richard Strauss, the "Waltz Dream" of the Viennese Oscar Straus, or any one of dozens of waltzes composed by the father or the various sons of Johann Strauss. As a matter of fact, both father and son Johann Strauss were natives of Vienna who lived and died there; Oscar Straus was also a Viennese who tried Hollywood and went back to die in his dear Bad Ischl in Austria's lake country; Eduard Strauss was one of the Strauss sons known in America because he came here on tour; and Richard Strauss of Munich belongs to our story only because he directed the Vienna opera (he was director from 1919 to 1924 with Franz Schalk who also directed in New York), composed operas like "Der Rosenkavalier" (1909) and "Ariadne auf Naxos" (1911) in the best and most gay Vienna tradition, and because the Austrian Hofmannsthal did libretti for some of his finest operas, "Elektra" (1909) and "Die Frau ohne Schatten" (1919) as well as "Rosenkavalier," that were far above the usual mediocrity of libretti.

The Jubilee for World Peace in Boston in 1872 has long since been forgotten but its most famous foreign guest, Johann Strauss (1825–1899), left behind him a tremendous enduring interest in the Vienna waltz and operetta. It was the younger Johann whom Boston brought over to conduct more than a dozen huge concerts and a couple of sensational balls. They paid him $ 100,000 plus expenses, they built him a hall to accommodate 100,000 people, and they received him with flamboyant posters showing him as the king of music ruling the entire globe. Strauss didn't like such crowds, he was a bad traveler and only the $ 100,000 had persuaded him to leave home, and he resented having to shave off locks of his own hair and even some from his dog's coat to placate Boston's enthusiastic women.[52] But his tour was an amazing success. America played and sang nothing but Vienna music for months afterward. New York, where he conducted another pair of concerts, was equally enthusiastic and in two years the Thalia Theater there had presented the American premiere of "Fledermaus." His music must have impressed Mark Twain for that American, a kind of American counterpart to the great Austrian, visited him at his Vienna home on May 26, 1899, only a week before his death.[53]

Father Strauss (1804–1849), whose charming waltzes and marches had swept Europe, first in Vienna's Leopoldstadt where Johann played so long and composed so often for Sperl's modest wine garden,[54] and then on tour all the way from Budapest to London, never reached America, but very little of his music was overlooked by his American followers. In the 1890's, after Johann Strauss the son was too ill and too preoccupied with operetta to travel, another son, Eduard (1835–1916) brought his own orchestra to America, toured seventy-three cities, was surprised to find Americans unable to waltz, and proceeded to give the country a real education in the music of his father and brother. He made a fortune, lost it through family speculations, and returned to America to recoup the Strauss fortune.[55] America still plays the music that Eduard taught it.

Vienna melodies in this country did not end with the Strauss family. For instance, a young Vienna opera singer, Therese Foerster, was engaged in 1886 by the Metropolitan. When she came to New York she was pursued by her lover and future husband, a certain Irishman named Victor Herbert who had in 1882 played the cello in Johann Strauss's orchestra in Vienna. They remained in America and her husband became America's favorite composer of operettas with Vienna-like melodies.[56] Much light Vienna music was adapted for American use as when Moss Hart used Strauss tunes in his successful musical, "The Great Waltz," and "Rosalinda" was produced from Max Reinhardt's version of "Fledermaus."[57]

Vienna never got over its love for the light waltzes and operettas that had made it as famous for that kind of music as Paris had been in the 18th century for the minuet. Its operetta kings early in the 20th century included the Austrian Leo Fall who made a fortune from "The Dollar Princess" and his friends in the last happy but tragic days of Habsburg Vienna, Franz Lehár and Oscar Straus. Lehár (1870–1948) was born in Komorn, Hungary, educated in Prague, and died in Bad Ischl in Austria's eastern Alps. His family was Hungarian, Slav, and even partly French, "and he combined these musical roots into his own fascinating brand of newer Viennese music – the music of Vienna at twilight, sentimental and sensuous."[58] Like so many Austrian musicians he conducted Austrian military bands, from Poland to Trieste to Budapest, directed at the *Theater an der Wien*, saw in 1905 the world premiere of his "Merry Widow" in Vienna, made fortunes and lost them. The New York debut of the "Merry Widow" in 1907 was followed by a run of 421 more performances with seven different prima donnas in the title role, "merry widow" hats for women became famous on both sides of the Atlantic, and Lehár's later efforts, such as "The Count of Luxembourg," were good box office in the United States as in Central Europe. The "Merry Widow" was still drawing crowds in New York during World War II in spite of the fact that the aged Lehár, despising the Nazis who accused him of having a non-Aryan wife and contriving to escape Germany at all cost, was caught in Hitler's admiring embraces. "Die lustige Witwe" was Hitler's favorite operetta.

When Franz Lehár was dying in Ischl his colleague in operetta, Oscar Straus (b. Vienna, 1870 – d. Bad Ischl, 1951) came back from America to settle there. His triumphs had been in the Johann Strauss tradition: dozens of waltzes and twenty-five charming operettas including "The Waltz Dream" (1907), which made him, in Austrian terms, a millionaire, and, even better known in America, "The Chocolate Soldier" (in German "Der tapfere Soldat"). There were at one time ten different companies playing it in the United States![59] After a decade of cabaret, conducting, and composing in Berlin, Warner Brothers called him to Hollywood. He must come at once, so he set out in nine days – the beginning, doubtless, of his dislike for Hollywood's show-business ways. Arriving in 1930 before the emigré crowds of the thirties, he received a royal reception in New York and found there dozens of his old friends, from Jeritza to Dietrich and Korda. Even Hollywood gave him V.I.P. treatment. He went over to MGM, helped Lubitsch convert "The Waltz Dream" into a successful American musical that they called "The Smiling Lieutenant" and, satiated with Hollywood ways, went back to Berlin. His Jewish blood ended that saga, and Ischl was hospitable only until the Nazis took Austria when, thanks to a Nazi border official who loved his music, Straus escaped, via Paris, to America.

Straus's biographer points out that he had, in his last American years, charm and good manners that made him outstanding among the conductors of his day. He liked America well enough to take out citizenship – he even liked our musical comedies, especially "Oklahoma," and admitted that the world had moved beyond the operettas which had been close to his heart. But he could not forget the blue mountains and rushing streams of Bad Ischl to which he returned in 1948. The historian of immigration would note with interest that in little Ischl he spent happy days with such visitors or residents as Bing, Kálmán, Garbo, Lehár, and Jeritza – all names thoroughly familiar in contemporary America.[6]

America's gay inheritance of light operetta from the old monarchy in the Viennese tradition seemed never to end. Rudolf Friml was a Czech (b. Prague, 1879) who came to this country early in the century, composed for stage and film, and charmed America with such operettas as "Rose Marie" (1924) and "The Vagabond King" (1925). And Sigmund Romberg (b. Szeged, Hungary, 1887 – d. New York, 1951), who had been brought up in Hungary and educated at the University of Vienna, who had learned a bit of music from Vienna's noted Heuberger, and who had come penniless to America in 1909, gave up bridge engineering in the United States to turn to music. Many of his two thousand songs he composed for J. J. Schubert and there are few Americans who do not know and love some of his operettas: "Blossom Time," which was based on Franz Schubert melodies, "The Desert Song," "The Student Prince," and "Up, in Central Park." There were many others that made their mark on Broadway.

And Emmerich Kálmán (b. Siofok, Hungary, 1882 – d. Paris, 1953) was another master of operetta in the Vienna tradition who escaped from Nazi Austria in 1938 to arrive, via Paris, two years later in the United States. He composed "The Gypsy Princess" during the first World War, did "The Countess Maritza" which opened in Vienna in 1924, and another success, "The Circus Princess" in 1926. The German theater in New York was playing Kálmán soon after World War I and he went on composing operetta, some on American themes, until his death.[61]

The missionary period of European music in America, when occasional immigrants and a handful of American devotees of serious music were making sporadic efforts to convert audiences here to "good" music, drew to a close with the 19th century. As the country matured culturally, audiences demanded not only importations for presentation in foreign-language theaters and concert halls, and not only waltzes and operettas and sweet *Lieder*, but also the best of the more serious music that Europe had to offer. And since America was now rich enough, it began to build its own fine musical institutions and, not satisfied with immigrants or occasional musical visitors from Europe, to import the talent it needed. For it was still to be some generations before we could do without foreign talent. We have already mentioned Mahler, one of the finest of our musical imports.

A fascinating example of the role that Austria played during the half decade before World War I made German and Austrian musicians unpopular in the United States was its part in building the Boston Symphony Orchestra. For almost forty years after it was founded that orchestra was almost as Austrian as the Vienna Philharmonic.[62]

Young Henry Lee Higginson, scion of one of those old New England families which "had done less for the arts than for the virtues,"[63] failed to finish Harvard after eyesight trouble and so, about the time when Buchanan was in the White House, spent four years in Europe, chiefly in Vienna, studying music. The place, the people, and the music all appealed to him and he decided that he could bring some of Vienna – its music, at least – to Boston. Enormously wealthy, he found it possible to capitalize upon his Vienna experience and friends for guidance, to bring a German conductor named Georg Henschel to Boston, and to establish the Boston Symphony in 1881. "During some years of my youth, spent in Germany and especially in Austria," he wrote, "whither I went to study music, I conceived the hope to see an orchestra in Boston which should play as well as the great orchestras of Europe ..." Anything but a German or Austrian orchestra was inconceivable to him. The standards which he specified for the orchestra were all based on his experience over there: "From long knowledge of Austrian ways, I knew that all these points were essential ..." And it was the music of Austria and Germany that he wanted played. Beethoven, Gluck, Haydn, Schubert, Max Bruch, and Weber comprised the first concert in Boston's "Music Hall" on Winter Street.[64]

After three difficult years with Henschel trying to make bricks without straw, Henry Lee Higginson found his ideal conductor, Wilhelm Gericke (b. 1845 – d. Vienna, 1925), a native of Schwanberg near Graz who had conducted for the *Musikfreunde* and the opera in Vienna.[65] Higginson's Vienna friends had recommended the right man. Gericke, distressed with the raw material he found trying to make music for the new orchestra, went back to Vienna to recruit a competent concert-master, Franz Kneisel, and a good nucleus of trained musicians. And, as Higginson explained, "he taught those first violins to sing as violins sing in Vienna alone."

Wilhelm Gericke was a great musician and a demanding drill master. He made a superb instrument of his orchestra. He introduced the orchestra's Young People's Popular Concert, took it on tours of the West, survived the criticism that came inevitably when he tried such substantial numbers as Brahms' third and Bruckner's seventh symphonies, and became a first citizen in admiring, enthusiastic Boston. The Orchestra continued to recruit Vienna's best. Felix Winternitz, for instance (b. Linz, 1872 – d. Cambridge, Massachusetts, 1948), came over in 1889, giving up his career as violonist at the *Theater an der Wien* and the imperial opera, to play the violin with the Boston Symphony and teach at the New England Conservatory of Music.[66]

Bad health sent Gericke back to Austria in 1889 after yielding the baton to the orchestra's third conductor, also an Austro-Hungarian, Arthur Nikisch (b. 1855 – d. Leipzig, 1922). He was born in Hungary (Szent Miklos), recommended to Higginson by his Vienna friends, and lured away from Leipzig where he was first conductor at the *Stadttheater*. After four years with the Boston Symphony he went back to his native land to conduct in Budapest.

Another fine Austro-Hungarian musician, Emil Paur (b. Czernowitz, 1855 – d. ČSR, 1932), was recruited by Mr. Higginson in 1893.[67] Born in the Bukowina in Austria's part of the monarchy, Paur called himself Austrian. He studied music in Vienna, played the first violin at the opera there, and became famous in Austria as well as in Germany. He arrived during a year of bad business in America when audiences were as sparse as contributions to musical causes and yet he became another giant of the young American musical world. His vivid personality appealed to provincial and to Boston audiences, and Professor Faust was able to compare his influence upon music in the East with that of the great Theodore Thomas in the West.[68] From Boston he went to New York and some years later he was to succeed Karl Muck as Kapellmeister of the Berlin Orchestra when Muck came to conduct the Boston Symphony just before the World War.

Wilhelm Gericke's return in 1898 to Boston to direct the Boston Symphony for eight more triumphal years was another high point in the orchestra's history. By 1906 Austrian, or Austro-Hungarian, conductors had occupied the podium for twenty-two years and had built what many still call America's finest orchestra. When in 1918 wartime passions had forced old Henry Lee Higginson to turn away from Vienna and appoint a French conductor he wrote to Gericke: "Rabaud, an admirable French conductor, is at the head and the work should go on. But I often long for a concert such as you gave us – Haydn, Mozart, Beethoven, Schubert. Only a *Wiener Kind* can play Schubert."[69]

Boston has never attracted many Austrians; New York has been their favorite refuge for a century or more and New York's musical world has not only welcomed Austrian immigrants but has, like Henry Higginson in Boston, lured many more with lucrative offers that Vienna could not equal.

The long-since forgotten grandaddy of the Austrian musical fortune-hunters was a certain Anthony Philip Heinrich (b. Schönbüchel, Bohemia, 1781 – d. New York, 1861) who has been called "The Beethoven of America" and "the most commanding composer in the United States before 1860." This native of Bohemia who has been variously described as an Austrian and a German, came to America in his mid-twenties, and entered upon a fantastic, erratic career that ended in poverty in New York. He tried Kentucky, directed a theater in Philadelphia before he was thirty, played the organ in Boston's Old South Church, presided over the founding of the New York Philharmonic Society, and composed an enormous amount of grandiose music with the accent upon Americanism. He still found time for concerts in Prague and Graz and to compete, unsuccessfully, for a prize for a symphony in Vienna. He was important chiefly as a pioneer in the effort to create a distinctive, if bombastic, style of American music.[70]

Maurice Grau (1849–1907), a Jewish Austrian, born in Brünn, came to New York with his parents at the tender age of five to become one of America's great impresarios.[71] He, or his firm, managed Rubinstein, Sara Bernhardt, Patti, Henry Irving, and Ellen Terry. He managed the Maurice Grau Opera Company and, in London, the Covent Garden Opera. He imported, for his own Maurice Grau Opera, the Vienna-born Franz Schalk, one of the greatest directors of the Vienna *Staatsoper* (1918–1931), whose career had begun as concert violinist in Vienna and who had later conducted from Graz to Prague and to Berlin. And Grau became manager of the young Metropolitan Opera in New York.[72]

A far more significant champion of cultural Americanism than Anthony Philip Heinrich was Heinrich Conried (b. 1855 – d. Meran, 1909), who, as Grau's successor in 1903, helped mightily to hammer the Metropolitan into one of the world's great operas. This son of Bielitz in Austrian Silesia, born of Jewish parents named Cohn, was at the age of eighteen taking parts at the fine *Hof-Burgtheater* in Vienna. Before he was thirty he was managing German theater in New York City and producing gay operetta as well as contemporary comedy and German classics. He never succeeded in giving reality to his dream of an American national theater but he gave life and vigor to the Metropolitan and fought Oscar Hammerstein's rival Manhattan Opera tooth and nail. It was an exciting period. Conried imported some great names for his Met: Caruso, Chaliapin, Farrar, and to conduct, the able Gustav Mahler.

He brought over Felix Mottl (1856–1911), a native of the Vienna suburb Unter St. Veit and a graduate of the Vienna Conservatory who had helped Wagner prepare the first Bayreuth Festival.[73] Mottl conducted the opera that inaugurated the Conried regime, Wagner's "Parsifal."But the Wagner family objected to this production despite its tremendous success, and the all-powerful boxholders of the Metropolitan objected strenuously to Conried's production of the "immoral Salome." Wrangling and poor health forced his resignation and he died a year later in Munich.[74]

A mainstay of the Manhattan Opera which Conried so disliked was a fellow-countryman of his, Hugo Riesenfeld. Thirty years younger than Conried, he had been born in Vienna, educated there at the conservatory and the university, and imported to New York in 1907 to serve for four years as concertmaster of the Manhattan. He not only composed some musical comedies like his "Betty be Good" but he also managed several well known New York theaters and, in 1928–1930, became musical director for United Artists in Hollywood.

There were still more Austrians who achieved fame in the New York music world. There was the genial Anton Seidl(b. Pest, 1850 – d. New York, 1898) who was born "of German stock," studied in Leipzig, served as concertmaster at the Vienna opera, worked for Wagner at Bayreuth, and came to New York at the behest of Walter Damrosch to conduct German opera at the Met. As a Wagnerian he began with "Lohengrin" and introduced a whole series of other Wagner operas to America. Appointed in 1891 permanent conductor of the New York Philharmonic, his untimely death by ptomaine poisoning was a tragedy for music in his adopted country. The standard "Baker's Biographical Dictionary of Musicians" calls him the Philharmonic's most brilliant conductor before the advent of Mahler.[75] And his successor was Emil Paur who came from the Boston Symphony and who carried on in the Wagnerian tradition. At the Metropolitan Seidl's successor was Franz Schalk (b. Vienna, 1863 – d. Edlach, Lower Austria, 1931), pupil of Bruckner and a fine director of Vienna's opera. Felix von Weingartner (b. Zara, Dalmatia, 1863 – d. Switzerland, 1942) who was to succeed Mahler in 1908 as director of the Vienna opera was a frequent visitor to America where he made his debut with the New York Philharmonic Orchestra in 1905.[76]

Another distinguished name in German repertory at the Metropolitan Opera was the Viennese conductor Artur Bodanzky (b. Vienna, 1877 – d. 1939) who had conducted concerts for the *Musikfreunde* and opera under Mahler at the imperial opera in Vienna, moved on to Mannheim in 1909, conducted the London premiere of "Parsifal," and achieved such success that he was called to the Met in 1915. He was the original conductor of the New York Symphony Orchestra, which was to merge with the Philharmonic, but he retained his connection with the Metropolitan until 1939 when he died there in New York.[77] The competent conductor Karl Heinrich Riedel (b. Vienna 1879 – d. 1946) began his long career at the Metropolitan in 1922.[78]

The Austro-Hungarian musical immigration pushed out, in lesser numbers, far beyond New York. From Vorarlberg came Edward Josef Stark (b. Hohenems, 1858 – d. 1918), cantor and composer who loved the music of the synagogue, brought his baritone voice to Brooklyn in 1871, but composed sacred music and operetta for two decades in San Francisco.[79] Emil Paur conducted at Pittsburgh as well as at Boston and New York. The handsome, soldier-like Carl Pohlig, born at Teplitz, Bohemia, back in 1864, who followed Liszt from Weimar to Rome and Budapest, toured most of Europe, served as concert master at Graz and with Mahler in Hamburg, came to Philadelphia in 1907 to serve for five years as conductor of its orchestra.[80]

And there was Maurice Rosenfeld (1867 – 1939), a boy immigrant from his native Vienna who taught piano for many years at the Chicago Musical College and, after 1916, at his own Piano School in the windy city. He was for years musical editor of the "Chicago Examiner" and, unlike so many of his fellow immigrants, he chose to remember his foreign origins through membership in the *Verein Deutsche Presse* and the *Verband Deutsch-Amerikanischer Journalisten*.[81] There was the Vienna-born violinist Eric Sorantin (b. 1905), an immigrant of 1924, who reorganized the Chicago Little Philharmonic Orchestra and found his home in San Antonio where he founded its Symphony Orchestra after working with its Chamber Music Society and Civic Opera.[82]

Adolf Schmid (b. Hannsdorf, Moravia, 1868) who came from Austria in 1915, via London, conducted the Boston Grand Opera Company and the Pavlova Ballet Russe, composed for years for radio and taught at the Juilliard School.[83] And Ernst Kunwald (b. Vienna, 1868 – d. Vienna, 1939) who earned his doctorate in law at the University of Vienna while he was studying piano and composition, became in 1912 the regular conductor of the Cincinnati Symphony Orchestra. Little wonder that, after having been arrested during the unpleasantness of 1917 as an enemy alien and interned, he returned to Europe.[84]

There were of course dozens of adventurous virtuosos and singers who heeded the call of the New World and its growing interest in music. The nearly forgotten ones included, for instance, Erich Wolff (b. Vienna, 1874 – d. New York, 1913), one of the fine accompanists of his time who turned composer of sentimental songs in the vain hope of taking his place among the great Austrian writers of *Lieder*. His name can still be found in the catalogs of the better recorded music.[85] Emma Juch, another Viennese (b. 1863 – d. New York, 1939), learned singing with her father, made her debut in opera in London, came to the United States and boldly attempted what da Ponte and Thomas had tried without success, establishing her own opera company. She found that in 1889 America's provincial cities were not quite ready for her pioneer efforts.[86]

Little Fannie Bloomfield Zeisler (b. Bielitz, Austrian Silesia, 1863 – d. Chicago, 1927) came when a child to Chicago with her parents but managed to return so often to Europe that she must be classified as an internationalist in music. That would identify her as a typical Austro-Hungarian. Faust called her a "German-American." She made her piano debut in Chicago in 1875, returned later to study with the famous Leschetizky in Vienna, gave concerts all over America and Europe, and died in Chicago, her adopted home.[87] Marcella Sembrich, who was born Praxede Marcelline Kochanska (b. Wisniewczyk, Galicia, 1858 – d. New York, 1935), was an even better known internationalist who began her training in voice in Lemberg in Austrian Galicia, went to Vienna at Liszt's suggestion to study with Rokitansky, made her debut in Athens, and sang at the Dresden opera and in London before she appeared at the Metropolitan in New York in 1883. She settled there in 1898 for nine great years at the Met before she retired to teaching at the Curtis Institute of Music.[88] And in the 1880's there came to the Metropolitan two other fine Austrian singers, Marianne Brandt (b. Vienna, 1842 – d. Vienna, 1921) and Amalia Materna (b. St. Georgen, Styria, 1844 – d. Vienna, 1918) who had sung Brünnhilde at Bayreuth's first Wagner festival.[89]

Great virtuosos and singers from the old monarchy came year after year to the Metropolitan Opera and were at home there among their fellow countrymen. Richard Mayr (b. Henndorf near Salzburg, 1877 – d. Vienna, 1935) whom Mahler had brought to the opera on the Ringstrasse, became famous at the Met as Wotan and Baron Ochs; and Selma Kurz (b. Bielitz, Austrian Silesia, 1875 – d. Vienna, 1933), another Mahler recruit in Vienna made her reputation here, often with her soprano daughter, on the concert platform. Fritzi Scheff (b. Vienna, 1879 – d. New York, 1954), who came to the Met back in 1900, in "Fidelio" won the hearts of America's males later when she shifted to light opera.[90]

Madame Ernestine Schumann-Heink (born Rössler) was, despite her birth in Lieben near Prague, Austrian and not Czech.[91] This charming prima donna (b. 1861 – d. Hollywood, 1936) was always ready to sing at a German-American *Sängerfest* or a charity concert. She never outgrew her devotion to Wagner and appeared in "Rheingold" at the Met when she was sixty-four.

Leo Slezak (b. Mährisch Schönberg, Moravia, 1873 – d. Tegernsee, Bavaria, 1946), the man-mountain from Bohemia, was one of the commuting artists who interrupted his twenty-five years at the Vienna opera to come to the Metropolitan for guest performances in 1909 and until the war. It was Toscanini's "Othello" that introduced him to New York and started him on the American road to fame. That great tenor, a beloved *Kammersänger* in Austria and a redoubtable rival of his dear friend Caruso in America, was always ready to play opposite his famous countrywoman Maria Jeritza because, she maintained, her slimness enabled his tremendous girth to approach close enough for required embraces without detaching any buttons.[92]

The Chicago Opera Company in 1911 and the Metropolitan in 1924 welcomed the baritone Friedrich Schorr (b. Nagyvarád, Hungary, 1888 – d. Farmington, Conn., 1953) who had studied law and the voice in Vienna and sung in Graz before he essayed Prague and Germany. The soprano Melanie Kurt (b. Vienna, 1880 – d. New York, 1941), a guest at the Met in 1915, settled in our metropolis in 1939, and the contralto Maria Olczewska (b. Wertingen, Bavaria, 1892) of the Vienna Opera sang in Chicago and New York between 1928 and 1935 and later, like so many of the visiting artists who were never entirely at home here, returned to Austria, in her case to teach at the Vienna Conservatory.[93]

The violinist Erica Morini (b. Vienna, 1904) began her American career in 1921 and a year later Margarethe Dessoff (b. Vienna, 1874 – d. Locarno, Switzerland, 1944) came to New York where she established the famous Dessoff Choir.[94]

And the great solo dancer with the shaved head, Harald Kreutzberg (b. Reichenberg, Bohemia, 1902), grandson of "Professor" Charles Kreutzberg who visited America with side-show freaks and wax figures, made well over a dozen American tours. He achieved fame in Germany, came on tour with Reinhardt to the United States in the twenties, lived at Austrian Seefeld, and taught Americans, along with others, not only at his dance seminars in Bern and the Salzburg Mozarteum but also in Hollywood and at some of America's best universities. Some called him the world's greatest dancer.[95]

"One of the greatest violinists of any age, and very possibly the most beloved musician before the public for a generation"[96] was Fritz Kreisler (b. 1875–d. New York, 1962). He had studied music in his native Vienna and in Paris, tried medicine and art, and returned to the violin. He was so much in demand for recitals and concerts that, according to Rachmaninoff, he seldom had to do any additional practicing. His American debut in Boston in 1888 was followed by concert tours here in 1900–1901 and in 1914, carrying his audiences by storm.

Kreisler spent more and more time in America, enjoying his many musical friendships here and especially Victor Herbert's Pittsburgh home where he played his favorite Mozart for his host. But the Kreisler who had been wounded fighting in the Austrian army early in the first World War found wartime prejudice so prevalent that in 1917 he terminated his American contracts and retired to his home in Maine because of the "bitter attacks ... made on me as an Austrian." His was one of those sweet personalities that found it difficult to understand hate. "I am not only an Austrian, but, more than that, I am a human being and have no right to hate anybody ..." He had always had his charities, especially among the children of Vienna, and when he played soon after the war in Carnegie Hall for their milk fund, he received such an ovation that wartime wounds were quickly forgotten. The former "enemy alien" became an American citizen in 1940.[97]

Fritz Kreisler composed dozens of violin pieces and even a pair of operettas. He received high honors from all over the world and especially from his native Austria which will always claim him despite the appearance of his name in our catalogs as "the great American violinist of the generation." America has a habit of adopting Austrians without giving credit!

[1] Ralph Hill, *Liszt*, N.Y. 1949, p. 12.

[2] P. H. Lang and Otto Bettmann, *Pictorial History of Music*, N.Y. 1960, pp. 94–95.

[3] Hugo Zelzer in *Österreich und die angelsächsische Welt*, Wien 1961, pp. 542–43; Willi Apel, *Harvard Dictionary of Music*, Cambridge 1961, pp. 29–30; A. B. Faust, *German Element in the United States*, 2 vols., Boston and N.Y. 1909, II, pp. 254f. Essential for the American background is Gilbert Chase, *America's Music*, N.Y. 1955, ch. I.

[4] *Ibid., passim; Dictionary of American Biography.*

[5] Cf. article on Rudel by Winthrop Sargeant, *New Yorker*, 20 Oct. 1962, pp. 57ff.

[6] *Das Buch der Deutschen in Amerika*, Philadelphia 1907, pp. 357–59; Faust, *op. cit.*, II, pp. 254–57; Apel, *op. cit.*, p. 31.

[7] 28 Sept. 1874, p. 8.

[8] *Das Buch der Deutschen*, p. 362.

[9] J. T. Howard, *Our American Music*, N.Y. 1946, pp. 212–14.

[10] Dieter Cunz, *The Maryland Germans*, Princeton 1948, pp. 244–45.

[11] Faust, *op. cit.*, II, p. 261; Carl Wittke, *Refugees of Revolution*, Philadelphia 1952, p. 13.

[12] *Das Buch der Deutschen*, p. 359.

[13] H. A. Pochmann, *German Culture in America*, Madison 1957, p. 450.

[14] Faust, *op. cit.*, II, p. 265.

[15] *Das Buch der Deutschen*, p. 719.

[16] *American-German Review*, Dec. 1946, p. 6.

[17] *Ibid.*, Aug. 1941, p. 17; H. Simonhoff, *Jewish Notables in America*, N.Y. 1956, pp. 243ff.

[18] Constant v. Wurzbach, *Biographisches Lexikon des Kaiserthums Oesterreich*, 60 parts, Wien 1856–91, IV, p. 28; M. R. Werner, *Barnum*, N.Y. 1926, p. 49; Walter Terry, *Dance in America*, N.Y. 1957, p. 31.

[19] Howard, *op. cit.*, pp. 174f.; Wurzbach, *op. cit.*, XXIV, pp. 281–84. For "The singing Hutchinsons" see Chase, *op. cit.*, p. 173.

[20] *American-German Review*, June-Aug. 1947, p. 41; article "Maria Augusta Trapp," *Who's Who*, 1962–63; Hoehn, *Catholic Authors*, 1952, pp. 589–91.

[21] Howard, *op. cit.*, p. 204; *Baker's Biographical Dictionary of Musicians*, 4th ed., N.Y. 1940.

[22] Howard, *op. cit.*, p. 211.

[23] Thomas Čapek, *The Čechs (Bohemians) in America*, Boston and N.Y. 1920, p. 229.

[24] Howard, *op. cit.*, pp. 272–73; Josef Nadler, *Literaturgeschichte des deutschen Volkes*, 4 vols. Berlin 1939–1941, IV, p. 120; Wittke, *op. cit.*, pp. 258, 292–95; Baker, *op. cit.*, p. 78.

[25] *Ibid.*, 1958 ed.

[26] Henry Dwight Sedgwick, *Vienna*, Indianapolis and N.Y. 1939, pp. 121–23.

[27] The *Schwann LP Record Catalog*, Sept. 1961, lists 16 Gluck items. This catalog and similar ones have been used for checking recent American interest in composers mentioned in this chapter.

[28] Chase, *op. cit.*, pp. 110–17, 120.

[29] Chase, op. cit., *passim*; Howard, *op. cit.*, pp. 28, 75–77, 147, 270; Cunz, *op. cit.*, p. 349; F. A. Wister, *Twenty-five Years of the Philadelphia Orchestra*, Philadelphia 1925, p. 8.

[30] *Music and Letters*, Apr. 1951, pp. 199f.; *High Fidelity*, Feb. 1957, p. 53.

[31] *Op. cit.*, II, p. 293.

[32] See, for instance, *Schwann LP Record Catalog*, Sept. 1961, and the *Gramophone Shop Encyclopedia of Recorded Music*, N.Y. 1948, which indicate that Mozart leads all the world composers in the number of items listed – the lead generally being by very wide margins.

[33] Article by H. C. Robbins Landon, *High Fidelity*, Apr. 1960, pp. 40ff.

[34] Gustav Pollak, *Franz Grillparzer and the Austrian Drama*, N.Y. 1907, p. 429.

[35] David Hall, *The Record Book*, N.Y. 1940, pp. 16ff.

[36] Howard, *op. cit.*, p. 98, awards the palm to Lexington in 1817.

[37] He may have decided finally to compose it for the *Gesellschaft der Musikfreunde* in Vienna. *American-German Review*, June 1942, pp. 4f.

[38] *Ibid.*, June 1936.

[39] *Gramophone Shop Encyclopedia of Recorded Music*, N.Y. 1948. Schubert did not score as well in some other record catalogs. Cf. P. H. Lang and Otto Bettmann, *A Pictorial History of Music*, N.Y. 1960, pp. 94–100.

[40] *Grove's Dictionary of Music and Musicians*, 3rd ed., 6 vols., 1 suppl., N.Y. 1944, I, article "Czerny."

[41] Ralph Hill, *op. cit.* Cf. *Arbeiter-Zeitung*, Wien, 16 May 1961, for account of 150th anniversary celebration of his birth at Raiding, now a small Austrian village.

[42] Grove, *op. cit.*; David Ewen, *Composers of Yesterday*, N.Y. 1937.

[43] According to *Musical America*, July 1963, p. 31, the most-often-played composers by American and Canadian symphony orchestras in 1962–63 were Beethoven, Mozart, and Brahms, in that order. *The Gramophone Shop Encyclopedia of Recorded Music*, N.Y. 1948, shows Brahms as one of the "big three" with Mozart and Beethoven. Mason is quoted in Chase, *op. cit.*, p. 365.

[44] M. Bauer and Ethel Peyser, *How Music Grew*, N.Y. and London 1939. Hall, *op. cit.*, gives Wolf two columns of listings compared with, for instance, half a column each for Mahler and Stravinsky.

[45] Cf. *Saturday Review*, 16 Dec. 1961, p. 35; Dika Newlin, *Bruckner, Mahler, and Schoenberg*, N.Y. 1947, *passim*; M. A. De Wolfe Howe, *Boston Symphony Orchestra*, Boston and N.Y. 1931, p. 63; Willi Apel, "Anton Bruckner," *American-German Review*, Apr. 1944, p. 10.

[46] Čapek, *op. cit.*, p. 231, points out that Mahler was not Czech for his affiliations were with the "Germans" of Bohemia.

[47] Hall, *op. cit.*, p. 12.

[48] R. Berges, "Mahler in America," *American-German Review*, Apr.-May 1960, p. 13.

[49] Walter is quoted in the *International Celebrity Register*, U.S. ed., p. 804. Cf. Dika Newlin, *op. cit., passim;* and Alma Mahler-Werfel, *And the Bridge is Love*, N.Y. 1958.

[50] E. g. Leonard Fischer's *Encyclopedia of Jazz*, N.Y. 1955, yields almost no Austrian names.

[51] Paul Nettl articles in the *American-German Review*, June-Aug. 1947 and Feb. 1949, on college songs and the old national anthem. Nettl points out that Austria had the world's only national anthem by a great composer.

[52] H. E. Jacob, *Johann Strauss Father and Son; a century of light music*, N.Y. 1940, p. 357; *American-German Review*, Aug. 1943, p. 21.

[53] P. H. Lang, *One Hundred Years of Music in America*, N.Y. 1961, p. 59. Otto Hietsch wrote of the Strauss meeting with Mark Twain in the *Jahrbuch für Amerikastudien*, vol. VIII, Heidelberg 1963, pp. 210–11.

[54] Johann Sohn began his career conducting at a similar establishment, Dommayer's, in the more elegant Hietzing quarter of the city. Grove, *op. cit.*, pp. 158–60.

[55] Jacob, *op. cit.*, p. 357.

[56] Chase, *op. cit.*, p. 620; Howard, *op. cit.*, p. 653; Apel, *op. cit.*, p. 35.

[57] Glenn Hughes, *History of the American Theater*, N.Y. 1951, pp. 433, 456.

[58] Quoted from the program of "Vienna on Parade" which toured the United States in 1962.

[59] *Austro-American Tribune*, Oct. 1943, p. 7; Werfel, *op. cit.*, p. 274; Bernard Grun, *Prince of Vienna*, London 1955, *passim.*

[60] This brief account of Oscar Straus is based largely upon his biography by Bernard Grun. According to the *Universal Jewish Encyclopedia* he became a French citizen in 1939.

[61] *Riemann Musiklexikon*, Personenteil L–Z, Mainz 1961. *Die Presse*, 26 Nov. 1961, p. 7, mentions the N.Y. productions of Kálmán by Rudolf Bach after World War I. Cf. *Gramophone Shop Encyclopedia of Recorded Music*, N.Y. 1948, p. 278, and his alphabetical listing referring to seven operettas. He lived in Vienna and considered himself an Austrian.

[62] Howe, *op. cit.*, has been relied upon very heavily for this story.

[63] *Ibid.*, p. 7.

[64] *Ibid.*, pp. 27–28.

[65] Cf. articles on Gericke in the *Dictionary of American Biography* and *Who's Who*, 1899–1900.

[66] *Ascap Biographical Dictionary.*

[67] *Who's Who*, 1899–1900; Howe, *op. cit.*; Grove, *op. cit.*

[68] Faust, *op. cit.*, II, p. 266.

[69] Howe, *op. cit.*, p. 138. Gericke died in Vienna.

[70] H. D. McKinney and W. R. Anderson, *Music in History*, N.Y. 1957, p. 708; *Dictionary of American Biography*; *National Cyclopaedia of American Biography*, VIII, p. 447. The latter gives 1858 as the year of his death.

[71] *Who's Who*, 1899–1900.

[72] *Ibid.*

[73] David Ewen, *Encyclopedia of the Opera*, N.Y., 1955, p. 332.

[74] *Das Buch der Deutschen in Amerika*, p. 431; *American-German Review*, Mar. 1936, p. 8; *Cambridge History of American Literature*, 3 vols., N.Y. and Cambridge 1961, II, pp. 588–89.

[75] Page 1492. Cf. Faust, *op. cit.*, II, p. 282.

[76] Baker, *op. cit.*, 1958 ed.

[77] *Who's Who*, 1938–39; Oscar Thompson, ed., *International Cyclopedia of Music and Musicians*, N.Y. 1952.

[78] *Who's Who*, 1938–39.

[79] *Dictionary of American Biography.*

[80] Wister, *op. cit.*, pp. 89, 94.

[81] *Who's Who*, 1938–39.

[82] Hope Stoddard, *Symphony Conductors*, N.Y. 1957.

[83] *Ascap Biographical Dictionary*, p. 439.

[84] Baker, *op. cit.*, p. 886.

[85] Grove, *op. cit.*, 5th ed., 9 vols., 1 suppl., London and N.Y. 1954–1961, IX, p. 349. *The Gramophone Shop Encyclopedia of Recorded Music*, N.Y. 1942, has several Wolff listings on p. 539.

[86] Faust, *op. cit.*, II, p. 454.

[87] *Ibid.*, p. 455; *Who's Who*, 1899–1900.

[88] *Hobbies*, magazine, July 1960, pp. 30–32.

[89] Baker, *op. cit.*; Marianne Brandt was born Marie Bischof.

[90] *Ibid.*

[91] Čapek, *op. cit.*, p. 231; F. J. Brown and J. S. Roucek, *Our Racial and National Minorities*, N.Y. 1937, pp. 304–05; *Who's Who*, 1930–31.

[92] Maria Jeritza, *Sunlight and Song*, N.Y. and London 1924, p. 234; Walter Slezak, *What Time's the Next Swan*, N.Y. 1962; Lang, *op. cit.*, p. 72. Leo Slezak hated the Nazi regime yet refused to come to America. His property in Germany and language difficulties were mentioned as reasons.

[93] Baker, *op. cit.*, Olczewska was born Berchtenbreiter.

[94] *Ibid.*

[95] Emil Pirchan, *Harald Kreutzberg*, Wien 1950; *Wer ist Wer*, XIII; *Dance*, May 1958, p.. 44

[96] According to critic Paul Hume, *Washington Post*, 30 Jan. 1962, p. B4.

[97] *Ibid.* for obituary; *Who's Who in America*; *American-German Review*, Feb. 1951, pp. 36–38; Baker, *op. cit.*, p. 869.

CHAPTER X

CONTEMPORARY MUSIC

Hitler gave America the two grea est figures in the development of musical modernism, Stravinsky and Schönberg. Both found refuge in the United States. Of the two Arnold Schönberg (b. 1874 – d. Los Angeles, 1951) was Viennese. He was one of those many rather unhappy Austrians who, like Mesmer and Freud in mental therapy, Mozart in music, and Adolf Loos in architecture, were so far ahead of their native land that their works were far better appreciated abroad than in the land that had given them their careers. Schönberg was, indeed, so much ahead of his time that many lovers of the older music still find it hard to appreciate him. The historian of music, however, can hardly fail to appreciate his importance as an experimentalist. He and his disciples, Berg and Webern, according to music critic Gilbert Chase, left "to the world a fecund musical legacy in the form of some indisputable masterpieces, a profoundly elaborated theory, and the makings of a genuinely new tradition in the art music of Western civilization."[1]

This father of the twelve-tone system who began to work in music's romantic period and discovered in the first decade of our century that he could advance beyond the old ideas of harmony and tonality, learned music in an innocuous *Realschule* in Vienna and then as a pupil of the able Zemlinsky who was to come to America and died at Larchmont, New York, in 1942. Vienna accepted his early, more-or-less romantic compositions. Mahler supported him. But after his iconoclasm had broken out in what many call atonality – his twelve-tone technique, he was derided in Paris and Berlin and his "Kammersymphonie" in Vienna in 1907 brought on "the greatest uproar ... in a Vienna concert hall in the memory of the oldest critic ..."[2]

There were long-haired Viennese who soon came to accept Schönberg and his ways. In 1913 his "Gurrelieder" were received with enthusiasm by the Viennese. And he was called to Berlin where his fame grew until the Brown Shirts took over and the Jewish radical moved on to Paris and then to the U.S.A. Some of his piano pieces were already known here. His "Die glückliche Hand" had had its premiere in Philadelphia, and his "Accompaniment to a Film Scene" (in German "Begleitungsmusik zu einer Lichtspielszene") had been played in the Hollywood Bowl. America, curious to see the "wild man" of music, greeted him with considerable fanfare. The Malkin Conservatory in Boston welcomed him as a teacher in 1933 but the winter was too severe and he moved on to continue his teaching at the University of Southern California and then at the University of California at Los Angeles where he taught until his retirement in 1944. His compositions were often tonal, not atonal, in this American period. Which leads one to wonder whether the stresses and strains of Vienna might not produce more revolutionary idiosyncrasies than the contentments of the American democracy. Schönberg died at his California home in 1951, respected by all and enthusiastically admired by an ever increasing few.

This man who had broken with the musical past and ignored beauty in music in every conventional sense had been more important as a pathfinder and a teacher than as a composer for the millions. He taught hundreds in America with success but without, his biographer, Dika Newlin, points out, establishing a "group" or a "school" here as he had in Vienna.[3]

Both of Schönberg's principal disciples were Vienna-born composers; both, unlike their master, were Aryan;[4] yet the music of both was decreed decadent and was outlawed by the Nazis. One died before the *Anschluss*, the other survived the war to be shot at its close by an American soldier.

Alban Berg (b. 1885 – d. Vienna, 1935), whose early works showed the romantic influence of Wagner and Mahler, studied only under Schönberg, turned to the twelve-tone technique in the middle twenties, and taught composition in Vienna. His music was never popular. His opera "Wozzeck," his best-known work, was derided in Berlin, Prague, and Vienna. Here, after Stokowski had given it its American premiere, the critics found it significant and interesting. He composed rather little.[5]

The third in this interesting trinity of musical rebels was Anton von Webern (b. Vienna, 1883 – d. Mittersill, Salzburg, 1945). His atonal compositions were even more advanced than those of his master and, like Schönberg, he scandalized Vienna's musical world. Even in New York where the League of Composers introduced his Symphony for a Chamber Orchestra in 1929 there was only a bitter reaction and his music long remained more significant than beloved. Recently, however, Webern's music, like that of Schönberg and Berg, has captured a very substantial American audience. Eyebrows are no longer raised when any of the three Austrian rebels are named on the programs of our most conservative orchestras. Indeed, Seattle had its First International Webern Festival in 1962.

Yet Webern's death by an American bullet was a tragedy for warworn Austria that was losing so much of its talent. He had taken his whole family in 1945 to Mittersill in Salzburg to escape the Soviet army and find refuge behind the American lines. There his brother-in-law was in trouble with the U.S. occupation troops for black-marketeering in cigarettes. One of the detachment which came to pick up the offender was the company cook who remained outside in the dark of the evening, came upon someone smoking a cigarette, drew his revolver and shot him three times. The victim who was fatally wounded was Anton von Webern. His bewildered assassin was overcome with a sense of guilt, took to drink, and died of it ten years later.[6] It was only one of many tragedies during the ten years of the occupation of Austria.

The Austrian musicians who came to America to enrich American musical life when the Nazis took over Austria were legion. Who can say how many might have come after 1938 had there been no Hitler and no *Anschluss*? If the bad times of the early thirties, anti-Semitism, and the ideological conflict of the reds and the blacks that had plagued the little republic had continued, America might still have profited immensely as Austria's musicians sought security and opportunity and fortunes in the United States.

As it was, the advent of Hitlerism compounded Austria's woes and stifled her cultural life. Thousands of her finest figures sought refuge in Switzerland and Paris and more especially in Britain and America. The advent of the musical Thirty-eighters was a milestone of no small significance in American music.

A decade after Pearl Harbor, for instance, the Austrian-born ranked next in importance to the English, Russian and German-born in the membership of the important American Society of Composers, Authors and Publishers — despite the enormously greater populations of Great Britain, Russia and Germany and their much higher totals in immigration statistics. And in 1962 an American critic could point out that Austrian impresarios had taken the lead over the Italians who had been earlier in the vanguard.[7]

It is, of course, impossible to compute statistically anything as intangible as a cultural loss or a cultural gain. And the Austrian Thirty-eighters are especially difficult to tabulate because they came and were confused with thousands of German refugees and, having for the most part no intention of returning to their homeland, they were so quickly assimilated into American life. They lived apart in areas like Yorkville in New York City only for the first months of their life in the adopted country. The more fortunate and able, even though they might return to Yorkville now and then for a nostalgic *Wiener Schnitzel* and some *Palatschinken* soon found a career elsewhere. Americans in all corners of the United States were eager to help the refugees from Hitler and the immigrant musicians were free to practice without having to meet requirements like those that handicapped their friends in law and medicine.

Erich Wolfgang Korngold (1897—1957), one of the most prominent of the composer group, emigrated from the sad Vienna of 1934. He had been born in Brünn when it was under the Habsburgs but had, like his critic father, found his musical career in Vienna. A child prodigy, he studied under Fuchs and Zemlinsky, composed at the age of twelve, and at the age of twenty-three did his opera "Die tote Stadt" which was introduced to America along with Jeritza at the Metropolitan in New York. He worked with Max Reinhardt who brought him to Hollywood to arrange Mendelssohn's music for Reinhardt's "Midsummer Night's Dream" and stayed on to write a violin concerto in 1946 and compose and conduct music for a whole series of successful films such as "Anthony Adverse," "Private Lives of Elizabeth and

Essex," and "Escape Me Never," with some Academy Awards for distinction. He occasionally found his way back to Vienna but was naturalized in America (1943) and died in Hollywood.[8]

Ernst Toch (b. Vienna, 1887 – d. Los Angeles, 1964) was a Pulitzer Prize winner for his Symphony No. 3, in 1956. He had tried medicine, distinguished himself as a composer in his teens, served in imperial ranks during World War I, lived in Germany for four years and moved on to London in 1933 when Hitler took over. Like Korngold, he found his career and his home in California in the mid-thirties. His friend, Alvin Johnson, the director of New York's New School for Social Research, not only engaged him as a lecturer but also introduced him to the Pinocchio story during his first months in America and he wrote his "Pinocchio, A Merry Overture," whose gaiety charmed his American friends. In California he taught composition at the University of California.[9]

When the flood gates opened in 1938 Vienna lost to America one of its great musical iconoclasts, an expressionist who followed Mahler, married his daughter, and adopted Schönberg's twelve-tone system, Ernst Křenek (b. 1900). This Vassar professor was, despite his non-Germanic name, a native of Vienna who had lived in Berlin and Zurich, represented the German "Frankfurter Zeitung" in Vienna, and achieved fame by toying with jazz in his opera "Jonny spielt auf." This appealing story of an American Negro's conquest of degenerate Europe has somehow overshadowed all his other works. "Baker's Dictionary of Musicians" states that "Jonny" was translated into eighteen languages, played at the Metropolitan in 1929, and remembered only because a popular brand of Austrian cigarettes was named after it. In America Křenek taught at Hamline University as well as Vassar, and then settled in Los Angeles to find time for prolific composition in styles more mellow than the Viennese-Schönberg school of his younger days. America has seldom encouraged Austrian radicals to persist in their extremism.[10]

The composer of "Dantons Tod" and "Der Prozess," which had a more successful debut in Salzburg in 1953 than it had in New York, was the exciting modernist, the composer Gottfried von Einem. Born in Bern, Switzerland (1918), to the Austrian branch of a Lower Saxon family, he was brought to Austria when a child, and educated there, made some contributions to music in Germany, spent a few months in a Nazi concentration camp, and settled in Salzburg and Vienna.[11] His operas soon became classics in even the less progressive of American opera houses. His "Dantons Tod" was produced in English by the Austrian-born director of the New York City Opera, Julius Rudel, in his new Lincoln Center home of the New York City Opera.

Quite a different figure on the side of popular music was Hans Lengsfelder (b. Vienna, 1903) who wrote dozens of reviews, operettas and plays, like "Why Do You Lie, Cherie?," that were played all over Europe. He came here in 1939, was naturalized in the minimum five years, founded Your Theater, Incorporated, and went on composing in a popular vein.[12] Jacques de Menasce (b. Bad Ischl, 1905 – d. Switzerland, 1960) was another Thirty-eighter, a composer in the neo-classic style, who found his place in the American music world.[13]

The most appealing of the recent Austrian composers in this country were undoubtedly Robert Stolz of "Frühling im Prater" and "Two Hearts in Three-quarters Time" and Frederick Loewe of "My Fair Lady." Stolz (b. 1882), a native of Graz, had sacrificed all his European fame – the product of twelve years of conducting at the *Theater an der Wien* and the composing of hundreds of *Lieder* and dozens of Viennese operettas that were nearly the last of their kind – Stolz had given up his German contracts, sought refuge in Vienna in 1933, and gone on to Paris after the *Anschluss*. Hitler wanted the "Aryan" composer of good Germanic music to return. "Tell him," Stolz replied, "that the only thing I would be interested in is to compose his funeral march, and would love to play this gay composition the sooner the better."[14] The Nazis confiscated everything of his they could put their hands on and he came to New York. There he organized Austrian evenings with light music and operettas and conducted Vienna Nights at Lewissohn Stadium. He toured the continent until after the war, homesick, he returned to Vienna. His pleasant tunes are still heard on stage, film, radio and television in America as in Central Europe.

There is probably no contemporary music in present-day America that is better known than the entrancing bars that Frederick Loewe (b. 1904) wrote for Lerner's lyrics in "Brigadoon," "Gigi," "My Fair Lady" and "Camelot." A native of Vienna, his father was famous as a tenor in operetta – especially as the original star of "The Chocolate Soldier" and the creator of the Prince Danilo role in "The Merry Widow."[15] His father introduced Frederick to music, prepared him for his first concert at the age of eleven, and brought him to America when he was twenty. Failing in concert work he turned, like many a misfit immigrant, to odd jobs: bus boy in a cafeteria, boxer, and cow puncher. Then he began composing, married a Vienna girl who managed the fashion shops of another famous Austrian, Hattie Carnegie, met Alan Jay Lerner who tried writing lyrics for Loewe's music, and together they marched on to fame and fortune on Broadway and in Hollywood. "On Broadway," it was said, "nothing succeeds like Lerner and Loewe."

Frederick Loewe was a gay little man fully charged with the melodic sweetness that had been so typical of Vienna in its operetta era. His accent remained definitely Teutonic and he was generally referred to by the journalists as the "German" member of the Lerner and Loewe team. He came first to the United States in 1924 as a concert pianist.

Everything Lerner and Loewe did was tops on Main Street as on Broadway. And "My Fair Lady" (1956), that charming musical version of "Pygmalion," was the greatest of them all. On the stage it grossed twelve millions in two years in New York alone and its music sold 1,600,000 records in eighteen months![16] George Bernard Shaw's estate paid a larger amount to its beneficiaries from the royalties for "My Fair Lady" than from all the fine products of Shaw's pen. Shaw would doubtless have resented the success of the American Lerner and of the Austrian Loewe. Whether Lerner needed Shaw or Loewe, his productions immediately following "My Fair Lady" achieved only minor successes.

The musical Thirty-eighters were as varied in their interests as they were useful in their adopted country. Some like Max Graf (b. Vienna, 1873 – d. Vienna, 1958), the fine critic, came to escape Hitler. Graf taught in the New School for Social Research but returned home after the war to help with the rehabilitation of Austria.[17] Most of them, like Max Graf's son Herbert, came to stay. Herbert Graf (b. Vienna, 1903), after staging several productions for the Philadelphia opera, moved on to become stage director at the Metropolitan in New York and was in 1949 appointed head of the opera department at Philadelphia's Curtis Institute.[18] Gustav Kotany, who worked with Robert Stolz to organize the Austrian evenings of music and operetta in New York, settled permanently in New York.[19]

An art director for stage and film who had worked for Max Reinhardt was Harry Horner (b. Vienna, 1910). In 1932 he received the League of Nations Award for the best film script on a peace theme, came to America three years later, and did stage sets for the Metropolitan and for dozens of fine stage productions on Broadway. He directed for Twentieth Century Fox, serialized the Canadian Mounted Police for TV and made Beverly Hills his home.[20] Another Viennese, William L. Weissel, came in the year of the *Anschluss* to manage the "New York Times" radio station, the Little Orchestra Society, and, as assistant manager, the New York Philharmonic.[21]

The advent of Hitler even brought us a musical therapist, Vally (Pick) Weigl (b. Vienna, 1894). She was a product of the University of Vienna, Columbia University, and Manhattan College who applied her musical therapy to work with children at the New York Psychiatric Institute.[22] Her husband was the Austrian composer Karl Weigl (b. Vienna, 1881 – d. New York, 1949). Another Viennese musical figure with an unusual field of interest, Emanuel Winternitz (b. Vienna, 1898), has long been an authority on musical instruments who lectured at Harvard, Columbia, and Yale and served for years as custodian of musical instruments at the Metropolitan Museum of Art in New York.[23] And George Richard Marek (b. Vienna, 1902), who came to New York in 1920, was an advertising agency executive who, like so many Austrians, failed to resist the appeal of music. He became music editor of "Good Housekeeping," vice president of RCA, and after 1957, general manger of RCA Victor's record division. He wrote several books on opera.[24]

Writing books on music, chiefly in English, seems to have been a major industry among our musical Austro-Americans. Most prolific has been David Ewen (b. 1907), a native of Lemberg in Austrian Galicia, who came when a boy to New York to serve later as music critic of "Cue" and "Stage" and to turn out a large crop of reference books, such as "Twentieth Century Composers," "Musical Vienna," and "American Musical Theater."[25] The magazine "Time" called him "music's interpreter to the American people." And the Gershwin family chose him to write the definitive biography of America's beloved George Gershwin. Frederick Dorian (b. Friedrich Deutsch in Vienna, 1902), the Vienna musicologist and Thirty-eighter who had been music critic for German and Austrian papers, came to America in 1936 to teach at Carnegie Tech and to write his "A History of Music in Performance" and "Musical Workshop."

The president of the American Musicological Society in the middle 1950's, Karl Geiringer (b. Vienna, 1899) of Boston University has also written about musical instruments and on Haydn, Brahms and Bach.[26] He was a former curator of the Society of the Friends of Music. And, unlike the great majority of the Austrian Thirty-eighters, he became himself a Methodist.

There were other professors of music, most of them Vienna-born. Paul Amadeus Pisk (b. Vienna, 1893) of the University of Texas since 1951, was a religious maverick, a Presbyterian. That pupil of the radical Schönberg had taught in Vienna's *Volkshochschulen* and written for the Social-Democratic "Arbeiter-Zeitung": in America he listed himself as a Democrat. After fourteen years at the University of the Redlands he went to Texas to win four Texas Composers' Guild prizes in the fifties.[27]

Vienna, Budapest, and Harvard trained Dr. Conrad H. Rawski (b. Vienna, 1914), a medievalist in musicology, for his position in Western Reserve's library school.[28] And the universities of Vienna and Chicago gave doctorates to Professor Paul L. Frank (b. Vienna, 1905) who was appointed in 1946 to teach music at Otterbein College. Professor Siegmund Levarie (b. Austria, 1914), chairman of the music department of Brooklyn College, came to America in his late teens but returned for work at the Vienna Conservatory and the University of Vienna (Ph. D. 1938) before teaching at the University of Chicago (1938–52), with leave of absence to serve, like so many Austrian immigrants, in the U.S. army, and become dean of the Chicago Musical College.[29]

The newcomers in music were remarkably successful in finding places in this country. For popular appreciation of music had been growing in America ever since the eighteenth century. Imported music and imported musicians had helped the cause of music here mightily in the earlier years. And in recent generations the phonograph, radio and television have all helped to make more converts to music, serious and popular. Orchestras, bands, choral groups and such have sprung up on an unprecedented scale in smaller communities as well as in the larger cities; and in thousands of schools and colleges music has been taught to its eager new devotees.

Immigrant teachers of music, as well as musicians, were welcomed all over the country. America could pay far better than could Austria in the sorry days between the two world wars when only Wagnerians and old-school exponents of German culture were in favor. Thus, America offered both opportunity and profit. The Austrian musical world suffered severely when it lost not only its finest musicians but also dozens of its best teachers of music.

Such professorial musicians were not all to be found in New York. The pianist Walter Robert (b. Trieste, 1908), for instance, recipient of a Bösendorfer Award from the Vienna Academy before World War II, combined concert work with years of teaching at Indiana University.[30] George Robert, a Viennese (b. 1919) who had studied with von Webern, settled at the University of New Mexico.[31] The pianist Margaret Grete Neufeld, also a Viennese, established in the forties her own music studio in Seattle. And the distinguished concert pianist Rudolf Serkin (b. Eger, 1903) was named head of the piano department at the Curtis Institute in Philadelphia. Serkin is described as a musical internationalist: born in Bohemia, his father of Russian stock, his musical education in Vienna (in composition with J. Marx and Schönberg), his debut at the age of twelve with the Vienna Symphony, and his American debut eighteen years later at a Coolidge Festival in Washington. This American citizen has been called "one of the most persistently admired, beloved, and influential musical figures throughout the entire world."[33]

There were also artists of the voice who turned to teaching. There was the daughter of David Schwarz who invented the rigid airship for Count Zeppelin. She was Vera Schwarz, a soprano from the Vienna opera, who taught in New York when she found refuge there as a Thirty-eighter.[34] The Viennese contralto Herta Glaz taught at the Manhattan School of Music while she distinguished herself singing with most of the fine American orchestras and operas. And the baritone Ralph Herbert (b. Vienna, 1909), a newcomer of 1939, not only sang at the New York City Center, San Francisco, and Metropolitan operas but he also taught stage direction at the Mannes College of Music and, more recently, assumed a chair of music at the University of Michigan.[35]

There were famous musical names that were less professorial. There was the singer Margaret Matzenauer (b. Temesvár, Hungary, 1881 – d. United States, 1963), daughter of two great musical names in Vienna, who made her debut at the Metropolitan in 1911 and stooped only once to the films when she played in "Mr. Deeds Goes to Town."[36] The immortal soprano Lotte Lehmann, was a German with so many roots in Vienna – she received the highly honorific Austrian title of *Kammersängerin* – that Schlag seems justified in listing her as an Austrian Thirty-eighter.[37]

Jeritza – originally Maria Jedlitzka – (b. Brünn 1887) was another immortal. She was one of the many Austrians born over the line in what, long after her girlhood days, became Czechoslovakia.[38] Her fame was made in Vienna and New York.

She studied music in her native Brünn, sang there and in Germany, and was a member of the Vienna Opera from 1912 to 1935. Typically enough she had in the meanwhile, in 1920, come to the Metropolitan in New York, made her debut in the United States premiere of Korngold's "Die tote Stadt" (1921), and become a fixture at the Metropolitan.

Maria Jeritza, a significant example of the artists who never gave up their old-world homes, tells in her frothy little volume, "Sunlight and Song" (New York and London 1924), how she had arrived in New York in 1920 with few friends and less English, how she came to tour the country and to love it, and how proud she was of the musical citizenship conferred on her by her membership in the Metropolitan Opera. "I have felt . . .," she wrote, "that a European singer is less a foreigner in the United States than she is in European countries outside her own." Americans, even after a war, were less nationalistic. American women were more vital than European women. She might still shop in Vienna and Paris, she might regret finding so few American friends, but she enjoyed New York and returned time and again. She regretted only that opera was not so much a part of the New Yorker's life as it was of the European's. "If we have an important political article already set up in type," a Vienna editor told her, "and we get some opera news at the last moment, the serious political article goes out . . ."[39] We ourselves have seen the chancellor of Austria arrive at a public occasion and receive far less applause than Jeritza received a few minutes later. A Jeritza is admired in America; she is beloved in Austria.

Little wonder that many of the Austrians go back to settle down in the Vienna of thunderous applause, even for the idols of past years who would be written off by American critics as ghosts of the past. A fine bass like Emanuel List (b. Vienna, 1891 – d. Vienna, 1967),[40] once a chorister at the *Theater an der Wien*, a star at the *Volksoper*, a Wagnerian in Berlin, and a glorious Baron Ochs in "Rosenkavalier," could sing with distinction in the Metropolitan (debut in 1933), take American citizenship but find himself back enjoying the wines and cafés of Vienna after the war. Not all Austrians become so completely assimilated in America that they can ignore the spell of the Danube and the Alps. And then there was the fine tenor Richard Tauber (b. Ernst Geiffert in Linz, 1892 – d. London, 1948) a frequent visitor in America who found his post-Nazi home not here but in Britain.[41]

". . . as exciting as anything I've ever heard, and bold enough to suit anyone, . . . She is tremendous . . ." was a critic's comment on another great Viennese singer, Lotte Lenya (b. Vienna) when she, Lenya, played in the off-Broadway success of 1962, "Brecht on Brecht."[42] She had been a star in Germany between the two wars, had married Kurt Weill, come to know Brecht through her husband, and starred in the Weill-Brecht "Dreigroschenoper," the "Three Penny Opera" that had run for years since its Berlin success. She fled from Hitler, went from Paris to America in 1935, contributed to the Austrian refugee "Players from Abroad" during the second World War, specialized in everything that Weill or Brecht did for Broadway, and did herself many superb recordings.[43] She is so prominent in American theater circles that no one stops to think of her as an importation from Austria.

There were two far more recent importations in folk singing: Martha Schlamme (b. Vienna) and Theodore Bikel (b. Vienna, 1924). Both were refugees from Hitler, both had escaped to Britain (Bikel went first to Israel and from there to London), and both have become famous in America through their popular recordings as well as through concerts. The new-comer Bikel played the male lead in "The Sound of Music" opposite Mary Martin whose reputation overshadowed him.[44]

There came, chiefly from Vienna, scores of virtuosos who found their places in the United States. There was the harpsichordist, Yella Pessl (b. Vienna, 1906), who had specialized in Vienna in the harpsichord music of the 17th and 18th centuries and in Bach, who founded a Bach Circle in New York in 1937,[45] and taught at the University of Southern California. Less well known here was the visiting harpsichordist Isolde Ahlgrimm. Among the violinists were Paul Kling (b.Vienna, 1919) who taught at the University of Louisville, Erica Morini (b. Vienna, 1904) who studied at Smith College and settled in New York, and Irving Ilmer whose career has been chiefly in the Middle West with excursions into recorded music and television. The violinist Paul Doktor (b. Vienna, 1919), a former choir master of the Vienna *Sängerknaben*, or Boys' Choir, immigrated in 1947 to teach at the University of Michigan and Mannes College of Music and, like so many of the Austrians, to produce recordings that were sold over the entire land [46]

One of the finest of the pianists was Artur Schnabel (b. Lipnik, Galicia, 1882 – d. Axenstein, Switzerland, 1951), a great interpreter of Beethoven and lover of Brahms, who studied in Vienna, taught in Berlin, found refuge from the Nazis in Switzerland, settled in America in 1939, and returned later to Europe. His compositions and his books on musical criticism were less famous than the concerts that he gave over the entire western world.[47] Adolph Baller was another pianist who came to the United States, became a member of the fine Alma Trio that was organized at Alma, Yehudi Menuhin's estate in California, and made a reputation here in chamber music before returning to Vienna.[48] The "little giant of the piano," Moriz Rosenthal (b. Lemberg, 1862 – d. New York, 1946), who had come to Vienna when he was a boy to study philosophy, had returned to music, his first love, and had made an enviable reputation in Europe and in America on twelve tours from 1887 on, for fifty-one long years, until he settled here in 1938.[49] On the lighter side was Tilli Dieterle (b. Feldkirch), a pupil of Schönberg who became staff pianist for Rodgers and Hammerstein, invaded the night club field, broke into television, and went to work for United Artists Records.[50]

A fascinating figure among the pianists was Paul Wittgenstein (b. Vienna, 1887 – d. Manhasset, L. I., 1961) who made his concert debut in Vienna in 1913, lost his right arm on the Russian front in World War I, but made a career of playing with one hand. Richard Strauss, Korngold, Ravel and Prokofieff wrote music for the left hand especially for Wittgenstein. He found his way to America – Ravel's Piano Concerto for the Left Hand was first performed by Wittgenstein in 1931 in Carnegie Hall with the Boston Symphony – settled in New York after the *Anschluss* and died there at the age of seventy-three, in 1961.[51]

The conductors and managers, the makers of programs and the builders of operas and orchestras, have a very considerable voice in the music world. Here the Austrians, and Austro-Hungarians with a Vienna background, have become pre-eminent in the United States. Of this group some like Karl Heinrich Riedel (b. Vienna, 1879) who came to the Metropolitan in 1922,[52] Rodzinski, Bing and Krips fall outside of the Thirty-eighter category.

Artur Rodzinski (b. Split, Dalmatia, 1894 – d. Philadelphia, 1958)[53] came to the United States in 1925 at Stokowski's invitation who made him his assistant conductor at Philadelphia. In Vienna he had studied law before he went to the Academy of Music and his apprenticeship in conducting was in what had been Austrian Poland. From Philadelphia he went to the Los Angeles Philharmonic and then to Cleveland where he introduced operas in concert form. He was honored by an invitation from the Salzburg Festival where he introduced American symphonic music; he organized the N.B.C. Symphony for Toscanini, spent four years of triumph and controversy at the New York Philharmonic, tried Chicago for a few months, toured the world, settled in Rome, and returned to live in New York. His impact here was far more than that of a European introducing Europe to America.

In 1950 Rudolf Bing (b. Vienna, 1902)[54] became general manager of the Metropolitan Opera. His career as an impressario had begun in Vienna and Berlin and after Hitler's rise to power he had worked for years with the Glyndebourne Opera in England and the Edinburgh Festival. His distinguished career was honored with decorations of the Order of the British Empire and the French Legion of Honor and a high Austrian decoration.

Another distinguished figure who fell out with the Nazi regime worked during the war in a food-processing plant in his native land. He was the pleasantly rotund Josef Krips (b. Vienna, 1902) who had played the violin at the *Volksoper* at the age of fifteen, directed music for Karlsruhe in Germany and returned in the Brown-Shirt year, 1933, to conduct at the *Staatsoper* and teach at the Academy. After the war he worked in the ruins to revive Vienna music and left the Philharmonic on its way back to greatness when he went to the London Symphony Orchestra for five years. His first season with the Buffalo Symphony Orchestra was 1954–55. He liked Buffalo from the start and Buffalo made him its "Citizen of the Year" (1957) and its university awarded him its Chancellor's Medal. Continuing his work there he was made permanent conductor of the San Francisco Orchestra in 1962 while he was accepting invitations to guest appearances with the New York Philharmonic and the Vienna Opera. "Some People Say the Conductor of the Buffalo Philharmonic is the Last of the Great Viennese School," a critic declared in 1961. While one may smile as he recalls how often the obituary of "the Great Viennese School" has been written, he must accept the statement as a genuine compliment to Josef Krips.[55]

Graz was the birthplace of another itinerant conductor who made his first American appearance in 1956 with the Chicago Symphony. He was Karl Böhm (b. 1894), a familiar figure in Vienna, who has conducted all the way from Graz to Hamburg, has directed the *Wiener Staatsoper*, and who by 1963 promised to become a familiar figure in New York at the Metropolitan and the Lincoln Center's new Philharmonic Hall. By 1966 and 1967 he was such a fixture that he was no longer identified as Austrian.

We have mentioned a few Thirty-eighters. But there were many more. They represented a tremendous agglomeration of talent that reached our shores, unsolicited for the most part, for sale to the highest bidder, and yet remarkably successful in finding places in the young and eager American world of music. Many were Jews who had to leave Nazi Europe; many were Gentiles who simply could not stomach the Nazi regime. Many left tragedy, death and concentration camps behind them. Many left relatives and friends in peril in Austria – after all, the entire population could not emigrate. Many came with reservations. They loved the homeland and they hoped to go back. Many came with only hate for the cruelties that they had left behind. Some like Alexander von Zemlinsky (b. Vienna, 1872 – d. Larchmont, New York, 1942), the great teacher of Schönberg and Korngold and Bodansky, came in their old age with no hope of finding a career in a new world. In any event it was fortunate that America had outlived the worst of its 19th century nativism and was ready to accept the musical fugitives, not only as reinforcements for American musical life, but as human beings in desperate straights.

There were dozens of them, even in the conductor group, who became very useful but not famous in their adopted country.

Richard Johannes Lert (b. Vienna, 1885), who married the Austro-American novelist Vicki Baum, came in 1938 to conduct in Pasadena, California. He was the brother of the Ernst Lert (b. Vienna, 1883 – d. Baltimore, 1955) who became a stage director at the Met in the mid-thirties and a teacher of music in the best music schools of Philadelphia and Baltimore.[56] Victor Zuckerkandl (b. Vienna, 1897 – d. Switzerland, 1965) was a fine figure in musical theory and the piano who, after conducting orchestras and writing criticism in Austria and Germany, came in 1940 to teach at Wellesley College, the New School for Social Research, and St. John's College at Annapolis. He died in 1965 a much regretted scholar of classical music.[57] Milton Weber (b. Graz, 1910)[58] arrived in 1941 and found a career directing orchestra in Waukesha, Wisconsin. Fritz Berens (b. Vienna, 1907)[59] became in 1950 the conductor of the Sacramento Philharmonic Orchestra. And Karl Kritz (b. Vienna), who had conducted Berlin's State Opera before emigrating in 1937, conducted not only in New York and San Francisco but also in Cincinnati, Pittsburgh, Fort Worth, and Syracuse. Robert Scholz (b. Steyr, Upper Austria, 1902), a product of Salzburg's famous music school the *Mozarteum*, conducted for years at the Henry Street Settlement in New York before he turned to the American Chamber Orchestra in 1952.[60] And Paul Breisach (b. Vienna, 1896) was a Thirty-eighter with a background in the great opera houses of Vienna and Berlin who found a place in summer opera in Cincinnati as well as in the great operas of New York and San Francisco.[61] Thanks to Hitler, American cities which had formerly had to content themselves with the minimum of musical talent were coming to enjoy the best. Another example: Gustav Mahler's nephew Fritz (b. Vienna, 1901) who came to America in 1935, equipped with a musical education from masters like Schönberg, Berg, and Webern and five years of experience conducting at the *Wiener Volksoper*, not only taught at Juilliard and served as music director of the National Youth Administration in New York, but has also conducted some of America's better radio orchestras and other orchestras in Erie, Hartford, Denver, and Newark.[62]

The conductor and composer Herbert Zipper (b. Vienna, 1904) was a musical "missionary" in the Far East who, having fled from Hitler, found himself a Japanese prisoner in the Philippines. Despite his work with the Brooklyn Symphony, the Business Men's Orchestra of Chicago, and the New School for Social Research, he maintained his interest in the Philippines and the Manila Symphony and in 1959 was awarded the medal of the President of the Philippines.[63] A Jewish Wagnerian from Cracow who studied music in Vienna also found himself in the Far East: Joseph Rosenstock (b. Cracow, 1895) conducted the Nippon Philharmonic Orchestra before the war, came to the United States for the period of the war, and spent another year in Tokyo before he returned to conduct for the New York Center Opera and, later, after two years with the Cologne opera, at the Metropolitan.[64] The *Wunderkind* who played with the Vienna Symphony Orchestra at the age of seven, Paul Kling of the Louisville, Kentucky, Orchestra, also served, as concert master, in Japan.

The great magnet for most of the Thirty-eighter conductors was New York. There was Carl Bamberger (b. Vienna, 1902) who came in 1937 to found the New Choral Group of Manhattan, to teach at Mannes College and, later, to conduct for the New York City Opera.[65] And Frederic Kurzweil (b. Vienna, 1912) after trying St. Louis and Philadelphia, returned to teach in New York and conduct at the City Center.[66] Fritz Stiedry (b. Vienna, 1883), who had studied law and music in Vienna and conducted in Berlin and Leningrad, conducted the New Friends of Music Orchestra in New York for eight years, did Wagner and Verdi at the Met and more contemporary things at his own concerts.[67] Walter Taussig, another Viennese (b. 1908), served for some years at the Metropolitan. And Kurt Herbert

Adler (b. Vienna, 1905), with decorations from the Austrian, German, and Italian governments, worked under Reinhardt in Vienna, assisted Toscanini at the *Mozarteum* and at the 1936 Salzburg Festival, conducted for the Chicago and San Francisco operas and the New Opera Company in New York. In 1953 he became artistic director of the San Francisco Opera where many Viennese singers made their first appearances in this country and a bit later also became director of the Baltimore Symphony.[68] He was a figure of no small importance at the Met.

Two of the most significant names among the conductors of the Thirty-eighter era should be mentioned despite the fact that they were not Austrian-born. Bruno Walter, originally Schlesinger (b. 1876 – d. Beverly Hills, Calif., 1962) was a Berliner who fell in love with two Austrians, Mozart and Mahler, came to Vienna when Hitler put his hand on Germany, and took Austrian citizenship. In Austria he became the towering figure of the Salzburg Festivals and the Vienna Philharmonic and *Staatsoper*. Then the *Anschluss* brought him permanently to the United States which he had visited occasionally ever since Damrosch brought him over in 1923. Here his fine recordings have perhaps made him known to more lovers of fine music than his great work at the New York Philharmonic and the Metropolitan. He became so closely associated with the American music world that the author of an obituary could say in all seriousness that he was almost as well known in Vienna and Salzburg as in the United States.[69] He left $ 60,000 to the Philharmonic Orchestra in his beloved Vienna.[70]

Another world-famous name was of Austro-Hungarian origin. George Szell, who has brought the Cleveland Orchestra to renown, was born in Budapest in the days of the Habsburg monarchy (1897), was taken to Vienna at the tender age of three, appeared with the Vienna Symphony when he was ten, found his musical education in Vienna, contributed his great ability to the Salzburg Festivals, and conducted over most of the western world. His mother was Czech and he liked to think of himself as a Czech. His piano concerts became famous in Prague and Germany as well as in Austria. And as orchestra conductor he became a beloved disciplinarian. In 1939 he found himself in the United States and seven years later commenced his famous career at Cleveland. America recognized his genius. He taught at the New School for Social Research and at Mannes, he conducted most of America's fine orchestras and the Met, and he has produced numerous recordings that the critics have praised to the skies.[71] "To work with Szell on . . . Beethoven . . . is like getting the word from God," reported an American critic in 1962 who recognized Szell as one of the greatest. Vienna properly proclaimed him to be one of the greatest of American conductors when he returned to direct his own Cleveland orchestra at the Vienna *Festwochen* in 1965.

Two of the finest of the Austro-American conductors who came in 1938 were Vienna-born: Erich Leinsdorf (b. 1912) and Julius Rudel (b. 1921). Leinsdorf was a product of the Vienna Academy and the University of Vienna who had worked first with the piano and choral music, then as orchestra conductor including work with Bruno Walter and Toscanini at the Salzburg Festivals. But there was no future for a Jew in Austria. In America he came directly to the Metropolitan, achieved success with his debut there in the opera "Die Walküre" and fell heir at the age of twenty-seven to German opera on Bodansky's death. The Metropolitan's prima donna, Kirsten Flagstad, threatened to resign if the young Leinsdorf remained, but manager Johnston refused to drop Leinsdorf, Flagstad finally relented, and the young conductor stayed on. He achieved more fame in Cleveland and Rochester. The New York City Center found General Director Leinsdorf too ambitious financially for its pocketbook and he went back to the Met and then on to the Boston Symphony where he has maintained the finest Austrian traditions of that fine orchestra.[72]

Vienna had an interesting musical experience in 1956 when Marcel Prawy, a young Austrian who had fallen in love with the light music in America during the war and returned to introduce it to the Austrians, persuaded the *Volksoper* to offer Cole Porter's "Kiss Me, Kate." It took Vienna by storm and remained on the *Volksoper* repertoire for many months.

The producer of "Kiss Me, Kate" in Vienna was Julius Rudel, a Viennese who has done yeoman service as a great exponent of contemporary American music. He studied at the Vienna Academy but came to New York at the age of seventeen, received most of his musical education here, and found his interest in the newer music whether European or American. That was partly because at the age of twenty-two he was called to the New York City Opera, a secondary opera in New York where one almost had to try new talent, new productions, and new music in order to avoid being a pallid reflection of the Metropolitan. That Julius Rudel enjoyed. Even his excursions away from the City Opera and the City Center were to the neglected institutions – he directed for the Third Street Music School Settlement and for the Chautauqua Opera Association and more recently received an honorary degree for bringing his opera to the University of Vermont.

Rudel, a serious person without the flare of most conductors for flamboyancy, had a genius for subordinating himself to the work. He was content to let the great names come and go on the Metropolitan's ever changing assembly line while he built up a membership of lesser-known artists, chiefly American "finds," who would have a loyalty to the City Center that was unusual among the international stars at the older opera houses.

After he followed Leinsdorf in 1957 as the General Director of the New York City Center he could indulge his passion for the lesser-known and the new. He was indefatigable in his search for talent among singers and composers. He developed stars who went on to the Met or on tour to Europe but who were generally eager to return when Rudel needed them. He has done many of the interesting but neglected

European operas but he has been enormously interested in contemporary American opera. The Ford Foundation has helped him take the more promising of them on American tours. In brief, Rudel was one of the finest of the many Austro-American masters of music whose feeling for music was orginally Austrian but who have devoted themselves to the development of an American school of music.[73]

After the Hitler period there were very few great Austrian musical figures who came to America to stay. Austria's own cultural life had again become vibrant with recovery and optimism, and, fortunately for the republic on the Danube, Austrian artists were going on tour to America only to return to Vienna. There was an occasional arrival like Hans Rosbaud (b. Graz, 1895) who came in 1960 to conduct the New York Philharmonic, but the vast majority of the new names in the arts were those of visitors and not of immigrants.

It is indeed fortunate that musical Austrians have invaded America in such numbers because American students of music have not crowded into Austria. In the 19th century Americans went to Germany for their music or to Paris and even to Switzerland in preference to Austria. Vienna was somehow not in the American orbit and it might become the mecca for young Ruben Goldmark, because he was the nephew of the Austrian composer Carl Goldmark, but it was *terra incognita* for Americans like composer MacDowell who studied in Paris and all over Germany without more than a pleasant visit to Vienna's music shrines. Composer Reginald De Koven, a native of Connecticut, was one of the few to study on the banks of the Danube and his best-known works were, perhaps for that reason, operettas.[74]

A few more American music students found Vienna in the 20th century. William Schuman studied conducting at Salzburg.[75] And soon after World War II H. C. Robbins Landon, the distinguished American musicologist and founder of the Haydn Society, went to Vienna to delve into the mysteries of Haydn.[76] A flood of young American music students came over in the 1950's with Senator Fulbright's exchange program that was simultaneously sending young Austrians — but fewer in music — over to the United States. And World War II was not only followed by music tours and summer courses for musically-minded American visitors but there appeared some more substantial projects like Oberlin's "junior year" for its music students at the Salzburg *Mozarteum*. In 1960 Oberlin gave an honorary degree to Director Preussner of the Salzburg *Mozarteum*.[77]

From Caruso's time on, the opera stars and the composers from America have been rather well represented in Austria. Caruso gave guest performances there year after year.[78] John Philip Sousa included Vienna in his European tour although he had to ask whether Austrians were still familiar with "The Blue Danube."[79] Dimitri Mitropoulos was so well known there that his death in 1960 was mourned in Vienna as it was in New York.[80] And more than a handful of Americans have braved a very modest *honorarium* to sing in Vienna.

Regina Resnik of the Metropolitan appeared at the *Staatsoper*. And George London, Leontyne Price, Therese Stich-Randall, Camilla Williams, and Jean Madeira are all stars of the first magnitude who are doubtless even more at home at the *Staatsoper* than on the boards at the Metropolitan. When the historic *Theater an der Wien* was reopened in 1963 with Berg's "Lulu," Evelyn Lear, the American soprano, sang in the title role. American Fulbright program grantees, like Fred Guthrie at the State Opera and Eleanor Schneider at the *Volksoper*, were to be found in the provincial operas as well as in Vienna.

Austrian performers of music, even more than the Americans, are constantly on tour and the Austrian musical invasion of the United States continues with the arrival every season of Austrian artists and musical groups and their recordings and films and television appearances. Musicians are usually internationalists and those of little Austria even more so than those of the larger lands. And they began visiting America after mid-century, not as outcasts seeking refuge or because American dollars are enticing, but because the American musical world has become a vital, interesting place.

This Austrian musical invasion included such fine groups as the Wiener Oktett, composed of members of the Philharmonic Orchestra, which came often in the post-war years, and the chamber orchestra, the Wiener Solisten, a fourteen-man string ensemble, that first invaded the United States in 1964. The superb Vienna Philharmonic Orchestra came, which Krips and American food packages[81] had helped to revive at the end of the war.

By 1963 the younger Vienna Symphony with its interest in contemporary music of the Schönberg school was packing for its American premiere. The charming *Sängerknaben*, the Vienna Choir Boys, who dated back to the Emperor Maximilian I and had included Haydn and Schubert in their ranks, were visiting the United States annually soon after the war's end. And Walt Disney's "Almost Angels," a delightful film of the *Sängerknaben*, reached the United States in 1962. The German-made Trapp-family film, "The Sound of Music," seemed to go on forever from one motion picture theater to another. But the Rodgers and Hammerstein version with the same title and Julie Andrews in the star role was the most amazing film success that America had ever seen. It broke all world records!

In America the Salzburg Music Festivals remained, with the possible exception of the Spanish Riding School in Vienna, Austria's best-known institution. Americans visited the Festivals in swarms and the music was heard almost everywhere on the American radio. The Vienna and Bregenz festivals were also broadcast here on dozens of stations and there were "repeats" on many a program throughout the year.[82] The Salzburg performance of "Rosenkavalier" came in 1963 in its entirety as a magnificent color film. The Austrian ensemble "Vienna on Parade" brought the more popular Austrian waltz, march and operetta music to America's large music halls in 1958 and the following years.

Some of the musical Austrians who come and go are so well known here that they appear among the few foreign-born in "Who's Who in America." There was the handsome soprano Leonie Rysanek-Grossmann (b. Vienna, 1928) who sang in opera at San Francisco and at the Metropolitan, the baritone Eberhard von Wächter (b. Vienna, 1929) who came to Dallas and the Met in 1960 and the tenor Sebastian Feiersinger (b. Austria, 1913) who also made guest appearances at the Metropolitan and in San Francisco.

"Who's Who in America" also listed two fine young Austrian pianists, Jörg Demus (b. St. Pölten, 1928) and Paul Badura-Skoda (b. Vienna, 1927) who discovered America in the 1950's. And Vienna's superb Friedrich Gulda (b. Vienna, 1930) made his American debut at Carnegie Hall when he was twenty and remained a favorite among pianists on the American concert platform and in our recordings.[83] The promising young pianist, Alfred Brendel (b. Wiesenberg, Moravia, 1931), already known here through his recordings, toured America in 1963 and in later years.[84]

The great voices of the *Staatsoper* were always to be heard in New York and frequently throughout musical America. There were Elisabeth Höngen and Erich Kunz and Walter Berry, Otto Edelmann and Carl Dönch. Elisabeth Schwarzkopf (b. Jarotschin, then West Prussia, now Poland, 1915) who became so dear to the Viennese has visited here time after time. She sang with the San Francisco opera in 1955, with the Metropolitan for the first time in 1964—65, and with the great American orchestras in other cities extracting superlatives from the critics: "Her art is one of the supreme displays in the world of music . . . flawless singer . . . Schwarzkopf Recital Tops Rare Feast of Music."[85] Soprano Irmgard Seefried (b. Köngetried, Bavaria, 1919) was another of the most charming of the visitors at America's Metropolitan Opera from Vienna where she had played at the opera since 1943.[86] She reminded some of Elisabeth Schumann (b. Merseburg, 1885 — d. New York, 1952), another German-born soprano with a great following at Vienna's opera, who had come to America in the "Rosenkavalier" back in 1914 and had returned here to settle with the Thirty-eighters and to teach at the Curtis Institute.[87] Vienna's Ljuba Welitsch (b. Borissowo near Varna, 1913), the "Bulgarian soprano" who first played her famous "Salome" role on the banks of the Danube in 1944, found fame in the same role at the Met in 1949.[88] Paul Schöffler (b. Dresden, 1897), the baritone who appeared year after year at the Met, was also for years a star of the Vienna opera. Another baritone, Otto Wiener, made his Metropolitan debut as Hans Sachs in 1962. Sena Jurinac, originally Strebenka (b. Travnik, Yugoslavia, 1921; Vienna opera debut 1945) made her Metropolitan debut in 1960.[89] And Hilde Güden (b. Vienna, 1922), one of the darlings of the Vienna opera, found the Metropolitan on Rudolf Bing's invitation in 1951 and appeared here so often that "Who's Who" listed her and gave New York as her home.

It was doubtless fortunate for both Austria and the United States that the dictator of Austrian music and opera in the early 1960's, Herbert von Karajan (b. Salzburg, 1908), came so often to conduct in the United States. He was a student of the Salzburg *Mozarteum* who gave up the piano to conduct and to manage, first in Germany and then in Vienna and at the Salzburg Festivals. He had appointments later in Berlin and Milan while his Austrian assignments gave him responsibilities for virtually all Austrian state music and opera. A man of tremendous energy he still found time for an occasional American visit and his fine recordings are innumerable. In 1961, for instance, he came with another guest conductor from Vienna, Karl Böhm, on tour with the Berlin Philharmonic Orchestra. His name, while he was associated primarily with Vienna and later when he transferred his loyalties to Berlin became a familiar one to the American world of music.[90]

Karajan's presence in the United States was an indication that the musical partnership of the two lands had been well established.The Austrians contributed mightily to the emergence of fine music in America and they continue, even now that musical America has come of age, to make their contributions to it.

[1] Gilbert Chase, *America's Music*, N.Y. 1955, ch. XXVIII.

[2] *Ibid.*, pp. 597ff.; W. Jenks, *Vienna and the Young Hitler*, N.Y. 1960, p. 202; Dika Newlin, *Bruckner, Mahler and Schoenberg* N. Y. 1947, pp. 221ff.; Everett Helm, "Six German Composers," *American-German Review*, Dec. Jan. 1956–57, p. 12.

[3] Newlin, *op. cit.*, p. 276.

[4] *Neue Österreichische Biographie*, vol. XII, Wien 1957, p. 209.

[5] *Ibid.*; David Ewen, *Twentieth Century Music*, N.Y. 1952, p. 20; Marion Bauer, *Twentieth Century Music*, N.Y. and London 1947, pp. 227–28.

[6] *Die Presse*, Wien, 19 Apr. 1962; Hans Moldenhauer, *The Death of Anton Webern*, N.Y. 1961.

[7] *ASCAP Biographical Dictionary, 1952*, and Winthrop Sargeant in the *New Yorker*, 20 Oct. 1962, p. 62.

[8] *Who's Who*, 1952–53; David Ewen, *Composers of Today*, N.Y. 1934; *Baker's Biographical Dictionary of Musicians*, 4th ed., N.Y. 1940.

[9] *Who's Who in America*, 1962–63; David Ewen, *Complete Book of Twentieth Century Music*, 1959, pp. 438–39. Elizabeth Gyring, a Viennese, may also be mentioned as a composer who came to the U.S. before World War II. Her music was contemporary in character. Cf. article by V. Tauber in *American-German Review*, Aug.-Sept. 1962, p. 30.

[10] *Who's Who*, 1962–63; *Books Abroad*, Spring 1959, p. 157; David Ewen, *The Book of Modern Composers*, N.Y. 1950, pp. 353, 358.

[11] David Ewen, *Encyclopedia of the Opera*, N.Y. 1955.

[12] *ASCAP Biographical Dictionary*, p. 300.

[13] Marion Bauer, *op. cit.*, p. 369.

[14] For the quotation and other information on Stolz, see *Austrian Information*, 14 Apr. 1962. See also *Wer ist Wer in Österreich*, Wien 1957, p. 192, and Baker, *op. cit.*, p. 1577. Baker and Brockhaus give 1882 as the year of his birth.

[15] *Current Biography*, 1958, pp. 242–43; *TV Guide*, Feb. 10–16, 1962, pp. 6–10.

[16] *Current Biography*, 1958; *TV Guide*, Feb. 10–16, 1962; numerous reviews and articles. According to the *Washington Post* of 3 Dec. 1965, Loewe decided after the great success of "Camelot" that he was not going to work any more. The royalties he donated to the Palm Springs (Calif.) Hospital may have reached the million dollar mark.

[17] *Universal Jewish Encyclopedia*, V, p. 81; *Who's Who in Austria*, 1954. Graf worked with the U.S. occupation authorities in Vienna.

[18] *Ibid.*; Baker, *op. cit.*

[19] *Austrian Information*, 14 Apr. 1962, p. 8.

[20] *Who's Who*, 1962–63.

[21] *Austrian Information*, 31 Dec. 1961.

[22] *Who's Who of American Women*, 2nd ed., 1961.

[23] Baker, *op. cit.*

[24] *Who's Who in Commerce and Industry*, Chicago, 1959.

[25] *Who's Who*, 1952–53; Baker, *op. cit.*, p. 451.

[26] Cf. biographical note in his *Brahms, His Life and Work*, N.Y. 1961; *Who's Who*, 1962–63.

[27] *Who's Who*, 1962–63.

[28] *Directory of American Scholars*, 3rd ed.

[29] *Who's Who*, 1962–63.

[30] *Austrian Information*, 16 Dec. 1961.

[31] *International Who is Who in Music*, 1951.

[32] *Who's Who of American Women*, 2nd ed., 1961.

[33] Quoted from Abram Chasins, *Speaking of Pianists*. See also *Who's Who*, 1962–63.

[34] Walter Slezak, *What Time's the Next Swan*, N.Y. 1962, p. 192. Miss Schwarz died in Vienna in 1964.

[35] *Who's Who*, 1962–63.

[36] *Washington Post*, 20 May 1963, p. B6.

[37] In his article in *Österreich und die angelsächsische Welt*, Wien–Stuttgart 1961. See also *Who's Who*, 1952–53, and *Who's Who in Central Europe*, Zurich 1937, which calls her Austrian.

[38] F. J. Brown and J. S. Roucek, *Our Racial and National Minorities*, p. 305, states that Jeritza was Austrian.

[39] *Ibid.*, p. 154.

[40] Baker, *op. cit.*, p. 962.

[41] *Op. cit.*, p. 1620.

[42] *New Yorker*, 13 Jan. 1962, p. 64.

[43] *Current Biography*, 1959, pp. 254–56.

[44] For Bikel see *Current Biography*, 1960. Schlamme's numerous recordings carry biographical information on the jackets.

[45] *Who's Who*, 1952–53.

[46] *Austrian Information*, 16 Dec. 1961, has a note on Kling. Morini and Ilmer appear in *Who's Who*, 1962–63, Doktor in *Who's Who in Austria*, 1959–1960.

[47] *Grove's Dictionary of Music and Musicians*, 5th ed., 9 vols., 1 Supp., London and N.Y., 1954–61, VII, pp. 502–03; David Ewen, ed., *Living Musicians*, 1st Supp., 1957, p. 136.

[48] *Die Presse*, 1 May 1962.

[49] Baker, *op. cit.*, p. 1317.

[50] *Who's Who of American Women*, 2nd, ed.

[51] *Die Presse*, 6 March 1961; *Austrian Information*, 18 Mar. 1961.

[52] *Who's Who*, 1938–39.

[53] *Who's Who*, 1952–53; Baker, *op. cit.*; Hope Stoddard, *Symphony Conductors*, N.Y. 1957, pp. 365–66.

[54] *Who's Who*, 1962–63; *Who's Who in Austria*, 1954. Bing became a British citizen in 1946.

[55] Shirley Fleming, "Josef Krips," *High Fidelity*, Oct. 1961, p. 8. See also Stoddard, *op. cit.*, pp. 112–16; David Ewen, *Encyclopedia of Concert Music*, N.Y. 1959, p. 243; *Austrian Information*, 28 Apr. and 15 Sept. 1962.

[56] Baker, *op. cit.*, 1958 ed.

[57] *Washington Post*, 2 May 1965.

[58] Stoddard, *op. cit.*, p. 386.

[59] *Ibid.*

[60] *Ibid.*

[61] *Who's Who*, 1952–53; Stoddard, *op. cit.*, p. 307.

[62] Stoddard, *op. cit.*, p. 352; *Who's Who*, 1952–53.

[63] *Who's Who*, 1962–63.

[64] Baker, *op. cit.*, p. 1370; *Austrian Information*, 14 Jan. 1961.

[65] Stoddard, *op. cit.*, p. 300.

[66] *Ibid.*, p. 347.

[67] *Riemann Musiklexikon*, Personenteil: L–Z, Mainz 1961; Baker, *op. cit.*, p. 1572.

[68] Stoddard, *op. cit.*, p. 295; *Who's Who*, 1952–53; *Austrian Information*, 7 Aug. 1961.

[69] *Washington Post*, 18 Feb. 1962. Cf. *International Celebrity Register*, U.S. ed., p. 804; Ruth Berger, "Bruno Walter," *American-German Review*, Oct.-Nov. 1960; David Hall, *The Record Book*, N.Y. 1940, p. 12.

[70] *Austrian Information*, 31 Mar. 1962.

[71] Stoddard, *op. cit.*, pp. 236–42; *Who's Who*, 1962–63.

[72] *Who's Who*, 1960–61; *Saturday Review*, 13 Febr. 1960; David Ewen, *Dictators of the Baton*, Chicago and N.Y. 1943, pp. 205–15.

[73] *Who's Who*, 1960–61; "Rudel of City Center" by Kolodin, *Saturday Review*, 13 Febr. 1960; Winthrop Sargeant, "Portraits," *New Yorker*, 20 Oct. 1962, pp. 57–82.

[74] Chase, *op. cit.*, pp. 619–20; J. T. Howard, *Our American Music*, N.Y. 1946, p. 655.

[75] Howard, *op. cit.*, mentions several little-known names.

[76] Baker, *op. cit.*, p. 904; *High Fidelity*, Apr. 1960, p. 40.

[77] *American-German Review*, Mar. 1961.

[78] Maria Jeritza, *Sunlight and Song*, N.Y. and London 1924, pp. 157–59.

[79] H. E. Jacob, *Johann Strauss, Father and Son; a century of light music*, N.Y. 1940, p. 361.

[80] *Austrian Information*, 12 Nov. 1960.

[81] Dr. Carleton Smith received Austria's Great Medal of Honor in 1960 for his administration of American relief to help the desperate Philharmonic Orchestra in 1945. *Austrian Information*, 26 Nov. 1960.

[82] The Salzburg Festival of 1961 was heard on 28 American radio stations, the Vienna Festival on 26 and that of Bregenz on 10. *Austrian Information*, 13, Jan. 1962.

[83] Baker, *op. cit.*, p. 628; *Austrian Information*, 29 Oct. 1960.

[84] *Austrian Information*, 26 Jan. 1963.

[85] *Washington Post*, 5 Dec. 1960, p. A27. Cf. David Ewen, *Encyclopedia of Opera*.

[86] *Baker's Biographical Dictionary of Musicians*, 5th ed., N. Y. 1958.

[87] *Ibid.*

[88] *Ibid.*

[89] *Austrian Information*, 27 May 1961, p. 9.

[90] *Österreicher der Gegenwart*, Wien 1951, p. 139; *Die Presse*, 2 Mar. 1961, p. 7; Baker, *op. cit.*

CHAPTER XI

THE AUSTRIAN IN JOURNALISM

Austria has had little influence upon American journalism. Its sons in America have had, considering the language barrier, considerable. In the second half of the 19th century the Austrian pen was most significant in the German-language press and the German-language press was in those years not be discounted. It was by far the most potent foreign-language press in melting-pot America.

Francis Joseph Grund (b. Klosterneuburg, 1798 – d. Philadelphia, 1863) was typical of the Austro-American as journalist. He was known in America as a German. The solid volume that he wrote as "the Jacksonian Tocqueville" was called, in its Harper Torchbook edition (1959), "Aristocracy in America: from the sketch-book of a German Nobleman." And Grund was typical in that he began as a German-language editor (his early Philadelphia venture was the "Allgemeine Deutsche Zeitung"[1]) but soon found himself, long before he became Washington correspondent of the "Philadelphia Public Ledger," using English and playing a vigorous and ever-changing part in American political life.[2]

Grund, who had had a liberal education at the University of Vienna and had fled his native land as a consequence of the reactionary *Karlsbader Beschlüsse*, came to Boston to teach in 1823, wrote campaign biographies for Van Buren and Harrison, received a couple of consular appointments, changed his politics time and again, and died of apoplexy in a police station when, the story goes, he thought himself pursued by the Democrats after his turn to Republicanism.

Grund was a fascinating figure whose "Aristocracy in America" might well have ranked with Tocqueville's "Democracy in America," had the titles been reversed.[3] Grund was a keen, intelligent observer and admirer of American democracy. It was a sad commentary upon American letters, however, that Grund had to go to London to get a publisher for such a book on America (it was published in London in 1839) and the first American edition appeared, almost unheralded, 120 years later!

We have already mentioned another refugee from the repression of the Metternich era (the censor in his case), Dr. Samuel Ludvigh, born in 1801 on the Hungarian border of Styria and best known in America as the radical Baltimore editor of the free-thought *Literaturblatt*, "Die Fackel."[4] He had seen the Far East and the Near East, come to Philadelphia almost penniless in 1837, moved on to Baltimore where he championed tolerance, pre-Marxian socialism, anti-slavery, anti-clericalism, and Van Buren for President. Ludvigh died in 1869 in Cincinnati, one of those fascinating revolutionaries who were too advanced for both Metternich and American democracy.

Ludvigh was a forerunner of the Forty-eighters – not typical, for the Forty-eighters were individualists who conformed to no type. They were, in any event – and especially the refugee journalists – men of conviction whom conservative Austria could ill afford to lose and whom America, even if the nativist movement was to use them for whipping boys, was fortunate to acquire.

Of all the radical Austrian Forty-eighters Friedrich Hassaurek (b. Vienna, 1831 – d. Paris, 1885) was the first. He was brilliant, a great speaker in both German and English, a bold opponent of Metternich reaction in Europe and of slavery in America, a champion of the immigrants who were swindled at America's ports of entry, an agnostic, and a violent anti-clerical.

The young Hassaurek had of course risked his neck in the 1848 Revolution, was wounded fighting in the Student Legion, and fled to Cincinnati where he became a significant figure. His newspaper "Der Hochwächter" was radically utopian. Hassaurek assumed leadership of the liberal Germans in his area, supported Lincoln with his fiery tongue, and only became conservative when the "German Fenians" called upon him to support their plans for a liberal world revolution based upon America. Lincoln made him American minister to Ecuador.

Hassaurek's radicalism was diluted a bit in his later years. His "Cincinnati Volksblatt," which he edited after the Civil War with help from his half brother Leopold Markbreit (b. Vienna, 1842 – d. Cincinnati, 1909),[5] was less radical than the "Hochwächter." He opposed Republican reconstruction in the South, and he supported his fellow journalist Horace Greeley for president in 1872. He was a prophet to the more liberal of the Forty-eighters, a menace to the conservative German Lutherans and Catholics.[6]

The refugees of 1848 were, almost to a man, abolitionists. Most of them joined the new Republican Party and helped to elect Lincoln. Benedict Prieth, for instance, was a Tyrolese whose service in the Vienna Student Legion ended in a Salzburg prison, who turned to journalism, and who emigrated in the late fifties to Newark. There he founded the pro-Republican "New Jersey Freie Zeitung," the state's principal German newspaper, which lasted for generations after Prieth's death in 1879.[7] Karl Burgthal's "Union and Washington Correspondent," published partly in German and partly in English, was established in 1856 to champion the Republican cause.[8]

Heinrich Börnstein's two autobiographical volumes, "Fünfundsiebzig Jahre" (Leipzig 1884), constitute a fascinating account of a talented Forty-eighter journalist, whom we have already mentioned, who spent a very useful decade in the United States before Lincoln sent him to Bremen as American consul. He was a native of Hamburg (b. 1805 – d. Vienna, 1892) who had sampled medicine, the theater, and journalism in his early years in Vienna. He arrived with his wife at New Orleans in

1849 with 24 trunks and means enough to try to escape from the coffee that he couldn't distinguish from tea by pushing on to St. Louis. He never did like American food. In St. Louis he performed miracles for the German theater and opera, promoted a kind of Vienna-coffeehouse-readingroom where newspapers and magazines were available at five cents a visit, tried to improve the beer of St. Louis, and edited and then acquired the ultra-liberal "Anzeiger des Westens," one of the most important of America's German sheets.[9]

In St. Louis an Austrian prophet of conservatism, Franz Joseph Saler (b. Vorarlberg, 1808 – d. 1893),[10] rose up to oppose the deistic "Anzeiger des Westens" of the prophet of free-thought, Heinrich Börnstein. Saler was a mason's apprentice at twenty-five when he emigrated to Great Falls, New York. He reached St. Louis by way of a soap factory where he worked in Pittsburgh. In St. Louis he turned to religion and found a way to operate two godly papers, the "Tageschronik" and the "Herold des Glaubens." The former was, we are told, the second German Catholic daily published in this country. The second, a weekly which Saler only rescued from oblivion, was doubtless more important than his German Catholic calendar, the first in the country, that he inaugurated in 1855. Germans and Austrians have made calendars vastly more important, and charming, than we have in America. As one might expect the battle in St. Louis between Börnstein and Saler was thought of by the American element as a battle of two trouble-makers within the German camp.

Börnstein was of Christian parentage; the Forty-eighter Isidor Bush (sic) was not only a Jew and the Vienna publisher of Jewish periodicals, he was said to have been the grandson of the first Jew ever raised to the nobility in Austria. And, before he left New York to go on to St. Louis to try his hand at farming and business and emancipation (he was a radical abolitionist), Bush published the first Jewish weekly in America, the short-lived "Israel's Herold."[11]

Bush had been born in Prague and had come to Vienna to learn printing there with his father. He was only one of a considerable group of "Germans" born in Bohemia and Moravia who had come to Vienna, involved themselves in the unhappy revolution of 1848, and distinguished themselves later in journalism in America. Heinrich Binder of the "Illinois-Staatszeitung" and "Puck" was a Vienna-born exception.[12] Better known was another editor of the "Illinois-Staatszeitung," Adolf Wiener (b. Prague, 1807 – d. New York, 1867) who had changed his name to Wiesner when he changed his religion from Judaism to Catholicism. He had tried the law unsuccessfully in Vienna, the *Burgtheater* showed little interest in his dramas, the censor jailed him for publishing without approval, and he served as a leftist at the Frankfurt Parliament. Wiesner was too much of a fire-eater for Austria. His attempts at literary and political journalism in New York, Baltimore, and Chicago brought him some fame but he was homesick and died in New York on his way back to Europe.[13]

One of the Vienna law students who came to America because the Austrian regime had sentenced them to death was the roving journalist Johann Rittig (b. Prague, 1820 – d. 1885). The titles of two of his American ventures, "Unabhängige" and "Die Menschenrechte," indicated that his politics were not conservative. He became an editor of the "New-Yorker Staats-Zeitung" in 1857.[14]

The "Staats-Zeitung" was to become, through the years, the most significant of all the many German-language papers in the United States. And its greatest editor and publisher, the man who brought it to the zenith of its fame,[15] was another Austrian, Oswald Ottendorfer (b. Zwittau, Moravia, 1826 – d. New York, 1900). Ottendorfer who had studied law in Vienna as well as in Prague, had become so involved in the upheavals of '48, first in Vienna's Student Legion and then in Germany, that he fled via Switzerland to New York. There he was friendless, found first a factory job and then a haven with the "Staats-Zeitung," soon married the widow of its owner-publisher, gave up all his early hopes of returning to his dear Vienna, and became a "first citizen" of New York.

Ottendorfer's was a kind of Horatio Alger career. He injected his liberal (but not radical) philosophy into his newspaper and his concept of good citizenship into his daily life. His charities (including a home for the aged and a free library) were numerous. He refused his salary as alderman of the city. His politics was suspect only with those who called even reform-Democrats Copperheads. He fought Tammany, was nominated for mayor of New York by the anti-Tammany Democrats (his bad health preventing his campaigning for the position) and supported every liberal Democrat. His admirer, Grover Cleveland, declared that "I look to him as to a father." Oswald Ottendorfer was far more than an immigrant journalist.[16]

The German Thomas Nast was not the only Central European to distinguish himself in political caricature in America. Joseph Keppler (b. Vienna, 1838 – d. New York, 1894), who learned drawing at the Vienna Academy of Applied Arts, may have been less significant politically than Nast but more important for his contributions to the art of political cartooning.[17] He was the innovator of the color cartoon and the owner of the delightful humorous magazine "Puck." His full-page cartoons had an exciting freshness about them utterly unlike the uninspiring American cartoons of the mid-century.

Father Keppler had migrated to Missouri in 1848 and Joseph, who had tried the stage back in Austria with no great success, followed in 1867. His first humorous weekly, "Die Vehme," was short-lived and he established another in German that he called "Puck." He moved on to New York, worked for "Leslie's Illustrated Magazine," revived the German-language "Puck," and then tried a companion edition in English. It was a success and by 1890 it had 23,000 subscribers.

Joseph Keppler was a liberal, anti-Tammany Democrat. He was conservative on the labor issue but his fine cartoons contributed mightily to decency in politics and sane Reconstruction in the South. He found a few Austrians for his staff, like the Viennese Emil Knotser who had worked in Milwaukee on the "Seebote,"[18] and he imported some from the homeland. The German "Puck" died with Keppler but the English edition went on through the first World War.

Since Keppler's day there have been other newcomers from Austria with their journalistic specialties. Charles P. B. Medlenka, a "Bohemian German," published "Die Deutsche Post" three times a week at Houston, Texas, in the early 1880's and seems to have intrigued and bewildered his readers with his brand of German that, unlike most good Bohemian German that both Austrians and Germans have been happy to claim, was decidedly difficult to comprehend.[19] John Francis Knott (b. 1878), a cartoonist after 1905 with the "Dallas News," received honorable mention in a Pulitzer Prize competition.[20] The work of William Sharp, born in 1900 or 1901 in Austrian Galicia and exiled from Germany for his anti-Nazi cartoons, can be seen in the Metropolitan Museum of Art and the Library of Congress.[21] The Vienna-born Elizabeth Clawson produced distinguished photography for America's best-known magazines.[22] Another Viennese, George Gershon Shor (b. 1884), served his journalistic apprenticeship in Providence and Boston, managed some big-city newspapers and news services and retired in 1953 from a long career with the "American Weekly."[23] William Frisch (b. Austria 1854) came to Baltimore as a boy and made a career with the "Baltimore American."[24]

On the unusual side among the Austro-American journalists were the editor of the great "Jewish Encyclopedia" (12 vols., 1901–05), Isidore Singer (b. Mährisch-Weisskirchen, Moravia, 1859–d. New York, 1939) with a journalistic background in Vienna, Berlin and Paris;[25] the Vienna-born Alfred Jacobson who managed the "Neue Zeitung," the vigorous American occupation newspaper in Berlin after World War II and who became an American Foreign Service Officer; and three fashion experts from Vienna, Francis Hutter (b. 1881), who immigrated before World War I to manage the McCall pattern department for several decades; Berta Mohr who started her own syndicated fashion column in 1946, and Trude Allma who did features in the world of design for "Parents Magazine," "Look," and "Life." It is surprising that so many Austrians born in German-speaking homes could make themselves so completely at home in English-language journalism.

Hungarians and Germans both claim Joseph Pulitzer (b. Mako, Hungary, 1847 – d. Charleston, S. C., 1911), founder of the "St. Louis Post-Dispatch" and owner of the "New York World," one of the greatest names in American journalism. A Solomon would doubtless judge him half Hungarian and half Austrian: his father was Jewish-Hungarian and he lived in Hungary, but his mother, born Louise Berger, was Catholic-Austrian, a branch of his father's family was Austrian, and German was his native tongue. The Austrian army rejected him, not because of his nationality but because of his health, and he went to Hamburg, enlisted with an agent of the

Union army, and came to America in 1864. The Austro-German claimants to the young Pulitzer might also point out that his regiment in the Union forces was largely German and Austrian and that his early journalistic and political career in St. Louis was not with the Hungarians but with the German-Americans and in the German language. The well-known "Westliche Post" of St. Louis was his first journalistic venture. And when he was naturalized in March 1867 he described himself as a subject of the Emperor of Austria. Even as late as 1872 he felt competent to campaign for Greeley for president only in German-speaking areas and in the German language. The Vienna-born founder of "Puck," Joseph Keppler, was one of Pulitzer's closest friends. Austria assuredly has some claim to this greatest of all American journalists born on Habsburg soil.[26]

Concerning Gustav Pollak's (b. Vienna, 1849 – d. Cambridge, Mass., 1919) nationality there can be no doubt. He was born and brought up in Vienna, found a distinguished career in New York, with "The Nation" and the "Evening Post," essayed politics (he was a Gold Democrat in 1896), and, unlike too many Austro-Americans, never denied his origins. He helped to found the German-American Reform Union in 1892 and over ten years later he was lecturing at Johns Hopkins University on the Austrian dramatists and publishing his "Franz Grillparzer and the Austrian Drama" (1907). He became one of America's finest literary journalists.[27]

The Austrian role in America's German-language press is difficult to assess. Editors like Ottendorfer of the "Staats-Zeitung," whose Austrian news was worse than indifferent, were known as Germans, not as Austrians. Their journals sold chiefly to German-Americans, with a weak intermixture of Austro-Americans.

And within the German-language press, which led the foreign press in America by wide margins, there were no Austrian ventures of any consequence. Arndt's fine volume on "German-American Newspapers" has even to question the dates of publication of the "Oesterreichisch-Ungarische Zeitung" and of the "Oesterreichisch-Amerikanische Zeitung" which were published in New York and Chicago and which, after merging in New York, had a sorry circulation in 1890 of only 4,000.[28] The weekly "Illustrierte Nachrichten aus Deutschland, Oesterreich und der Schweiz," which Arndt believes may have been inaugurated in New York about 1880, had a circulation of only 5,500 in 1881.[29] The papers published for peoples outside core-Austria (e. g. "Hungaria" in New York and "Siebenbürgisch-Amerikanisches Volksblatt" later in Cleveland[30]) were far more prominent than the almost non-existent "Austrian" press before 1914. The Austrians must have read the German papers. Austrian immigrants like Hans Raid (b. Bregenz, 1889) and Walter Palme (b. 1886 in "Austria Hungary") worked on the German papers. Both Raid and Palme edited the German-language "Baltimore Correspondent" during the second quarter of the 20th century and Palme went on, in 1947, to the "New-Yorker Staats-Zeitung."[31]

Hugo Karl Tippmann (b. Bohemia, 1875), the writer of ballads and drinking songs after he came to America in 1910, employed the journalistic experience he received in Styria, Salzburg, and Vienna in founding a German-American newspaper in the ill-fated year 1914. He called it first "Die Oesterreich-Amerikanische Zeitung" and later "Der Patriot." His monthly "Zeppelin" changed its name in 1917 to "Eulenspiegel" but the war was unfavorable to any German title and it died like all his other ventures. Tippmann was still trying in 1938 by taking over the New York edition of the "American Herold."[32]

The "Oesterreich-Ungarische Post" of 1914 was a Milwaukee venture that was so unsuccessful that Arndt merely lists it as having been traced in the city directory for 1914.[33] The weekly "Austria" is another item about which Arndt is undecided even as to the year of its establishment (1909?) although he indicates that it had a circulation of 7,850 in 1912. There was, unfortunately, no doubt about "The American Monthly: fair play for Germany and Austria-Hungary," which editor George Sylvester Viereck damned with his not-too-popular name in 1914–15 in a very futile effort to counteract what Viereck called British war propaganda.[34] The Germans and the Austrians needed champions but Viereck the propagandist was not the St. George that they needed. And the fact that Louis N. Hammerling of the American Association of Foreign Language Newspapers (b. Honolulu, 1874), who acquired the reputation of being a racketeer in the sale of advertizing for the foreign press, was dishonestly advertized by the nativists as being foreign-born was no help to the Austro-German cause. He had, indeed, graduated from the University of Lemberg. He was accused of having made a small fortune in helping the Republicans harvest the German vote, in being similarly helpful to the Brewer's Association, and in spending a subsidy from the Austrian, as well as from the German, government. He was "exposed" by the editor of the Croat "Narodni List" when the Habsburg nationalities were venting their spleen upon anything they thought to be Austrian.[35]

The proliferation in the 20th century of papers representing other segments of the old monarchy was no help to the Austrian cause. One Hungarian monthly might promote the candidacy of Otto of Habsburg to the Hungarian throne but the highly nationalistic Czech, Slavic, and Magyar press used German Austria only as a whipping boy. There were forty Hungarian-language papers in America by 1947 and they were all, it is safe to say, anti-Austrian. A Hungarian-American editor could write in 1917 that "If German militarism were destroyed today, it should be resurrected tomorrow that it might save civilization." But a year later, when Austria had lost the war, the same editor declared, "For several centuries the Austrian double-eagle has dug its talons deeply into the entrails of the Hungarian national body . . ."[36] Even the Croats, who had been comparatively loyal to the Habsburgs, and long-suffering under the Hungarians, joined all of the other monarchy nationalities striving for independence by denouncing the German Austrians. And the American press, patriotic enough during the war to condemn anything Austrian, was quick to support the cause of the "oppressed" nationalities. The German Austrians had always been slow to assert themselves in the United States; the war forced even the finest of them, like the great Fritz Kreisler, into seclusion.

After World War I the name Austria all but disappeared from the foreign-language press. "Eintracht," a weekly which began publication in Chicago in 1922 and reached a circulation of 4,000 in 1940, called itself the "Offizielles Organ der deutsch-österreich-ungarischen Vereine – Unabhängiges Organ der Österreicher, Burgenländer und Deutsch-Ungarn in Nord-Amerika" and the *Burgenländer* but not the Austrians appeared in the subtitle of the "Deutsch-Ungarischer Familien Kalender" (1939–1952).[37] But "Aufbau," a substantial sheet published in New York since the early Nazi days for Jewish refugees and still boasting a circulation of over 30,000 in 1959, was doubtless the most influential paper among the Austrian new-comers.[38]

The refugees' Assembly for a Democratic Austrian Republic, which helped to keep alive the concept of a free Austria, brought out its first paper in 1942, "Freiheit für Österreich." Both the Assembly and the paper changed names with confusing frequency. The latter soon became the "Austro-American Tribune" and then, finally, in 1948, "Forum and Tribune." The émigré group in New York also published a monthly for youth, "Freie Österreichische Jugend" (1941–43) and "Jugend im Kampf" was its successor (published by Austrian Action Inc., Free Austrian Movement, and their Free Austrian Youth). The Catholic Austrian American League had its "Austria" in 1941 and some time later the Friends of Austrian Labor brought its monthly "Austrian Labor" across the sea from Graz and Vienna to New York.[39]

"Freiheit für Österreich" and its successors attracted more reputable contributors – people like Paul Muni, Einstein, Sforza, and Dorothy Thompson – than circulation. They gloated over every Nazi setback, rejoiced in stories of Austrian desertions from the Hitler armies, and ridiculed the idea of a Habsburg restoration. Although such papers appeared partly in English it is unlikely that they had any impact upon the general public.[4]

It is interesting to notice that of the forty-one Austrian-exile papers of the sorry years 1934 to 1946 eight were published in France, nine in Britain, and twelve in the United States. The others were published in Czechoslovakia, before the Nazis took over, Switzerland, Canada, the Argentine, Belgium, Sweden, and Uruguay.[41] Refugee Austrians were spread over much of the western world with the largest representation in the United States.

There were relatively few Austrian refugees of 1938 to establish themselves in American journalism. The language was the obvious barrier. Thus, personalities like Emilio von Hofmannsthal (b. Vienna, 1884), a gifted feature writer and scholar, who came in the troubled times by way of South America to New York, continued writing in German. Hofmannsthal made a career for himself as correspondent at the United Nations and at the age of eighty is still contributing to Vienna's "Die Furche" as well as to New York's "Staatszeitung."[42]

The few who could achieve bilingualism found places in American journalism. Henry Anatole Grunwald immigrated in 1940 to become a senior editor of "Time."[43] The Viennese Kurt D. Singer (b. 1911), who had edited an underground weekly in Berlin and contributed to the anti-Nazi cause in London, also reached New York in 1940 to lecture, write, and serve the North American Newspaper Alliance.[44] William S. Schlamm (b. Přzemysl, Galicia, 1904), who had received a degree from the University of Vienna and served a journalistic apprenticeship in both Vienna and Prague, came to serve the Luce publications and to write anti-Nazi books on world affairs.[45] And well-known among the handmaidens of journalism was Inge Moerath, a suberb photographer from Vienna, whose marriage to the even better-known American playwright, Arthur Miller, was deeply regretted in European journalistic circles.

Years before Hitler's tragic advent, Raoul H. Fleischmann's (b. Bad Ischl, 1885) parents had brought him to this country. He received an education at Princeton and Williams, worked four years in the Fleischmann family bakery and fourteen more years for General Baking Company after it had bought out the Fleischmann plant, and in 1925 he joined editor James Ross in a venture far removed from baking, the building of the "New Yorker" magazine. The "New Yorker" barely survived its first years. But the imagination and business competence of Fleischmann, combined with the editorial genius of Ross, saved it, and Fleischmann remained its president for many years, into the 1960's.[46]

Familiarity with the European scene when the American public was becoming increasingly interested in it and when the United States press had still a paucity of journalists who knew Europe well offered opportunities to a few gifted newcomers from Austria. Otto Zausmer, for instance, now associate editor of the "Boston Globe," found language no barrier and a European background a genuine asset. A self-confessed "frustrated psychiatrist" who had applied psychiatry in Austria to his studies in culture and literature (he had taken his doctorate at the University of Vienna, 1934, in German and Latin when psychiatry seemed economically unrewarding), Dr. Zausmer used much the same techniques that he had used in Vienna when he came to write of foreign and domestic affairs and social problems in "The Globe."

And Ernest S. Pisko, an editor of the "Christian Science Monitor," was one of the amazing Austrians who, in his case, required only three months in America before he was writing in English, first for the "Christian Century" and shortly afterwards for the "Monitor." Pisko was born and educated in Vienna, the son of a Viennese mother and a father of a Moravian family. He served in World War I on the Russian and Italian fronts. He then turned to publishing, worked with Steyrermühl's great publishing operation, edited several of its magazines, and found himself in trouble with the post-*Anschluss* regime. He was, however, released from prison after three months and told to leave "Greater Germany." He and his family came by way of Czechoslovakia to England, where he served as a butler, and then, in 1940, to the United States. He still professes his pride in his cultural heritage, which includes Goethe and Kant as well as Kafka and Mozart and Freud. He has received a Sigma Delta Chi award (1952) for a series of articles on Stalin, he has also the Austrian republic's Golden Honor Award, and, more important, he has the loyalty of readers of the "Monitor," one of America's influential papers, who follow his reporting on events in Europe and, occasionally, in Austria.[47]

One of the "New Yorker's" most brilliant writers and staff members was the Thirty-eighter Joseph Wechsberg (b. Mährisch-Ostrau, Moravia, 1907).[48] He studied, not only in Prague and Paris, but also at the *Hochschule für Welthandel* and the Conservatory of Music in Vienna, joined the "claque" at the Vienna opera, pursued his love of music as a violinist on a French boat, tried the Czech army, suffered suppression of his writing and arrest by the Gestapo, and found refuge for a time in the United States. He soon returned to Europe to enter Prague with the American army, discover that he could write books and articles in English, and do for the "New Yorker" some of the best of that magazine's many fine articles interpreting post-war Europe. Some of his articles were on the Austrian scene but, to the regret of many of his readers, the Austrian theme became neglected as Austria settled down after the treaty of 1955 and came to have less appeal for the American reader.

That was perhaps too typical of the history of Austrian journalism in America. Few of the Austrians who have plied the journalistic trade in this country have undertaken to tell the Austrian story here.

[1] K. J. R. Arndt, *German-American Newspapers*, Heidelberg 1961, p. 549.

[2] For Grund's career see the introduction to *Aristocracy in America*, N.Y. 1959; Wilhelm Schlag, "A Survey of Austrian Emigration to the United States," *Österreich und die angelsächsische Welt*, Wien 1961, p. 151; and, for an unfavorable criticism, Ernest Bruncken, *German Political Refugees in the United States during the Period from 1815—1860*, Chicago 1904, p. 25.

[3] Tocqueville wrote his book after ten months here, Grund his after over ten years.

[4] *Der Deutsche Pionier*, Feb. 1870, pp. 354—60, has a good article on Ludvigh, See also A. J. Schem, *Deutsch-amerikanisches Conversations-Lexikon*, 11 vols., N.Y. 1869—1874, VI, p. 657, and *Das Buch der Deutschen in Amerika*, Philadelphia 1909, which states that Ludvigh took over Minnesota's first German paper in the 1850's. He was the founder of "Die Fackel" in Baltimore.

[5] *Das Buch der Deutschen in Amerika*, p. 534.

[6] *Dictionary of American Biography;* Arndt, *op. cit.*, p. 446; Josef Nadler, *Literaturgeschichte des deutschen Volkes*, 4 vols., Berlin 1938—1941, IV, p. 115; Carl Wittke, *Refugees of Revolution*, Philadelphia 1952, *passim.*

[7] *Das Buch der Deutschen in Amerika*, pp. 520–21. This volume mentions relatively few Austrian journalists.

[8] Wittke, *op. cit.*, p. 208.

[9] *Fünfundsiebzig Jahre*, II, pp. 120–23. Wittke, *op. cit.*, has an excellent account of Börnstein.

[10] George Timpe, *Kath. Deutschtum in den Vereinigten Staaten von Amerika*, Freiburg 1937, pp. 9, 136.

[11] H. Simonhoff, *Jewish Notables in America*, N.Y. 1956, pp. 340–42; Wittke, *op. cit.*, p. 88; Schlag, *op. cit.*, p. 159; Max Grunwald, *Vienna*, Philadelphia 1936, p. 500.

[12] *Das Buch der Deutschen in Amerika*, p. 377.

[13] Constant v. Wurzbach, *Biographisches Lexikon des Kaiserthums Oesterreich*, 60 parts, Wien 1856–91, LVI, pp. 78–82. David Schwarz, Jewish Forty-eighter, achieved such a name in Cleveland journalism that the city's shops all closed for his funeral. Grunwald, *op. cit.*, pp. 512–13.

[14] E. W. Dobert, *Deutsche Demokraten in Amerika*, Göttingen 1958, p. 172. According to Dobert "*Rittig war Österreicher*" despite his place of birth.

[15] Wittke, *op. cit.*, p. 270.

[16] *Who's Who*, 1899–1900; Wittke, *op. cit.*, pp. 270–71; *Das Buch der Deutschen in Amerika*, pp. 527–28. For his nomination at Cooper Institute as mayor with the support of conservative Republicans see the *Staats-Zeitung*, 21 Oct. 1874.

[17] Arndt, *op. cit.*, pp. 389–90, stresses Keppler's importance. See also *the Dictionary of American Biography;* A. B. Faust, *German Element in the United States*, 2 vols., Boston and N.Y. 1909, II, pp. 363–64; and *Puck*, N.Y. 1876–1918.

[18] *Das Buch der Deutschen in Amerika*, p. 381.

[19] Arndt, *op. cit.*, pp. 624f.

[20] *Who's Who*, 1952–53.

[21] Obit. in *Washington Post*, 3 Apr. 1961.

[22] *Who's Who of American Women*, 2nd ed., 1961.

[23] *Who's Who*, 1962–63.

[24] *Who's Who*, 1899–1900.

[25] *Who's Who*, 1938–39.

[26] Emil Lengyel, *Americans from Hungary*, Philadelphia and N. Y. 1948, pp. 84–86; H. A. Pochmann, *German Culture in America*, Madison 1957, p. 260; *Das Buch der Deutschen in Amerika*, p. 578; Arndt, *op. cit.*, p. 196; R. Du Bois, *Germans in American Life*, N.Y. 1936, p. 144; D. C. Seitz, *Joseph Pulitzer*, N.Y. 1924.

[27] *Dictionary of American Biography; Who Was Who in America*, 1897–1942.

[28] Arndt, *op. cit.*, pp. 81, 387–88.

[29] *Ibid.*, p. 372.

[30] *Ibid.*, *passim.*

[31] Dieter Cunz, *Maryland Germans*, Baltimore 1948, pp. 406–07.

[32] Article by Erich Posselt, *American-German Review*, Oct. 1950, pp. 25–26.

[33] *Op. cit.*, p. 689.

[34] *Ibid.*, p. 336.

[35] R. E. Park, *Immigrant Press and its Control*, N.Y. and London, 1922, pp. 377–411, and *Who's Who*, 1920–21.

[36] Lengyel, *op. cit.*, pp. 194–203.

[37] Arndt, *op. cit.*, pp. 68, 234.

[38] *New York Times*, 23 Nov. 1959, pp. 57–58.

[39] Arndt, *op. cit.*, pp. 343, 359, 361.

[40] See *Freiheit für Österreich*, etc., in Library of Congress.

[41] A. C. Breycha-Vauthier, *Die Zeitschriften der Österreichischen Emigration 1934–1946*, Wien 1960.

[42] *Die Furche*, Wien, 18 Dec. 1964. Hofmannsthal has long been a regular contributor to the weekly "Die Furche," Austria's finest, conservative, cultural publication.

[43] *Who's Who*, 1962–63.

[44] *Ibid.*

[45] *Ibid.*

[46] James Thurber, *My Years with Ross, passim; Who's Who in Commerce and Industry*, 11th ed.

[47] Letters to the author from Dr. Otto Zausmer and Dr. Ernest S. Pisko.

[48] *Who's Who*, 1960–61; *Current Biography*, 1955, p. 638; *The Author's and Writer's Who's Who*, London 1960.

CHAPTER XII

AUSTRIANS IN BUSINESS

Few Americans associate the term "business" with Austrians. Austrian "big business" has seldom put its trade mark upon any of the products that have become world famous. Most Americans would be hard put to it to name a single Austrian who has become nationally renowned in the American business world. He would be correct in his assumption that Austrians are seldom made of the stuff that builds big business, but he would be surprised to learn that some well-known names, scattered here and there in American business and industry during the last century, were Austrian.[1]

Drexel and Company, the great banking house of Philadelphia which helped establish the House of Morgan, was founded a century and a quarter ago by Franz Martin Drexel (1792–1863) of Dornbirn in what is now Vorarlberg. It was Drexel and Company that helped import European capital in the second half of the 19th century to support America's young industry. And it was the Drexels who, in 1871, teamed up with J. P. Morgan to found Drexel, Morgan& Company of 23 Wall Street.

As a young man Franz Martin Drexel[2] had studied art in Italy, painted portraits all over Europe, returned briefly to Austria after Napoleon's defeat, reached Philadelphia in 1817, given up portrait painting in favor of world travel, and opened a brokerage office in Louisville in 1837. The American President had killed off the United States Bank and Franz Drexel moved on to Philadelphia to mop up a very considerable business from the ruins. He prospered, but it was his sons who took over the business after his death in a railroad accident and who joined with Morgan to create the country's greatest financial power.

Another Austrian success story was the Brentano bookstore venture. August Brentano (b. 1831 – d. Chicago, 1886), a penniless Austrian immigrant, began his career by selling newspapers in the streets of New York. He acquired a newsstand in 1853, imported European dailies as no American had ever before done, and later established a "Literary Emporium" which moved in 1870 to Union Square, then to Fifth Avenue at 27th Street and later, to keep pace with the city's top-hat trade, to Fifth and 47th. The Brentano bookstores spawned branches in San Francisco, New York and Washington and an independent firm, Kroch and Brentano, used the name in Chicago and Paris. Adolph Kroch (b. 1882) who directed the Chicago-Paris firm was an Austrian. Not until 1933 did the Brentano family sell its major interest in the world-famous business.[3]

Very few Austrian immigrants have founded significant family dynasties in the United States. There were the Krochs whom we have just mentioned. There was, quite different, the fine sculptor, Karl Bitter (b. Vienna, 1867 – d. New York, 1915), whose daughter became a renowned harpist, one son a dean of the physics department at Massachusetts Institute of Technology, and another son the dean of music at the University of Miami.[4] And there were the Kohlers of Wisconsin. They were perhaps, a generation ago, second only to the La Follettes in prominence in that State.

There is in the town of Kohler in Wisconsin a house in the style of the Vorarlberg city of Bregenz that was designed in the 1930's by two Vorarlberger architects for the fifth Kohler generation in this country. The Kohler story varies a bit according to the source. It seems, however, that Johann Michael Kohler (b. 1806 – d. 1874) lived near Bregenz, that he was a weaver who left his homeland with his family in a huff in 1854 when the authorities denied him permission to dam a stream there to erect a mill, and who emigrated to St. Paul, bought a farm and found himself reduced financially to one golden florin.

The Kohler family history was an interesting one. Son John (1844–1900) apparently went to Chicago, left there after the great fire, and settled in 1871 in Sheboygan, Wisconsin. In Sheboygan the family manufactured Vorarlberg lace, presumably with the help of new-comers from Austria. In any event, after a marriage with Lillie Vollrath, daughter of a German manufacturer of sanitary equipment, the Kohler plumbing equipment business soon throve. Kohler began to furnish millions of American bathrooms, and scores of Vorarlbergers and Germans were imported to Kohler Town. Kohler became a great name in public service as well as in industry and two twentieth century governors of Wisconsin were Kohlers.[5]

There were, however, few other well known Austrian names in American business and industry until well into the twentieth century. The Fleischmann yeast family was Austro-Hungarian. Charles (b. near Budapest, 1834 – d. Avondale, 1897) and Maxim brought their renowned *Hebemittel* yeast, to Cincinnati in 1860 and made it famous with their exhibit at the Philadelphia Centennial of 1876. Nine years later a member of that family, Raoul, migrated from his home in Bad Ischl, Austria. He worked later for the Fleischmann bakeries, the General Baking Company, and made his greatest American contribution, with editor James Ross, in building the "New Yorker" magazine.[6]

Raoul Fleischmann came to America as an infant. Others came already equipped with European schooling or experience. There was, for instance, Erwin Reginald Lederer (b. Vienna, 1882)[7] who came in 1912 with degrees from the University of Vienna and the *Technische Hochschule* and with experience with Vacuum Oil in chemical engineering. He served several of the great American oil companies before he became president of the Bradford Oil Refining Company in 1936. Ernst Mahler (b. Austria, 1887) was another chemical engineer, trained at Darmstadt, who immigrated in 1912 to find a career in Wisconsin in paper (he was long vice-president of Kimberly-Clark) with a vigorous finger in other branches of big industry. A gold medal from the paper industry and an honorary doctorate from Brown University were indicative of his American success story.[8] Leo L. Beck (b. Austria, 1901), who came over as a child, was another chemical engineer who rose to high executive position in American industry.[9]

Louis Yaeger (b. Austria, 1899), the New York investment consultant, also came to this country as a child as did his fellow countryman Anthony Michael Golubich (b. 1896) who established in 1925 his own firm of general brokers and manufacturers' agents in Cleveland.[10] An Austrian candy magnate, John Heller, has established a branch factory over here and a part-time residence in suburban New York.

Austria, a tourist country, has supplied America with several names in the hotel and restaurant business. Jennie Grossinger (b. Vienna, 1892) of Grossinger, New York, a co-founder with her Austrian-born husband of the hotel-like Grossinger Country Club, has had an almost un-Austrian urge to advertise her fine retreat.[11] Ralph Hitz (b. Vienna, 1891 – d. United States, 1940) migrated in 1906 and managed hotels in Cleveland and Cincinnati before he became director and president of the Hotel New Yorker.[12] The operator of the Hotel Governor Clinton in New York after 1938 was Herman Fiedelbaum (b. Austria, 1889, emigrated 1905) who had tried dress manufacturing, building construction, and insurance before turning his hand to running hotels.[13] The general counsel of the Sheraton Hotel Corporation of America was the New York lawyer, Irvine J. Schubert, born in Austria in 1902.[14]

The Jews among these business figures were remarkable for their charities – Jewish and Gentile. Jennie Grossinger and Herman Fiedelbaum were cases in point. There were dozens of others. There was, for instance, Benjamin Samuel Katz (b. Austria, 1892), who delivered papers while he attended New York's public schools and worked his way through Wanamaker's store, photo supply shops, a branch of Ingersoll watches and jewelry manufacturing to the presidency of the Gruen Watch Company at Racine. Katz also found time for service with the National Conference of Christians and Jews, the board of governors of Hebrew Union College, and many lesser known welfare ventures.[15] Similarly, Abraham Blumenkrantz (b. Austria, 1898), who founded the General Investment Corporation in 1923 and helped for decades to guide it upon its epoch-making way to become one of America's "big ones," found time for his charities, including the vice-presidency of the Beth Israel Hospital of New York.[16]

There was doubtless a realization among these Jewish emigrants that their European co-religionists had, despite the old and the new anti-Semitism, been playing a great role in Austria's cultural life, and hence they had a desire to reveal here all of the fineness of which the race was capable.

There were relatively few Austrians directing the heavy industries that employed so many laborers from the ethnically non-Germanic lands of the Habsburg empire. Karl C. Jursek (b. Vienna, 1890)[17] who grew up in Pittsburgh, became president of the Lifetime Stainless Steel Corporation in Massachusetts. Joseph John Rosecky[18] (b. Austria, 1903), a graduate of the University of Wisconsin, climbed to the top with Allis Chalmers, the Heil Company, and some other giants in Pennsylvania and New York industry. John Bass (b. Vienna, 1891), with a Vienna education and a Vienna—Hamburg—Paris business background, manufactured sugar chiefly in Puerto Rico. And, like so many new-comers from Austria he kept up his music and composed and published it.[19]

One of the prominent names in American—and world-wide—metallurgy, is Paul Schwarzkopf (b. Prague, 1886). He was educated in his native city and in Berlin, served in the Habsburg army during World War I, and established his business in the Tyrol in 1921. By 1929 he was in business in Lewiston, Maine, having founded the American Electro Metal Corporation, which by 1939 had research laboratories in Yonkers, New York. Without relinquishing his interests in Germany, Holland, Great Britain and the Tyrol, he made his Schwarzkopf Development Corporation of New York one of the big ones in the field. Like so many Austrians who settled here he maintained also an Austrian home—at Reutte in the Tyrol.[20]

A Vienna businessman, Bernard Altmann (b. Austria 1888), found himself in 1941 in business in San Antonio, Texas, settled in New York as chairman of the board of the Bernard Altmann Company and made a fortune in manufacturing wool products.[21] He is not, however, to be confused with the American-born founder of the B. Altmann department store. He is in character with the many Austro-Hungarians who came here to find success and fortunes in the clothing industry and to employ so many of the Austro-Hungarian tailors who emigrated to America; many of whom were Jewish.

Charles Emmanuel Gelb (b. Austria-Hungary, 1898) made Chicago his home and, after ventures into architecture, commercial art, and advertising, became in 1938 president of Society Brand Clothes.[22] Paul Gelles of California and New York (b. Vienna, 1905) also made a career of clothing and textiles: Manhattan Shirts, Reis underwear, Onyx Knitting Mills and, after 1951, became chairman of the board of the B. V. D. Company.[23] The "New York Times" (obituary 16 May 1958) called Harry Frechtel of Austria "one of the nation's leading designers and manufacturers of women's suits and coats ..." His Austrian apprenticeship as a tailor ended at the age of fifteen when he came to New York to help dictate styles for American women. He was a figure of considerable importance in the more exciting areas of American design.

The department store magnates among the Austro-Americans included Nathan M. Ohrbach (b. Vienna, 1885) founder of the famous Ohrbach stores and Joe Weinstein (b. Austria, 1894) founder of the May stores. Ohrbach came to America as a child,

Weinstein at the age of fifteen. Both settled in New York and both opened their first stores in Brooklyn, branching out later to New York City and beyond. Both were Jewish and both were involved in literally dozens of charities and civic projects. That such men were far more than merchants is evidenced by the fact that Nathan Ohrbach received the decorations of the French Legion of Honor and of the Italian Star of Solidarity.[24]

The best-known Austrian name in the United States has for some years been Hertz. John David Hertz (b. 1879 – d. 1961) was the founder of the Hertz Rent-A-Car system. His was a Horatio Alger career. Although born across the Austrian border at Ruttka in present-day Czechoslovakia he seems to have considered himself an Austrian.[25] He came to Chicago with his father, "an Austrian immigrant junk dealer," ran away from home and never completed elementary school, tried his hand at boxing, driving a delivery wagon, reporting, and running a cut-rate taxi service in Chicago. By 1915 he had established the famous Yellow Cab system; two years later he merged the Chicago Coach Company with the Fifth Avenue Coach Company. His director of psychological research for the Yellow Cab Company was Dr. Adolph Snow who was born in the city of Austrian Poland that he called "Rzeszow, Austria," in 1894. Some months after he started the Hertz Drive-Your-Self system he sold the Yellow Cabs, in 1925, to General Motors for thirty million dollars. Just before his death in 1961 it was announced that the Hertz Corporation expected record revenues that year of 140 million dollars.[26] Hertz had inaugurated one of the most exciting successes in the history of American business.

Long before 1961, John David Hertz had begun to develop his hobbies and sidelines. He became famous in the sporting world for the race horses that he bred, including two Kentucky Derby winners. He sat on the board of some giant corporations, helped Harry Hopkins in 1941 straighten out the kinks in the Army's Motor Transport Division, developed some useful medical charities, and established the Hertz Engineering Scholarship Fund generously enough endowed to assist a hundred would-be engineers annually. It was an amazing career.

The well-known Teutonic names in brewing seem to have been German rather than Austrian. One of the few Austro-Americans in that industry was Alfred Epstein, chairman of the Pfeiffer Brewing Company at Detroit and a director of the Detroit Symphony Orchestra.

It is interesting to note that the great majority of the recent Austro-American men of business remained in the East. Relatively few went far to the south. Rudolph H. Bunzl a native of Vienna (b. 1922) was educated at Georgia Tech and became vice-president of the United States Filter Corporation in Richmond, and Samuel Hausman (b. Austria, 1897), became president of the Weldon Mills in Emporia, Virginia; but Hausman lived in New York. Public accountant Joseph Pelej (b. Vienna, 1899), a partner in Price Waterhouse and Company, lived close to New York in New Jersey, and the management consultant Rudolf Modley (b. Vienna, 1906) had his offices in New York and Washington. Only occasionally did a Viennese like Sam Regenstreif reach as far west as Indiana where he became vice-president in charge of the Philco Corporation's Connersville plant.

The Thirty-eighters in business and industry seemed especially to concentrate in and around New York – a concentration that was doubtless more obvious in this field than in some others such as teaching and music. A large proportion was Vienna-born and, as city dwellers, had no desire to push on from New York to smaller towns. Almost all of them, as refugees from Nazism, came because they had to and settled where they first found a foothold. Some came with the help of aid-the-refugee organizations with scarcely a groschen in their pockets. The best of them were capable enough to find a foothold in their first months here, in or near to New York, and they saw no need for moving on. New York was after all the business capital of America and it had always been the favorite point of refuge for Austrians in distress.

The distinguished Austro-American business men of the Hitler era were interesting people. Among them were Catholics as well as Jews and money makers as well as gentlemen of culture who devoted much of their gains in their adopted country to the finest of causes. They were in general mature men and women. That was understandable: they came because they were old enough to have realized the monstrous terror of Nazism and, generally, to have incurred its enmity. That story of the many Austrians who fled from one of the most horrible things that the twentieth century had yet produced, is yet to be written.

There was, for instance, the Jewish James Kassner (b. Vienna, 1905) who had a doctorate from the University of Vienna and years of experience with Julius Kassner & Sons of Vienna up to 1938, who came to the United States because the Nazis did not like Jews. He did well in silver and in maternity modes in Chicago and in 1957 became president of the celebrated Russek's Fifth Avenue in New York. That was doing rather well for an immigrant from a land four thousand miles away that spoke a different and difficult language.[27]

Only a few of these people got as far as Massachusetts. Otto Lobl, for instance, born in Vienna in 1897, educated there in what was, depending upon his own strange translation into English, probably the *Hochschule für Welthandel*, and a partner in a Vienna advertising agency before he established his own, came here in 1938 and found a place in the Hero Company of Middleboro, Massachusetts.[28] Emil Michael Bonyhady (b. Graz, 1905) who had supervised shoe factories in Germany and Yugoslavia found a place in shoes and shoe machinery in Massachusetts after his arrival there in 1938. He was one of the many Austrian Thirty-eighters who managed to get American citizenship in the minimum of five years – as contrasted with the somewhat more leisurely pre-Hitler years when the Austrian new-comers took ten or a dozen years, not because they did not mean to remain but because their world was not yet falling apart and there was no overwhelming urgency.[29]

Frank Gerard Back (b. Vienna, 1902)[30] was another five-year citizen. His doctorate from Vienna's *Technische Hochschule* and his engineering background in Vienna gave him an interest here in television as president of Zoomar, Incorporated. He not only became a fellow of the Royal Photographical Society but also, as a result of his interest in motion pictures and television engineering, received in 1948 the gold medal of the TV Broadcasters' Association. Few realized that the president of Locust Valley, New York, who had received such an honor, had been born in Vienna.

There was also the Vienna-born (1907) Hans Peter Kraus[31] who had graduated from one of the several commercial academies in Vienna. His interest was in books and rare books, in Kraus Periodicals Incorporated, of New York City, and his contributions in the book field were so great that France decorated him as Chevalier of the Legion d'Honneur. America has, unfortunately, no such devices for honoring the foreigners who have come to its shores.

Three other Thirty-eighters may be mentioned. One of the three has been called "one of the richest men in America"—with a fortune of about $ 250 millions. He was Karl Francis Landegger (b. Vienna, 1905) who owned a paper factory at Wels in Upper Austria (*Welser Papierfabrik*), escaped Hitler and came to America in 1940 (was naturalized in 1946), found a way into the paper industry in such far-flung lands as Brazil, Mexico, France, and England, kept up his vast interests in Austrian paper and American paper, and called himself at home in New York and Ridgefield, Connecticut. His son Carl Clement Landegger (b. Vienna, 1930), who had emigrated three years earlier, followed in his father's American footsteps, with emphasis upon machinery manufactering, and even returned for two years to Austria in the 1950's to manage the Wels paper factory.

Their fellow-countryman who made use of paper, Frederik Amos Praeger (b. Vienna, 1915), was a Thirty-eighter with a publisher's background who came over to make ventures in jewelry, serve in the United States army, act as publications officer with American military government in German Hessen, and set up a publishing firm in New York under his own name. He was far more interested in books on communism and the exciting underdeveloped world than in publishing books about his home country. He had, however, an occasional interest in such an Austrian book as Henderson's fine life of Prince Eugene, perhaps the first English biography of the man whom Napoleon called one of the seven greatest military geniuses in world history. And the Austro-American element in New York's book business was reinforced by the successes of a scholarly refugee from the Nazis, Frederick Ungar, whose publishing firm began in the early 1960's to find representation in all of the better book listings. He did not object, unlike Praeger, who seems to have come out of nowhere, to being described in Charles M. Madison's "Book Publishing in America" (N.Y. 1966) as a

Vienna publisher of considerable importance who had founded there the Phaidon Press. Ungar has been publishing the soundest of titles, from Rousseau to Allen Nevins, with no concern for the Book-of-the-Month Club. He still maintains his interest in the large Austrian segment of German-language writing when, for instance, he publishes in English with considerable pride that early Austrian classic, Grillparzer's "Poor Musician" and three beloved, early Austrian plays by Nestroy translated, with his editorial colleague, by Max Knight, a Viennese for half of his life and later an editor of the University of California Press. The matter of translation serves to remind us that two of the recent presidents of the American Society of Translators, Henry Fischbach and Kurt Gingold, were Viennese in origin.[32]

Another American success story began with Henrietta Kanengeiser (b. Vienna, 1889) better known as Hattie Carnegie.[33] She was brought to America as a child and started on her amazing career as a dictator of women's fashions at the age of twenty. The story is told that she found a seamstress partner because she herself couldn't sew a seam. She had, however, an innate love of good clothes. They chose the name Carnegie because they liked it, charged high prices, and did so well that in four years they opened a swank Manhattan shop. Henrietta bought out her partner, soon formed Hattie Carnegie Incorporated, moved the shop to East 49th Street, and began welcoming the richest and best dressed American women. She was a character, a dynamic woman who didn't hesitate to tell either an employee or a customer when a dress was unsuitable. She collected awards for good design as well as customers who took pride in that utterly un-Austrian name, Hattie Carnegie.

Long before Hitler, in 1899, the child Nettie Rosenstein (b. Vienna, 1893) arrived in New York. She set up her own business as a fashion designer during the first World War, designed costume jewelry as well as clothing, received the Lord and Taylor and the Coty awards, and designed Mrs. Eisenhower's gowns for two presidential inaugurations.[34] The man who scandalized America with topless bathing suits in the early 1960's was, some might hesitate to point out, also an Austrian. He was the bold Rudi Gernreich.[35]

There were Austro-Americans in other areas of the fashion world. Adolf van Stondeg (b. Austria, c. 1876 – d. Washington, 1963) founded a fashionable dress shop in Washington in 1915 and operated it until his death years later.[36] Ellis Jourman (b. Austria, 1898) of St. Louis became in 1944 editor of "Fashion Forecasts Magazine"[37] and Vera Hahn (b. Vienna, 1922), who had done display work for R. H. Macy's and Bamberger's stores, became fashion editor of the Fairchild Publications.[38]

In another area of design Paul Theodore Frankl (b. Vienna, 1881)[39] became a prominent figure. Coming to New York in 1914 he established his own Frankl Galleries, and lectured across the country from New York University and the Metropolitan Museum of Art to the University of California at Los Angeles. The University of Pittsburgh's professor emeritus, Walter Sobotka (b. Vienna, 1888), learned architecture and design in his native city, made the latter skill a career in commercial New York in the late 1930's, and then turned to teaching at Carnegie Institute of Technology and the University of Pittsburgh. Leopold Kleiner, president of his own firm in New York of interior design based upon modern psychological principles, was honored in 1964 by an award from President Schärf of Austria. The Hohenberg Art Gallery in Chicago was established in 1951 by Marguerite Hohenberg (b. Vienna, 1883), interior decorator and artist.

The Thirty-eighter group included Liane Fischer Zimbler (b. Prerau, Moravia, 1897), the Los Angeles interior decorator who had studied art and architecture in Vienna during World War I, practiced architecture in Vienna and Prague, and lectured in adult education schools in Vienna until the *Anschluss*. The interior designer Maria Bergson (b. Vienna) came in 1940 to establish her firm in New York. And, more recently, Rita St. Clair (b. Vienna, 1928) has practised interior decoration in Baltimore.[40]

The individuals and the categories mentioned in this chapter represent only a fraction of the Austrian contribution to American business and industry. Others appear in our other chapters. Thousands are unknown to us. Tens of thousands of little businessmen, shopkeepers, artisans, craftsmen, clerks and mechanics will always remain unknown to the historian. And the humble laborers whose role in American industry was as useful as that of the notables who appear in "Who's Who" can only be treated in the mass in our sections on immigration.

It is scarcely necessary to point out that the immigrant has been Austria's greatest contribution to America's economic life. Austro-American trade before World War II was of no great importance to either country. For Austria, less than one twenty-fifth as populous as the United States, Austro-American trade has in recent years been of real significance. For us it has been inconsequential.

The "burning disgrace" of United States representation at the great Vienna World's Fair of 1873 was indicative of our indifference during the last century. Our contributions to the earlier London and Paris fairs had been no triumphs. But we seem to have struck a new low at Vienna. There our exhibits, thanks to the opposition of all sections of the United States except the most industrialized ones, to wasting our resources on frills abroad, have been called the least creditable parts of the entire exposition. And the scandals that corruption among the American commissioners and the sale of duty-free American whiskey gave rise to, contributed a good deal less than nothing to our good relations with Austria-Hungary. We seemed destined in those days to strike sour notes during any attempts at an Austro-American symphony.[41]

After World War II, in 1950, war-devastated Austria exported goods worth only $ 16,386,000 to the United States while, thanks to the Marshall plan which was to help work a miracle in the little republic, it was able to import wares worth $ 105,999,000 from this country.[42] But after the Austrian economic miracle of the fifties, Austria had reduced the value of the imports it needed from America to a bit over eighty millions.[43] The United States was Austria's third most important trade partner, for both imports and exports, after only Germany and Italy.[44] And the United States was the largest foreign investor in Austria.[45] Even so the totals were so small as to have almost no significance in any evaluation of Austrian impact upon the United States economy.

More significant was the fact that the little republic had by 1962 so recovered its economic footing (the rate of growth of its gross national product in the decade of the fifties was second only to that of much-publicized West Germany!)[46] that it was helping support the American dollar by setting aside $ 50,000,000 (for the purpose) from its dollar reserves. That was a happy reversal of its sad history between the two wars when it could only beg help from us and the League of Nations.[47]

Indeed, it was the collapse in 1931 of Austria's great bank, the *Credit-Anstalt*, which toppled Europe's whole financial structure and made the American panic of 1929 a world-wide tragedy. "The shocks of this earthquake," said President Hoover at Des Moines in 1932, trying to pin our troubles upon the Austrians, "ran from Vienna to Berlin, from Berlin to London, from London to Asia and South America. From all these countries they came to this country, to every city and farm in the United States."[48] Hoover seems to have favored a Federal Reserve loan to save the *Credit-Anstalt* but the French objected and the President tried his famous moratorium on Europe's debts to the United States which failed to avert the crash. The transformation of the bankrupt Austria of the 1930's into the prosperous little country of the 1960's gave the United States no very important customer for its wares[49], but it did represent an element of economic stability that American business could be grateful for. And Americans who were troubled by the drain of gold could also be grateful for the country's favorable balance in its trade with Austria.

Of all of Austria's sales to Americans, tourist services were doubtless the most significant to any study of Austrian influences. Whereas 19th century Americans visited Austria by the dozens they were coming, a decade after World War II, by the tens of thousands – chiefly to Salzburg, Vienna, and Innsbruck. America's great critic of the "boobocracy," H. L. Mencken, was intrigued by Vienna's "innocent gaiety" that he found a welcome relief from New York's "commercialized bawdiness." He defended Austria, along with some of the rest of Europe, "as a haven of refuge for snobs of the better class."[50] In 1963, it was estimated, American tourists, despite their preference for some six other countries, spent some 900,000 nights in the little republic. The American press, poorly represented in Austria, gave less publicity to Austria's attractions than it gave to half a dozen other lands with smaller tourist totals, yet only four or five European countries outranked the United States in the Austrian tourist industry.[51]

It was perhaps the tourist business that brought the Bank of America in 1965 to open the first American banking establishment (aside from the ubiquitous American

Express — a kind of bank) in Vienna. And the Intercontinental Hotel, that opened recently in Vienna after the city refused to donate a part of its fine city park to the American hotel-builder, Hilton, was Vienna's first blatantly American hotel.

On the whole, America's interest in Austria's productive capacity has been disappointingly small. When an American ambassador to Austria, James W. Riddleberger, faced retirement from his Vienna post in 1967, he pleaded for an increase in American capital investments in Austria. He pointed out, in his completely objective, Riddleberger way (he was an undemonstrative career diplomat) that Americans had invested less than a hundred million dollars in Austria. That amounted to about .07% (a remarkably small proportion) of the total American investment of some fourteen billions in Europe. A greater American investment in Austria might have helped to relieve the pressure upon Austria to escape from its commitments to Britain and the Outer Seven and find an associate membership in the European Common Market, which Austria needed so desperately. But America has never been very much interested in the economy of Austria.[52]

All together, with the Americans, foreign tourists enabled Austria by 1963 to rank third in all Europe in tourism and to improve its total balance of payments by over one hundred million dollars. Americans missed the American drinks that they could find in Paris or Rome, but Americans who visited the music festivals, the theaters and concert halls, the finer municipal housing projects and recreation centers, the Winter Olympics in 1964, the entrancing ski resorts in Salzburg, Tyrol, and Vorarlberg, and the SOS Childrens' Villages, as well as the lakes and mountains and ancient monuments, were discovering that even the little Austria of the post-war era was making significant and unique contributions to contemporary life. But Austria has not been the rich man's tourist paradise and has made no "snob appeal" to wealthy Americans in the press.

Through the channels of commerce Austria has recently been taking chiefly grains and raw materials, machinery and heavy motor vehicles from the United States.

This country has bought the finished products of fine Austrian craftsmanship. The best known of the recent Austrian exports to this country have been the luxury goods: skis and ski equipment, fine hunting rifles, the famous Viennese petit-point bags, embroidered women's blouses, dirndls from Salzburg, Tyrolese hats, handwork from the provinces, rhinestones and costume jewelry, a bit of choice china from the Augarten shops, crystal dinner ware and chandeliers, pianos, and goods for gift shops like the fine enamel-on-copper ash trays and demitasse sets. We have bought most of Austria's recent export of bicycles. There has been a conspicuous absence of shoddy or mass-production products. In technical terms, apparel was in 1964 Austria's first export to America, then glassware (and the Austrian government's gift to New York in 1966 of lighting fixtures for the new Metropolitan Opera was doubtless designed to foster Austria's exports of fine crystal), then sporting goods, iron and steel, and then viscose fibres. Very few of the imports from Austria have been sold in the shops with any kind of Austrian label. Lanz of Salzburg, the famous creators of Austrian peasant ware for the "carriage trade" and of ski costumes in genuine Austrian style, established a fashionable shop in New York; and Austrian-born promoters of skiing in the United States often established their own shops for selling skis and everything connected with skiing. But they never gave such shops an Austrian label. There has been, in the good Austrian tradition, no blatant advertising of Austrian wares. Indeed, our imports from Austria have been like that country: small, highly specialized, and charming.

[1] The Austrian-born listed in *Who's Who in Commerce and Industry*, Chicago 1959, total 38. That is a small percentage of the whole (some 17,000) and the names are not well known.

[2] *Dictionary of American Biography*; Frederick F. Schrader, *Germans in the Making of America*, Boston 1924, p. 232. For a summary of the part of the Drexel firm in Drexel, Morgan & Co., see *Fortune*, Jan. 1962, pp. 108–10.

[3] *N. Y. Times*, 5 April 1962; *Universal Jewish Encyclopedia*, II, p. 520–21; Adolph Kroch will be found in *Who's Who in Industry and Commerce*, Chicago 1959.

[4] Wilhelm Schlag, "A Survey of Austrian Emigration to the United States," in *Österreich und die Angelsächsische Welt*, Wien 1961, p. 173. We have not generally in this study concerned ourselves with second generation Austrians but Dr. Schlag, Austrian cultural attaché in New York, confirms our conclusion that there have been few Austrian family dynasties in this country.

[5] *Die Presse*, Wien, 3 Dec. 1961, p. 27, has a lengthy account of the Kohler family. See also the article on Gov. Walter J. Kohler, Jr., *Current Biography*, 1953; *Who's Who*, etc. See also pp. XV, XVI and 2 of W. H. Uphoff, *Kohler on Strike*, Boston 1966.

[6] See chapter on journalists in this volume.

[7] *Who's Who*, 1938–39.

[8] *Who's Who*, 1952–53.

[9] *Who's Who in Commerce and Industry*, 1959.

[10] *Ibid.* for Golubich; *Who's Who*, 1952–53 for Yaeger.

[11] *Who's Who*, 1962–63.

[12] *Who Was Who in America*, 1897–1942.

[13] *Who's Who*, 1962–63. Fiedelbaum was also chairman of the board of Fields Hotels.

[14] *Who's Who in Commerce and Industry*, 1959.

[15] *Ibid; Who's Who*, 1952–53.

[16] *Who's Who*, 1962–63.

[17] *Who's Who in Commerce and Inaustry*, 1959.

[18] *Who's Who*, 1962–63.

[19] *Who's Who*, 1952–53.

[20] *Who's Who in Austria*, 1959–60.

[21] *Who's Who in Commerce and Industry*, 1959.

[22] *Who's Who*, 1952–53.

[23] *Who's Who in Commerce and Industry*, 1959.

[24] *Who's Who* for 1960–61 and 1962–63.

[25] Cf. *Who's Who*, 1962–63; his obit. in *N.Y. Times*, 10 Oct. 1961; *Newsweek*, 30 Sept. 1957, p. 47; *Time*, 20 Oct. 1961.

[26] *Washington Post*, 24 May 1961.

[27] *Who's Who in Commerce and Industry*, 1959.

[28] *Ibid.*

[29] *Ibid.*

[30] *Who's Who*, 1962–63.

[31] *Who's Who in Commerce and Industry*, 1959; *Who's Who*, 1962–63.

[32] *Who's Who*, 1962–63, and *Who's Who in Commerce and Industry*, 1959. See especially the article on Landegger in *Fortune*, Nov. 1964. For Ungar and Praeger see Charles A. Madison, *Book Publishing in America*, N.Y. 1966, pp. 526 and 540.

[33] *Who's Who*, 1952–53; *Washington Post*, 11 July 1961.

[34] *Who's Who*, 1962–63.

[35] *Parade*, magazine, 2 Aug. 1964, p. 2.

[36] *Washington Post*, 6 Jan. 1963, for his obituary.

[37] *Who's Who in Commerce and Industry*, 1959.

[38] *Who's Who of American Women*, 2nd ed., 1961.

[39] *Who's Who*, 1952–53; *International World Who's Who*, N.Y. 1949.

[40] *Who's Who*, 1962–63, and *Who's Who of American Women*, 2nd ed., 1961.

[41] Merle Curti, "America at the World Fairs," *American Historical Review*, July 1950, pp. 638ff., is a most significant account by an outstanding American historian.

[42] *Statistical Abstract of the United States*, 1958, p. 895.

[43] Department of Commerce figures cited in *World Almanac*, 1962, p. 674. Official Austrian figures appear not to correspond with U.S. totals.

[44] *Jahresbericht 1959 der Vereinigung Österreichischer Industrieller*, Wien 1960, p. 46.

[45] *Austrian Information*, 14 Apr. 1962, p. 3.

[46] *Washington Post*, 9 July 1962, p. A12.

[47] For the 1962 arrangement between the Federal Reserve system and the Austrian National Bank see *Austrian Information*, 16 Nov. 1962.

[48] Quoted from R. L. Wilbur and A. M. Hyde, *The Hoover Policies*, N.Y. 1937, p. 404. See also J. D. Hicks, *Republican Ascendancy 1921–1933*, N.Y. 1960, p. 245.

[49] It is interesting to note that, while there were many American automobiles on Austrian highways soon after World War II (many of them old cars sold by U.S. occupation soldiers) the Austrians were buying by 1960 only small European cars. Cf. *Die Presse*, Wien, 12 Mar. 1961, p. 16.

[50] Cushing Strout, *The American Image of the Old World*, N.Y. 1963, p. 181.

[51] West Germany, Britain, France, The Netherlands and in some areas Italy. *Austrian Information*, 26. Nov. 1960. For a more complete summary of the American share in Austrian tourism see *ibid.*, 1 Jan. 1965. Useful for the nineteenth century background is Foster Rhea Dulles, *Americans Abroad*, Ann Arbor 1964, which makes it clear that even though the Baedeker Guidebooks were printing in English from 1861 on and Americans found by that time that English was spoken as far east as Vienna, Austria was not included in the typical American's Grand Tour. He found himself much more at home in Switzerland.

[52] *Austrian News*, Austrian American Federation, N.Y., Apr.-May, 1967.

CHAPTER XIII

ERUDITE AUSTRIANS

The Austrian-born in America's academic groves have generally been educators but not educationalists. A few of the early arrivals like the Forty-eighter Anton Füster might champion free secular schools in the United States, Francis J. Grund could father a normal school for German teachers when normal schools were only beginning to appear on the American scene, and Dr. Godfrey Aigner might achieve a modest reputation as the scholarly Viennese on the board of regents of the infant University of Wisconsin.[1] Yet the Austrian contribution was not often in the science of education.

More Austrian-born educators made their reputations here in the present century. Father Francis Joseph Wenninger of Burgenland, brought here in infancy, became in 1923 dean of Notre Dame's College of Science[2] and Max Schoen (also born in 1888) became two years later head of the department of education at Pittsburgh's Carnegie Tech.[3] And among the talented Thirty-eighters were Kurt Maximilian Hertzfeld, business manager of the University of Rochester and vice president of Boston University;[4] Rose Mary Scheider, the expert in educational testing;[5] and the University of Chicago's Bruno Bettelheim (b. Vienna 1903) who has taught educational psychology and written on emotionally disturbed children.[6] And there was a goodly group of other psychologists and psychiatrists, from Freud and Adler to the recent arrivals in the United States, who have had a very important impact upon American education. Ernst Papanek of Queens College, for instance, who had helped reform the Austrian school system between the two world wars, became a director here at the Alfred Adler Mental Hygiene Clinic.

The educators who were not educationalists very naturally included, outside the fields of medical and natural science, the teachers of German. They represented a surprisingly small element among the "Who's Who" figures of their time, doubtless because Germans rather than Austrians filled so many chairs of German in the American universities. And because, in part, we were so often content with American teachers of German. The noted historian George Bancroft told James Russell Lowell that his German teacher at Harvard was self-taught and so had no notion of the pronunciation.[7] And when distinguished American scholars like Bancroft, Longfellow, Everett, and Prescott did visit Europe they spent far more time in Germany than in Austria and returned with little or no enthusiasm for bringing Austrian scholars to this country.

There were, however, even in the nineteenth century, some interesting immigrants here teaching German. The Czech Charles Hruby came in 1834 to teach in a small Ohio college.[8] John Eiselmeier (b. near Linz, 1861 – d. 1947) immigrated in 1876 to teach German for years in our Middle West where like a good Austrian language teacher, he stressed phonetics.[9] Max Winkler (b. 1866), educated in the best American schools and a dramatist of some distinction, long headed the German department at the University of Michigan.[10]

And at the turn of the century there came one of the greatest of the language teachers, Eduard Prokosch (b. Eger, Bohemia, 1878 – d. New Haven, 1938), a brilliant student at the gymnasium in his native Eger and at the German University at Prague and the University of Vienna, whose tremendous energy, charm, and scholarship made him in 1937 the president of America's huge Modern Language Association. From Austria's consulate at Milwaukee he went on to study and teach at the University of Chicago, spent some months in Germany, taught again in America until the prejudices of "the first war" lost him his position at Texas; but Bryn Mawr used him for a decade, New York University found him, and Yale gave him a distinguished professorship until his death in 1938. He was also, as his presidency of the Linguistic Society of America (1930) might indicate, an exponent of language instruction by direct method – the exclusive use of German in the German-language classroom. Prokosch was known and respected in Europe's German-speaking world as he was in America.[11]

Few of these Austro-American German teachers were primarily concerned, like Arthur Burkhard,[12] who in 1961 reversed the usual order of migration by taking his fine and authoritative interest in Grillparzer from Harvard to Graz, in specialization in things Austrian. Austrians often have an unfortunate reluctance to specialize in Austrian themes.

Typical was the distinguished Germanist, Walter Reichart (b. Pressburg, 1903), who rose to a professorship at the University of Michigan as a specialist on the German dramatist Hauptmann.[13] And Anthony Eugene Sokol (b. Vienna, 1897), whose career as an Austrian naval officer was terminated by the treaty of St. Germain, turned from German literature to Asiatic and Slavic studies at Stanford University. He was one of the Austrian notables whom the Fulbright exchange program took back to teach in his native Vienna.[14] We should also mention Professor Erich Kahler (b. Prague, 1885) who took his doctorate at the University of Vienna before he came to the United States to instruct at the New School for Social Research (1941 – 43), Cornell, Princeton and Ohio State University; Dr. Stefan F. Horn (b. Vienna, 1900, immigrated 1948), a president of the American Austrian Society in the nation's capital, who has interpreted at the Nürnberg War Crimes Trials and at numerous international conferences, was decorated in 1958 by the Austrian Government, and heads the Division of Interpretation and Translation of Georgetown University's

Institute of Language and Linguistics as the first and only Professor of Interpretation and Translation in the United States;[15] the Austro-Hungarian Fritz Moore (b. Uj-Verbasz, 1901) who came to America as a child and later headed Kansas State University's modern language department; Paul O. Straubinger (b. Vienna, 1910) who went to the University of California in 1954; and Heinz Politzer (b. 1911) whose poetry was inspired by his native, charming Salzkammergut. The Viennese Politzer, a brilliant essayist and joint editor of a significant edition of Kafka, has long occupied the chair of German literature at the University of California.[16]

There were many other Austrian teachers of German who helped convince Americans that Vienna's good German, if one avoided the dialect that all Viennese love just as all Hamburgers and all Berliners love their special dialects, was proper German in the best sense of the word. Despite their reluctance to emphasize the Austrian element in German literature they doubtless justified themselves by pointing out that Vienna's great *Burgtheater* has for generations been renowned for its superb German.

That any prejudices against the German language as spoken in Austria have been forgotten is evidenced by the fact that Austria has sprouted since the war a tremendous (for a small land) crop of summer schools inviting Americans to come to learn German and its literature. They can study ballet in Vienna and the philosophy of an integrated Europe at the Alpbach College and music (dancing under Harald Kreutzberg and conducting and voice and composition) at Salzburg's *Mozarteum* and history at the University of Vienna's fine English-language summer school — they can even learn mountain climbing from the University of Innsbruck — but at almost all of these schools, plus the junior-year schools from some excellent American universities, they can learn how to use the German language.[17] That was important in an era after the two world wars when German had lost so much of its prestige.

A few Austrians have even come to America to help Americans use their own language. Notable was Professor Hans Kurath (b. Villach, 1891) a president of the Linguistic Society of America (1942), editor of the "Linguistic Atlas of the United States and Canada" and of the fine "Middle English Dictionary,"[18] and Rudolf Flesch (b. Vienna, 1911) who was, surprisingly soon after his immigration in 1938, writing books like "The Art of Plain Talk" and "Why Johnny Can't Read" which one would scarcely expect from a doctor of law from the University of Vienna.[19]

The Austro-Americans represented dozens of other far-flung areas of scholarship. Maurice Bloomfield (b. Austrian Silesia, 1855 — d. San Francisco, 1928) of Johns Hopkins, who was perhaps more Austro-Hungarian than German Austrian in background, achieved fame in Sanskrit[20] and Leo Spitzer (b. Vienna, 1887) also achieved a chair at Johns Hopkins but in Latin literature and linguistics.[21] And among the Thirty-eighters were Elfrieda Frank (b. Vienna) who taught the classics at Cornell and the Texas Technical College and René Wellek (b. Vienna, 1903), so much at home in English literature that he could co-author a book on "Literary Scholarship" with

Norman Foerster and teach English at the University of Iowa, who nevertheless turned in 1946 to Slavic and comparative literature at Yale.

Another Viennese who did not come to America to promote his own native tongue was the orientalist Gustave von Grunebaum (b. Vienna, 1909) who took his doctorate at the University of Vienna in 1931, taught there at its Oriental Institute, emigrated to New York and its Asia Institute in 1938, a half decade later began a distinguished career in Arabic at the University of Chicago,[22] and went still later to the University of California at Los Angeles.

These Austrians had a way of being erudite in the most varied and surprising fields. The Viennese Edwin Mueller (d. U.S., 1962) came to be recognized here as "one of the truly great philatelic authorities."[23] Adolph K. Placzek (b. Vienna, 1913), who had studied medicine and fine arts at Vienna's higher institutions of learning, became librarian of Columbia's excellent library of architecture.[24] Austrian librarians have not crowded the profession in the United States but it should be noted that the *Meister* of all Austrian librarians, DDr. Josef Stummvoll (b. Baden near Vienna, 1902), was for four years (instead of the usual two-year term) chief librarian of the United Nations and was therefore the first Austrian director and the organizer of its fine Dag Hammarskjöld Library.[25]

The standard book on the Crow Indians was written in 1935 by Robert Heinrich Lowie (b. Vienna, 1883), an ethnologist specializing in American Indians who immigrated as a boy to study at New York's City College and Columbia, and in 1925 to accept a professorial chair at the University of California.[26] A more recent expert on Indians was the anthropologist Erika Eichhorn Bourguignon (b. Vienna, 1924) who has taught for some years at Ohio State University.[27] And widely known for his much-publicized studies of the pygmies was Father Martin Gusinde (b. Breslau, 1886), a University of Vienna product who came from Chile to the Catholic University of America.[28] He was an anthropologist with enthusiasms for primitive peoples including not only African pygmies, Bushmen and Hottentots but North and South American Indians as well.

In sociology and social work there came a few with a conscience-laden Social Democratic background, which would inevitably lead them into social service. But, significantly enough, the Austro-Americans in these fields have been so gloriously vague about their old world backgrounds that it would require a special study to discover whether America had inherited from Austria chiefly social workers in the Socialist tradition or from the conservative side.

Hermann Gmeiner whose fame as founder of the SOS Children's Villages reached even to America was a devout Catholic from Vorarlberg and Tyrol. His villages had spread from Austria to much of Europe and to some of the Far East before Vermont began to build one in 1963. The concept of a children's home founded upon the idea of the family, with a "permanent" mother in each stable household of nine children of both sexes and all ages, happily threatened to supersede most of the traditional ideas for institutions for orphans. Gmeiner came to America in 1963 only to help found the Vermont village and take a degree from Fordham University.

In any event this country acquired some very useful people in social service. Some came early like Sidonie Matsner Gruenberg (b. Austria, 1881), who brought but little of Austria with her, an expert on child guidance.[29] Dr. Emil Frankel (b. Vienna, 1886; emigrated 1905) also came early to work in the Labor Department and in social work, briefly with the State of Pennsylvania and for years, since 1927, with the State of New Jersey.[30] Elizabeth Dolde (b. Austria-Hungary, 1899) came as a child to work in Ohio and to achieve naturalization by special act of Congress.[31] Ernest John Bohn (b. Austria-Hungary, 1901) settled in Cleveland and found his interests in municipal housing and the problems of the aged.[32] Louis Schneider (b. Vienna, 1915), president of the Ohio Valley Sociological Society in 1959–60, has taught sociology in some of his adopted country's best universities.[33] Henrietta Etta Saloshin of Vienna, who taught social work at several famed American universities, became professor at Minnesota in 1959.[34] And Helmut Schoeck (b. Graz, 1922), who managed to stay in Germany during the war, came in 1950 to teach at Fairmont College in West Virginia and Emory University in Georgia.[35]

The most distinguished of the Austrian-born sociologists was doubtless Paul Felix Lazarsfeld (b. Vienna, 1901), a veteran of psychological studies in Vienna, who came to Columbia University in the thirties and became later chairman of Columbia's sociology department. His books – some on radio research – became everything short of best-sellers in the American market.[36]

Austrian contributions to American thought have not come primarily with the immigrant. Sigmund Freud's gospel, which caused one of the major revolutions in Western thought, was the gospel of a towering figure who only once visited this country. His teachings came here with the printed page and with his disciples who lived and practiced here. Logical Positivism, the philosophy of the Vienna Circle which was to assume a major role in our philosophical thinking, lived out its formative period in Europe before it began its conquest of our academic groves. And Martin Buber, "the greatest living Jewish philosopher,"[37] visited here like Freud to receive the acclaim of his followers but refused to be weaned away from the Old World.

There were others who did come to America like Francis J. Grund, the early nineteenth-century philosopher of democracy, and Richard von Mises, the contemporary Harvard mathematician and philosopher of the meaning of science, who, like Freud, will be found in our other chapters where they seem to belong more appropriately. There are relatively few whom we should mention here.

The enigmatical, long-since-forgotten Otto Weininger (b. Vienna, 1880 – d. Vienna, 1903) aroused only a brief storm of abhorrent dissent in the United States. He was an abnormal young Jewish genius whose doctoral dissertation, "Geschlecht und Charakter," swept through six German editions and was published in English under the title "Sex and Character." It was a denunciation of the female sex. Man is all. Woman is nothing – without soul or heart or shame. "The meaning of woman is to be meaningless." Her beauty exists only in man's imagination.

The American critics pounced upon "Sex and Character." It was "preposterous charlatanry." "There are parts so poor, illogical, and stupid that they would not be accepted in a college boy's essay, and other parts worthy of Kant..." "The Outlook's" critic was not surprised that the author had died by his own hand at the age of twenty-three.[38] The book certainly did not help to enhance the prestige of Austrian scholarship in America.

On the positive side of the ledger there was Franz Brentano (b. Marienberg, 1838 – d. Zurich, 1917), a Rhinelander who came to the University of Vienna back in 1871 and whose learned tomes on "Psychology from the Empirical Standpoint" and the "Origin of Knowledge" had their impact on America principally perhaps by way of such great English philosophers as G. E. Moore. The Austrian in America came so often via England. And his disciple Alexius Meinong (1853–1920), who brought fame to the University of Graz, developed Brentano's "intentional psychology" and an "object-theory" concerned with subsistence in reality. His realism had its influence in America as well as in Britain.[39]

The great Jewish philosopher Martin Buber (b. 1878 – d. Jerusalem, 1965), born in Vienna only two years before Weininger, was a completely different figure. When Dag Hammarskjöld of the United Nations was killed in deepest Africa he had in his pocket a copy of "Ich und Du" ("I and Thou" in its English editions) which was Martin Buber's principal work and which Dag was translating into his native Swedish, thus underscoring the fact that Buber was not only the outstanding Jewish thinker of the middle of the twentieth century but also a philosopher with a powerful message for men of all creeds. Hermann Hesse called him "a master who has enriched world literature as has no other living author."[40]

This grand old man of Jewry spent his infancy in Austria, his childhood in Austrian Galicia, his university years in Vienna (where he received his doctorate), Berlin, Zurich and Florence, and was converted to Zionism, not in Vienna where its founder Herzl worked so long, and where Buber soon found a Zionist magazine to edit, but in Leipzig. He became a great figure. Geniuses like Kafka knew him and drew their inspiration from him. From the year of the *Anschluss*, 1938, to 1951 he taught philosophy at the Hebrew University in Jerusalem. And that was a philosophy of passionate concern for humanity, a unique kind of existentialism,[41] with Polish Hasidism and Nietzsche and Herzl and Kierkegaard mixed in. He brought together the Jewish enlightenment with the Western tradition of logical criticism. Like so many of his fellow philosophers he worked to reconcile religious experience with modern science.

A "New York Times" article of 1961 estimated that 860 volumes bearing his name had been printed in fourteen different languages. Ludwig Lewisohn classed him with Freud, Einstein, and Bergson as one of the greatest living geniuses.[42] Certainly his doctrines had attracted millions of men and women of good will before he came to America in 1951 and 1952. Here his disciples rallied about him, he addressed 2500 enthusiasts in Carnegie Hall, gave dozens of eloquent lectures, and received honors from Union Theological Seminary in New York and Hebrew Union College in Cincinnati. That he remains a philosophical prophet to millions of Americans is evidenced by his ubiquity in American periodical literature and book shops.[43]

More distinctively Austrian was the *Wiener Kreis*, the Vienna Circle. Long before World War II a German-born philosopher named Moritz Schlick (b. Berlin, 1882) had married a young lady from Boston, found his life work at the University of Vienna, and been assassinated by an unhappy student there in 1936 while he, Schlick, was enjoying fame as the leader of one of the great philosophical "schools" of our century.

The Boston lady was in the early 1960's still a charming old lady in the Vienna which she and her husband had adopted.[44] And the philosophical gospel of her husband, a kind of neo-positivism, had become more significant in contemporary philosophical thought in England, Scandinavia, and the United States than in its Vienna cradle. It had become recognized by some as "the most significant of serious philosophical movements in the period between the two world-wars."[45]

This was logical positivism, a scientific approach to philosophy. It purported to demonstrate the futility of metaphysics, it represented the reaction to nineteenth century idealism, it endeavored to reconcile science and philosophy, and, through logic, semantics, physics, and mathematics, to provide philosophy with a sound foundation. It died in Austria because Schlick was murdered and because Hitler destroyed Austrian scholarship in general and the *Wiener Kreis* in particular.[46] It lived in England because Bertrand Russell and Whitehead and the "Cambridge school" had been adherents of what might be regarded as a form of logical positivism, and it caught on in America because of English influences and the teachings of immigrants from Vienna.[47]

The Austrian John the Baptist of the movement was the physicist-philosopher Ernst Mach (b. Turas, Moravia, 1838 – d. near Munich, 1916) who taught at Graz, Prague, and Vienna, developed "Mach's postulate" which was a denial of the conception of the "absolute," influenced Einstein, and led into logical positivism. His striking impact upon European thinking was comparable only to America's too frequent neglect of him and his message. His significance is noted in passing in a few American treatises.[48] Mach was the first to hold the chair of inductive science at the University of Vienna which was later held by Boltzmann[49] and Schlick.

Logical positivism proper started, some maintain, with one of the very greatest of modern philosophers, Ludwig Josef Johann Wittgenstein (b. Vienna, 1889 – d.

Cambridge, England, 1951). He was schooled in Vienna and Linz and Berlin, settled in England because Vienna's Boltzmann died before he could study under him, became a convert to Bertrand Russell's philosophy, and ultimately became a British subject and one of the very greatest names in British philosophy. His excursions to Vienna, before his Jewish blood put a stop to all that, made him the connecting link between the *Wiener Kreis* (of which he was never a member and with which he came more and more to differ) and the Cambridge school of analysis. And while he was still in Vienna he published his great book, his "Tractatus Logico-Philosophicus" (1921). It was, Bergmann points out, the beginning of logical positivism.[50] Wittgenstein received an honored chair at Cambridge University, visited America in 1949 and decided he did not want to live and die here, but achieved here a reasonable fraction of the acclaim that he received in Britain where he ranked with the greatest. Even though his direct influence upon the United States has doubtless been far less than his indirect impact via his British associates, American philosophical students of his era went crazy over him and over the analytic philosophy that he represented.[51]

In 1922 Schlick was called to Mach's chair of philosophy at the University of Vienna, a few months after Wittgenstein's "Tractatus" had appeared. Rudolf Carnap (b. Wuppertal, Germany, 1891) and Otto Neurath (b. Vienna, 1882 – d. Oxford, 1945) enjoyed their years of fame in Vienna as logical positivism developed. Carnap's great empiricist volume "Der logische Aufbau der Welt" appeared in 1928, the peak of the constructive period of the *Wiener Kreis*. The culmination came only a few years later with Schlick's "Gesammelte Aufsätze" (1936) and Carnap's "The Logical Syntax of Language" (Vienna 1934; New York 1937). It was a great period for the philosophical faculty of the ancient University of Vienna.

Logical positivism, which some called logical empiricism, spread rapidly. Its devotees met, during its heydays 1929–1938, in almost annual congresses in various European cities. Professor Schlick visited the United States to lecture at California's two greatest universities half a dozen years before his death to introduce his positivism to America where its influence grew among what Americans called the school of analytic philosophy. The British philosopher Alfred Jules Ayer achieved fame in America in 1936 with his book on the Vienna Circle and its philosophy and American students of philosophy included Ayer in their hero-worship of Wittgenstein. There was a group at Berlin which kept in touch with the Vienna group. Professor Hans Reichenbach (b. Hamburg, 1891 – d. Los Angeles, 1953) of Berlin, and later of Los Angeles, was a full-fledged member of the Vienna Circle and a collaborator in the work on its journal, "Erkenntnis." There were Wittgenstein and his associates in positivism and realism in Britain. And in 1931 Carnap went to the University of Prague to work with the physicist Philipp Frank (b. Vienna, 1884) in developing a cell of logical positivists in Czechoslovakia.

In Vienna logical positivism was losing its lifeblood. Schlick was assassinated, Frank and Carnap were at Prague, the Nazis had prodded Neurath into emigrating to England, and America, as well as Britain, began to acquire men whom Vienna so badly needed.

Rudolf Carnap came in 1936. Harvard gave him an honorary degree and Chicago a chair of philosophy. He moved to Princeton in 1952 and to the University of California at Los Angeles two years later. California has in recent years been a favorite refuge for Austrians who could bring themselves to go beyond New York. And there are few greater names in California cultural history than those of her Austro-Americans, from Reinhardt to Neutra and Carnap.

Gustav Bergmann (b. Vienna, 1906), author of "The Metaphysics of Logical Positivism" (1954), came to the United States in 1938 for a career at Iowa State University. Richard von Mises (b. Lemberg, 1883 – d. Boston, 1953), a well-known associate of the logical positivists, and Philipp Frank both came to Harvard in the year of the *Anschluss*. Another prominent member of the Vienna Circle, Dr. Zilsel, died here before the end of the war. Herbert Feigl (b. Reichenberg, Bohemia, 1902) had come earlier. He was a product of the University of Vienna who had lectured in Vienna's *Volkshochschulen*, adult education schools, before he researched at Harvard in 1930, taught at Iowa State, and received the chair of philosophy at the University of Minnesota in 1940. He has been called "Schlick's heir."

These were all philosophers of significance. Their presence here represented a serious loss for Central European philosophy but it represented an equivalent gain for American philosophy. Logical positivism has made itself at home among the analytic philosophers in the United States. It has had its impact upon the empiricists and the realists as well as upon its American counterparts, the analytical philosophers. Bochenski[52] could write some years after the death of Schlick that neopositivism, driven out of the Third Reich by the Nazis, had become "the principal school" in England and of first rate importance in the United States.

The Austrians were not all members of the Vienna Circle. Professor Alfred Stern (b. Baden near Vienna, 1899), for instance, a former president of the Pacific branch of the American Philosophical Association, has taught the philosophy of values and of history at California Institute of Technology for about two decades and his books have appeared in five languages. He is typical of dozens of Austro-American philosophers who were not disciples of Moritz Schlick.[53]

Austrian economists, like Austrian philosophers and Austrian psychiatrists, have made a significant, easily-recognizable contribution to American thought. Like the philosophers and the psychiatrists they have been well represented in the United States by disciples, often notable ones, of the Austrian masters. Indeed, some of the masters themselves have come here.

The best-known of the older Austrian schools of economics was the "marginal value" or "marginal utility" school of Karl Menger (b. Neu Sandez, Austrian Galicia, 1840 – d. Vienna, 1921), Eugen von Böhm-Bawerk (b. Brünn, 1851 – d. Kramsach, Tyrol, 1914) and Friedrich Freiherr von Wieser (b. Vienna, 1851 – d. Brunwinkel on Wolfgangsee, 1926) at Vienna. Their empirical-theoretical methods represented a break with the historical methods of the Germans. They explained prices and distribution in terms of social value, of human need, and of the marginal utility that determined the greater value of a product vis-a-vis its competitors.

British political economy had been supreme until well after the 19th century. The Austrians and their colleagues elsewhere on the Continent created a refreshingly new approach to the subject. American economists in general continued for years to follow the British, and, only recently in this century, with the actual arrival of Austrians and other Europeans at the American scene, has American economic thought been strongly influenced by the new schools. Of those the French, Italian and Viennese were outstanding. American thought on marginal value has, especially, come from the Austrians. When Irving Fisher, one of America's greatest recent economists, could dedicate a book to the Austrian Böhm-Bawerk "who laid the foundations upon which I have endeavored to build," it was clear that the Austrians had had an impact in this country.[54]

Most of the Austrian economists have been strongly anti-Marxist. Lekachman in his book on economic ideas called Böhm-Bawerk "Marx's most damaging critic." Menger's teachings were based upon confidence in the utility of capitalism. Some of the Austrians who came to America were out-and-out crusaders for capitalism.

Joseph Alois Schumpeter (b. Triesch, Moravia, 1883 – d. Cambridge, 1950), one of the most notable of the Austro-American economists, was a leading critic of Marxism although he predicted the end of capitalism. Educated in Vienna he had doctorates from Vienna, Columbia, and Sofia. He taught in Vienna, Czernowitz, Graz, Bonn, and, during the Hitler years and until his death, at Harvard. He was Austrian Minister of Finance in the new republic's cabinet in 1919–1920. He was an authority upon business cycles which was a specialty among Vienna economists. His method was more historical than that of most of his friends of the Vienna School. The fact that over half a dozen of his learned books were still available in the American book trade a decade after his death indicates how much he was read in his adopted country.[55]

Ludwig von Mises of New York University (b. Lemberg, 1881), the Vienna-educated founder of the Austrian Institute for Research in Business Cycles and secretary of the influential Austrian chamber of commerce, was a distinguished refugee from Nazism. He taught economics at the University of Vienna and at Geneva's Institute of International Studies before he came to New York University's School of Business Administration in 1945. Von Mises was a critic of planned economy and so notable as an anti-Marxist that "U.S. News and World Report" could, on October 19, 1956, spread his article on "The Anti-Capitalistic Mentality" as its feature of the week. In 1962 he was decorated by the Austrian government.[56]

A younger colleague of von Mises who came to America back in 1920 was Professor Marcus Nadler born in 1895 in Kimpolung, Bucovina, that is now Rumania. He has served as Federal Reserve Board economist and associate editor of the New York "Journal of Commerce" as well as New York University's professor of banking and finance.[57]

Although relatively few Austro-Americans have entered politics in their adopted country, a very considerable group, and especially among the economists, has served the Executive branch of the Federal government. The statistician Max Sasuly (b. 1888) who came to America in his teens has made a career with such branches as the Bureau of Standards, the New Deal's NRA, and the Social Security Board.[58] Kurt Edward Rosinger (b. Vienna, 1904) who immigrated as a child served in several of the Federal economic agencies during World War II.[59] Well known in Germany as a champion of Stresemann's liberal politics, member of the Reichstag, and editor of economic journals was the Austrian-born, Vienna-educated Gustav Stolper (b. Vienna, 1888 – d. 1947) who fled from Hitler in 1933 to New York, became chairman of the Conference of American Business Economists, and died of the strain involved in helping ex-President Hoover prepare his proposals for the revival of the German economy.[60]

David Weintraub (b. Kozlow, Austrian Galicia, 1904) immigrated in the twenties and served the United States government during World War II before he became, in 1946, director of the U.N.'s division of economic stability and development.[61] Another familiar Austro-American at the U.N. since its founding at which he participated has been the State Department's Walter Kotschnig (b. Judenburg, Styria, 1901). The product of the universities at Graz and Kiel, since 1954 director of the Department's strategic Office of Economic Affairs, the able Kotschnig has helped guide the Department through a maze of conferences and programs in the fields of international organization, culture and economics.[62]

One of the most useful members of the U.S. Mission to European Communities at Brussels (appointed 1958) was the former Vienna banker, Oscar Zaglits (b. Petersdorf, Burgenland, 1897), who came in 1939 to serve as chief of the international monetary branch of the Department of Agriculture.[63] The Vienna-born Bert F. Hoselitz (b. 1913; emigrated 1939), since 1953 professor of social science at the University of Chicago, was a consultant to the U.N. and, briefly, advisor to the government of India. And Robert Eisenberg (b. Waidhofen, Lower Austria, 1908), in 1955–1956 in charge of the U.S. mission to the European Coal and Steel Community, became in 1945, four years after his arrival in the country, one of the State Department's useful group of Austrian-born officers.[64]

The notable university professors among the economists were far more widely known than the public officials. We have already mentioned some of them. Alexander

Gerschenkron was professor of economics at Harvard. A president of the American Catholic Economics Association (1949—1950) was Professor Josef Solterer (b. Vienna, 1897), a veteran of the Austrian navy during World War I and of navigation in the Dutch East Indies, who came to America in 1924.[65] Most of the better-known worked in the eastern half of the country. There was Professor Frank Tannenbaum of Columbia (b. Austria, 1893; immigrated 1905), whose newspaper career in Mexico in the early twenties led him into Latin-American history and whose book on Mexico, which he knew from burro-back, intrigued tens of thousands of American readers.[66]

And Professor Peter F. Drucker (b. Vienna, 1909) of Bennington and New York University, arrived in the New World as late as 1937 to become one of America's favorite economic prophets with books like "The End of Economic Man" (1937) and "The New Society." Somehow his articles in "Harpers" and other influential magazines seemed properly to interpret contemporary America to thousands of Americans. It is probable that a European education, at Vienna and Frankfurt in Drucker's case, enables the observer to see his adopted country through different and often exciting perspectives.[67]

Fritz Machlup (b. Wiener-Neustadt, 1902) came to Princeton in 1960 some twenty-seven years after his arrival in America with a distinguished career from Harvard to Johns Hopkins and a whole series of much-read books on economics for the thoughtful reader to his credit.[68] American economics would clearly have been much the poorer without the contribution of these scholars who came here to place their Austrian training or experience at our disposal.

The name Friedrich August von Hayek (b. Vienna, 1899) is a major reminder of the tremendous losses that Austria has suffered through the emigration of so much talent. And Hayek, student of von Wieser and of von Mises, and director of von Mises' new Vienna Institute for Research in Business Cycles, left his native land for Britain, to teach at London University, long before Hitler threatened Austria, in 1931. He returned only for summers in Innsbruck to climb the Alps that he missed so much. His fame grew in London, he published the correspondence of John Stuart Mill and Harriet Taylor (U. Chicago Press), found that he could write a best-seller, "The Road to Serfdom" (1944) to popularize his economic views, including his conviction that Socialism had become respectable while still dangerous, and in 1950 accepted the position of social and moral sciences on the Committee on Social Thought in the University of Chicago. His books have been read by more than the academes in the United States.[69] His brothers, Erich the head of the Chemical Institute of the University of Innsbruck and Heinrich the director of the Anatomical Institute of the University of Vienna, are known by reputation here in America.

We must also mention the distinguished Professor Gottfried von Haberler of Harvard (b. Purkersdorf near Vienna, 1900) who took his doctorates at the University of Vienna in 1923 and 1925 and taught there until he went to Harvard in the early thirties. He became known in the United Nations and in all the universities of Europe and Latin America where he lectured. He contributed to Washington's price-control program during the war, and became so prominent as to achieve election to the presidency of both the International Economic Association and the American Economic Association. Haberler was a free trader and an expert on business cycles.[70] His works on world trade became classics and he himself became one of America's greatest economists. Many of his students, like the Troppau-born Emil Spitzer whom he recommended to the United Nations' International Monetary Fund, have spread his economic gospel.

And to Princeton in 1938 came the German-born Professor Oskar Morgenstern (b. Görlitz, Silesia, 1902) who had studied and taught at the University of Vienna and directed there von Mises's Institute for Research in Business Cycles. Morgenstern, like so many of the finer Austro-American economists, had often contributed to public service, in his case in advising the Austrian Ministry of Commerce, the League of Nations, and the U.S. Atomic Energy Commission.[71] Indeed, to list all of his public services together with all his academic distinctions would be a major undertaking. The student may wonder whether the uprooting of such figures, passing them through the stimulating Vienna atmosphere of hope and despair, and then subjecting them to a refreshing American experience, is what produces genius. In any event it is clear that much American talent in the field of economics came out of Vienna.

[1] I. H. U. Lacher, *German Element in Wisconsin*, Steuben Soc. 1925. Aigner served 1851–53.

[2] *Who's Who*, 1938–39.

[3] *Universal Jewish Encyclopedia.*

[4] *Who's Who*, 1962–63.

[5] *Who's Who of American Women*, 2nd ed., 1961.

[6] *Who's Who*, 1962–63.

[7] H. A. Pochmann, *German Culture in America*, Madison 1957, p. 19.

[8] Thomas Čapek, *Čechs (Bohemians) in America*, N.Y. and Boston 1920, p. 93.

[9] *American-German Review*, Apr. 1947, p. 34.

[10] *Das Buch der Deutschen in Amerika*, Philadelphia 1907, p. 322.

[11] Articles by Herbert Penzl in *Dictionary of American Biography*, Supp. II, and in *Österreich und die angelsächsische Welt*, Wien 1961, pp. 217ff. See also *Who's Who*, 1938–39. Herbert Penzl (b. Neufelden, 1910), himself an Austrian of distinction, educated at Brown University and Vienna, received his professorship at the University of Michigan in 1953: *Directory of American Scholars*, 3rd ed.

[12] See his *Franz Grillparzer in England and America*, Wien 1960, and his many translations of Grillparzer's plays, etc.

[13] *Kürschners Deutscher Gelehrten-Kalender*, Berlin 1954.

[14] *Who's Who*, 1962–63.

[15] See for Kahler the *Directory of American Scholars*, vol. III, N.Y. 1964; and for Horn the ms. list of Austrian-born in the Humanities at the Austrian Institute, N.Y., compiled 1960. See also the *Directory of American Scholars.*

[16] *Books Abroad*, Summer 1961, p. 265.

[17] *Austrian Information* publishes frequent items on these schools, e. g. 16 Feb. 1961, pp. 4–6.

[18] *Who's Who*, 1960–61; article by Penzl in *Österreich und die angelsächsische Welt*, p. 221.

[19] *Who's Who*, 1962–63.

[20] *Who's Who*, 1899–1900.

[21] *Who's Who*, 1952–53.

[22] *Ibid.*

[23] Obit. in *Washington Post*, 14 Oct. 1962, p. G9.

[24] *Who's Who in Library Service*, 3rd ed., p. 387.

[25] *Austrian Information*, 15 Nov. 1961, 9 Feb. 1963.

[26] *Who's Who*, 1938–39.

[27] *Who's Who of American Women*, 2nd ed, 1961.

[28] *American Men of Science*, 9th ed., vol. III, N.Y. 1956, *Time*, 22 Oct. 1956 and 15 July 1957; *Austrian Information*, 6 May 1961.

[29] *Who's Who*, 1952–53.

[30] *American Men of Science*, 9th ed., III; *International World Who's Who*, N.Y. 1949, p. 712.

[31] *Who's Who of American Women*, 2nd ed., 1961.

[32] *Who's Who*, 1962–63.

[33] He was appointed at the U. of Illinois in 1960. *Who's Who*, 1962–63.

[34] *Who's Who of American Women*, 2nd ed., 1961.

[35] *Who's Who*, 1962–63.

[36] *Who's Who*, 1960–61.

[37] Buber was so called by Reinhold Niebuhr. *Current Biography*, June 1953, p. 94.

[38] David Abrahamson, *The Mind and Death of a Genius*, Columbia U. Press 1946, is a biography of Weininger. For reviews of his book see *The Critic*, May 1906, pp. 414–15; *Book Review Digest*, vol. I, 1905–06, p. 372.

[39] *Concise Encyclopedia of Western Philosophy*, N.Y. 1960.

[40] *New York Times Magazine*, 3 Dec. 1961, pp. 43ff. See also *Current Biography*, June 1953, pp. 94–95; and the pocket book, *The Writings of Martin Buber*, N.Y. 1956, edited by Will Herberg. Dozens of his books are available in American libraries.

[41] See M. L. Diamond, *Jewish Existentialist*, N.Y. 1960.

[42] In 1927. See *Current Biography*, *loc. cit.*, which states that Max Lerner listed him with the 25 political, intellectual, and moral rulers of the world in 1949.

[43] There were, for instance, twenty Buber catalog cards in the Washington, D.C. public library in 1962. The Library of Congress had many times that number.

[44] In 1962 Blanche Hardy Schlick published in Vienna the *Aphorismen von Moritz Schlick.*

[45] V. Kraft, *Vienna Circle*, N.Y. 1953, pp. V and IX.

[46] The Nazis forbade publication of its literature including its journal *Erkenntnis*. Kraft, *op. cit.*, p. 8.

[47] Philosophical literature contains much information on the Vienna Circle. See especially G. Bergmann, *Metaphysics of Logical Positivism*, 1954; *Concise Encyclopedia of Western Philosophy* . . ., pp. 77, 402; W. H. Werkmeister, *A History of Philosophical Ideas in America*, N.Y. 1949, p. 565; W. E. Hocking, *Types of Philosophy*, N.Y. 1959, pp. 88–90.

[48] See, for instance, the *Concise Encyclopedia of Western Philosophy*, pp. 244–46. See also *Chamber's Dictionary of Scientists*, London 1961, p. 298. Mach is, however, one of the dozen immortals included in H. D. Aiken's *Age of Ideology*, Boston 1957, receiving more space than Schopenhauer.

[49] We Americans now know Ludwig Boltzmann chiefly as the man who gave his name to the *Gasse* where the U.S. embassy is located. He was a great mathematician and philosopher.

[50] *Metaphysics of Logical Positivism*, p. 2.

[51] Bergmann, *op. cit.*, p. 2; Norman Malcolm, *Ludwig Wittgenstein*, London 1958, *passim;* Philipp Frank, *Modern Science and its Philosophy*, Harvard 1949, p. 32; D. D. Runes, *Pictorial History of Philosophy*, N.Y. 1959, pp. 272, 338; *Concise Encyclopedia of Western Philosophy*, pp. 408–11. The author is also indebted to Prof. Boyd Graves of the University of Virginia for his suggestions.

[52] I. M. Bochenski, *Contemporary European Philosophy*, Berkeley 1961, pp. 52–53. See also B. A. G. Fuller, *History of Philosophy*, N.Y. 1957, p. 593.

[53] Biographical information regarding these philosophers will be found in many of the sources cited above in this chapter. See also *Who's Who* for those who came to the U.S.A. Runes, *op. cit.*, has some easily understandable passages, e. g. p. 337 for Schlick. See also the Schlick obituary, *N.Y. Times*, 23 June 1936, p. 9. We have also drawn upon Fuller, *op. cit.*, pp. 592ff. Schlick's reputation here is underscored by the publication in 1963 of a fourth edition of his *Space and Time in Contemporary Physics* (Dover Publications, New York). His wife, the late Mrs. Blanche Schlick (b. Massachusetts) has been most kind in supplying information and Countess Amethe von Zeppelin of Vienna has assisted in supplying a statement regarding Professor Schlick. For Stern see the *Directory of American Scholars*, IV, N.Y. 1964. Stern's letter of 5 July 1966 to Dr. W. Schlag of the Austrian Institute makes it clear that he did not belong to the *Wiener Kreis.*

[54] Robert Lekachman, *History of Economic Ideas*, N.Y. 1959, pp. 248ff; H. A. Mills and R. E. Montgomery, *Labor's Progress*, N.Y. 1938, p. 177; Charles Gide and Charles Rist, *History of Economic Doctrines*, 2nd English ed., p. 638. A cursory check of books on economic thought in the author's local public libraries indicates that however much the doctrines of the Austrians may have permeated world thinking, it is the British and French books, and not the American authorities, which recognize the Austrians by name and origin. Even Austro-American names seem to appear more frequently in British and French general studies than in American ones.

[55] *Books in Print*, 1960; *Dictionary of American Scholars*, 1942; Lekachman, *op. cit.*, *passim.*

[56] *Wer ist Wer*, XIII; *Der Grosse Brockhaus*, 1955; *Universal Jewish Encyclopedia; Austrian Information*, 31 Oct. 1962; *American Men of Science*, 9th ed., III.

[57] *Who's Who*, 1962–63.

[58] *Who's Who*, 1952–53.

[59] *Who's Who*, 1962–63.

[60] *American Historical Review*, Jan. 1962, pp. 488–89.

[61] *Who's Who in the United Nations*, 1951; *Who's Who*, 1962–63.

[62] *Ibid.*

[63] *Ibid.*

[64] *Ibid.*

[65] *Ibid.*

[66] *Ibid.*

[67] *Harpers*, June 1962, pp. 40 and 41.

[68] *Who's Who*, 1952–53.

[69] *American Men of Science*, 9th ed., III; *Twentieth Century Authors*, 1st Supp.

[70] Gide and Rist, *op. cit.*, pp. 697 and 751; *Who's Who in Austria*, 1954; *Who's Who*, 1962–63.

[71] *Ibid.*

CHAPTER XIV

SCIENTISTS

Hiroshima might never have been the first victim of an atomic bomb in 1945 had it not been for a shy little Austrian physicist named Lise Meitner. "The atom age began," it has been said, "in a woman's mind," and that woman was Lise Meitner.[1] Not that the atom age would not have come without Dr. Meitner (b. Vienna, 1878) but it can be demonstrated that it came when and where it did because her inquiring mind awoke to the significance of the researches in which she had collaborated back in Berlin in 1938 before she fled the Jew-baters to go to Copenhagen and Stockholm.

In Berlin Lise Meitner had helped Otto Hahn and Fritz Strassmann bombard uranium atoms. It was only, however, after she had in Scandinavia applied what she had learned from Einstein to the bewildering results of the Berlin experiments that she realized the mighty significance of it all. Dr. Meitner called the breaking of the atom "fission" and she realized its enormous potential for creating energy.

So, while the Germans were still thinking of atomic energy as a mere form of fuel, their enemies started work on the atomic bomb. Dr. Meitner's Danish colleague Niels Bohr, and her nephew Otto Frisch came to America and through them, early in 1939, the epoch-making story was revealed. Scientists like Fermi and Einstein confirmed the Meitner hypothesis, Roosevelt was convinced, and the New Mexico desert heard the first appalling atomic explosion in 1945. Without Dr. Meitner the secret of fission might have remained unrealized for long critical months in Berlin.

The little Austrian scientist (she had lived and worked in Vienna until she went to Germany at the age of thirty) was shocked by the application of her work. Anti-Nazi as she was, she was horrified by the destructive feature of her discoveries. She doubtless visited America more because it was her sisters' home than to receive acclaim. And living later in Stockholm and Cambridge, England, she modestly accepted homage (she received, among many other honors, the Achievement Award of the Women's National Press Club in Washington, and Sweden distinguished her as one of the only three women in two hundred years to receive election to its Academy of Science) but she never sought fame and she seems to have shown little satisfaction in her role in changing history.[2] It was only in 1966 that the United States officially recognized her contribution to the atomic age by presenting her, and Otto Hahn and Fritz Strassmann, both Germans, with the significant Enrico Fermi award. Dr. Meitner was the first woman ever to receive that award.

The German Austrians, like the Germans to the north of them, have had a long and distinguished record in science. And many of those achievements, like the work of Lise Meitner, have been so notable as to be of genuine significance to scientifically-minded America. And in science the Habsburg empire was often as international as Lise Meitner's career. The famous expounder of the Copernican system of the universe, Johannes Kepler (1571–1630), for instance, was a Württemberger by birth who came in his early twenties to teach and turn from theology to astronomy at the University of Graz, practice mathematics at Linz, and become world-famous at Prague before spending his last four years at Ulm.[3]

More provincial was Gregor Mendel (b. Heinzendorf, Austrian Silesia, 1822 – d. 1884), "the little Austrian monk," who died in Brünn in obscurity only to be rediscovered and recognized as the Father of Genetics by Erich Tschermak von Seysenegg (b. Vienna, 1871 – d. Vienna, 1962) and his colleagues in 1900. Mendel's iconoclastic study of his experiments with peas was first ignored by Brünn's Natural History Society at a session that was simply preoccupied with the impacts of Darwinism. And another irony in his career was the fact that Mendel, "the father of genetics," failed in Vienna to qualify for teaching biology and had to return home and learn Czech so that he could teach in something beside his native German.[4]

Nineteenth-century Austrians with inquiring minds, finding boldness in the social sciences and in belles-lettres frowned upon by Metternich and too many of his successors, turned to science. There was in consequence a long series of scientific immortals, known to every American student in science and medicine – men like the physicist Josef Stefan (b. near Klagenfurt, Carinthia, 1835 – d. Vienna, 1893) and his disciples Ludwig Boltzmann (b. Vienna, 1844 – d. near Görz, 1906) whose "Lectures on Gas Theory" were first published in English by the University of California Press in 1964, and Friederich Hasenöhrl (b. Vienna, 1874 – d. at the front 1915) whose work on light and heat radiation "served as a starting point from which the great bulk of our knowledge in this field up to this day has been acquired." Stefan made it possible to estimate the intensity of the sun's heat.[5] Hasenöhrl's formula of 1904, $E = mc^2$, which is engraved on the walls of the Austrian National Library, became more famous later when Einstein used it for his prediction on the deflection of light. The great majority of these famous figures worked at the University of Vienna. Some taught briefly in Germany. Almost none came to the United States.

The twentieth century, on the other hand, saw many of the most notable of the Austrian-born scientists coming to this country. That was especially true in physics.

Of Austria's four Nobel Prize winners in physics three came to live and work in America and the fourth, Erwin Schrödinger (b. Vienna, 1887 – d. Vienna, 1961), a great mathematical physicist, spent some time here during his refugee period.[6]

Victor Franz Hess (b. Waldstein near Graz, 1883—d. Mt. Vernon, N.Y., 1964), student and teacher in both Graz and Vienna and professor at Innsbruck, received a chair in physics at Fordham in 1938 two years after receiving the Nobel Prize for his epoch-making discovery of cosmic rays.[7] That discovery, which dated back to his work at the University of Vienna, brought him fame in America as well as in Europe. He advised the United States Radium Corporation as early as 1921—1923 and, when his marriage to a Jewess brought on his dismissal from the University of Graz in Austria's first Nazi year, Hess was doubtless more than welcome at Fordham. Switzerland had given him and his wife temporary asylum.

"Fortune" magazine's "Great American Scientists" (1960) describes Isidor Isaac Rabi (b. Rymanov, Austrian Galicia, 1898) of Columbia and the President's Science Advisory Committee as the oldest of the great group of men who have shaped American physics. He came to America as an infant and received the Nobel award in 1944. Wolfgang Pauli (b. Vienna, 1900) on the other hand was educated in Vienna and Munich and taught for years in Europe before he came to Princeton during the Nazi years. This last of the Big Four received his Nobel Prize in 1945.[8]

Three of these four Austrian-born Nobel Prize winners were designated by American Nobel Laureates polled by "Fortune" magazine's editors in 1960, as ranking among the fifteen Nobel "immortals" in physics.

In American defence work the Austrian-born scientists played a fascinating role. Some came before and during World War II to bear evidence to the determination of thousands of Austrians to rid Europe of the Austrian-born menace named Hitler. And some who had used their scientific abilities on behalf of the Third Reich were brought over at the end of the war under "Operation Paper Clip" to work in America's laboratories on ordnance, nuclear problems, rockets and the like. The U.S. Army, for instance, picked up Friedrich von Doblhoff (b. Budapest, 1916)[9], the chief engineer of the Wiener Neustadt Aircraft Works in 1945 and used him for some months as an interpreter before he was shipped off to the United States where for ten years he built helicopters for McDonnell Aircraft in St. Louis. He was an aero engineer, a product of Vienna's *Technische Hochschule*. American firms, and even anonymous government agencies, rushed to Vienna to outbid Austria for the most likely of its scientists. Austria did indeed lose many of its best.[10]

An intriguing figure, who never came to America but whose patents fell into the hands of the victors at the end of World War II, was Georg Stetter (b. Vienna, 1895) who anticipated the later development of nuclear-reactor research. His original patent of June 1939 was "for a contrivance for the technical production of energy with the help of nuclear reaction." His findings, developed at the First Physical Institute of the University of Vienna, were declared secret by the German patent office and were doubtless acquired too late by the Allies to contribute to American nuclear development. "A minor Austrian miracle," as the Vienna press called it when the story was told in 1963, it had remained like so many miracles in far-away Austria, unrecognized and unsung.[11]

Notable among the Austrian-born physicists at the Oak-Ridge-Nuclear-Project and Atomic Energy Commission were Philip Sporn (b. 1896) whose career at Columbia University was recognized with academic honors here and abroad;[12] Ernest H. Kalmus (b. Vienna, 1899) in biophysics who was one of the late-comers at the Los Alamos atomic laboratory; Victor F. Weisskopf, born in Vienna in 1908, educated there and at Göttingen, and later, after 1937, professor of physics at Rochester and Massachusetts Institute of Technology, who was an earlier comer at Los Alamos;[14] and another Los Alamos physicist, Martin Deutsch (b. Vienna, 1917) who immigrated in 1935 and achieved his M.I.T. professorship in 1953.[15]

Austro-Americans also contributed to the development of rockets and missiles. The president of the American Rocket Society in 1958 was George Paul Sutton (b. Austria, 1920), immigrant of 1938, who taught at M.I.T. and engineered rockets for North American Aviation.[16] And notorious in early 1963 when Israel objected to the work "German" scientists were doing for Nasser's Egypt, was Eugen Sänger (b. Presnitz, Bohemia, 1905 – d. Berlin, 1964)[17] who worked until 1936 at the *Technische Hochschule* in Vienna before he went to Germany to make rockets for the armed forces there. His *formulae*, West German sources declared, had enabled the U.S. Air Force to launch its Project Dyna-Soar and design the fabulous X-15 that broke so many speed and altitude records. And a Viennese who had pioneered in radar in Germany during the war was Carl L. Kober (b. 1913) who came only in 1949 to the United States to continue his career in the field of radio and missiles.[18]

Perhaps the most impressive of all the Austro-Americans in the defence effort was the inventor of the all-important counter-radar device – an invention that made it possible for American ships and planes to hide from enemy radar. He was Otto Halpern (b. 1899), a native of Vienna, who worked out his project during World War II when he was teaching at New York University and M.I.T. After long years of litigation Halpern received in 1959 an award of $ 340,000 for his invention which thereupon became the property of the government. The Secretary of Defence admitted at that time that the top-secret Halpern invention was still the basis for America's radar defence.[19]

A few of the outstanding University of Vienna physicists came only to visit: the impressive Jewish refugee Professor Felix Ehrenhaft (b. Vienna, 1879) who stayed long enough to take American citizenship; Michael Higatsberger (b. near Krems, 1924) who taught briefly at the University of Minnesota and returned to direct Vienna's nuclear reactor center, and the well-known Hans Thirring (b. Vienna, 1888) who came in 1961 on a visit that had been too long deferred by the now-despised security boys of the McCarthy period. His son Walter Thirring (b. Vienna, 1927), one of the University of Vienna's ablest young nuclear physicists, worked briefly at the Massachusetts Institute of Technology and in Princeton and Seattle. Dr. Peter Weinzierl, nuclear physicist with Austria's reactor plant near Vienna, was one of the many Austrian Fulbright-scholarship grantees who studied here before embarking upon useful careers in their native land.

Of the professorial physicists who came long before World War II or well after it, as well as during the tragic era, there were many. Some like Karl Lark-Horovitz (b. Vienna, 1893) who headed Purdue's physics department for many years, and Selig Hecht of Columbia, whose book "Explaining the Atom" was a best-seller, were among the very best. Dozens of them, even though they might earlier have worn Austrian uniforms, contributed to American defence work. They were well distributed, from Wisconsin to Texas, and from California to the Middle Atlantic states. Most of them were natives of Vienna.[20]

Many of the Austro-American scientists went into the commercial field. The Austrian army veteran Ernst Anton Lederer, born in Prague in 1895, educated in Vienna, employed by Westinghouse Austria and, after 1923, by Westinghouse U.S.A., was honored after World War II with citations from the War Department and the War Production Board.[21] In Nazi days came another Prager, Paul Schwarzkopf (b. 1886), a pioneer in powder metallurgy,[22] and John Hans Troll (b. Vienna, 1919) in electronics at Cambridge in Massachusetts, Franz Urbach (b. Vienna, 1902) of Vienna's pioneer Institute for Radium Research to work with Eastman Kodak, and, well after Hitler, Richard Franz Karl Herzog (b. Vienna, 1911) to work in Massachusetts with the Geophysics Corporation of America.

Most successful of all the industrial scientists from Austria was Frederic de Hoffmann (b. Vienna, 1924), an immigrant of 1941 who studied at Harvard, worked at Los Alamos on the bomb and, a bit later at the early age of thirty-one came to be a vice president of one of our greatest defense industries, General Dynamics. The "New Yorker" surmised in 1958 that he might well have been the only thirty-three-year-old senior vice president of a billion dollar corporation.[23] He became the corporation's president two years later.

Einstein's associate Walter Mayer (1887—1948), long a professor of mathematics at the University of Vienna and after 1933 connected with the Princeton Institute of Advanced Study, was famous for the Einstein-Mayer unified-field theory.[24] The Austro-American mathematicians came to comprise what was apparently, after medicine, physics and chemistry, the largest group of Austro-American scientists.[25]

Perhaps the best known among the mathematicians was Richard von Mises (b. Lemberg, 1883—d. Boston, 1953), with a typically Austro-Hungarian career that led from his birthplace in Lemberg to study in Vienna and Brünn, to teaching in Germany, flight from the Nazis to occupy the chair of mathematics at Istanbul and, finally, coming to America in 1938, to distinguish himself at Harvard. Von Mises married the Vienna-born mathematician Hilda Geiringer who taught mathematics here at Bryn Mawr and Wheaton colleges. His interests were broad, from aerodynamics and applied mathematics to literature (he published a Rilke bibliography in English) and philosophy. His volume on "Positivism" (1951) revealed his conception of science as the basis of philosophy and of philosophy as a primary objective of scientific study.[26]

There came in Austria's republican period a notable group of biologists. Theodore Spaeth Hauschka (b. Reichenau, Lower Austria, 1908) and Erna Alture Werber (b. Vienna), the first educated in America and the second in Vienna. They went into research work, Hauschka with American Cyanamid and Werber with Squibb and the Jacques Loewe Foundation in Brooklyn.[27] Many went into teaching—Hauschka at the University of Buffalo. Jacob Yerushalmy (b. Vienna, 1904; immigrated 1924), the biostatistician who worked for years for the health services of New York and the United States, achieved a professorship at the University of California;[28] the biologist Paul Weiss (b. Vienna, 1898) to whom Frankfurt gave an honorary doctorate in 1949, came to Yale in 1931, went on to Chicago, and later joined the Rockefeller Institute for Medical Research;[29] and the younger prodigy, Henry Koffler (b. Vienna, 1922), immigrated in 1939, was promptly naturalized, like most of the Thirty-eighters, in 1945, and found himself in 1959 a full professor of biology at Purdue University.[30] It was amazing how these newcomers from Austria found their places in the greater American world.

The Cornell University Press published in 1950 the important volume on "Bees" that was the work of Karl von Frisch (b. Vienna, 1886), an animal behaviorist with a University of Vienna doctorate who had worked chiefly at Munich and briefly at Graz but not in America. The zoologist Nathan Fasten (b. Lezaysk, Austrian Galicia, 1887) of Oregon and Washington seems to have considered himself an Austrian.[31] And there were other charming invaders in zoology and botany, usually distinguished by the long "A" that even the Austrian-born, with all their skill in foreign languages, found it difficult to shake off. Two of them, at least, achieved pocket-book popularity in America. The brilliant Konrad Lorenz (b. Vienna, 1903), whose importance was widely proclaimed in the 1960's, published some intriguing and highly significant studies on social relationships in birds and other creatures, representing the revival of interest in animal behavior that followed the era of interest, after the rediscovery of Mendel in 1900, in genetics. His fascinating "King Solomon's Ring" (Crowell 1952; Crowell paperback 1961) was a highly readable and yet important book on animals and their behavior. Far more significant was his highly readable volume, "On Aggression," which became almost immediately a classic in the America that was then so much concerned with man's aggressive urges in far outposts like Viet Nam. Americans who opposed their country's Viet Nam venture, found the fascinating findings of Lorenz a kind of Bible. Lorenz was widely honored in his field by, for instance, the New York Zoological Society with its golden medal and the American

Academy of Arts and Science with an honorary membership.[32] And the books of Hans Hass about marine adventure and sharks and other predatory ocean monsters, especially his "Manta Under the Red Sea" (Rand McNally 1952), have become classics.[33]

A significant figure in botany and Orientalia was Joseph F. Rock (b. Vienna, 1884) who worked in Hawaii well before World War I, came to the U.S. Department of Agriculture and, later, during the second war to the Army Map Service. He devoted himself for years to Chinese plant research, directed the National Geographic Society's Yunnan-Tibet expedition and Harvard's explorations into the same area of northwest China.[34]

There were other early arrivals in the natural sciences. Adolf Carl Noé (b. Graz, 1873), recipient of a gold medal from the University of Vienna in 1923, twenty-four years after his arrival in the United States, taught German at Stanford and Chicago before Chicago allowed him to turn to paleobotany where he became so well-known.[35]

In astronomy there was the Jesuit Johann Georg Hagen (b. Bregenz, 1847 – d. Rome, 1930) who came here in 1880 to direct Georgetown College's observatory, and almost eighty years later Professor Thomas Gold (b. Vienna, 1920) who came from England to Harvard and Cornell.[36] The chairman of the Rutgers Department of Meteorology from 1946 was Erwin R. Biel (b. Vienna, 1899), a Thirty-eighter who had taught at the *Volkshochschulen* in Vienna, those admirable upper schools for Viennese unable to fit into the more formal universities.[37]

Although, as we have seen, America attracted three of the four Austrian Nobel laureates in physics, none of the Austrian-born laureates in chemistry came here to live and work: Fritz Pregl whose career was chiefly at the University of Graz, or Richard Zsigmondy and Richard Kuhn, both Vienna-born chemists who worked in Germany. Actually Kuhn never received his award because the Nazis forbade him to accept it.[38]

Dozens of other Austrian-born did come in the twentieth century to distinguish themselves here in chemistry. A few like Ludwig F. Andrieth (b. Vienna, 1901) in inorganic chemistry at the University of Illinois were brought here in their infancy.[39] Most of them, like internationally-known Oskar Paul Wintersteiner (b. Bruck/Mur, Styria, 1898), came with Austrian training and experience. Wintersteiner, for instance, who in 1948 received the Presidential Certificate of Merit after 22 distinguished years in the United States, was a product of the University of Graz, famous for its work in chemistry.[40] Anton Alexander Benedetti-Pichler (b. Vienna, 1894 – d. South Carolina, 1964) was another fine name in chemistry with a Graz background who immigrated soon after Wintersteiner to teach at Queens College.[41] Erich Mosettig (b. Vienna, 1898 – d. 1962) came in the same year, with a Vienna background, to work at the University of Virginia and to fill key positions at the National Institutes of Health.[42]

There was a substantial group of chemists that came during the long Hitler years. Austria's chief chemist of World War I, Ernst Berl (b. Austrian Silesia, 1877 – d. Pittsburgh, Pa., 1946), came as one of the earliest refugees to work with the American military services on explosives and chemical warfare.[43] Later there came Hans Neurath (b. Vienna, 1909) to become head of the department at the University of Washington, Walter Berl (b. Vienna, 1917) who was to work at Johns Hopkins, Ernst Hauser (b. Vienna, 1896) who taught at the Massachusetts Institute of Technology, and younger fugitives like Kurt Clark Schreiber (b. Vienna, 1922) who went to Duquesne University and Ruth Hubbard (b. Vienna, 1922) who went to Harvard.

One of the most-honored of all the Thirty-eighter chemists was the "zestful Viennese," Hermann Francis Mark (b. Vienna, 1895) who came via two years in Canada to build in Brooklyn upon his vast Old-World reputation for work in synthetic plastics, fibers, and rubbers. After work at the Kaiser Wilhelm Institute in Berlin and a short term with I. G. Farben, Dr. Mark developed polymer chemistry at the University of Vienna. Arrested by the Gestapo in 1938 he made his way to Switzerland and financed his escape in part with coat-hangers of platinum that he had devised for the purpose. Later, at Brooklyn Polytechnic Institute his polymer chemistry drew dozens of able disciples and his reputation for practical achievement made him consultant to du Pont for eighteen years. At his Polymer Research Institute of the Brooklyn Institute of Technology (founded by him in 1946) he helped develop a whole range of synthetic materials including Nylon, Orlon, Dacron, and Polystyrene. He became a rich man but never lost his zest for Vienna's light music and drinking songs.[44]

Otto Eisenschiml (b. Vienna, 1880 – d. Chicago, 1963), whose hobby was Lincoln and the American Civil War and writing books about them, was one of the earliest of the Vienna-educated chemists devoted to industrial chemistry in the United States. He worked with Carnegie Steel and then made his reputation in the field of vegetable oils. He was first president of the National Soybean Manufacturers Association.[45] Eisenschiml's fascination for writing Lincoln books (his "Why was Lincoln Murdered" was the best known of them all) might remind one vaguely of another fine industrial chemist, Norbert Lewis Lederer, an American born and educated in Austria, whose hobby was writing crime stories.[46]

Out of Graz before the refugee years came Ralph Norbert Lulek (b. Graz, 1901) to work in industrial chemistry and develop 75 patents, and Joseph Berthold Niederl (b. Graz, 1899) of N.Y. University and J. B. Niederl & Associates who in 1947 was placed by the experts among the first ten in American analytical chemistry.[47]

Later, in the Nazi period, the industrial chemists came to America from Vienna rather than from Graz. And here they were well distributed without the usual Austrian tendency to concentrate in New York. Many worked for the nation's biggest firms, some established their own laboratories under their own names, some taught on the side and many gave time and effort to government service.[48]

The cumulative contribution of these Austrians to American scientific endeavor was obviously of huge importance. Their loss to little Austria must have been tremendous. A third of Austria's university graduates were emigrating as late as 1961, long after the Nazi period and simply because a small country could not use all of the talent that it was developing.[49] Certainly the laboratories of America owe a debt of gratitude to the Austrian universities which, in the sound old European manner, have been furnishing so much fine grist for the American mill.

[1] Roberta Silman, "Atom Age Mona Lisa: Dr. Lise Meitner," *Saturday Review*, 6 June 1959; article by P. M. Plechl in *Die Presse*, Wien, 2–3 Nov. 1963.

[2] *Who's Who*, 1962–63; *Current Biography*, 1945; James Stokeley, *New World of the Atom*, N.Y. 1957, pp. 53ff; Friedrich Klemm, *A History of Western Technology*, N.Y. 1959, pp. 370–71; D. Lang, *Early Tales of the Atomic Age*, Garden City 1948, p. 24.

[3] Philipp Lenard, *Great Men of Science*, London 1950.

[4] Harry Scotin, *Gregor Mendel*, N.Y. 1959; Grove Wilson, *Great Men of Science*, N.Y. 1942, pp. 334–40.

[5] Lenard, *op. cit., passim;* N. H. de V. Heathcote, *Nobel Prize Winners in Physics*, N.Y. 1953, p. 98.

[6] *Austrian Information*, 14 Jan. 1961.

[7] Heathcote, *op. cit.*, pp. 334–40.

[8] *Ibid.*, p. 411; Harrie Massey, *New Age in Physics*, N.Y. 1960, *passim.*

[9] *Who's Who in Commerce and Industry*, 1959.

[10] Wilhelm Schlag's article in *Österreich und die angelsächsische Welt*, Wien 1961.

[11] Austrian American Federation, *Austrian News*, Aug. 1963, p. 3; *Die Presse*, Wien, 13–14 July 1963, p. 6.

[12] *Who's Who in Commerce and Industry*, 11th ed.

[13] *American Men of Science*, 10th ed.

[14] *Ibid.*, 9th ed., vol. I, Lancaster, N.Y. 1955.

[15] *Who's Who*, 1962–63.

[16] *Ibid.*

[17] *Washington Post*, 12 Aug. 1962; *Die Presse*, Wien, 11 Feb. 1964.

[16] *Who's Who*, 1962–63.

[19] See *N.Y. Times Index* 1959 and especially *N.Y. Times*, 2 July 1959, p. 9.

[20] Many can be found in the various issues of *American Men of Science* and the various *Who's Who* publications: e.g. Henry Paul Kalmus in electronics most recently with the U.S. Army; Karl Ferdinand Herzfeld of Johns Hopkins and Catholic University; Siegfried Fred Singer and Charles Maria Herzfeld of the University of Maryland; John Christian Michael Brentano of Northwestern; Walter Heinrich Munk of California; Joseph Eisinger of Rice Institute; and even some women including Sulamitt Goldhaber who came to California via Jerusalem, Wisconsin and Columbia; and Ilse Lisl Gal who studied and worked at Hunter, Radcliffe, Wellesley, Cornell, and Yale.

[21] *American Men oj Science*, 9th ed., I.

[22] Schlag, *op. cit.*

[23] Issue of 4 Jan 1958, p 40. This issue contains a ong biographical sketch of de Hoffmann. See also *Who's Who*, 1962–63.

[24] Brown and Roucek, *One America*, 1957, p. 219; obit. in *School and Society*, 18 Sept. 1948.

[25] Typical were the following who appear in *American Men of Science* and/or *Who's Who in America:* Emil Artin (b. Vienna, 1898) of Princeton; Karl Menger (b. Vienna, 1902) of the Illinois Institute of Technology; Otto Neugebauer (b. Innsbruck, 1899) of Brown University; Kurt Gödel (b. Brünn, 1906; Privatdozent University Vienna, 1933–38) of the Princeton Institute for Advanced Study; and Friedrich Ignaz Mautner (b. Vienna, 1921) of Johns Hopkins.

[26] *Universal Jewish Encyclopedia; School and Society*, 25 July 1953; *Wilson Library Bulletin*, Sept. 1953; *Science*, 11 June 1954.

[27] *Who's Who*, 1962–63; *Who's Who of American Women*, 2nd ed., 1961.

[28] *Who's Who*, 1962–63.

[29] *American Men of Science*, 9th ed., I.

[30] *Who's Who*, 1962–63.

[31] *Universal Jewish Encyclopedia*, N.Y. 1948.

[32] *Who's Who in Germany*, Munich 1960; *Book Review Digest*, 1952. For Lorenz and von Frisch see J. P. Scott, *Animal Behavior*, U. Chicago 1958. Lorenz's volume *On Aggression* (N.Y. 1966) has attracted much favorable criticism. Its author was then director of the Max Planck Institute for Behavioral Psychology in Bavaria.

[33] A. C. Spectorsky, ed., *Book of the Sea*, N.Y. 1954, p. 299. Reference should also be made to the zoologist Jerry John Kollbros (b. Vienna, 1917), professor at the State University of Iowa, *Who's Who*, 1962–63.

[34] *American Men of Science*, 9th ed., I.

[35] *Who's Who*, 1938–39.

[36] *Who's Who*, 1899–1900 and 1962–63.

[37] *American Men of Science*, 9th ed., I.

[38] Eduard Farber, *Nobel Prize Winners in Chemistry*, N.Y. 1953.

[39] *American Men of Science*, 9th ed., I.

[40] *Chemical Who's Who*, N.Y. 1956.

[41] *American Men of Science*, 9th ed., I.

[42] Obit. in *Washington Post*, 3 June 1962.

[43] According to Maurice R. Davie, *Refugees in America*, N.Y. 1947, Berl discovered methods for artificially producing coal and oil.

[44] *Fortune* editors, *Great American Scientists*, 1960, p. 123; *Chemical Who's Who*, 1956; M. M. Hunt, "Profile," *New Yorker*, 13 Sept. 1958.

[45] *Chemical Who's Who*, 1956.

[46] Born Vienna 1888, *Who's Who*, 1952–53.

[47] *Who's Who*, 1962–63 and 1952–53.

[49] From the various editions of *Who's Who* and *American Men of Science* we note especially Francis Joseph Weiss (b. Vienna, 1898) who immigrated in 1938; Otto Schwartzkopf (b. Linz, 1903) the director of the Schwartzkopf Laboratories; Helmut Rudolf Pichler (b. Vienna, 1904) of Hydrocarbon Research, Inc.; Robert Steckler (b. Vienna, 1914) the president of Synthetic Organics and owner of the Steckler Laboratories in Cleveland; Henry Robert Linden (b. Vienna, 1922) with his patents for gasification processes and research at the Illinois Institute of Technology; and Joana Thimm Nakofske (b. Vienna, 1923), vice president of Bultoni Foods in Los Angeles.

[49] U.S. Office of Naval Research, London, *European Scientific Notes*, 15 July 1961, p. 161.

CHAPTER XV

ARCHITECTS

There has long been a dichotomy about Austrian institutions that has been reflected in some of the most fascinating of the Austrian immigrant groups in the United States. In the homeland it has shown itself too often in violent form: right vs. left; Catholic vs. Protestant in the era of Reformation and Counter-Reformation; Black vs. Red in politics since World War I; Nazi vs. anti-Nazi in 1938; or, in the field of culture, the beloved conservatives like Grillparzer and Haydn vs. the scarcely tolerated prophets of the new like Freud and Schönberg. The Austrian has often been an extremist in his mild-mannered way.

This dichotomy has marked the Austrian's architectural impact upon America. And, in spite of the glory of Austria's churches and monasteries, palaces and castles, town houses and Alpine villas, and its fascinating baroque and rococo, the impact of the architectural radicals has been of far more significance across the Atlantic than the influence of its own most treasured architectural names like Fischer von Erlach, Hildebrandt or Prandtauer. Austria has seldom been able to export what it most admires. For instance the charming German Renaissance room of about 1585 from the Stiegerhof near Villach in Carinthia which Henry Dolfinger gave the Pennsylvania Museum of Art a generation ago has attracted attention but few imitators.[1]

Austria was, around the turn of the century, one of the three or four principal hotbeds of the modern spirit in architecture. Its great city planner, Camillo Sitte,[2] published his epoch-making attack upon cities planned only for their grand boulevards and right angles, back in 1889. It appeared in America literally fifty-six years later!

"The Nation,"[3] called it "a back number" on "how to compose a plaza so as to provide a proper setting for a given edifice." Yet even in 1945 an American expert could write that "there is no question about Sitte's timeliness. We have learned our lesson and are ready to admit that there has been something radically wrong in the type of controls which have shaped the growth of our metropolitan areas . . . had there been some understanding of Sitte in America . . . Americans might have avoided some of the mistakes of the great building boom."[4] We in America had clung to the Haussmann-French school of formality and grandeur with but little concern for function and livability. The Sitte doctrines have had, nevertheless, some influence in Britain and America. Eliel Saarinen, a European whose voice was by no means lost in the American wilderness, accepted the Sitte gospel and applied it to some of his great designs such as that of the Chicago lake front and his Detroit River project of 1924.[5] And by 1963 Professor George Collins of Columbia was preparing a new translation of the Sitte volume. That tremendous gap between 1889, when Sitte's first edition "burst like a demolition bomb on the city planning practices of Europe," and 1945 when an American reviewer called it a "back number" was only too typical of the gap between Austria and America.

Americans were perhaps more understandably indifferent to Vienna's great housing program that began in the late twenties and is still housing hundreds of thousands of Viennese. An English woman might call it "the greatest housing achievement of the century"[6] and point out that it was "first recognized in Vienna that shelter is not enough, that human beings need companionship and recreation, need beauty in environment, need the help that can be given to parents still in slums by taking their children into nursery schools." But Americans did not even crowd the lovely grounds of the *George Washington Hof* (which was in the Soviet Sector after World War II and yet kept its name) to discover that, typical of the municipal apartments, it had over twenty-one acres of park to eight acres of building plus kindergartens and other prerequisites of civilized life.

Before the sad events of 1934 stopped the "Red Vienna" building program, the municipality had built some 75,000 units. An important Brookings Institution publication emanating from Washington in that same year indicated that the cessation of private building in the United States in the great depression might compel us to imitate the Vienna experiment.[7] We were not sympathetic, however, to Socialist projects in deepest Europe; the architecture of the Vienna project was not so exciting as to attract our architects; and we believed, in any event, in private enterprise.[8] It was to be long years before the Vienna-born Victor Gruen would apply what he had learned from the Vienna apartment houses to his gigantic shopping-housing-working centers in America.

We Americans wanted no conscience-burdened city planners. We could, however, welcome the Austrian-born prophets of the nineteenth century who merely represented the Viennese eclecticism that was rebuilding the *Ringstrasse* without contributing too much to any school of architecture.

Leopold Eidlitz (1823–1908),[9] for instance, who was born in Prague under the Austrian flag and educated in both Prague and Vienna, arrived here at the age of twenty to become one of the very greatest of our nineteenth century architects.[10] He was a disciple of the medieval revival and put his stamp upon a multitude of American Gothic churches. His association with the great American-born architects, H. H. Richardson and F. L. Olmstead, in the construction of the state capitol at Albany (and he is said to have done much of the actual work of design with his friend Richardson) is evidence that the excellent basic training in architecture[11] that he had brought with him from Vienna had raised him to the top in his profession here in America. He not only designed the old Produce Exchange in New York but he did what has been called the first fireproof commercial structure in New York, the American Exchange National Bank.

The other great Austrian figure in 19th century American architecture was doubtless the sculptor Karl Bitter (b. Vienna, 1867 – d. New York, 1915). He had worked on the monumental buildings which rose during his youth in his native Vienna on the new *Ringstrasse*, site of the earlier city bastions. Architect Richard M. Hunt, one of New York's finest, welcomed the fugitive from the Austrian army. Together they worked on the Administration Building at Chicago's Columbian Exposition and Bitter found himself already established in his mid-twenties as a leading figure in the new American sculpture.[12] In consequence of his striking successes the young immigrant was placed in charge of sculpture at the three major expositions that followed: the Pan American Exposition at Buffalo, the World's Fair at St. Louis, and the Panama-Pacific Exposition at San Francisco. Many thought that the sculpture at San Francisco was the best that the new world had yet seen.[13] Bitter and Hunt put their stamp on some of the most noble of New York's Fifth Avenue mansions. Bitter did the Dewey Arch and the gates of Trinity Church, public buildings, and homes for the Vanderbilts and John Jacob Astor. ". . . there was fluency in his whipped-cream baroque." He had "Teutonic exuberance touched with the gaity of the Viennese." Unlike so many immigrants he seems to have made no effort to throw off his Austrian traits. Some of the critics might object to what they called lack of restraint and what may well have been a recrudescence of the baroque tendencies of his homeland. But Oswald Garrison Villard maintained that: "Coming from abroad with fresh eyes that looked beneath the surface, Bitter saw and felt things that were veiled to the multitude born to Americanism."[14]

Far less well-known than Karl Bitter was the Vienna-born architect of one of the best-known buildings in the United States, the Library of Congress. One has to hunt carefully for traces of the John L. Smithmeyer (d. Washington, 1908) who was born in the Vienna of 1832 as Johann Schmitmeyer, who was a fugitive of the Revolution of 1848 but who avoided the eagle eye of the multitude of historians of that revolution, who escaped the reaction by settling in Chicago (where he studied architecture), moving on to Indianapolis (where his ability must have impressed the state fathers because he designed the so-called old court house at South Bend and some other reputable public buildings), and who contributed to the Union triumph in the Civil War as commander of an artillery depot. That a young Austrian should wear the Union uniform was nothing as surprising as it would have been had he crossed the Ohio to wear the Confederate grey.[15]

Certainly his army service did not disqualify Schmitmeyer for a position after the war in the Office of the Supervising Architect where he was placed in charge of the design of Federal buildings in the far South. The historians of architecture mention his triumphs in New Orleans, Mobile and Charleston but seem to have been mostly impressed with his Army and Navy Hospital at Hot Springs, Arkansas. In later years Smithmeyer alone, or with his partner, was to design other landmarks like the old Hotel Chamberlain at Fortress Monroe, Georgetown College in Washington and the Carnegie Library at Alleghany, Pennsylvania. We may still admire the monumental old Georgetown College Gothic cathedral-of-learning but we cannot insist that it changed the trends in American architecture.

Smithmeyer's monument across from the Capitol in Washinton, on the other hand, has undoubtly had as much influence upon public architecture in America as any other single structure. It became a landmark because it was the one great public building in Washington between the era of the building of the Capitol and the new era of the Lincoln Memorial which has found a place in the heart of the American tourist to Washington. Critics suggest the demolition of dozens of other aging Washington buildings: they suggest only annexes to Smithmeyer's Library of Congress.

It was due to the Library project that Smithmeyer's career ended in tragedy. That was not because he was foreign-born. An able German-American historian might criticize Schmitmeyer for anglicizing his name.[16] But he became a victim of Congressional tyranny as an American and not as a foreigner.

His partnership with the German-born Paul J. Pelz should have been a milestone in American architectural history. Pelz was a decade or so younger than Smithmeyer; he had received part of his architectural education in Vienna, and he had won first prize for light-house design at the Vienna World Exposition of 1873.

And the firm of Smithmeyer and Pelz won the first prize of $ 1500 in 1873, among 28 competitors, for a design of a building for a national library of the United States. A few years later, in 1880, Smithmeyer was one of three experts named by the Congress to decide whether the Capitol could be extended to include an adequate national library. Although his firm had drawn plans for such an extension, Smithmeyer and his colleagues recommended a new building that would house a national library capable of upholding America's cultural position among the greater world powers.[17]

For thirteen years plans were drawn for the new library. Smithmeyer went to Europe to study the great European libraries while his colleague Pelz drew blueprints with the firm's staff in Washington. The firm won a second competition and that established Smithmeyer and Pelz firmly in the position of the anointed for the designing of the new library. More than a dozen plans for the library, in German Renaissance, Tudor, Gothic, French Renaissance, Romanesque and other styles were produced by the busy firm of Smithmeyer and Pelz, and all were finally discarded in favor of Italian Renaissance. Nothing called Austrian or Viennese had ever entered into the strange conglomeration of plans that the firm had produced.

The tragedy was a bureaucratic one. Congress decided by law in 1886 that the library building should be constructed "substantially according to the plan submitted . . . by John L. Smithmeyer, in the Italian Renaissance style of architecture . . ." And all went well until the architect refused to accept an inferior concrete mix. He refused to let the work go on. And the inevitable happened. His contractor won the fight through his Congressman and, by 1888, Smithmeyer was removed.[18] The brigadier general of engineers, T. L. Casey, replaced Smithmeyer and found a happy opportunity to appoint his 25-year-old son Edward, who had been reveling in an architectural education in Paris, as the architect in charge. Young Casey got rid of Smithmeyer's colleague Pelz by 1892.

Smithmeyer himself died penniless and "heartbroken at the ingratitude of the people of his adopted country."[19] He and Pelz had received a few thousand dollars in prizes and fees – nothing compared to what architects had a right to expect for a major work. By the time that Congress got around to appropriating a fairly adequate amount, in 1908, Smithmeyer was dead. Four U.S. Senators were among his pallbearers. "The architectural world," declared the "Washington Post," had "lost a leading figure."[20] He had been "genial, sociable, and lovable," a man of "transcendent genius and ability."

The all-important role that Austria played in the development of modern architecture and design is all but unknown to most Americans. That Mies van der Rohe, Corbusier, and Gropius are well-known names on this side of the water while Otto Wagner, Adolf Loos and Joseph Hoffmann are utter strangers underscores the unhappy significance of those few additional miles from Western Europe eastward to Vienna.

The Austrian architects who remained at home in Europe were doubtless even more important in the development of the new architecture of the twentieth century, which means so much to America, than the remarkable group of Austrian-born immigrants who rank so high in the story of our architecture. Pevsner, in his "Pioneers of Modern Design,"[21] could point out that "The first architects to admire the machine and to understand its essential character and its consequences on the relation of architecture and design to ornamentation were two Austrians, two Americans and a Belgian: Otto Wagner (1841–1918), Adolf Loos (1870–1933), Louis Sullivan (1850–1924), Frank Lloyd Wright (1869–1959) and Henri van de Velde (1863–1957)." Of the two Austrians, Loos, the extremist, was the pupil of Wagner, the pioneer.

The elegant, stately Wagner was Viennese from his birth to his death. He was a practising architect from the middle twenties and a teacher of architecture at the Academy of Fine Arts from 1894 when he made his presidential inaugural the declaration of independence from tradition in architecture. "Our starting point for artistic creation is to be found only in modern life."[22] He doubtless knew of the work of William Morris and his arts and crafts movement in England, and he made Austria an advanced stronghold of the Art Nouveau, or *Jugendstil*, that mildly revolutionary school of design whose curved lines suggested by plant forms pointed so directly into our architectural future. The *Sezession*, or secession from all architecture's time-honored styles, was Austria's Art Nouveau. Wagner and this Austrian mainstream of modernism repudiated the stress upon ornament that the conservatives of the *Sezession* still clung to and insisted that architecture should seek "to derive form and motives from purpose, construction, and materials."[23] This was indeed the key to modern architecture. Little wonder that the architect Frederick Kiesler calls Wagner one of the great fathers of that modernism.[24] That Austria and the Low Countries led even Germany and France into architectural modernism was due largely, as far as Austria was concerned, to Otto Wagner.[25]

Wagner knew Frank Lloyd Wright (whom Europe accepted twenty years before America!)[26] chiefly through his colleague Adolf Loos who had worked with Wright. It is unlikely that America's Chicago school had much influence upon Wagner. His Vienna designs which shocked the conservatives neither shocked nor delighted America. They were generally unnoticed here. Yet the "structural rationalism"[27] that he had exemplified – his paternity of contemporary architecture and design – has found its way into almost every competent American history of architecture.

His disciple Joseph Maria Olbrich (b. Austrian Silesia, 1867 – d. Düsseldorf, Germany, 1908) was another of the Vienna iconoclasts who helped to create the *Sezession* (Olbrich designed the bold *Sezession* gallery which still stands near the heart of the city); he became a favorite *Sezession* designer; and then he went on, like Wagner, to help set off the reaction against the Art Noveau and all its curious works that were so quickly to give way to the simpler and more boldly functional styles of the 20th century.[28] Olbrich was by no means well known in America although he created the German pavilion at the St. Louis Exposition of 1903.[29]

The names of early German radicals like Peter Behrens, who had studied with Otto Wagner of Vienna, were as unknown in America's first 20th century years as those of the Austrians. It was only when Gropius (who was for a time an Austrian "in-law" by marriage to Gustav Mahler's widow) created the world-famous *Bauhaus* in Weimar, Germany, that central European modernism became more than a vague uncertainty in the United States.[30] And in the early stages of the *Bauhaus*, Johannes Itten, who came from Vienna, played an important role.[31] Yet, with or without the names, the impact was there. Burchard and Bush-Brown, for instance, in their fine volume on our architecture point out that the notable efforts at modern design which distinguished the major expositions at New York and San Francisco in 1939 were chiefly "derived from European work of the twenties in the manner of Loos and Hoffmann; long planes of white plaster, incised by strip windows, flat roofs and terraces."[32] The statement is significant to our theme because Loos and Hoffmann were both Vienna architects. They rank with Wagner and Olbrich as leaders of that Vienna group which distressed the turn-of-the-century Viennese with their iconoclasm and left more of an impact on Berlin and Weimar, New York and Chicago, than upon the noble streets of old Vienna.

Loos and Hoffmann were both born in 1870 and born over the line in the Czechoslovakia of today. Josef Hoffmann (d. Vienna, 1956), born in Pirnitz in 1870, studied under Otto Wagner in Vienna, served as professor at the school of applied art, did some splended town houses in Vienna and some exposition buildings in Rome (1911) and Cologne (1914). His early work, the Stoclet House in Brussels (1905), was an architectural landmark of such importance that it became well known in America. As director of the *Wiener Werkstätte*, or Vienna Workshops, which he founded in 1903, he discovered his inspiration in the machines of the modern world and never surrendered to the decorative strivings, plant forms, and tulip curves of the Art Nouveau. The famous Corbusier came to Vienna with plans to work under Hoffmann.[33]

His leadership was so significant, Henry-Russell Hitchcock pointed out, that Vienna had stolen the primacy in the arts and crafts of decoration, during his active period, from Paris. Indeed, the Paris Exhibition of Decorative Arts in 1925, for which Hoffmann designed the Austrian pavilion, was designed to recover the prestige that, due largely to Hoffmann, Paris had lost to Vienna.[34]

Adolf Loos, "one of the greatest creators in modern architecture,"[35] was an internationalist in the usual Austrian way: born in Brünn, educated in Dresden and for three or four years in the mid-nineties in the United States; he spent four years in Paris in the twenties. He practiced most of his life in Vienna where he died in 1933. Relatively unknown during his lifetime, he is doubtless best known to posterity for his essay of 1898 called "Ornament and Crime." Noting that eighty percent of the prisoners in certain jails bore tattoo marks he concluded that the tendency for such self-decoration was a sign of degeneracy and maintained that, similarly, any ornamentation in architecture "was proof of the criminal tendency of the designer." "The progress of civilization is synonymous with the stripping of all ornament from objects of everyday use." Engineers and plumbers had contributed far more to culture than artists.[36] Before the turn of the century he was doing shops and houses with no ornamentation whatsoever and was denouncing the few fragments of ornament that Olbrich had used on the *Sezession* building on the *Naschmarkt*. He was one of the rare Viennese who were too extreme for America. The none-too-modern design that he submitted in the "Chicago Tribune" competition of 1922 lost out to the Gothic tower whose traditionalism he despised.[37] Called one of the four or five greatest architects of his generation,[38] he remains almost unknown in America. He is recalled here with reverence chiefly by the men who studied under him such as Professor E. Brandl of Notre Dame University.

A couple of generations ago when Austrians of genius were still scarce in America and those few were still categorized as Germans, Joseph Urban's was the great Austro-

American name in architecture and design.[39] Born in 1872 in Vienna when Franz Joseph was still young, Urban (d. New York, 1933) had a sound education at the Academy of Fine Arts and the *Technische Hochschule*, and as the pupil of Hasenauer. He worked with the exhilarating masters of the *Sezession*, visited Russia to help bridge the Neva, and Egypt to build a palace for the Khedive. Back on the Danube he designed for the opera (to which he also turned his hand in Paris and London), did some well-known, but not strikingly modern, interiors for the Vienna Rathaus and other public buildings, and found success in designing Austrian buildings for international expositions. At the Paris exposition of 1900 he won the grand prize for decoration and he repeated that feat at the St. Louis exhibition only a few months later.

Having achieved fame in America he emigrated to Boston in 1911 to do stage sets for the new opera house there. His successes brought him in three years to the Met and a new career in New York. There he could escape from the classic seriousness of the opera to do commercial design or to put his stamp upon the breath-taking sets of Flo Ziegfeld's Follies or digress to Florida to lend color to the Palm Beach scene. It was a distinguished career.

On the serious side he joined with moderns like Kahn and Saarinen in doing rooms on the theme of industrial art in America for the Metropolitan Museum. He still reflected his Austrian origins, and his design for the New School for Social Research had, according to the experts, the horizontal lines that American architecture was borrowing from Urban and other Europeans. He had become such an exponent of modernism that he was putting his stamp upon the new domestic architecture of the Atlantic coast before most of the native architects had caught up.[40] And his color scheme for the Century of Progress exposition at Chicago was sensational. Urban was one of the many sons of conservative Vienna whose training had prepared them to grow with, or even beyond, their times.

There were, however, to be others. Considering that Austria's own most fascinating architecture has very seldom stirred the American builder to the point of imitation this country has been blessed with a remarkably large number of really distinguished Austrian-born architects. Some of the recent arrivals were useful if not sensational. A small group was so progressive as to be excitingly sensational. Many, like the Viennese Felix Augenfeld (b. 1893) who received an award from the American Designers Institute, lived and practiced in New York City.[41] But California attracted some of the best of them and a few found distinction elsewhere. Willi Baumgarten, for instance, born in 1885 in the Tyrol with a first-rate Vienna background in training, teaching and practice, made his home in Raleigh, North Carolina.[42] Another immigrant of the thirties was the Vienna-born and educated Elizabeth Scheu Close who settled in Minneapolis and there, in partnership with her husband, designed the Civic Orchestra and the Ice Center. And associated for years with the

Rhode Island School of Design was the architect-designer with the manner and appearance of a gentleman of the old school who was anything but that in his creations, Professor Ernest H. Lichtblau (b. Vienna, 1883). He studied in Vienna with the famous Otto Wagner, designed some of Vienna's municipal apartments, and, in private practice, designed buildings like the Belgian embassy and private residences and interiors in Vienna and in New York – for R. H. Macy, for instance, in New York. The Celanese Corporation of America used his designs for textiles. And from the 1920's when a Paris exposition awarded him a gold medal, to his American period when he received honors in Chicago and in Rhode Island and in New York (Modern Art Museum) he found recognition as a designer and teacher of significance.[43]

Hans Adolph Vetter (b. 1897) who made Pittsburgh his American home was another Viennese[44] who escaped the Hitler regime; he went first to Britain and arrived in America in 1947. He had taught and practiced architecture for years in Vienna, with excursions to Paris and Warsaw. The city of Linz had given him its prize in town planning. Later in the fifties he was to renew his Austrian connections by directing the Salzburg School of Architecture. In Pittsburgh he has practiced, taught at the Carnegie Institute of Technology, and written poetry along with English history and architecture. In 1956 a younger Vienna architect, Eduard F. Sekler (b. Vienna, 1920), came to Harvard University as a guest professor. His work and study in England had not weaned him away from Vienna where he taught at the *Technische Hochschule* and was associated with such interesting tasks as the reconstruction of the *Volksprater* (a popular amusement park), the city's great housing program, and the restoration of the church on the Leopoldsberg overlooking the city.[45] With Carl Auboeck and Gerhard Karplus, an architect of Austrian descent, Professor Sekler has recently converted an off-Fifth Avenue mansion in New York into the republic's new Austrian Institute, an oasis of Austrian culture on Manhattan with what may be the best Austrian library in the United States.

No account of Austrian-born architects in the United States would be complete without mentioning five more notable contemporaries: Richard Neutra, R. M. Schindler, Herbert Wilhelm Bayer, Victor Gruen, and Frederick Kiesler. All were Vienna-born; all settled in the West except Kiesler who remained in New York; all except Gruen and Bayer migrated before Nazism was an issue; all of the five, and especially Kiesler, were so ultra-modern in their approach that they could never have become more than prophets of the future in their native city and were indeed suspect in all the more conservative corners of the U.S.A. In brief, this was a fascinating group.

Neutra and Schindler especially became great names in the American architectural world. Neutra might be too stark in his design to satisfy some of the more conservative American experts. Yet he insisted that his forthrightness was humanism. Buildings should be created to serve man's needs, not for style. The steel that Neutra used and his cement-covered horizontals did not have to be disguised. His vigorous cubic forms and the stucco that he had learned to use so freely in his homeland are so unembellished and forthright that he is accused of being less of an artist than such contemporaries as Wright and Corbusier. Actually he is a different kind of artist, and a great one.

Before he came to the United States in 1923 Richard Neutra (b. 1892) had studied at the *Technische Hochschule* in Vienna and had pursued his architectural education in Zurich and Berlin. He had worked with the iconoclast Adolf Loos, he had admired Otto Wagner, and he had known enough of the *Sezession* to have been made an honorary member years later in 1954. He was already a bold pioneer in his field before he came to the United States.

Here he worked some months for Frank Lloyd Wright. His Lovell house in Los Angeles, which intrigued Wright, and his Kaufmann house in Arizona and his Garden Apartments back in Los Angeles brought him fame. His houses clung to their lovely southwestern hillsides as though the slopes had been designed for the houses and not *vice versa*, and the stucco, glass, steel and cubic horizontal construction that he used were all bold and undisguised. And he built office buildings and wartime housing units and played with light and color and planned whole communities in the typical Southern Californian fashion.

Richard Neutra became California's greatest architect. He is "customarily named among the few pioneers who have changed the architecture of the United States in the twentieth century." And his voice, perhaps because it was in essence an international voice, was heard around the world. "A local boy of Vienna cannot help but be a sort of cosmopolitan boy," Neutra said when receiving a prize from his native city in 1958.[46]

R. M. Schindler's (1887–1953) has been a lesser name in American architecture but it is receiving more and more recognition as one of the great ones.[47] Educated with the best in Vienna, vitally impressed with the work of Otto Wagner, influenced by Adolf Loos, sharing Neutra's enthusiasm for Frank Lloyd Wright, he brought with him to America a record which showed that the architects of the future comprised a small more-or-less inter-related group who knew each other's work and worked for the same ends whether in Vienna or in Germany's *Bauhaus* or in Los Angeles.

Schindler, according to Burchard and Bush-Brown's recent book,[48] belonged to the group of "tough-minded aggressive designers" who came from Europe and promoted modern, technological architecture. He opposed mere functionalism, so dear to most modernists, and believed that it took more than so much stucco and stainless steel to create a structure. Like all Europeans he used concrete and the cube form and horizontal structure. But he pioneered with plywood and other woods. His was a new kind of Californian modernism – with infinite care for his design and less concern for his materials than his colleagues were showing.[49]

In the United States he found his way at the age of 28 into Wright's Chicago studio, met the great Louis Sullivan and kept in touch with him,[50] went to California with a mandate from Wright, stayed in Los Angeles for the rest of his life, quarreled mildly with the great Chicagoan and never saw him again. His masterpiece was "a plaster and wood house of dateless charm" on Catalina Island. He designed exciting furniture to fit in the little California homes which he planned in the conviction that they could be works of art and not parts of future suburban slums.

R. M. Schindler came to America because he had read a notice in 1914 in a Vienna paper that a Chicago firm needed draftsmen. Victor Gruen (b. Vienna, 1903), thirteen years younger, migrated in the tragic year 1938.[51] Like most of the Austrian-born in the architect group he had a sound and useful Vienna background: a good family, the *Technische Hochschule* and the Academy of Fine Arts, and some exhilarating experiments in commercial architecture during the half dozen years when he practiced in the then unhappy town.[52] The immigrant of 1938 spoke no English and had only eight dollars in his pocket. A few years later he was the subject of a feature article in "Fortune" magazine[53] that pointed out that his Los Angeles firm, Victor Gruen Associates, was making $ 4,200,000 a year and "... its impact on U.S. architecture and planning is so great that Victor Gruen Associates can be called one of the most influential elements in urban and suburban architecture." He began with store fronts and commercial interiors in Vienna and the United States. His aesthetics were completely practical. "We have no desire to create new fashions in architecture," this iconoclast remarked. "There is little value in the building of buildings alone. The only thing that really matters is taking a whole area and creating an environment, comfortable and convenient for the people who live there, work there, and shop there."[54]

What Gruen was designing for Los Angeles and Detroit and Fort Worth and other cities with imagination enough to accept his plans, was not mere super-shopping centers but community centers with places to live and earn money as well as shops for spending money. He often used the famous Ring around Vienna's inner city as inspiration for the designing of modern cities in America that seemed to need just such a *Ringstrasse* to intercept traffic and protect the heart of the community. It was surprising that the imagination for designing these tremendous living centers ("It is environmental architecture that really calls for imagination today. Architectural style is secondary."[55]) that shocked traditionally-minded Americans with their boldness should have come from a genius trained in little, conservative Austria.

Victor Gruen Associates, organized in 1950, achieved triumph after triumph. Gruen, who looked back with gratitude to the people in Vienna who had kept him alive as what he called a building superintendent from 1923 to 1932 and given him a practice in architecture for six more years, and to Morris Ketchum the New York architect who had taken him in in 1938, found himself in his adopted country a prophet of the future in architecture with awards from the American Institute of Architects and the flattery of imitation by town planners all over America.

Another prophet of modernism, trained at the *Bauhaus* as well as in Linz and Darmstadt, was the Thirty-eighter Herbert Wilhelm Bayer (b. Haag, Lower Austria, 1900).[56] He taught advertising layout and typography in Germany and in the United States combined industrial art, for Wanamaker and the Advertising Guild and the Container Corporation of America, with non-industrial architecture and design. He designed distinguished buildings at his home in Colorado for the Aspen Institute for Humanistic Studies and his public service included artistic work for the government's Coordinator of Inter-American Affairs. Bayer has been a figure of no little significance.

A much younger figure of genuine importance in contemporary architecture is Edward Durell Stone's associate, Burghard Engele (b. Innsbruck, 1925). His interest has been in the theater. In Austria, after a higher education in Vienna, he designed outstanding theater and stage projects for Clemens Holzmeister. Thousands of Americans know his new *Festspielhaus* at Salzburg. Other Americans are coming to know him through his New Jersey music center, his theater for Hamilton College, New York State University's theater in Albany, and his plans, under Stone's directions, for the John F. Kennedy Center for the Performing Arts in the nation's capital.[57] The future of American architecture lies with young architects like Engele.

Frederick John Kiesler (b. 1896 – d. New York, 1965) has been called the "greatest non-building architect of our time."[58] This great abstract artist designed interiors, operatic and stage and concert sets, furnishings, and the like in styles that are some light-years distant from that of the fine churches and palaces of his native Vienna. Even America has found him too advanced for practical industrial and domestic architecture.[59]

Kiesler was trained under Adolf Loos and in the *Technische Hochschule* and the Academy of Fine Arts in Vienna. He was a collaborator of the radical de Stijl school in Europe. Painter and sculptor as well as designer he was an artist of great versatility. He designed exciting "floating" buildings that cantilevered out from masts, and he experimented with spiral architecture that was later developed by Le Corbusier and Frank Lloyd Wright. His portion of the Austrian exhibit at Paris in 1925 brought him international fame and, after he came to the United States in 1926 he served with distinction designing for the Metropolitan Opera, the Juilliard School of Music, and the Architectural Laboratory of Columbia. Among his breath-taking creations was the Space House of 1934 "of continuous shell construction with continuous windows," his arrangements for displaying paintings without supports at the opening of the Peggy Guggenheim Museum in 1942, his Sanctuary for the Dead Sea Scrolls at Jerusalem, and his design for an Endless House of shell concrete for the garden of the Museum of Modern Art, both in 1959.

Frederick Kiesler has been described as one of the "under-recognized artists" of mid-century America. Properly recognized or not he certainly has a place in the impressive list of Austro-Americans who have made so many significant contributions to the architecture of their adopted country. And, indeed, Austria's only noteworthy contribution in that field after the Nazis had squeezed all that was decent out of Austrian art, came to us through the emigrant group.

[1] Article by Fiske Kimball, *American-German Review*, Dec. 1937, p. 47.

[2] E. Saarinen, *The City*, N.Y. 1943, pp. 116–32, treats at length of Sitte and explains how his book "has echoed an awakening herald in many a country and town, inspiring a new and wholesome movement in town-building."

[3] Cf. *Book Review Digest*, 1946. *Der Städtebau* was the original title. It was published in Spanish and French soon after the German edition.

[4] Suppl. chapter by Arthur C. Holden to Sitte, *The Art of Building Cities*, N.Y. 1945.

[5] J. Burchard and A. Bush-Brown, *The Architecture of America*, Boston 1961, p. 357. Sitte was born in Vienna in 1843 and died in 1903.

[6] Elizabeth Denby, *Europe Re-housed*, London 1938, p. 253.

[7] Cf. preface to C. O. Hardy, *The Housing Program of the City of Vienna*, Brookings, 1934. See also E. K. Winter, "Housing and Resettlement in Vienna," *National Muncipal Review*, Aug. 1937, p. 399–400.

[8] Useful is Henry-Russell Hitchcock, *Architecture in the 19th and 20th Centuries*, Baltimore 1958, pp. 351–2.

[9] Cf. *Century Cyclopedia of Names*. The German-American architect Pelz, who worked on the Library of Congress, praised him in a letter to Rudolf Cronau (Ms. in Carl Schurz Mem. Found., Phila.) as a famous compatriot. His brother Marc Eidlitz was perhaps New York's greatest builder.

[10] Quotation from page 192 of the *Biographical Dictionary of American Architects*, Los Angeles 1956.

[11] *Ibid.; Dictionary of American Biography*.

[12] F. Schevill, *Karl Bitter*, Chicago 1917.

[13] A H. Eaton, *Immigrant Gifts to American Life*, N.Y. 1932, p. 123.

[14] O. W. Larkin, *Art and Life in America*, N.Y. 1949, p. 314; A. B. Faust, *German Element in the United States*, 2 vols., Boston and N.Y. 1909, II, p. 308; Schevill, *op. cit.*, pp. 1–2.

[15] *Das Buch der Deutschen in Amerika*, Philadelphia 1907, pp. 352–3; *Biographical Dictionary of American Architects*, p. 562; obit. in *Washington Post*, 13 March 1908.

[16] Rudolf Cronau corresp. in Carl Schurz Mem. Foundation.

[17] David Mearns, *The Story Up To Now*, Washington 1947, p. 134 and 136 (re locating the library in the dome of the Capitol).

[18] Smithmeyer tells his story, well illustrated, in his booklet *The Library of Congress*, Washington, 1906.

[19] Letter of Simon Wolf (born in Bavaria, made U.S. Minister to Egypt, Jew, long resident of Washington) to *Washington Post*, 13 March, 1908.

[20] *Post*, 13 March 1908. Although General Casey's name appears above those of Smithmeyer and Pelz on the tablet in the entrance hall of the Library of Congress, and although young Casey claimed considerable credit for his work, the D.C. Chapter of the American Institute of Architects

and others made it clear in resolutions, editorials, etc. that only Smithmeyer and Pelz were entitled to credit as architects of the building. Cf. *Architecture and Buildings*, 3 April, 1897.

The Rudolf Cronau mss. in the Carl Schurz Mem. Foundation contain the whole story as seen by Pelz and Cronau who minimize the role of Smithmeyer as architect. This was doubtless because Pelz spent his time actually drafting plans while Smithmeyer toured Europe for ideas from its best libraries, sat on Congressionally-appointed committees as required, and was, in general, the promoter and contact man for the firm.

21 N.Y. 1949, p. 12.

22 Fiske Kimball and G. H. Edgell, *History of Architecture*, N.Y. 1918, p. 515, and Burchard and Bush-Brown, *op. cit.*, pp. 234f.

23 Kimball and Edgell, *op. cit.*, pp. 511–12; Grimschitz, *Ars Austriae*, Wien 1960, p. 62.

24 *Progressive Architecture*, July, 1961, p. 105.

25 Wagner's Postal Savings Building still stands near the Ringstrasse in Vienna.

26 Jos. Watterson, *Architecture*, N.Y. 1950, p. 373. Watterson writes, p. 376, that "the real leadership" in modernism came from Germany and Austria and he mentions Wagner and Hoffmann by name.

27 The term is from the *Columbia Encyclopedia*. Wagner's book *Modern Architecture* was translated into English in 1901. Cf. Faust, *op. cit.*, II, p. 318. Columbia published his lectures on city problems in 1911.

28 N. Pevsner, *Pioneers of Modern Design*, N.Y. 1949, p. 64; Kimball and Edgell, *op. cit.*, p. 515; Hitchcock, *op. cit.*, p. 349.

29 W. Jenks, *Vienna and the Young Hitler*, N.Y. 1960, p. 216.

30 O. W. Larkin, *op. cit.*, p. 353, calls the *Bauhaus* the focus of European modernism. Larkin's tendency is to stress the great German developments of the second decade of the century and he overlooks the Austrian influences of ten or fifteen years earlier; cf. p. 352.

31 According to Prof. Eduard Sekler who read this chapter in manuscript and made a number of invaluable corrections and suggestions.

32 *The Architecture of America*, p. 456.

33 Grimschitz, *op. cit.*, p. 52; Peter Blake, *The Master Builders*, N.Y. 1960, p. 7; J. M. Fitch, *Walter Gropius*, N.Y. 1960, p. 18; Jenks, *op. cit.*, p. 216.

34 Hitchcock, *op. cit.*, p. 351.

35 Pevsner, *op. cit.*, p. 124.

36 Wayne Andrews, *Architecture, Ambition and Americans*, N.Y., 1955, p. 267; Jenks, *op. cit.*, p. 217.

37 Jas. M. Fitch, *op. cit.*, Plate 12.

38 Hitchcock, *op. cit.*, p. 352.

39 *Dictionary of American Biography* has a good article on Joseph Urban (1872–1933). See also *Who Was Who in America*, I, and Burchard and Bush-Brown, *op. cit.*, pp. 353, 372, 457.

40 Burchard and Bush-Brown, *op. cit.*, pp. 353 and 372.

41 *American Architects Directory*, N.Y., 1955, p. 18. Augenfeld was born in 1893.

42 The late William Ludwig Baumgarten, consultant for Herzmansky's department store in Vienna, had his own architectural firm here from 1945 on. Cf. *American Architects Directory*, p. 31.

43 For E. S. Close see *Who's Who of American Women*, 2nd ed., 1961. For information regarding Lichtblau the author is indebted to the Dean of the Rhode Island School of Design.

44 *Who's Who*, 1962–63. He was born in 1897, studied at the Academy of Applied Art in Vienna, served as captain in the Austrian army in World War I. He was naturalized in 1954.

45 *Österreicher der Gegenwart*, Wien 1951, p. 282.

46 Quotations are from *Current Biography*, July, 1961, p. 33. For Neutra see also *Who's Who in Austria*, Zurich 1954; *Who's Who*, 1960–61; Larkin, *op. cit.*, pp. 446, 469; Burchard and Bush-

Brown, *op. cit.*, p. 242; V. Scully, jr., *Frank Lloyd Wright*, N.Y. 1960, pp. 26–7; Hitchcock, *op. cit.*, p. 381; *Encyclopedia of World Art*, vol. I., N.Y., 1959, Plate 412.

[47] Letter to the author from Prof. Eduard Sekler, 15 Oct. 1961.

[48] *Architecture in America*, p. 446.

[49] Cf. Esther McCoy, *Five California Architects*, N.Y. 1960, ch. on Schindler; and Andrews, *op. cit.*, pp. 274–6.

[50] *Journal of Architectural Historians*, Dec. 1961, pp. 179ff.

[51] *Who's Who*, 1962–63.

[52] *American Architects Directory*; Burchard and Bush-Brown, *op. cit.*, p. 500; Walter Guzzardi, jr., article on Gruen in *Fortune*, Jan. 1962, pp. 77ff.

[53] Jan. 1962, "An Architect of Environments."

[54] *Ibid.*, p. 77.

[55] *Ibid.; Die Presse*, Wien, 29–30 Jan. 1966.

[56] *Who's Who*, 1962–63.

[57] Announcement of Austrian Institute, May 1964.

[58] P. Johnson, "Three Architects," *Art in America*, 1960, No. 1, pp. 70–75.

[59] For Frederick John Kiesler see also *Who's Who*, 1962–63; Burchard and Bush-Brown, *op. cit.*, p. 447; *Progressive Architecture*, July, 1961, p. 104; "Design's Bad Boy," *Architectural Forum*, Feb. 1947; *ibid.*, Mar., 1939 for review of his book, *Contemporary Art*.

CHAPTER XVI

ARTISTS

Austrian artists may emigrate; the best Austrian art cannot emigrate. For much of it consists of the fine murals and statuary and wood carving that embellished palaces and churches of the 17th and 18th centuries – and the palaces and churches themselves.[1] Such masterpieces cannot be removed; they have, in recent times, been protected by the Federal Monuments Office whose purpose is to preserve them and prevent their exportation. Hence famous objects like the bronze figure of King Arthur, so familiar to every American schoolboy, that Peter Vischer did for the Innsbruck tomb of his friend, Emperor Maximilian I, will never leave Austria.

Austria's artistic contributions to America have come through less direct channels: from its Vienna porcelain factory, for instance, which recently found itself, after the disappearance of Meissen behind the iron curtain, the oldest porcelain manufactory in the Western World (founded 1717), or, a couple of centuries later, from Max Reinhardt's revolutionary innovations in theater and film production. Even expressionism, a school of art that was essentially Austrian and German with Austrian representation as notable as Richard Gerstl, Egon Schiele and Kokoschka, has excited far more interest than direct imitation in the American world of art.

But with or without conscious imitation the ever increasing number of Austrian exhibits in the art galleries of 20th century America shows an increasing awareness in this country of the significance of the Austrians – that the Guggenheim Museum in New York, for instance, could arrange for 1964 an exhibit of the fine Viennese Gustav Klimt (b. 1862 – d. 1918) who represented much of Austria's best art from 19th century naturalism to the *Sezession* (Austria's *Art Nouveau*) to expressionism.[2] And the expressionist Egon Schiele also deserves mention. Schiele (b. Tulln, Lower Austria, 1890 – d. Vienna, 1918) was one of those many revolutionary Austrians who were out of step with their native land. He was derided or ignored for years for his radicalism in art, was forced out of the academy, denounced for his eroticism, and criticized for his pacifism. Vienna discovered him too late. The editor of "The Dial" here in America discovered him in 1922 and reproduced his works in "The Dial." The Minneapolis Art Institute acquired a Schiele in 1955. Two years later Otto Kallir's Galerie St. Etienne in New York began showing him and in 1960 a substantial Schiele show of some seventy-five items went from the Boston Institute of Contemporary Art on to New York, Pittsburgh and Minneapolis. "The most talented artist to emerge from Austria in modern times" had finally been discovered in America.[3]

The men and women who actually came to the United States doubtless made a more important immediate impact. Dr. Otto Kallir, the Viennese discoverer of Grandma Moses and the imaginative owner of the St. Etienne Galerie in New York, has played a major role in introducing Austrian artists to New York. He has been one of the few Austrians in the United States with the ability and the inclination to introduce the best of Austria to his adopted country.[4]

A splendid history of the American frontier in pre-Civil War days is depicted in the water colors of Franz Hölzlhuber (b. near Steyr, 1826 – d. Vienna, 1898). He was an artist-musician who could write poetry and lecture and who put most of his talents to work when he came to Milwaukee in 1856, found that the German theater there had never received his letter accepting its position of choir master, and had therefore to finance his four year visit as best he could. Hölzlhuber seems to have done well in Milwaukee. He turned to painting signs and cooking Viennese pastries. As his reputation grew he did illustrations for Frank Leslie's and Harper's magazines, and he traveled during his vacations from Texas to Canada. He painted wherever he went and he seems to have wandered far from civilization. A group of his water colors that has recently turned up in Vienna shows frontier forts, Conestoga wagons and encampments with dogs and an intriguing deer in harness, as well as oxen, Indian folkways, early railroads, river boats, and Milwaukee itself. Austrians, who have always been interested in the Leatherstocking theme and in the American frontier in general, were doubtless fascinated by his lectures and paintings on his return home.[5]

There were a few other interesting Austrian men of art in America before the era of Hitler. There was the painter George Peter (b. Vienna, 1860) who studied at the *Akademie der bildenden Künste* and came to Milwaukee in 1885 to paint Civil War themes, decorate brewer Pabst's new German theater, and become the Milwaukee museum's art director.[6] The infant Richard Offner (b. Vienna, 1899 – d. New York, 1965) came to America to carve out for himself a distinguished career in teaching art, after 1923 at New York University.[7] In 1902 the Vienna-born (1871) artist Oscar Gross came overseas to work in portraiture and murals for public buildings and win awards from the Municipal League and Chicago's Association of Painters and Sculptors.[8] Joseph Urban (b. Vienna, 1872 – d. New York, 1933) was a great artist of the theater who was versatile enough to illustrate the Grimm and Anderson fairy tales and turn his hand to architecture.

There was Richard Alexander Loederer (b. Vienna, 1894) who came here in 1914 and who has done murals and portraits of famous Americans.[9] Puritan and Middle Class America were, in the nineteenth and early twentieth centuries, a bit suspicious of the arts but portrait painting, especially of famous national figures, was above suspicion and more than one Austrian-born artist realized this and turned to the art of portraiture. And Stephanie Okhanska Komarnitsky (b. Austria-Hungary, 1897), an immigrant of 1920, educated in Vienna, Bristol in Virginia, and New York, has both taught art and created it.[10] There was Joseph Margulies (b. Austria, 1896), the arti t of New York's ghetto who painted and etched Jewish and Mexican types as well as famous Americans and new Americans, from Einstein to Muni, and taught art in and around New York.[11] Another portrait painter was Fritz Werner (b. Vienna, 1898), an immigrant of 1932, who came with a substantial Austrian and international reputation and specialized in portraits of masters of industry.[12]

The son of a Viennese baker was the artist Frederic Taubes (b. Lemberg, Galicia, 1900) who ran away to poach game in the Tyrol, studied art in Vienna and Germany, painted cubist and dadaistic works, achieved some reputation in Vienna by 1921, and came to New York in 1930. In America he has taught art and painted it, had dozens of one-man shows and been represented even in the Metropolitan Museum.[13]

One of the four Austrian-born artists that the "Encyclopaedia Britannica" was proud to claim as contributors to its Collection of Contemporary American Painting was Hilde Kayn (b. Vienna, 1903) who came here in 1921 after World War I had swept away the family fortune. Fame came to her in the 1940's when American museums began to buy her works.[14]

Several of New England's museums are able to boast of their watercolors and etchings by Ludwig Mestler (b. Vienna, 1891 – d. 1959) who worked first as an architect in Vienna and, after World War I, in New York. His desire to turn to painting brought him back to Vienna for eight years in the 1930's but in 1939 he came to Boston, lived in Cambridge, and painted with no great financial success until his death. New York's Austrian Institute, that has recently attempted to introduce so many Austrian artists to an American public, exhibited works of Mestler in 1966.[15]

Maurice Sven Dimand (b. Vienna, 1892) came to New York in 1923 to become a few years later the curator for Near Eastern art in the Metropolitan Museum.[16] And Austria's best-known American museum director, René d'Harnoncourt (b. Vienna, 1901), educated at the University of Graz and at the *Technische Hochschule* in Vienna, came to the United States in 1931 to interest himself in Mexican art and teach art at Sarah Lawrence College. Washington used him on Indian and South American projects. And he became director of America's most important outpost of contemporary art, New York's Museum of Modern Art, in 1949.[17] That was a key position for a recent arrival from middle Europe.

Two very notable Austrian artists of our day whose work is well known in America's world of art are Alfred Kubin (b. Leitmeritz, Bohemia, 1877 – d. Zwickledt, Upper Austria, 1959) and Oskar Kokoschka (b. Pöchlarn, Lower Austria, 1886). Kubin, who lived most of his long life in an ancestral castle at Wernstein on the River Inn was primarily an illustrator, a unique expressionist who combined the fantasy of the fairytale world with much that was earthy and psychotic and frightening. Otto Kallir has tried more than once without too much success to popularize Kubin in America with exhibits at the St. Etienne Galerie. The illustrations he did for authors like Poe and Dostoyevski have, however, ensured him a place in modern art.[18]

The works of Oskar Kokoschka, the greatest name in contemporary Austrian art, are avidly sought by American museums and collectors. He was a pet aversion of Hitler when Hitler denounced the Jewish degeneracy of the art of Germany's Weimar Republic. Born on the Danube of a Czech father and a Styrian mother, and educated in Vienna, he worked and taught in Germany, traveled over most of the Western World, found refuge for a time in Britain, visited America in 1949 with a one-man show of his exciting, expressionistic work. He has been teaching art in Salzburg since 1953. Vienna which was savagely disapproving when Kokoschka first exhibited there in 1907 and America which long neglected him have come to honor him as one of the greatest.[19]

The art historian of the future may be able to estimate the degree to which Austrian art was impoverished by Nazi persecution and the degree to which art in America and England and Switzerland profited by the immigration of dozens of competent artists whom Austria could so ill afford to lose. A few of them returned at the end of the war like the renowned abstract sculptor Fritz Wotruba (b. Vienna, 1907) who spent the war years in Switzerland, has exhibited all over Europe and in America, and is the central figure of the brilliant group which has made Vienna today "one of the capitals of sculpture."[20] Otto Benesch (b. Ebenfurth, 1896—d. Vienna, 1964), the art historian who worked and taught at Harvard during the war returned to become director of Vienna's *Albertina*.[21] Otto Demus (b. Harland, Lower Austria, 1902) a refugee in London in 1939, returned to direct the all-important Federal Monuments Office with a year out to teach at Harvard in 1949. Later he accepted a chair for art history at the University of Vienna.

A famous cover of "Time" magazine showing Hitler playing his Hymn of Hate on a gruesome organ was the work of another Austrian artist, Rudolf von Ripper (1905—1960), who suffered in a German concentration camp, was severely wounded as a U.S. paratrooper and returned with a fascinating blond American wife, who seemed twice Rudi's height, to Vienna and Mallorca to draw and paint the abstract and the grotesque.[22]

Most of the able Thirty-eighters, however, whether they intended to adopt America or not, did in fact remain. And since so many achieved United States citizenship in the minimum five-year period, we may assume that they intended from the first never to return to the land where they had suffered so much. Emanuel Winternitz (b. Vienna, 1898), for instance, who had studied music and law in Vienna, arrived in America in 1938 and was naturalized in 1943. He turned to art, became a curator of collections at the Metropolitan Museum, and taught music at Yale.[23] The artist Hans Jelinek (b. Vienna, 1910) who has taught at the College of the City of New York and the New School for Social Research also received citizenship in five years.[24]

There were other curators and professors who came in 1938 or thereafter such as those two graduates of the Vienna Academy of Fine Arts, Viktor Löwenfeld (b. Linz, 1903 – d. 1960) long a professor of art education at Pennsylvania State University, and Ala Story (b. Hruscha, Austria, 1907)[26] who spent years in London before he came to New York to work in films and went on to become director of the Santa Barbara Museum in California. Some Austrian artists, like William Unger of Vienna and Kirksville, Missouri, grandson of a well-known Vienna artist of the same name whose portrait of Kaiser Franz Joseph his grandson has found in a little Wisconsin town a couple of generations later, came some years after the National Socialist period – but they were relatively few.

An Austrian tragedy in America was the sad death of the really distinguished co-founder of the Munich *Sezession* and representative of fine modernism in Graz up to 1931, Wilhelm Thoeny (b. Graz, 1888 – d. New York, 1949). His delicate paintings of Vienna's *Karlskirche* and of Paris and New York's Battery have entranced thousands. He and his wife emigrated to New York to escape the Nazis; he lost virtually all of his glorious paintings by fire in 1948, and died grief-stricken the next year. And Thoeny was one of the best among the Austrian emigrants whose paintings are valued collector's items even in distant America. They are to be found in museums all the way from San Francisco to New York's Metropolitan.[27]

If most Austrian artists had not been internationalists who concerned themselves with art and not with any chauvinistic inclinations to promote the art of Austria, the dozens of Austrian-born artists in America might have attracted far more attention than they have to the best of Austrian art. Actually, almost none of the immigrant artists have propagandized for anything Austrian. There are fortunate exceptions like Otto Kallir with his art gallery in New York. Franz Bader in the nation's capital has occasionally exhibited contemporary Austrians like the printmaker Fred Nowak. And two Viennese named Lloyd and Fischer have developed the prominent Marlborough-Gerson Gallery in New York where they have shown the works of contemporary Austrians like Wotruba. But most of the emigrés have been too content to be called German or, later, American artists. Yet the many Austrian-born artists who came to this country during the tragic Hitler years have certainly left somewhere the impact of Waldmüller, Klimt, Schiele, Kokoschka and the other fine Austrians.

There were dozens of these Austrians. There was Hans Tietze, native of Prague[28] (b. 1880 – d. New York, 1954), who helped the Austrian government organize its museums and taught art history until he came to America in 1938 to instruct at the Toledo Museum and work in New York with the Metropolitan.[29] There were the painters Franz Lerch (b. Vienna, 1895), the expressionist who came to New York in 1939, and another expressionist Max Oppenheimer (b. Vienna, 1885 – d. 1956) known as Mopp, and Ernst Lothar (b. Vienna, 1906 – d. Washington, 1961) who taught at the University of Santo Domingo, at Hampton Institute and Baltimore and in Washington where he lived and exhibited at the best galleries.[30]

Hans Böhler (b. Vienna, 1884 – d. Vienna, 1961), son of the silhouettist of Brahms and Bruckner, brought his very considerable European reputation to New York in 1936. When he died on a visit to his native Vienna, he left fine examples of his work in the Boston Institute of Contemporary Art and the New York Museum Purchase Fund Collection as in Vienna's galleries.[31] Joseph Floch (b. Vienna, 1895) was another genuinely distinguished 38er, a professor at the New School for Social Research in New York, whose excellent modernism has been purchased by many of the world's best museums from the *Jeu de Paume* in Paris and the *Albertina* in Vienna to the Whitney and the Metropolitan in New York and the Toledo Museum.[32]

"My Parents," painted in 1946 by a fine refugee artist in New York portrays two old folks walking in their beloved Vienna Woods, a certain Herr and Frau Körner who refused to flee from the Nazis and who were subsequently "liquidated." Their son, Henry Körner (b. Vienna, 1915) fled to Italy, reached New York in 1939 with the help of a Brooklyn uncle, found success in commercial art, served in the American army, and later settled in Pittsburgh. Körner sketched for the military, did posters for the U.S. government, covers for "Time," taught in Pennsylvania, maintained a foothold in New York, and painted and drew "genre scenes (which) have a Neo-Romantic flavor in almost Surrealist symbolism."[33]

The 38er group included graphic artists like John W. Winkler (b. Vienna, 1890) of Berkeley, California whose reputation rests partly on his San Francisco etchings of many famous names,[34] and the Washington portrait photographer Hans Strenitz-Glogau (b. Vienna, 1894) who had experienced a none-too-happy Russian prison camp when, as an Austrian soldier of the first World War, he was captured on the eastern front.[35] There was also among the Thirty-eighters Oskar Stössel of New York who painted Franklin D. Roosevelt and produced many distinguished folio etchings before returning to Vienna in 1959, and Benjamin Strasser (b. Vienna, 1888 – d. New York, 1955), the portrait painter who fled the Nazis to England and Switzerland and found America only in 1951.[36] There was the cartoonist Eric A. Peters (b. Vienna, 1909) who did work for popular magazines like "Colliers" and the "Saturday Evening Post" but whose work was distinguished enough to find a place in the Austrian National Library.[37] And the younger Henry Wolf (b. Vienna, 1925) who came to New York to work in commericial art received several gold medals for magazine design from the New York Art Directors' Club.[38]

The majority of the women artists among the 38ers were also from Vienna rather than from the *Länder*. But most of them were specialists. The significant Wally Wieseltier (b. Vienna, 1895 – d. U.S.A. 1945) who came to New York in 1929 was an artist in ceramics, glass, and textiles.[39] Gertrud Natzler (b. Vienna, 1908) of Los Angeles, for instance, was a potter – distinguished enough to be represented in museums like the Chicago Art Institute and Seattle and the Metropolitan.[40] Lisl Weil (b. Vienna) has done fascinating work with children's books and TV programs for children.[41] Emmy Lichtwitz Krasso (b. Troppau) who studied art in Vienna and Budapest, taught it in Vienna and Bombay, and is represented in the *Albertina*, has also worked with children.[42] Cipe Pineles Golden (b. Vienna, 1910) did magazine art work in New York and Elise Rosen (b. Vienna), a graphic artist with a French decoration of honor, has exhibited in Vienna, Paris and New York.[43]

President Kennedy in 1961 expressed regret at the death of the Austrian-born Enit Kaufman who had painted dozens of famous Americans including the presidents from Hoover on, and had taken an abstract turn in her later years.[44] And there were other Vienna-born women artists: Gertrude Quastler (b. 1909) of Long Island who is represented in such significant galleries as the New York Museum of Modern Art and Helen Wolf (b. 1912) of New York City who has been honored with the medal of the Knickerbocker Artists.[45] Helen Siegl of Philadelphia, represented by the Weyhe Gallerie in New York, produced fine woodcuts.

And there were other and equally interesting specialists among the artists of the other sex. A well-known craftsman of genuine distinction was the painter – calligrapher – printer Victor Karl Hammer (b. Vienna, 1882) who had worked as a boy in the studio of Vienna's famous city planner, Camillo Sitte, taught at the Academy of Fine Art, spent a dozen years in Florence, and achieved an Austrian reputation as a portrait painter. He left Austria secretly in 1939, found an opportunity to teach at Wells College, pursued his interest in the making of fine books, and created the distinguished, beautiful, American uncial type. He became known as a sober, talented, modest artist, unique in his unusual combination of interests.[46]

All of these Austrians whose art has been known and respected in the United States or who have come here and practiced their art may not have created any such immediate response as the magnificent "Art Treasures from the Vienna Collections" from the finest Vienna collections that toured America in 1950; but they have doubtless had a more important, lasting influence, year in and year out, upon American artists and students and art lovers in this country. Even though many of the names have been thought of as being "German" and though Austrian immigrants have a strange reluctance to promote the achievements of their mother country, the work of Fischer von Erlach and Schiele and Kokoschka and Victor Karl Hammer of Wells College (and all of the other émigrés) has come to mean more and more in America.

There were few finer artists in 19th century America than the sculptor Karl Bitter (b. Vienna, 1867 – d. New York, 1915) who never threw off his Austrianism yet became American enough to design the Dewey Arch in New York and the Thomas Jefferson statue at the University of Virginia. Bitter represented "one of the greatest influences in the field of sculpture our country has known."[47] He had, as we are noting in our chapter on architecture, worked on Vienna's public buildings, escaped the Austrian "draft" by coming to America, and found such a place in American architecture that, before he died in a New York traffic accident, he was twice president of our national association of sculptors. Winning John Jacob Astor's money in a competition for designs for the new doors of New York's Trinity Church established Karl Bitter's American reputation sixteen months after the young Viennese arrived in this country. He did dozens of other splendid works which few Americans have ever attributed to a draft-dodger from Austria. But his most telling contributions were doubtless those that he made in design at the series of American "world fairs," before and after the turning of the century. Those fairs set American taste in sculpture for decades to come, and Bitter was their key figure in sculpture.

Many of Bitter's Austro-American successors have, despite the fact that sculpture was the last of the major arts to develop in America, distinguished themselves in public service. His disciple Max Mauch worked with him at the Chicago and St. Louis expositions.[48] Some of the buildings at Chicago's Columbian Exposition showed the work of the sculptor Isidore Konti (b. Vienna or Szombathely, Hungary, 1862 – d. 1938) who came to Chicago when he was twenty-nine, settled in New York, provided Bitter with groups for the Dewey Arch, received a gold medal for his contributions to the great fountain at the St. Louis exposition of 1903, and, among dozens of other notable sculptures, did the group representing South America on the famous Pan American Union Building in Washington.[49] Chaim Gross (b. Austria, 1904) came to New York as a young man, achieved fame in sculpture, wood carvings, and illustrations for children's books, designed innumerable high spots in public buildings such as the door panel for the Federal Trade Commission Building in Washington, and won representation in most of our finest art museums.[50]

In June 1961 President Kennedy unveiled a figure of a space-age-man, an award to be given annually to the Air Force man contributing most to the conquest of space, that was the work of the Vienna-born Felix Weihs de Weldon (b. 1907). One wonders why Felix Weiss should have changed his name to something as un-Austrian and un-American as Weihs de Weldon. But the new name has obviously been no handicap. He received sculpture prizes in Vienna and Washington and Canada, and he has done some of America's favourite sculpture: Commodore Perry's statue in Tokyo, the Iwo Jima Flag Raising group on the banks of the Potomac, the equestrian statue of Bolivar two blocks from the White House, the Richard E. Byrd statue at the entrance to Arlington Cemetery, and the Speaker Sam Rayburn statue down in Bonham, Texas. The Greeks were something less than enthusiastic about the huge Harry S. Truman statue that de Weldon did for Athens. He designed the medal for America's favourite astronaut John Glenn and he has done innumerable busts of the famous of two continents.[51]

There have been a few Austro-Americans outside of the area of official sculpture. The Vienna-born Grete Schuller of New York City has received the prize of the National Association of Women Artists (1953) and the Elia Morgenthau Prize for Sculpture (1956).[52] Egon Weiner (b. Vienna, 1906) of Chicago's Art Institute, a

Thirty-eighter, has done several fine religious pieces like the Christ in the Rockefeller Chapel at the University of Chicago.[53] Leo Steppat (b. Vienna, 1910), a graduate of Vienna's Academy of Fine Arts, an associate of the New York Museum of Modern Art and a director of the Forum Gallery there, has taught art all the way from Washington, by way of Indiana and Mississippi, to the University of Wisconsin.[54] And one of Austria's finest moderns, Georg Ehrlich (b. Vienna, 1897), who went to London in 1937 to avoid the threat of Nazism, has taught sculpture in New York and Columbus.[55] And with distinction.

The Austrian contemporaries of the abstract Wotruba school (Fritz Wotruba was born in Vienna in 1907) have an international reputation that is only gradually reaching America. Wotruba was represented at the Philadelphia Museum of Art back in 1949 and at the Pittsburgh International Exhibition in 1961. American lovers of modernism in Vienna have found his modern Würthle Gallery and his work at the new Twentieth Century Museum a refreshing oasis. Some Americans are buying his fine pieces in bronze or limestone or marble. But the names of Wotruba's disciples are for the most part unknown in this country and we find it difficult to look four thousand miles away to distant Vienna to realize that Michael Seuphor may be correct in calling it one of today's capitals of sculpture.[56]

If the Austrian Institute of New York was correct, in 1966, in describing the Alan Gallery's exhibition of the Vienna School of Fantastic Realism as a glimpse at post-war Central Europe's most significant art movement, there is still reason to believe that modern Austrian art will attract America's attention. But the America that is so fond of contemporary French painting and of African primitives, is not likely to become intrigued with Vienna's "Fantastic Realism."[57]

[1] Alfred Werner, "Truly Austrian Art," *American-German Review*, Aug.-Sept. 1959, p. 4. Werner is a Viennese who has taught at the College of the City of New York and has written art criticism.

[2] *Austrian Information*, 28 July 1962. Alfred Werner in *Arts*, Oct. 1960, p. 49, and N. Pevsner in *Pioneers of Modern Design*, N.Y. 1949, p. 147, emphasize Klimt's significance in the development of modern art.

[3] *Arts*, Oct. 1960, pp. 46–49; *Austrian Information*, 12 Nov. 1960.

[4] Louis Calder is sometimes mentioned as the discoverer of Grandma Moses. According to Mrs. Kallir (letter to the author, 1 Aug. 1963), he found some Moses pictures in a drug store, was interested, and took them to Otto Kallir whose concern for folk art was well known and who was happy to exhibit and help develop Grandma Moses and her fascinating work.

[5] *Alte und moderne Kunst*, March-April 1964, pp. 31–34.

[6] *American-German Review*, Oct. 1946, p. 32.

[7] *Who's Who in American Art*, N.Y. 1959.

[8] *Who's Who*, 1938–39.

[9] *Who's Who*, 1952–53.

[10] *Who's Who of American Women*, 2nd ed., 1961.

[11] *Universal Jewish Encyclopedia*, N.Y. 1948; *Who's Who*, 1952–53.

[12] *Who's Who*, 1962–63.

[13] *Encyclopedia of Painting*, N.Y. 1955; *Current Biography*, 1943; *Britannica Collection of Contemporary American Painting*, Chicago 1946, no. 119.

[14] *Britannica Collection of Contemporary American Painting*, no. 66. Floch, Taubes and Thoeny were the other Austrians included.

[15] *Who's Who in American Art*, Washington 1940; announcement of Austrian Institute, May 1966.

[16] *Who's Who*, 1962–63.

[17] *Who's Who*, 1962–63. He has high honors from the French, German and Peruvian governments.

[18] Alfred Werner in *American-German Review*, Apr.-May 1960, pp. 8–9; Bernard S. Myers, *The German Expressionists*, N.Y. 1957, pp. 198, 256–58.

[19] Myers, *op. cit.*, p. 58; Bruno Grimschitz, *Ars Austriae*, Wien 1960; O. W. Larkin, *Art and Life in America*, N.Y. 1949, pp. 351, 430.

[20] Michael Seuphor, *Sculpture in this Century*, N.Y. 1960. He exhibited in Philadelphia in 1949: *Österreicher der Gegenwart*, Wien 1951, p. 345.

[21] *Who's Who in American Art*, 1959.

[22] *Art in America*, 1961, no. 1, p. 107.

[23] *Who's Who*, 1962–63.

[24] *Who's Who*, 1960–61; *Who's Who in American Art*, 1959.

[25] *Directory of American Scholars*, 1957.

[26] *Who's Who in American Art*, 1959.

[27] Grimschitz, *op. cit.*, p. 53; *American-German Review*, Aug.-Sept. 1959, p. 6; *Britannica Collection of Contemporary American Painting*, no. 120.

[28] *Universal Jewish Encyclopedia*, X, p. 249.

[29] *Ibid.*

[30] Obit. in *New York Times*, 2 Apr. 1961.

[31] *New York Times*, 19 Sept. 1961, p. 35; *Austrian Information*, 30 Sept. 1961.

[32] *Ibid.*, 31 Oct. 1962; *Who's Who in American Art*, 1959; *Encyclopaedia Britannica Collection of Contemporary American Painting*, no. 43.

[33] Alexander Eliot, *Three Hundred Years of American Painting*, N.Y. 1957, pp. 261–63. Quotation is from the *Encyclopedia of Painting*, N.Y. 1955.

[34] Winkler appears in *Who's Who*, 1962–63; Stössel in *Who's Who in American Art*, 1959.

[35] *Washington Post*, 4 May 1965, obituary.

[36] *New York Times*, 21 Sept. 1955, p. 33.

[37] *Who's Who in American Art*, 1959.

[38] *Who's Who*, 1962–63.

[39] Cf. N.Y. Times *Index* and Ulrich Thieme and Felix Becker, *Allgemeines Lexikon der bildenden Künstler*, 36 vols. and supplements, Leipzig 1907–47, XXXV. Concise data regarding many other artists mentioned in this chapter will be found in this *Lexikon* usually referred to as "Thieme-Becker."

[40] *Who's Who of American Women*, 2nd ed., 1961.

[41] *Who's Who*, 1962–63.

[42] *Who's Who of American Women*, 2nd. ed., 1961.

[43] *Ibid.*

[44] *American-German Review*, Apr.-May 1957; *Austrian Information*, 27 May 1961.

[45] *Who's Who of American Women*, 2nd ed., 1961.

[46] *American Artist*, June-Aug. 1956, pp. 44ff.; Joseph Graves, *Victor Hammer*, Charlottesville 1954.

[47] Allen H. Eaton, *Immigrant Gifts to American Life*, N.Y. 1932, p. 122. Authoritative is Ferdinand Schevill, *Karl Bitter*, Chicago 1917. See also Larkin, *op. cit.*, pp. 314 and 392.

[48] *Das Buch der Deutschen in Amerika*, Philadelphia 1907, p. 350.

[49] *Ibid.*, p. 349; Rachel Du Bois, *Germans in American Life*, N.Y. 1936, p. 138; *National Cyclopaedia of American Biography*, Supp. I, N.Y. 1910, p. 493. Thieme-Becker, *op. cit.*, XX, p. 283, states that Hungarians claim he was born in Hungary and the authority Eisenberg gives Vienna as his birthplace.

[50] *Who's Who*, 1962–63.

[51] *Who's Who in American Art*; *Washington Post*, 29 June 1961, p. A2; 12 Nov. 1962, p. A2.

[52] *Who's Who of American Women*, 2nd ed., 1961.

[53] *Who's Who*, 1962–63.

[54] *Ibid.*

[55] Grimschitz, *op. cit.*, p. 52.

[56] *The Sculpture of this Century*, N.Y. 1960, pp. 165–66. Also *Österreicher der Gegenwart; International Who's Who*, 1960; *Austrian Information*, 15 Sept. 1961.

[57] Austrian Institute (New York), announcement, March 1966.

CHAPTER XVII

PRACTICAL AUSTRIANS

Austrians are reputed to be impractical dreamers. Americans think of them as a race of musicians who love only their operas and orchestras and the wine gardens where they listen to their music and nibble on delectable pastries and dream about the glories of the old monarchy. Typical is the journalist's story that, back when all Europe was on the verge of crisis, the situation was reported in Berlin as serious but not hopeless while in Vienna the situation was reported as hopeless but not serious. It is easy to overlook the fact that Austrians, with all their artistry and *Gemütlichkeit*, have occasionally contributed to the practical arts and sciences, often in fields of direct concern to American life.

Austrian achievements, in the long years when few Americans visited there, usually reached America by devious routes. Her introduction of the postcard in 1869, for instance, reached us by way of Britain. Indeed, the entire concept of an international public postal service, not confined as in the Middle Ages to princes and their courts, seems to have reached us from Innsbruck by way of Western Europe long after the enterprising Franz von Taxis made a fortune in the business about the year 1500. Taxis, whose family had for centuries delivered messages for the Venetian nobility, came to Innsbruck, won the favor of Emperor Maximilian, carried his mails for him and, cheating a bit, began carrying letters on the side for all who would pay for the service. Another Taxis capitalized on the idea in Vienna. Maximilian offered no objections, and the new postal service became so renowned that Philip of Spain employed Franz von Taxis to introduce it into his part of Europe, from Madrid to Rome and the Netherlands. The Counts of Thurn and Taxis conducted a vast network of postal services for the better part of five centuries before Austria, and the last German states to use it, nationalized the service.[1]

The postcard was first initiated by the Austrian post in 1869. It is probable, also, that Austria established the first airmail service in the world. That was on April 1, 1918, between Vienna and Kiev, six weeks before the opening of America's first airmail service between Washington and Long Island.[2]

A few of Austria's practical men of invention should certainly be mentioned. Some like Dr. Joseph Goldmark, a refugee of 1848, who introduced amorphous sulphur into the United States revealed their inventive genius in America. This first non-poisonous type of sulphur had been discovered in Vienna in 1845 by Anton Schroetter – a godsend to workers in match factories! Goldmark discovered how to produce red phosphorus for safety matches while he was practising medicine about New York, and patented a mercury compound that proved valuable in making percussion caps for the Union Army during the Civil War.[3] Others, like Austria's pioneer railroad builders, Mathias von Schönerer of the horse-drawn railroad, who visited the United States in 1838 to bring back with him the first steam locomotive ever seen in Austria and Karl von Ghega who built Europe's first great tunnels through the Alps, were virtually unknown here.[4]

And there is a more interesting group who should doubtless be better known: Joseph Madersperger (b. Kufstein, 1768 – d. Vienna, 1850), a tailor who invented a sewing machine long before Elias Howe's; Siegfried Marcus (b. Mecklenburg, 1829 – d. Vienna, 1898), a mechanic who invented an automobile long before America ever saw one; and David Schwarz (b. Szala-Egerszeg, Hungary, 1845 – d. Vienna, 1897) who flew a lighter-than-air airship before Count Zeppelin. Madersperger's sewing machine of 1814, which was the first to use two threads to bind a seam, a full generation after the English Thomas Saint had patented his primitive machine but more than thirty years before the date of Elias Howe's American patent, quadrupled the speed of hand-workers. But Madersperger was the victim of the hostility of the Austrian tailors and, with no capital to develop his invention, died in a poorhouse.[5]

The Marcus automobile was another debacle resulting from inadequate promotion. His models of 1864 and 1874 were the first successful automobiles following the steam-engine era. For they used vaporized gasoline, a single-cylinder, four-cycle motor, water cooling, with electric ignition and jet carburation, and a throttle to regulate speed. They ran so rapidly and noisily in Vienna's streets that the police objected. Marcus lost his enthusiasm and left it to Daimler and Benz to put the first automobile into production over ten years afterwards. Yet when Henry Ford was sued a generation later for infringement of Selden's patent rights, Marcus's papers were brought to America (1900) in the conviction that they would show that it was Marcus and not Selden who had given the gasoline auto to the world. Unfortunately for Marcus's reputation in America, Ford won his suit without reference to the Marcus car.[6]

It was somewhat ironical that not the plodding, inventive Marcus but Austrian genius in the person of Dr. Ferdinand Porsche should create in Germany a motor car known for years all over America, the Volkswagen. After decades of automotive work in Austria, including the building of imperially elegant cars for the Habsburgs and fighting cars and trucks for Austrians and Germans in the first World War, Porsche transferred his work to Germany. He listened to Hitler's sensible demand for a cheap, practical car to serve the many without ostentation, and produced the little, air-cooled, rear-motored Volkswagen which sold after the second World War by the millions. In the early 1960's VW sold its every third car in America. The Porsche sport car that Dr. Ferdinand put into production in Germany in 1950 had enthusiastic devotees in this country but it never competed in numbers or importance with his basic product, the Volkswagen.[7]

The case of David Schwarz's first rigid airship is more evidence that invention is seldom a one-man, one-country affair as simple as the American or Austrian contention that one American or one Austrian invented the sewing machine. Most inventions have been the work of dozens of men of several nationalities. Surely the rigid airship that America credited to the German Count Zeppelin was the immediate descendent of the brain child of David Schwarz, born in Hungary, employed for years in Zagreb in Croatia, repudiated by the skeptical Austrian war ministry which saw nothing in his airship, and welcomed by the Berlin government if only his machine would fly. Unfortunately, Schwarz dropped dead in Vienna in 1897 just as he was called to Berlin to see his machine's first flight; the machine did fly but for only four miles before a minor defect brought it down; and Count Zeppelin bought the rights from Schwarz's widow.[8] Austrian indifference had again, as in the cases of sewing machines and automobiles, presented the lead in an important area of endeavor to another country. Americans interested in such endeavors have never thought of them as having any Austrian connections.

The typewriter is another case in point. According to Bruce Bliven Jr., in his "The Wonderful Writing Machine,"[9] if the inventor was not the English Henry Mill who may never have actually built one, "it was either Von Knaus or Count Neipperg of Vienna, in the early 1760's," or a Swiss or Frenchman twenty years later. Yet the American "World Almanac" (1961) agrees with the German encyclopedia "Der Grosse Brockhaus" (1956)[10] that the first practical typewriter was invented by Peter Mitterhofer (b. Partschins near Meran, 1822 – d. there, 1893) in Vienna in 1866. If the Sholes machine of 1867, which some Americans claim to have been the first, was not superior to the Mitterhofer models, the competition was close![11]

The screw propeller was still another case. Josef Ludwig Franz Ressel (b. Heinersdorf a. T., Bohemia, 1793 – d. Laibach, 1857) is generally credited with the practical, modern application of the rather ancient principle of the screw propeller. But his trial run in Trieste's harbor in 1829, successful until a boiler pipe broke, brought the police down on him, and he died years later, poor and embittered, while John Ericsson and other inventors in more sympathetic lands were reaping the credit for the development of the all-important screw propeller. That was one more Austrian tragedy in the field of invention, important to America but unrecognized here.[12]

There were some inventions by Austrians that were recognized in the United States. Wilhelm Gintl's duplex telegraph of 1853, that permitted the simultaneous transmission between two stations of two messages, was years later to be improved upon by Edison, but it was immensely important in the telegraph's early years. The armored train that was used to defend Vienna during the Revolution of 1848 may well have inspired the use of armored trains in the American Civil War.[13]

Also well known here, and especially among sportsmen, are the fine Mannlicher-Schoenauer rifles. Ferdinand Ritter von Mannlicher, who produced at the Steyr factory, which Werndl had made famous among war offices all over Europe, was, according to an American expert, never equalled among inventors of firearms "for prolific originality and mechanical wizardry." His military rifles, which the Austrian army never promoted in the way the German government promoted Mauser's, were used by several of Europe's armies and his hunting rifles appear in many handsome designs in American catalogs.[14]

The best-known Austrian name in all the ranks of inventors was in America doubtless Carl Freiherr Auer von Welsbach (b. Vienna, 1858 – d. Castle Welsbach, Carinthia, 1929) whose statue still marks the Vienna bus stop for the American embassy. His incandescent mantle gave gas a strong white glow that was far more effective than the gas lights that had but dimly lit American cities since the early 19th century. Welsbach mantles conquered America in the 1890's and the old Welsbach Street Illuminating Company came to own a vast majority of the gaslights in the streets of New York and San Francisco and other large American cities. The mantle tripled the candle power of the gas flame and it achieved a near monopoly of American street lighting. The electric light retired the gas light for a few generations but then, in the mid 20th century, nostalgia for the gas-light era plus a practical appreciation of the cheapness of gas, began to revive "the magic name" of Welsbach and the intense green-white glow of the Welsbach mantle began to reappear on Beacon Hill and Independence Square and even in Chicago and the sophisticated parts of dozens of other American cities. Welsbach is still a name to conjure with.[15]

Almost equally important were the Viennese Georg Sigl (b. Breitenfurt near Vienna, 1811 – d. Vienna, 1887) who in 1851 built the world's first power press, which was soon sold, with improvements by a French engineer, in America and Britain; Karl Klietsch, originally Klič (b. Arnau, Bohemia, 1841 – d. Vienna, 1926) who developed rotogravure for American Sunday newspapers,[16] and the Levy Brothers of half-tone fame. Louis Levy (b. Stenowitz, Bohemia, 1846 – d. 1919) was a Bohemian Jew, Max was American-born. Louis came to Detroit as a child with his parents, developed the photo-chemical engraving process he called "levytype" in 1875 in Baltimore, and in Philadelphia with his brother in later years he invented one of the finest methods of making half-tone plates. Credit for the first half-tone blocks in newspaper printing, in 1877, is generally given to the Jaffé brothers of Vienna.[17]

There were other Austrian inventors whose names have remained relatively unknown here in America whose findings have been nevertheless of genuine importance in American life. Of the field of motion pictures, for instance, it is most interesting to read in the great Oxford "History of Technology" that "the one and only fundamental discovery" was achieved in 1832 with spinning discs by a Belgian physicist and an Austrian geodesist and mathematician, Simon von Stampfer, and that the Austrian Baron Franz von Uchatius (b. Theresienfeld, Lower Austria, 1811 – d. Vienna, 1881) found the true solution to the problem of making motion pictures in 1853 when he devised a projector for the instruction of army officers.[18]

There was also the Vienna physicist Robert von Lieben (b. Vienna, 1878 – d. Vienna, 1913) whose *Lieben-Röhren*, or radio tubes, were of such significance in experimental physics as well as in radio development,[19] and Dr. Emanuel Rosenberg (b. Vienna, 1872 – d. 1962) whose *Querfeld-Dynamo*, or crossfield generator, has been used in building guided missiles.[20] Gustav Hoffmann invented coke ovens of the type used here late in the 19th century. America's largest turbines for developing water power have long been modeled upon the Kaplan turbines invented by Viktor Kaplan (b. Mürzzuschlag, 1876 – d. Unterach, Upper Austria, 1934) that the World Power Conference of 1936 recognized as one of the greatest achievements in the history of water power.[21]

In an entirely different field, it is said that the Austrian chemist Fran Seech, living in California, produced a new type of ink that made the popular ballpoint pen a success – "the greatest subsequent improvement" after the development of the ball-point by the Hungarian Biro.[22]

Austrian distinction has been in scientific, rather than in industrial inventions. Scientific discoverers like Lise Meitner whose escape from Berlin with the secrets of atomic research may well have deprived Nazi Germany of victory in World War II, belong in our chapter on science. Here we should only mention two important Austrian contributions to steel production. The first was the use of Austrian magnesite which "became supreme" among the refractories essential to world steel production. Austria's Leoben works used it in 1860; Cleveland, Ohio imported it first in 1885; and it was imported to America in huge quantities until the first World War shut it off.[23] And the LD (Linz-Donawitz) basic oxygen process for making steel, first developed in Austria and first used in the United States at Trenton, Michigan, in 1954, was by 1961 utilized in the production of nearly a quarter of the world's steel output. The American Iron and Steel Institute added in 1959 the basic oxygen process to the time-honored processes of the past: open-hearth, Bessemer, etc., only seven years after the first use of the new process at Linz in Austria. The United States Steel Corporation, announcing the building of three new basic oxygen furnaces at Gary in 1963, boasted that the new furnaces would make steel about eight times faster than the conventional open-hearth method.[24] International Harvester, claiming that its plant in South Chicago had become one of the first ten in America to introduce basic oxygen equipment, maintained that it could produce in 20 minutes what the open-hearth process could produce only in ten hours.[25] The supremacy of this Austrian process is especially interesting in view of the fact that, despite its modest iron and steel industry, Austria ranked only 17th in steel production in 1954 when the United

States first tried Austria's LD process. By the end of 1964 there were eighty LD plants on five continents with an annual capacity of 68 million tons.

In exploration there were early figures significant enough to be claimed by several nationalities including the Austrians: Augustin Herrman (b. Prague, 1621), claimed by Czechs and Germans, who mapped Maryland for Lord Baltimore;[26] John Lederer, very possibly a native of mid-17th-century Tyrol but more definitely at home in Hamburg, who sought the elusive Northwest Passage for Governor Berkeley in the Virginia and Carolina mountains;[27] and Father Eusebio Francisco Kino (b. Segno, 1644 – d. New Mexico, 1711), born Kühn, in what is now the Italian Tyrol and hence claimed by the Italians as well as the Austrians, whose explorations in our Arizona and Colorado River country and in Sonora and Lower California are an essential part of the story of the American West.[28]

There was indeed considerable Austrian interest in the Americas before their interest shifted, in the later 19th century, to Africa. In the 1780's there came the Austrian Imperial Botanical Expedition with a group of botanists under the leadership of Professor Franz Josef Maerter who journeyed from Pennsylvania to Florida. Sixty years later another botanist, Professor Karl Heller of Graz, traveled in the American South, and Clara von Gerstner came here in 1838–1840 to observe our social and economic institutions.[29]

Much later Joseph Francis Rock (b. Vienna, 1884) came to the United States as a young man to achieve some reputation as an explorer, orientalist, and botanist. Rock went to China for the United States Department of Agriculture soon after World War I and he led expeditions into China, Tibet, Annam, and Cambodia for Harvard, the National Geographic Society and the National Museum. He worked for years at the University of Hawaii where he died in 1962.[30] Another distinguished Orientalist, Gustave von Grunebaum (b. Vienna, 1909), was a Thirty-eighter who had been associated with the University of Vienna's Oriental Institute before he came to the Asia Institute in New York and, in 1943, went on to the University of Chicago to teach Arabic.[31]

Ernst von Hesse-Wartegg (b. Vienna, 1854 – d. Switzerland, 1918), the world traveler, geographer and writer, was known in America for his travel books, although he was doubtless better known as the husband of Minnie Hauck, beloved star of the Vienna (1870–74) and Berlin operas and of the Metropolitan.[32]

Of all the Austrian attempts at exploration in the last century, the one that most intrigued America and its press was the Austrian expedition of 1872–74 in the S.S. *Tegetthoff* which tried to find a Northeast Passage over the top of the world and succeeded in discovering the most northerly land of the Eastern Hemisphere. Franz Josephs Land, as they called it, was later re-explored by the Norwegian Nansen and its name changed to Fridtjof Nansen Land.[33]

Austro-Americans have seldom turned to agriculture. Some of the few Austrian immigrants of 1830 and 1848 may have gone west with the Germans to distinguish themselves as "Latin Farmers," those Teutonic immigrants who were far more at home with Virgil and Horace than with the hoe and plow. They loved their music and their German classics, they hung a Tyrolean hat or two on the walls and visited on Sunday with any German-speaking neighbors within walking distance. Their American neighbors considered them all as the "damned Dutch" who put on airs despite their incompetence at farming.[34]

But the Austrian pine (*pinus austriaca*), valuable both as an ornamental and a forest tree, and the Tyrolean Haflinger horses, bred to provide the farmer with a practical multiple-use draft animal, have not been the only American imports from the Austria of garden and forest. Anton Donnersberger (b. Moravia, 1790 – d. United States, 1862) who had practiced horticulture in Vienna, Germany, and Holland, as well as in his native Moravia, sailed to New Orleans in 1819, moved on to Cincinnati three years later, imported seeds and plants and know-how from Europe, and created some of Cincinnati's finest gardens for the wealthy Nicholas Longworth.[35]

A more famous horticulturist was the Forty-eighter Ignaz Anton Pilat (b. St. Agatha, Upper Austria, 1820 – d. New York, 1870) who had learned gardening at the *Kaiser's* Schönnbrunn palace and had laid out a park for Prince Metternich before he came to America to landscape some fine estates in the South and to help America's famous 19th century architect, Frederick Law Olmstead, lay out Central Park in New York.[36] Another landscape gardener trained on the grounds of Schönbrunn was Adolf Strauch (b. Silesia) who visited America in 1854, designed a number of fine private parks, and made Cincinnati's Spring Grove Cemetery a model for American cemetery design.[37] Max Schling (b. Austria, 1874 – d. 1943), who was educated in Vienna, came to New York as a young man to prosper in the florist and seed business. He made outstanding contributions to the development of the city's Botanical Garden.[38]

The Austrian-born are conspicuous by their absence in the recent "American Who's Who in Engineering." There have, however, been some few notable ones in the United States. Franz Anton von Gerstner (b. Prague, 1793 – d. Philadelphia, 1840), the "celebrated Austrian engineer"[39] who had built Russia's first railroad, lived here only two years before his death. Marc Eidlitz, also born in Prague (b. 1826 – d. New York, 1892), with an Austrian background, was doubtless for years New York's foremost builder. He migrated as a young man, started his own business in 1852, and built Steinway Hall, the J. P. Morgan residence and dozens of other famous structures. His brother Leopold, a graduate of Vienna's *Technische Hochschule*, became equally famous in New York architecture.[40]

Another distinguished figure was the Austrian-born Gustav Lindenthal (b. Brünn, Moravia, 1850 – d. Metuchin, New Jersey, 1935) who came in 1874 to achieve fame among New York's greatest engineers. His best-known projects included the Hell

Gate Bridge over the East River and the Pennsylvania tunnels under the East River and the Hudson.[41]

There is a monument near Beaumont, Texas, to the man who made Texas rich with oil. He was Anthony Francis Lucas (b. Dalmatia, 1855 – d. Washington, D.C., 1921), who, educated in Austria to be a sailor, emigrated to America in 1879 where he changed his name from the Montenegrin Luchich to the "American" Lucas, and was naturalized in 1885. Lucas, disregarding the opinions of the experts, was certain that there was oil off the Louisiana and Texas coasts – and proved it. His great find, Spindle Top, near Beaumont, was the biggest well ever opened in the United States. It made Texas as great in oil as in area. Lucas became a Texan hero.[42]

There were more Austrian engineers in this country during the early years of the Twentieth Century. Some, like Philip Sporn (b. Galicia, Austria, 1896), the president of the Electric Power Service Corporation, consultant on the Oak Ridge Nuclear Power Project and member of the Atomic Energy Commission, were educated in the United States,[43] while others, like Professor Arthur Casagrande (b. Haidenschaft, Görz, 1902), professor of soil mechanics and foundation engineering at Harvard,[44] had learned their engineering in Austria, usually at the *Technische Hochschule* in Vienna, before they emigrated. Many of them were honored by foreign governments and by foreign and American universities.[45]

Austria lost more of its engineering talent to the United States during the Hitler years and immediately afterwards. Some taught at America's best universities, some engaged in construction and some in industrial engineering. Like so many of the Austrian new-comers they generally remained in the East or went all the way across the continent to California.[46]

Some thirty years ago Averell Harriman, then Chairman of the Board of the Union Pacific Railroad, discovered one of the most useful and fascinating of all recent Austrian exports. Skiing in Austria he met Count Felix Schaffgotsch and persuaded him to come to America to locate a ski resort on the Union Pacific line. The result was Sun Valley. There the Austrian Hans Hauser inaugurated an Austrian ski school of some seventy instructors. Brilliantly successful, it became the largest ski school in the world and had by 1961, its twenty-fifth anniversary, given lessons to over 100,000 skiers.

That was neither the beginning nor the end of the Austrian ski invasion. Sig Buchmayr and his assistant Otto Lange had already established a ski school at Franconia, New Hampshire; Hans Schroll taught skiing in the West, Sepp Ruschp of Linz helped make Stowe, Vermont, an important ski center, and Benno Rybizka developed a school at Jackson, New Hampshire. A bit later, in 1938, the most famous figure in skiing, Hannes Schneider (b. St. Anton, 1890 – d. North Conway, 1955), a refugee from Nazism, arrived at Jackson. He was the greatest advocate of the almost universally adopted Arlberg technique in skiing – the Austrian technique that the layman identifies most easily by noting the frequent use of the snow-plow position of the skis that gives the skier more control than the parallel position. Indeed, the "American method" of skiing in the 1960's is an adaptation of Austrian techniques.

The Austrian ski invasion, encouraged by Austrian victories in world championship matches and by the publicity that Innsbruck reaped as the location of the Winter Olympics in 1964, continued apace. Resorts like Aspen and Heavenly Valley bristled with Austrian ski instructors as this winter sport found a new and booming popularity in the United States. Even in the Southeastern mountains the passion for skiing revived bankrupt resorts that had merely vegetated for years: Sepp Kober of Innsbruck, for instance, had by 1963 fourteen instructors on his staff at The Homestead, a fine old Virginia resort that had seemed close to the end of its career, and he was welcoming nearly 20,000 would-be skiers in one winter.

The ski fever even reached New York City where the Ski Club-Austria, U.S.A., was established in 1960 to arrange excursions into the ski country and where Sig Buchmayr ran his "fashion center for the 'complete' skier from six to sixty." Americans might buy chiefly their own made-in-America metal skis, but half of Austria's ski production was being exported and some of it came here.[47]

Austria's ski triumphs contributed, of course, to the prestige of the ski equipment that the republic exported. In eighteen recent Alpine ski championship meets the Austrians have led by goodly margins in the capture of gold, silver, and bronze medals. The Swiss, Germans, French, and Americans, following in that order, have never threatened Austrian supremecy. Austrian stars have often failed to star but, on the whole, the Austrians have dominated the ski world.

Other Austrian sports have had little or no impact upon the United States. Indeed, it was the great American skater Jackson Haines (b. 1879) who skated to fame in Europe and founded the Vienna school of skating which, the American skater Dick Button declares, fostered the international style of skating still in vogue today.[48] But in skiing the Austrians not only helped to train the Tenth Mountain Division of the United States Army during World War II;[49] they are indoctrinating much of young America with the love of a new sport. Austrian skiing, like Austrian music, but unlike so many other Austrian achievements, they have been practical enough to export while maintaining their supremecy at home. For this export, at least, America has furnished a brisk market without contributing to the drying up of the source of supply.

The abyss between Austrian labor and America has been, until recent years, so appalling that it requires more than a footnote in any study of Austro-American relations. Americans thought of "Austria," in the last years of the Nineteenth Century, as the source of Hunkies and Polaks and Kikes and every other conceivable brand of cheap, unskilled, radical worker who immigrated to steal jobs from American laborers and depress American standards of living. They thought of them in terms of anarchist Johann Most, the "German trouble maker," who had published his radical papers in Austria as well as in Germany, and whom America jailed for sedition after the assassination of President McKinley. They thought of them as serfs from despotic Eastern Europe, often as unwelcome guests who came to make a few dollars and return home. They resented their pacifism and, in labor relations, their tendency to join the more radical labor unions like the I.W.W., their fondness for the extremists in the industrial unions and neglect of our favorite brand of trade unionism. They failed, of course, to distinguish between the core-Austrians who were emigrating in relatively small numbers and the outer peoples of the monarchy who were coming after 1880 by the hundreds of thousands. "Austria" was blamed for all.

The significance of this was that the more radical forms of labor organization in the United States suffered under the stigma of being foreign. Samuel Gompers, president of the American Federation of Labor, visited Europe in 1909, spent weeks discovering that Austria-Hungary's sorry (to him) labor movement was too much concerned with welfare programs and culture and political action to the neglect of practical working conditions. And Gompers and his A. F. of L. joined the crusade against unrestricted immigration. The fact that Austrian labor has always been identified with Austrian Socialism did not help in America where Socialism has never been a significant force. And in later years, after World War I, the fact that practical Austrian Socialism helped to build one of the only two successful democracies of Europe (Czechoslovakia is generally named as the other) to emerge after the controversial Treaty of St. Germain, seems never to have been of interest to American labor.

There were some elements on the positive side. The modest American apprenticeship laws have been based, with many modifications, upon the successful Austrian and German apprenticeship system. The thorough Austrian apprenticeship education in the trades and crafts, which has minimized Austria's teenager delinquency, has occasionally attracted American attention. Austrian public housing, a Socialist achievement since the 1920's, is becoming more interesting in an America that is finally discovering a need for public housing. And the success of the Austrian labor-Socialist front in reducing the Communist vote, so near to the Iron Curtain since 1945, to the entire elimination of the Communist Party from the Parliament was a satisfaction to every American newspaper reader.[50]

There were few Austrian names, laborite or liberal, that ever penetrated the United States. Theodor Hertzka's utopian novel "Freeland" (1890) swept Europe and America, and Freeland Associations sprang up here to spread his liberal economic and socialist doctrines. But Hertzka, economic editor of Vienna's best newspaper, the "Neue Freie Presse," and founder of the "Wiener Allgemeine Zeitung," was a liberal and not a Socialist. And his book was quickly forgotten.[51] More twentieth century Americans recall the prominent Socialist Karl Kautsky (b. Prague 1854 – d. Amsterdam 1938) who helped turn German Socialism away from Lenin, and lived many years in Vienna before he died in exile from the Nazis. Kautsky was for long more famous in America for the "Kautsky documents," his publication of German diplomatic correspondence intended to reveal the aggressive role of imperial Germany in bringing on World War I, than for his Socialist doctrine.[52]

Few of the prominent "Austrians" among the leaders of American labor came from core-Austria although many, like Charles Kreindler of the International Ladies Garment Workers Union who was born in Galicia, called themselves Austrians. The needle trades, even more than shop-keeping, attracted a tremendous number of the Jewish emigrants from the monarchy before and after the turn of the century. Herman Grossman of Austria was the first president of the Garment Workers (1900–03 and 1905–07) and other leaders of that union who came to America before the First World War included Vice President Moe Falikman and the amiable conservative, Isadore Nagler. Nathan Wertheimer (b. Austria, 1887), vice president of the Retail Clerks International Protective Association, was one of the few self-declared Austrians among America's twentieth-century labor leaders born in the old monarchy.[53]

Perhaps the most significant American labor leader of his day was Victor Berger (1860–1929), the pacifist-Socialist who was finally seated in the House of Representatives in Washington in 1923 after the House had for four years refused to seat him. Berger was born of German-speaking parents in Nieder-Rehbach, a village on the Austro-Hungarian border, and educated at the universities of Vienna and Budapest. He dodged the Austrian draft and came to Connecticut in 1878. He moved to Milwaukee, Wisconsin, two years later to teach school until suspended for his radical notions, and subsequently made a career of journalism and politics. It was, for an immigrant Socialist, a remarkable career. His popularity elected him to various Milwaukee city posts and in 1911 he became the first Socialist to sit at Washington in the House of Representatives. He converted Eugene V. Debs to Socialism and helped him build the Socialist Party. Judge Landis in 1919 sentenced him to twenty years' imprisonment for disloyalty as a pacifist, but his Milwaukee constituency retained its faith in him.[54] Victor Berger was doubtless Austria's most important contribution to the cause of American labor.

Far less significant and considerably less typical was Josef Peukert (b. near Gablonz, Bohemia, 1855 – d. 1910), the anarchist. The more famous anarchist, Johann Most (b. Bavaria, 1846 – d. Cincinnati, Ohio, 1906), who was for years a Vienna publisher, hated him as a rival, first when Peukert was publishing his anarchist sheet "Die Autonomie" in London and then when the *Autonomie* group appeared in New York and began operating in brazen disregard of Most's anarchist cells. The deadly-serious Peukert and his friends were influential enough to win Emma Goldman, that most prominent of American lady radicals, away from Most.

Peukert's association with Emma Goldman may have helped to persuade her to go to Vienna in 1895 to study nursing at the city hospital, the *Allgemeines Kranken-*

haus. Although she had to conceal her identity as an American radical and disassociate herself from the struggling Austrian Socialists, she found Vienna a charming city and regretted having to leave it. She even discovered an interest in Freud and his gospel back in those early times, the 1890's.[55] But she accomplished as little as did Gompers towards bringing Austrian labor into touch with America's young labor movement.

Only too typical of the latter days of the nineteenth century, when Austro-Hungarians were getting themselves involved in America's labor movement, were the Lattimer riots in Lattimer, Pennsylvania, in 1897 when ten Austro-Hungarians were killed and more of them were injured in the course of a strike of miners. The Austro-Hungarian embassy claimed an indemnity but the American government rejected the claim on the ground that the aliens in question had not exhausted the legal remedies open to them through the courts. All in all, it was a sad affair.[56]

That there was an American edition of Adelheid Popp's little autobiography of an Austrian Socialist was surprising.[57] That was a realistic story of a young anti-Jewish Viennese who suffered all the tortures of poverty in old Vienna and became one of the Continent's first Socialist leaders. The book knocked about American libraries for many years after the Socialist elements in the coalition that followed World War II contributed so much to elimination of Austrian Communism. But it is unlikely that any later American readers of the chatty little Popp volume ever thought of it in terms of the building of one great element in the Socialist-Peoples Party Coalition of the two decades following 1945 which gave Austria such a stable regime that, for the first time since World War I, the little Alpine republic soon needed no help from any world organization, or from the United States.

Since the Social Democratic Party of Austria had been made illegal in 1934 during the ideological battles between blacks and reds that were always so unhappily sharp in Austria, thousands of laborites — Social Democrats — came to America during the Fascist years. They did not publicize their leftist position. But their presence here is evidenced by the fact that they had a labor press in New York City. The Austrian Labor Committee published the "Austrian Labor News" from 1942 to 1945; the American Friends of Austrian Labor published later "The Austrian Republic" (1946—48), and "Austrian Labor Information" was edited during the last years of the war by Friedrich Adler, Karl Hans Sailer, who was to return to Vienna to help edit labor's daily "Arbeiter-Zeitung," and Wilhelm Ellenbogen, a Social Democratic veteran (b. Lundenburg over the present Czech border, 1863 — d. New York, 1951) who had immigrated after a distinguished career in the Austrian government with President Renner following World War I.

Ellenbogen, trained for medicine in Vienna, had turned to Socialist politics, served as acting minister for commerce, returned to Parliament, and migrated to America when he was too old to make a new career for himself.[58] He was, however, representative of a whole segment of Austrian life that was never adequately represented here.

The chairman of the Central Committee of the Austrian Socialist Party, during the significant years 1935–1938 when the Socialist Party had been driven underground by the Blacks, the Christian Socials of the Dollfuss-Schuschnigg era – was a certain Joseph Buttinger (b. Austria, 1906) who came to New York and became prosperous through a fortunate marriage. He not only wrote and published his sad story of the Austrian Socialists of the 1930's ("In the Twilight of Socialism," N.Y. 1953), which alienated some of his fellow freedom-fighters, but he also produced a standard volume on Vietnam ("The Smaller Dragon," N.Y. 1958) that was much in demand when our war in Vietnam began. His library in New York – the Library for Political Studies – became one of the few places in the United States where Americans could study the significant clashes in Austrian life that led to the triumph of totalitarianism in the *Anschluss* of 1938.[59]

[1] Laurin Zilliacus, *Mail for the World*, N.Y. 1958, pp. 58–67. The *Britannica*, 14th ed., XVIII, p. 306, mentions the introduction of the postcard.

[2] Wilhelm Schlag in *Austrian Information*, 15 March 1965, p. 7. *Austrian Information*, 15 March 1966.

[3] Carl Wittke, *Refugees of Revolution*, Philadelphia 1952, p. 333. For Schroetter's discovery of sulphur see Charles Singer *et al*, *History of Technology*, vol. V, Oxford 1958, p. 253.

[4] J. G. Leithäuser, *Inventor's Progress*, Cleveland and N.Y. 1959, pp. 89–94.

[5] Fred Reinfeld, *They Almost Made It*, N.Y. 1956, p. 157; Constant v. Wurzbach, *Biographisches Lexikon des Kaiserthums Oesterreich*, 60 parts, Wien 1856–91, XVI, p. 246; *Der Grosse Brockhaus*, vol. VII, Wiesbaden 1955; Leithäuser, *op. cit.*, p. 219.

[6] *Ibid.*, p. 119; *Der Grosse Brockhaus*, VI, 1955; Allan Nevins, *Ford*, N.Y. 1954, pp. 97–98, 308; Wm. Greenleaf, *Monopoly on Wheels*, Detroit 1961, p. 30. The Marcus car may be seen in Vienna's technical museum but the papers imported for use in the famous Selden case have been lost.

[7] J. H. Greene's article on Porsche in *The American-German Review*, Oct.-Nov. 1963, pp. 13–16.

[8] Leithäuser, *op. cit.*, p. 153; *Der Grosse Brockhaus*, X, 1956; *Universal Jewish Encyclopedia*, vol. IX, N.Y. 1948; Singer, *op. cit.*, V, pp. 402–03.

[9] Published N.Y. 1954.

[10] Vol. X, p. 479. The *World Almanac* states it was invented 1864. Two of Mitterhofer's first models are now in the Technical Museum in Vienna: Österreichische Akademie der Wissenschaften, *Österreichische Naturforscher und Techniker*, Wien 1951.

[11] *Encyclopedia Americana*, 1956, article "Typewriter," dates the Sholes machine as of 1868 but does not mention Mitterhofer.

[12] Leithäuser, *op. cit.*, pp. 104–05; *Encyclopedia Americana*, 1957, article "Screw Propeller," which gives full credit to Ressel; *Austrian Information*, 31 Oct. 1961, p. 6.

[13] Article "Telegraph," *Encyclopedia Britannica*, 1962, for the Gintl invention. See also C. R. Kutz, *War on Wheels*, Harrisburg 1940, p. 193.

[14] W. H. B. Smith, *Rifles*, National Rifle Assc., Washington 1948. Schoenauer worked with Mannlicher at the Steyr *Werke*.

[15] Arnold Nicholson, "The Return of the Gaslight," *Saturday Evening Post*, 5 Aug. 1961, pp. 24ff; article "Gas Illumination," *Encyclopedia Americana*, 1957.

[16] Singer, *op. cit.*, V, p. 707; Charles G. Abbot, *Great Inventions*, Smithsonian Inst. 1931, p. 371.

[17] W. Kaempffert, ed., *A Popular History of American Invention*, vol. I, N.Y. 1924, p. 415; *Dictionary of American Biography*, article on Louis Edward Levy; *The American Hebrew*, 28 Feb. 1919, p. 393; *Das Buch der Deutschen in Amerika*, Philadelphia 1909, p. 648; Singer, *op. cit.*, V, p. 704.

[18] Singer, *op. cit.*, V, p. 735.

[19] *Neue Österreichische Biographie*, vol. VI, Wien 1929, pp. 175–77; John Jewkes *et al*, *Sources of Invention*, London 1958, pp. 351–52.

[20] *Wer ist Wer*, Wien 1937; *Austrian Information*, 14 Apr. 1962, p. 6.

[21] For Kaplan see *Grosse Österreicher*, vol. X, Wien 1957, pp. 203ff; J. G. Crowther, *Discoveries and Inventions of the Twentieth Century*, N.Y. 1955, p. 5. *Brockhaus* dates the Kaplan turbine in 1912. The *Encyclopedia Americana*, 1956, treats of Hoffmann in its article "Coke."

[22] Jewkes, *op. cit.*, p. 269.

[23] Singer, *op. cit.*, V, p. 664.

[24] *Britannica Book of the Year*, 1956, p. 371; *Austrian Information*, 31 Oct. 1961, 28 Apr. 1962, 15 Nov. 1963. United States literature regarding this process found by the author deals largely with French utilization of the process to the complete neglect of the original Austrian contribution. Cf. *Journal of Metal*, July 1960, pp. 542–46.

[25] *International Harvester World*, No. 3, 1965, pp. 9ff. Cf. *Encyclopedia Americana*, XXIII, p. 567.

[26] Dieter Cunz, *Maryland Germans*, Princeton U. Press 1948, pp. 12–29.

[27] *Ibid.*, pp. 30–38; D. L. Rights and W. P. Cumming, *Discoveries of John Lederer*, U. Virginia Press 1958, pp. 69ff.

[28] H. E. Bolton, *Rim of Christendom*, N.Y. 1936, pp. 30ff; H. E. Bolton, *Kino's Historical Memoir of Pimeria Alta*, 2 vols., 1919, rev. 1948. See Ch. III above.

[29] See Hugo Hassinger, *Österreichs Anteil an der Erforschung der Erde*, Wien (1949), *passim;* and Wilhelm Schlag, *Österreichische Pioniere und Forscher in Nordamerika*, ms. in Austrian Institute, New York.

[30] *Washington Post*, 8 Dec. 1962, p. C4.

[31] *Who's Who*, 1952–53. His original name was Gustav von Grünebaum.

[32] *National Cyclopaedia of American Biography*, VIII, p. 154; *Österreichisches Biographisches Lexikon 1815–1950*, vol. II, Graz–Köln 1957.

[33] *Encyclopedia Americana*, XXII, p. 295a. Austrian-born geographers have been few in the United States. *Who's Who*, 1962–63, lists Guido Gustav Weigend (b. Steiermark, 1920) who immigrated in 1939 and who has taught at Rutgers University since 1957.

[34] For an account of an Austrian farmer in Michigan see *Der Deutsche Pionier*, Sept. 1876, pp. 214–16, and for Latin Farmers in general see Wittke, *op. cit.*, *passim.*

[35] *Der Deutsche Pionier*, II, pp. 3–4.

[36] Wilhelm Schlag, "A Survey on Austrian Emigration to the United States," in *Österreich und die angelsächsische Welt*, Wien 1961, p. 161; A. B. Faust, *German Element in the United States*, 2 vols., Boston and N.Y. 1909, II, p. 63.

[37] Rudolf Cronau, *German Achievements in America*, N.Y. 1916, p. 110.

[38] *Who's Who*, 1938–39.

[39] B. J. Blied, *Austrian Aid to American Catholics*, Milwaukee 1944, p. 40.

[40] *New York Times*, 16 Apr. 1892; *National Cyclopaedia of American Biography*. Cf. letter from Pelz in Cronau collection, Carl Schurz Mem. Foundation.

[41] *Columbia Encyclopedia*, 2nd ed., 1956.

[42] *National Cyclopaedia of American Biography*, XXIX, p. 262f.

[43] *Who's Who in Commerce and Industry*, 1959.

44 *Who's Who*, 1962–63.

45 See in *Who's Who*, 1962–63: John Joseph Chyle (b. Vienna, 1902), welding executive in Wisconsin; Sigmund Nicholas Fiala (b. Burstyn, Austria, 1900), chief engineer of the American Electric Service Corporation in New York; a significant arrival of 1930, Ernst Weber (b. Vienna, 1901), president of the Brooklyn Polytechnic Institute and recipient of a Presidential Certificate of Merit. Walter Jay Halpern (b. Vienna, 1906), former president of the Gotham Instrument Company, appears in *Who's Who in Commerce and Industry*, 11th ed.

46 Notable were Robert Schwarz (b. 1884–d. Los Angeles, 1961), publisher of engineering journals who settled in Hollywood; Wenceslaus Sivel (b. Lower Austria, 1901) who was a teacher and builder of roads and bridges in the San Francisco area; Henry H. Hausner (b. Vienna, 1901) and Hans Heinrich Bleich (b. Vienna, 1909), both active in industrial engineering, who taught at New York University and at Columbia respectively; George Winter (b. Vienna, 1907), Cornell's professor of structural engineering; Oscar George Garner (b. Vienna, 1915), vice president of the General Cable Company; Anselm Franz (b. Schladming, 1900), for five years with the Air Force, who engineered for AVCO; and Stefan Ludwig Grapnel (b. Vienna, 1912) also engaged in industrial engineering in Connecticut. Dr. Karl Terzaghi (b. Prague, 1883), educated at Graz and active in teaching and construction in Vienna and all the way from the Near East to Mexico, finally accepted a chair of engineering at Harvard.

47 The best account is in Dr. Schlag's article in *Österreich und die angelsächsische Welt*. See also *Austrian Information*, 25 Aug. and 29 Oct. 1960 and 30 Jan. and 2 Dec. 1961; *Washington Post*, 4 Feb. 1962, p. C7, and 4 Jan. 1963, p. A22.

48 Button, "America on Ice," *American Heritage*, Feb. 1963.

49 Schlag, *op. cit.*

50 Samuel Gompers, *Labor in Europe and America*, N.Y. 1910, and *Seventy Years of Life and Labor*, N.Y. 1925; G. D. H. Cole, *History of Socialist Thought*, 2 vols., London 1956; Adolf Sturmthal, *Tragedy of European Labor 1918–1939*, N.Y. 1943; Ralph C. Wenrich, "A Comparison of Vocational Education . . .," *Österreich und die angelsächsische Welt*, Wien 1961.

51 Cole, *op. cit.*, p. 559.

52 *Ibid.*, ch. 12; *Britannica*, 1958.

53 *Cutters' 1902–1962 Almanac*, 1962, pp. 59 and 88; Benjamin Stolberg, *Tailor's Progress*, Garden City 1944, pp. 224 and 330–31. For Wertheimer see *Who's Who in Labor*, N.Y. 1946.

54 Faust, *op. cit.*, II, p. 197 note; Emil Lengyel, *Americans from Hungary*, 1948, p. 72; *Milwaukee Leader*, 7 Aug. 1930 (Berger Memorial Edition); *Dictionary of American Biography*, supp. I.

55 Emma Goldman, *Living My Life*, N.Y. 1931; Henry David, *History of the Haymarket Affair*, N.Y. 1957. For Most and Peukert we have consulted Ludwig Brügel, *Geschichte der österreichischen Sozialdemokratie*, 5 vols., Wien 1922–25, and Josef Peukert, *Erinnerungen eines Proletariers*, Berlin 1913.

56 John Bassett Moore, *Digest of International Law*, vol. VI, Washington 1906, pp. 868ff.

57 *Autobiography of a Working Woman*, Chicago 1913, with introduction by Ramsey Macdonald.

58 A. C. Breycha-Vauthier, *Die Zeitschriften der Österr. Emigration*, Wien 1960; Walter G. Wieser, *Die Österreichischen Handels- und Arbeitsminister*, *Sonderdruck*, Wien 1961, p. 480.

59 There is very little about Buttinger in American sources. See the *Author's and Writer's Who's Who*, N.Y. 1963. His library is located at 10 East 87th Street, N.Y. 28.

CHAPTER XVIII

AUSTRIANS IN LAW, POLITICS AND HISTORY

One would not expect that the immigrants from any land outside our own Anglo-Saxon, common-law area would be able to contribute to the legal and political sciences in America. Indeed, relatively few of the Austrian-born have entered American politics.Dozens of the newcomers, especially in the Nazi period, had to give up legal practice and turn to other fields like teaching. Yet there have been some newcomers from Austria who have distinguished themselves in law.

The most famous of them all, called "the most influential single individual in the United States" during New Deal days by General Hugh S. Johnson of the NRA, was Felix Frankfurter (b. Vienna, 1882 – d. Washington, 1965). He came of an excellent Jewish family in Vienna. His scholarly uncle was librarian of the University of Vienna and his businessman father, Leopold, had means enough to visit the Chicago World's Fair in 1893 and to bring his large family with him to New York the following year. Felix lived on a German island in New York, learned English in the New York public schools, distinguished himself at New York's City College, learned law at Harvard and public service with United States Attorney Henry L. Stimson in New York and in Washington when Stimson became Secretary of War.

Felix Frankfurter was for twenty-five years professor of law at Harvard before Franklin D. Roosevelt appointed him to the United States Supreme Court. "One of this century's ablest legal minds," he was a Theodore Roosevelt liberal and a disciple of Justice Oliver Wendell Holmes and of Justice Louis D. Brandeis who, incidentally, also came of a good Austro-Hungarian family. Frankfurter has been called "the most important single figure in our whole judicial system" and its "outstanding disappointment." The conservatives feared his crusading zeal, the reputation he achieved when he denounced the Sacco-Vanzetti executions, and his Socratic but, they thought, academic, methods. And the liberals disliked him because he was more lawyer than crusader and, in his innumerable dissenting and concurring opinions on the Supreme Court, seemed too willing to have the Court leave the decisions to the legislative and executive branches. General Johnson was convinced that he controlled the Roosevelt New Deal through the many former Frankfurter students who were so devoted to him.

His biographer Helen S. Thomas believed that his Austrian education with "its emphasis on precision of statement and deductive reasoning" had left its mark upon Justice Frankfurter. But others maintained "he had nothing to show for his Vienna nativity but an eager spirit and a slight thickening of the letter S." It was perhaps only natural that Felix Frankfurter himself, while he was playing such an important role in American life, should have had so little to say about his Austrian youth. He was evidently one of the Austrians that Secretary Seward had noted some generations earlier who almost never confessed to being Austrian. In any event he remained for over 23 years one of the greatest figures on the Supreme Court.[1]

There were other fascinating figures in the law who came from Austria, beginning with some of the refugees from the abortive revolution of 1848. The Vienna-born August Bondi who had fought from behind the barricades of his native city remained a crusader in the New World, joining in an attempt to liberate Cuba and fighting with John Brown of Osawatomie.[2] The famous radical among the Forty-eighters, Friedrich Hassaurek (b. Vienna, 1831 – d. Paris, 1885),[3] who was more journalist than lawyer, helped educate his half-brother in the law. That was Leopold Markbreit (b. Vienna, 1842 – d. Cincinnati, 1909), junior partner in the Cincinnati law firm of Hayes and Markbreit, and Hayes was none other than Rutherford B. Hayes who was later to become President of the United States. After achieving a captaincy in the Union army and losing his health at Libby Prison, Markbreit returned as aide to Hayes, then governor of Ohio, was appointed President Grant's minister to Bolivia, essayed journalism, and in Washington served under Presidents Arthur and Cleveland as assistant treasurer of the United States.[4]

A well known biographer of Abraham Lincoln was the New York lawyer Emanuel Hertz (b. Butka, 1870 – d. New York, 1940) who was a Republican presidential elector in 1928.[5] Another Austro-Hungarian, who had learned his law in Vienna and at Northwestern University, was the husband of the famous pianist Fannie Bloomfield, Sigmund Zeisler (b. Bielitz, Austrian Silesia, 1860 – d. 1931). Practicing and teaching in Chicago, the high spot of Zeisler's career was his defence in 1886 of the Anarchists involved in the history-making Haymarket Riots. An historian of the Haymarket trials tells us that the young Zeisler, only two years after his admission to the Chicago bar, made an admirable plea for the defence, but the prosecuting counsel, with far more experience, capitalized upon the fact that the accused were foreigners who could speak little or no English, and all but one of them were condemned to death. Zeisler later became assistant attorney for the city of Chicago.[6]

There were many other notables in public service. One of the organizers of the Progressive Party in 1912, who voted years later as Presidential Elector for Dewey and Eisenhower, was Jacob L. Holtzmann (b. Austria, 1888) who came to New York as a child.[7] Carl Sherman, New York attorney general in the early 1920's, was born in 1890 in Olmütz where good King Wenceslaus defeated the Mongols, and wrote himself an Austrian.[8] Leffert Holz (b. Austria, 1896) was active in public life in New York, city and state.[9] And of the two Ellenbogen brothers from Vienna, Henry[10]

(b. 1900) of Pittsburgh served two terms in Congress before he received a state judgeship in 1937 and Theodore of Washington drafted proposed legislation for the Department of Health, Education and Welfare.

Even nudism was represented by an Austro-American lawyer. Alois Stock Knapp (b. Innsbruck, 1889), who taught school in his homeland, immigrated in 1911, practiced law in Chicago, owned a nudist resort in Indiana, and became president of the National Nudist Council.[11]

It was an Austrian-born, New York-educated lawyer, Joseph Heller (b. 1900),[12] who administered one of the New Deal's first devastating setbacks by winning the historic Schecter Poultry Case against the New Deal's National Recovery Administration in 1935. And four years later there came to this country one of Austria's most interesting women, Marianne Beth (b. von Weisl in Vienna, 1890) who was the first woman to be admitted to legal practice in her native land.[13]

One of Austria's little-known legal contributions has been in the field of criminology and what the great Austrian pioneer Hans Gross called Criminalistics.

Hans Gross (b. Graz, 1847 – d. Graz, 1915) attended a police congress in New York City and chagrined the American hosts by showing how far ahead the Austrians were in the field of criminology. As examining justice and public prosecutor in Graz, Gross had been disgusted with the crude justice administered by the soldier-like police. He not only made crime detection a science (by teaching the police microscopy, finger-printing, X-rays, ballistics, chemistry and the other sciences) but he rationalized treatment of the offender with the help of psychology. He preached objectivity in crime detection. He denounced the fallacy that two concurring witnesses must be right. In 1912 he gave the University of Graz what may have been the world's first university institute of criminology. He is regarded by some as the father of criminology. He was definately the originator of the science of criminal investigation that he called Criminalistics, and which he interpreted in such a broad sense that it became almost synonomous with criminology.

And while Ferri and Lombroso were working in Italy to humanize the treatment of criminals, Gross and his Graz colleague Franz von Liszt (b. Vienna, 1851 – d. Seeheim a. d. Bergstraße, Germany, 1919), who worked for years in Germany and took his place there with the top criminologists of the time, were making an exact science of the detection and treatment of crime. Gross's classic manual for the examining justice (1883) was published in edition after edition and in dozens of languages. It appeared in English under the title "Criminal Investigation" and became the Bible of the profession. Certainly the tribute that the American police captain Willemse paid to the Austrians at the police congress in New York showed that America had much to learn from the overseas criminologists.[14] And there was a substantial group of Austrian criminal lawyers who were innovators in the profession and not to be confused with the Germans who were also making an original contribution in those pioneer days.

A far better-known Austrian contribution to crime prevention was the creation of Interpol, the international cooperative for the prevention of crime. Vienna's police president, Johannes Schober, who was twice chancellor of the republic, was distressed by the amount of crime after World War I that prospered by finding asylum over international boundaries. The European police congress that Schober assembled at Vienna in 1923 had to admit that national police forces were inadequate to meet the post-war challenge and Interpol was established. The United States joined in 1924. Forty years later its Paris headquarters was serving 92 member states in the world's most significant crusade against international crime.[15]

The United States became in the Nazi era the adopted country of a very distinguished group of Austrians who were trained in the law and who made university teaching their profession. Most came here to stay; some of the Thirty-eighters returned home after World War II. Most of them taught by preference; some turned to teaching because they could not practice in America the kind of law they had learned in Austria.

Many of the legally-trained professors, with the help of American friends and organizations, found positions far beyond the borders of New York, so often the Austrian's Mecca. Josef Kunz (b. Vienna, 1890), for instance, who had taught law at the University of Vienna and written legal treatises for translation into half-a-dozen languages, became professor of international law at the University of Toledo in 1934.[16] More recently Francis Seidler (b. Vienna, 1913), who had studied at the Consular Academy in Vienna in the building which now houses the American Embassy, served the American occupation forces in Austria and then, in 1948, accepted a professorship at Georgetown University.[17] In Washington there was also Dr. Egon Ranshofen-Wertheimer (b. Castle Ranshofen near Braunau, Upper Austria, 1894—d. near New York, 1957) at American University.[18] A veteran of the Austrian high court for constitutional cases and draftsman of the Austrian labor code, Judge Arthur Lenhoff (b. Teplitz-Schönau, Bohemia, 1885) came to the University of Buffalo in 1939;[19] the Viennese Ernst Rabel (b. 1874 — d. Zurich, 1955) who had taught in Germany and Switzerland and served on several international tribunals came in the same year and went in 1942 to the University of Michigan; and two other notable Austrian jurists, the canon-law authority Willibald Maria Plöchl (b. St. Pölten, 1907) and the conflict-of-laws expert Albert Ehrenzweig (b. Herzogenburg, Lower Austria, 1906), came to the Catholic University of America and to the University of California respectively, Plöchl to teach for several years before returning to the University of Vienna and Ehrenzweig to remain in the States. Otto Zimbler who had edited the Austrian law review, "Juristische Blätter,"[20] was another Thirty-eighter.

Not only lawyers, but Austrian statesmen of renown have come to America. The republic's finance minister of 1918 and 1931, Joseph Redlich (b. Göding, Moravia, 1869 — d. Vienna, 1936), came in 1926 to teach comparative law for almost a decade at Harvard. He was a distinguished figure who had served in the Moravian regime in the 1890's, taught for many years at the University of Vienna, sat in the imperial parliament, and helped to establish the republic after the first world war. His books on Austrian government and Franz Joseph are still standard authorities in American libraries.[21] And the Austrian Minister who had the unpleasant tasks of closing the old Austro-Hungarian Embassy in Washington near the intersection of Connecticut Avenue and N Street (back when the embassies clustered about Connecticut Avenue) and of closing the later Austrian Legation when the Nazis took over, was Edgar Leo Prochnik (b. Indonesia, 1879 – d. Washington, 1964). After he left his Legation office that had Franz Joseph's picture over his desk, he lectured for 22 years in diplomatic history at hospitable Georgetown University.[22]

Two other makers of Austrian history have come in recent years, not to return to Vienna like Redlich, but to make a teaching career in the United States. Both were refugees. Hans Kelsen (b. Prague, 1881), whom Gulick called "probably the outstanding political scientist of Central Europe"[23] and Harvard's Manley O. Hudson described as the greatest living international lawyer, came here first in 1930 to receive a fine reception from Harvard and the University of California. For Dr. Kelsen had been legal adviser to the Austro-Hungarian war ministry during the first world war and, more significant, he had written, at President Renner's behest, the basic law, or constitution, of the Austrian republic that has recently given Austria one of Europe's most stable, and altogether satisfactory, political systems. Dr. Kelsen came again in 1940 to find a career and distinction at the University of California.[24]

And the most significant of this group of public figures, Kurt von Schuschnigg (b. Riva, Italy, then Austria, 1897), the ill-fated chancellor of Austria's sad middle thirties (1934–1938), successor to the assassinated Dollfuss, was the victim of Gestapo prisons until released by the American army in 1945. Schuschnigg like Chancellor Gorbach, his successor a quarter century later, and so many other public figures of the last thirty years, was evidence that it was not only the Jewish Austrians who spent years in the Nazi concentration camps. Schuschnigg was a conservative from Western Austria, a disciple of Seipel and Dollfuss. He settled in America in 1947 and taught for years at St. Louis University.[25] His book, "Austrian Requiem" (N.Y. 1946), was doubtless in the United States the most-read account of the fall of the Austrian republic to the Nazis.

It was a happy phenomenon that the United States could, especially in the tragic Hitler years, welcome both conservatives and left-wingers. Schuschnigg, for instance, who had been a member of the government which outlawed the Austrian Socialists, was welcomed as was Julius Deutsch (b. Lackenbach, Burgenland, 1884), a genial leftist, a victim of the fall of the Socialist *Schutzbund* in 1934, and a general in Spain's republican army in 1936. The scholarly Deutsch came to America to lecture at our universities, write for liberal journals like "The Nation," and serve for four years in the Office of War Information before he returned to Vienna in 1946.[26]

His presence in the United States must have done much to show his American friends that the Austrian left was a kind of New Deal, far removed from Soviet Communism, that might even help to make Central Europe safe for America's brand of democracy.

Austrians might occasionally show an interest in the American political system as when the Kremsier *Reichstag* of 1848 planned to give Austria an upper and lower house patterned upon the two houses of the American Congress, and a formulation of people's sovereignty adapted from the Texas republic's constitution of 1836.[27] Or when Archduke Franz Ferdinand became interested in the American constitution as pointing the way to a federal system that might solve Austria's nationality problem,[28] or when the Rumanian Popovici proposed in 1905 a United States of Austria to break the Hungarian strangle-hold on Transylvania.[29] But Americans have seldom concerned themselves with the Austrian governmental system. Our "inheritance" from Austria in this field has been the Austrian-born lawyers and political scientists who have taught at American universities.

Among the political scientists who came when Hitler was scarcely known outside of Munich was Robert Straus-Hupé (b. Vienna, 1903) of the University of Pennsylvania whose authoritative books and articles on foreign policy were to be found in every American bookshop[30] and whose distinguished conservatism qualified him to advise Senator Goldwater during his futile campaign for the Presidency in 1964. And later, during the Nazi years there came others including Georg Maria Alexich (b. Vienna, 1893), a veteran of Austria's foreign service, who was welcomed in 1943 to Georgetown University,[31] William Ebenstein (b. Austria, 1910) of Princeton and the University of California, Franz Schick (b. Vienna, 1901) of the University of Utah and Robert Gerhard Neumann (b. Vienna, 1916) who enlisted in the U.S. forces and was appointed to a professorship at the University of California at Los Angeles. When the distinguished Neumann (he held many distinctions including the French Legion of Honor) took his oath in 1966 as American ambassador to Afghanistan he was told that birth in cosmopolitan Vienna helps qualify a man for ambassadorial honors in any part of the world.

Another Viennese and adopted Californian of the same generation was Stefan T. Possony (b. 1913), a University of Vienna product who reached America during the war, advised the American armed services, taught international politics at Georgetown University, and then became the Hoover Institution's director of international political studies. Like so many of the Austro-Americans mentioned in this chapter, he wrote profusely and was well represented in American book shops.

In history, as in the humanities and in the social sciences, the Austrian influences in the United States have been cosmopolitan and internationalist. That was true, first, because Austrians have never been narrow nationalists at home, their interests have always exploded over and beyond Austria's own narrow borders, and, on the American side, Austrians have almost never specialized in anything Austrian. We have read many translations of Egon Conte Corti's readable histories, not for their Austrian history, but for the light which his privileged researches in the Vienna archives threw upon the greater European story where the Habsburgs, Metternich, Ludwig of Bavaria, and the Rothschilds played major roles.[32] And the University of Vienna's famous historian Alfred Francis Pribram (b. London, 1859 – d. London, 1942), who gave the Lowell Lectures in Boston in 1926 and lectured at Stanford and Harvard, Oxford and the London School of Economics, is known here less as a prophet of Austrian history than as the editor of "The Secret Treaties of Austria-Hungary, 1879–1914," which made possible a definitive study of the Triple Alliance and the aggressive motives of the Italians and Austrians in that ill-fated prelude to World War I.[33]

There were Austrian historians like Professor Frederick Engel-Janosi (b. Vienna, 1893) of the Catholic University of America who kept his interest in Austria and who eventually returned to Vienna. And the Tyrol-born Prince Hubertus Friedrich zu Löwenstein (b. near Kufstein, 1906) lectured here at dozens of universities under Carnegie auspices for almost a decade in the Nazi period and founded the American Guild for German Cultural Freedom, before he returned to his adopted Germany.[34]

But most of them came to stay. Walter Consuelo Langsam (b. Vienna, 1906) came as an infant to study later in New York's universities, became president first of Wagner College and then of the University of Cincinnati, and wrote significant studies on European history and history textbooks for thousands of American college students.[35] Saul K. Padover (b. Austria, 1905) came to receive his advanced education here, to contribute to American intelligence during the war, receive an award from President Truman, write widely for the best periodicals, and teach for years at the New School for Social Research.[36] And a genuinely distinguished historian from a Tyrolian family who was born in Berlin but educated at the University of Vienna and Harvard University was Professor Clemens von Klemperer whose interest in European history, in teaching at Harvard and Smith, was in German and not in Austrian backgrounds.

The Medieval Academy of America gave a gold medal to the Austrian, Gerhart Ladner (b. Vienna, 1905), who taught at Notre Dame, Howard, Fordham and the University of California at Los Angeles.[37] And two typical Austrians were Gotthard Deutsch (b. 1859 – d. 1921) who studied and taught Jewish history at Breslau, Vienna, Brünn, and the Hebrew Union College in Cincinnati,[38] and Oscar von Halecki (b. Vienna, 1891) who taught Polish history at Cracow and Warsaw, came to America with the help of the Kosciusko Foundation, and who later taught at Vassar and Fordham with occasional appearances at Columbia.[39]

"The Catholic Historical Review" could in its January 1961 issue, reviewing Alfred Diamant's "Austrian Catholics and the First Republic" (Princeton 1960), rejoice that "That avalanche of scholarly publications on Austrian political and intellectual history is an impressive testimony to the long overdue revival of interest in the specific problems of the First Republic."[40] There had through two centuries been little enough written in America about the Habsburg Empire and the troublesome little republic of 1919. William H. Prescott had used the Vienna collections along with many other archives, in researching for his story of Philip II.[41] Indeed, his friend Edward Everett, a famous but not always commendable president of Harvard College, had gloried in the gathering of archival notes in Vienna for Prescott. But he was an exception to the rule: the Austrian side of the European story was, generally speaking, outside the American orbit. America's historians who interpreted European history for us in the nineteenth century were Protestants with little understanding of Habsburg Catholicism. Protestant Britain was their chief interest, and there they had Whig sympathies—Whiggery was about as un-Austrian as anything one could imagine. France, our ally of the Revolution, and Italy, which won its independence much as we had won ours a few generations earlier, intrigued their interest. Austria seemed remote, aristocratic, and strange.

When Mark Twain and his family spent some months in Vienna's Hotel Metropole and then more in a charming apartment in the Hotel Kranz that offered a salon for many attractive Viennese like the great piano teacher Leschetizky, they loved the Viennese and the Viennese loved them to the extent that daughter Clara found admirers on all sides and the great pianist could describe the love-struck youths as having "delirium Clemens." Mark Twain was fascinated by the funeral of the martyred Empress Elisabeth, that he could see from his apartment windows.[42] Yet he never wrote anything about his Austrian days that would encourage any American to visit that country.

The happy increase in interest in Central European history referred to by the reviewer writing for the "Catholic Historical Review" in 1961 was due, among other things, to the refreshing and encouraging interest of the United States Committee to Promote Studies of the History of the Habsburg Monarchy which was flourishing by 1961.

That Committee could never have existed before the immigration of 1938. It represented many of the outstanding contributors to "Austrian" history: Hans Kohn of the College of the City of New York (b. Prague, 1891) whose studies of European nationalism became classics in his adopted country, was its first chairman; Robert A. Kann of Rutgers (b. Vienna, 1906), an Austrian whose fine study of "The Multinational Empire" has become a basic authority for all Austrian studies; Arthur J. May of the University of Rochester who had written the finest single American volume on the Habsburg Empire; and R. John Rath whose University of Texas and, later, Rice University defrayed the costs of Professor Rath's useful bibliographies and news-letters on Austrian-Habsburg history, were among the committee's members. Rath's enthusiasm for encouraging study in the often neglected Austrian field inspired plans for the inauguration, to replace the news-letter, of an Austrian History Yearbook. The recently established Institute for Advanced Studies in Vienna, maintained in part with Ford Foundation help, should also contribute to the maintenance of Austro-American relationships.

There are many like Professor Carl Schorske of California who have recently been doing distinguished work in Austrian history. And among the American Fulbright grantees who had visited Austria were George B. Fowler of the University of Pittsburgh who had done, years ago, his first study on Engelbert of Admont, the well-known Hajo Holborn of Yale, Andrew Whiteside of Queens College, Thomas Clark and his student Enno Kraehe of Kentucky, and William A. Jenks who wrote the volume on "Vienna and the Young Hitler" which may, with its sorry picture of Hitler's Vienna, not have been a best-seller among the Viennese. Much, indeed, of the Austrian history written here was a bit out of step with what was being written in Graz, Innsbruck or Vienna. Charles A. Gulick's tremendous, scholarly, two volumes on "Austria from Habsburg to Hitler" (U. Calif. Press 1948) was a major contribution to the Socialist interpretation of the rise of Austrian Nazism that was published in Austria in German but was studiously ignored in Austria's best university circles.

It is significant that some of the recent programs of the American Historical Association have been studded with the names of scholars of Austrian history. It may be that the historians, more than any other group outside of the musicians and the psychologists, will ultimately be found to have incorporated a bit of Austria into American thinking.

[1] Helen Shirley Thomas, *Felix Frankfurter*, Baltimore 1960; Fred Rodell, *Nine Men*, N.Y. 1955; H. B. Phillips, *Felix Frankfurter Reminisces*, N.Y. 1960; *Fortune*, Jan. 1936, pp. 63ff.; *Scribners*, Apr. 1939, p. 67.

[2] A. E. Zucker, ed., *Forty-eighters*, N.Y. 1950; p. 281.

[3] *Dictionary of American Biography*.

[4] *Who's Who*, 1899–1900; *Buch der Deutschen in Amerika*, Philadelphia 1909, pp. 534–35.

[5] *Who's Who*, 1938–39.

[6] *Buch der Deutschen in Amerika;* Frederick Trevor Hill, *Decisive Battles of the Law*, N.Y. and London 1907, pp. 240–68.

[7] *Who's Who*, 1962–63.

[8] *Who's Who*, 1938–39.

[9] *Who's Who*, 1962–63.

[10] *Biographical Directory of the American Congress.*

[11] *Who's Who in Commerce and Industry*, 1959.

[12] *Who's Who*, 1938–39.

[13] *Who's Who of American Women*, 2nd ed., 1961. Among the other notable Austro-American lawyers, men and women, appearing in the various editions of *Who's Who in America* were Max

D. Steuer (b. 1871) of New York, Isaac Pacht (b. 1890) of Los Angeles, Emil Baar (b. 1891) of Brooklyn, Sarah G. Vogel Needell of Rahway, N.J., Irvine Joseph Shubert (b. 1902) of New York, Hans A. Klagsbrunn (b. 1909) of Washington, D.C., and Caroline Birman (b. 1895) of New York. Many were Jewish, most were notable for their charities, and some gave time to public service.

[14] *Der Grosse Brockhaus*, vol. VII, Wiesbaden 1955; C. W. Willemse, *Behind the Green Lights*, N.Y. 1931. See also Hermann Mannheim, ed., *Pioneers in Criminology*, London 1960, and Leon Radzinowicz, *In Search of Criminology*, Harvard U. Press, 1962, for both Gross and von Liszt. These are both English books. A superficial check of "popular" American books in the field would indicate to the author that Gross and von Liszt are much better known across the seas than here. Cf. George Godwin, *Criminal Man*, N.Y. 1957, which has a whole section on Gross with scarcely a paragraph of substance concerning the man himself.

[15] *Die Presse*, Wien, 8 Oct. 1963, p. 3.

[16] *Who's Who*, 1952–53.

[17] *Who's Who in Commerce and Industry*, 1959.

[18] *Österreicher der Gegenwart*, Wien 1951.

[19] *Directory of American Scholars*, 3rd ed.

[20] File in Library of Congress.

[21] *Wer ist Wer in Österreich*, Wien 1937.

[22] Obituary in *Washington Post*, 2 Apr. 1964.

[23] Charles A. Gulick, *Austria from Habsburg to Hitler*, 2 vols., U. Calif. 1948, I, p. 50.

[24] *Austrian Information*, 31 Oct. 1961, p. 2.

[25] *Columbia Encyclopedia; Webster's Biographical Dictionary*, 1959.

[26] *Österreicher der Gegenwart*, Wien 1951. Deutsch died in Vienna in 1968.

[27] Hugo Hantsch, *Geschichte Österreichs*, 2 vols., Graz, Wien 1947–53, II, pp. 357–58; Robert A. Kann, The *Multinational Empire*, vol. II, N.Y. 1964, p. 325.

[28] A. J. May, "Archduke Francis Ferdinand in the United States," Ill. State Hist. Soc., *Journal*, XXXIX, 1946, p. 344.

[29] Gordon Brook-Shepherd, *Austrian Odyssey*, London 1957, p. 57.

[30] *Who's Who*, 1962–63.

[31] *Österreicher der Gegenwart*, Wien 1951.

[32] Cf. *Journal of Modern History*, Sept. 1961, pp. 238, 257–59.

[33] Österreichische Akademie der Wissenschaften, Wien, *Almanach*, LXXXXIX, 1950, pp. 240ff.; S. B. Fay, *Origins of the World War*, vol. I, N.Y. 1928, p. 37.

[34] *Who's Who*, 1962–63.

[35] *Who's Who*, 1952–53.

[36] *Ibid.*

[37] *Who's Who*, 1962–63.

[38] *Dictionary of American Biography*.

[39] *American Catholic Who's Who*, 1954–55; *Who's Who*, 1962–63.

[40] Page 495.

[41] Henry A. Pochmann, *German Culture in America*, Madison 1957, p. 75.

[42] Mark Twain, *Complete Works*, vol. XXIII, N.Y. 1935, pp. 339–65.

CHAPTER XIX

AUSTRIANS IN LITERATURE

Austrian belles-lettres of the present century have played a distinguished role in German literature. Some of Austria's most notable authors, and even more of its sons and daughters who have made no claim to literary preeminence — who have written as journalists or who have produced books as by-products of careers in other fields — have become as well known in the United States as in their native land.

America knew less and read less of Austria's notable nineteenth century authors like Lenau and Grillparzer and Nestroy and Stifter. They were read by the American scholars who were reading German literature in ever increasing numbers after the middle of the century. But, like German literature as a whole, they never became really popular here.

Indeed, Austrian literature had, like that of America, developed late — only a century and a half ago. What had come earlier was supranational or cosmopolitan like the Holy Roman Empire. It was simply German — not Austrian. Goethe's death in 1832 marked not only the end of a great period in the literature of Germany but it marked, approximately, the beginnings of Austria's characteristic literature. Grillparzer (1791 — 1872) was its first genius. And Grillparzer's pen was distinctly Austrian. Love for Austria was for him a dominating characteristic — *die Liebe zu seinem Vaterlande*, as Hofmannsthal expressed it decades later, in explaining Grillparzer's significant position as the first representative of writing that was uniquely Austrian. Hofmannsthal underscored this early nineteenth-century period as that of the awakening of Austrian consciousness by his emphasis on the year 1809 when Andreas Hofer won his victories in the Tyrol against the French-supported Bavarians and the Austrian armies defending Vienna defeated Napoleon at Aspern. The Holy Roman Empire had just been terminated and the Habsburg Kaiser Franz found himself the emperor, not of the Roman empire or of the Germans, but of Austria. The stage was set for Grillparzer and his successors, who would write as Austrians, not as Germans, in the great field of German literature.[1]

The brilliant contemporary essayist Herbert Eisenreich, in "Das grosse Erbe" (Graz and Vienna 1962), has described the various generations of Austrian writers, from the age of Grillparzer, through the age of the realists and neo-romanticists who were hardly known in America, to the great generation that wrote only after the fall of Austria-Hungary in 1918, and that was and is so well known here, to the homeless generation between the wars that found very little Austrian to write about, to the young generation of today that has again discovered Austria.

And all through the generations since Grillparzer, Austrian literature has been characterized, not by the subject matter that has often ignored core-Austria, but by characteristics that have been non-German: the influence of Vienna that has always been the focal point of cultural Austria; the impact of the tremendous Slavic element, and that of the Magyars, in the old empire; the Austrian concern for the concrete, often the psychological, as contrasted with the German interest in the philosophic; the Austrian aversion to largeness and power and noise and brutal change; and the ever-present baroque element in the Austrian, so difficult for the American to understand.

The finest Austrian prose, notable from Grillparzer to Doderer for its epic qualities, is well known in America for volumes like "The Sleepwalkers," "The Man without Qualities," and "The Demons." Only less well known is what has been written in Vienna for the stage: Da Ponte's librettos for Mozart, for instance, and Hofmannsthal's for Richard Strauss. Austria's penchant for lyric poetry, significant as Lenau and Rilke and Trakl have been in the German-speaking world, has had less of an impact in this country. And the Austrians' fondness for aphorisms and the essay form — the Austrians' pleasant substitutes for the Germans' didactic and philosophical writing — are much less well known in the United States. Most read in this country are the writings of refugees from Hitler like Werfel and Zweig, and of charming — but less important — figures like Bemelmans. Such people are, unfortunately, not in the main line of Austria's great contribution to world literature.

There is one typically Austrian characteristic of its literature that must be mentioned — the Austrian's love of his countryside. The Austrian may criticize his politicians and his men of business and his labor barons, but he loves his mountains and his rivers and their charms. The great Hofmannsthal could not restrain himself, only a half century ago, in his expressions of love for the beauties of his country. He felt that the beauties of the little *Gau* or district, or of the individual Crown Lands of the old monarchy, awakened his Austrian compatriots to write and compose and so produce literature in its finest sense.[2] Hofmannsthal was always spilling over with love of that Austrian countryside that has charmed so many other Austrian writers and has, in recent years, brought some of them back from America to the land of the Danube and the Drau.

Americans have not always been avid to read what Austrians have written. Grillparzer lamented that unless a German (and he included the Austrians in that category) was called Schiller or Goethe, the world ignored him.[3] That was perhaps, a century ago when few native-born Americans were really competent in German, because the translations were seldom distinguished. Oskar Seidlin wrote recently in the "American-German Review" that "Most of the old translations are so poor as to make any exposure to them positively painful."[4] Poetry especially is very difficult to translate effectively. "*Ein Dichter lässt sich nicht übersetzen*" as Grillparzer wrote.[5] Review after review in American journals of sensitive authors like Rilke and Hofmannsthal complain that English translations fail to catch the sense of the original. American publishers are generally reluctant to publish translations when no competent translators are available, and thus the writing of some fine Austrians remain untranslated.

The translation barrier is of course not unique to America's understanding of Austrian writers. It is a common problem as between peoples who speak different tongues. The well known Russian author, Boris Pasternak, discovered and admired the Austrian poet, Rilke, but regretted that all translations of him into Russian had been so unsuccessful. When Berg's "Wozzeck" returned recently to the Metropolitan Opera in New York most of the critics discussed the difficulties of rendering the German text into English.[5] Translation is now, however, far less of a barrier than it was a century ago when publishers were less conscious of the problems involved. The appearance of fine scholars like Arthur Burkhard, who has translated all of Grillparzer's plays, may eventually supply American readers with competent translations of many of the Austrians who have hitherto been but little read in the United States. The charming Austrian dialect – a kind of second language that is spoken by the common folk, understood by most of the sophisticated, and regarded with considerable merriment by the North Germans who prefer their own dialects – has long been considered untranslatable. Very recently, two editors of the University of California Press, who originated in Austria, have attempted to solve the problem of dialect – Max Knight and Joseph Fabry. And Max Knight, a product of the University of Vienna, has lectured at New York's Austrian Institute and elsewhere about the translator who wants to interpret the wit and dialect of a genuine Austrian like Nestroy into English. The Austrian-born Frederick Ungar has recently published three Nestroy comedies translated by Knight and Fabry. But translation remains a major problem. Ungar has not yet minted great profits from Nestroy.

Austria's men of letters have very generally, and very naturally, been confused in the United States with their German counterparts. Many are referred to as "German writers." The Austrians have been often so much in the mainstream of German literature that they were widely published in Germany, included in anthologies of German literature, and thought of in America as Germans. All that was a tribute to the important role that they were playing in German literature. It has resulted, however, in a tendency to associate them with the Germans and so give them no recognition as Austrians. The "Germanic Review," for instance, could in 1948 criticize the "Columbia Dictionary of Modern European Literature" for giving Czech and Slovak literature far more adequate attention than it gave to the Austrian.[7] That was doubtless because the Austrians of significance were drained off into the German portion of the story. Only recently, after the end of the Nazi and occupation periods, do we see signs of impatience among the younger Austrian writers with the tendency of Germans to consider Austrians as German writers. One critic, Ivar Ivask, points out that while no one doubts that America has a literature of its own distinct from England's, German critics judge Austrian writers as they would Germans, without regard to the basic differences between the two – ethnical and historical, geographical and ideological, that have persisted, with the exception of the confused generation of the World War II period, since Grillparzer and Lenau.[8] The Austrian characteristics, even as basic and as obvious as the Vienna impact and the baroque stamp, are often overlooked by American critics who, more often than not, review Austrian books as they would German ones.

"But all the stories have a strange alien quality, set among unfamiliar Eastern European cities and neglecting the description of familiar, orienting things and events."[9] That statement of an American reviewer of a book by the really significant Austrian writer, Robert Musil, may be indicative of another barrier between American readers and Austrian writers. Americans recognize Balzac's Paris and Dickens' London. They know less of the Middle Europe of Musil and his compatriots and they do not read Austrian books merely because they know and love the remote back streets of Vienna and Central Europe. They do not feel so much at home in Musil's Europe as in the countries of the west.

Two world wars have contributed, linguistically, to America's separation from German-speaking Central Europe. It is estimated that from twelve to twenty millions in America in 1914 spoke German and that by 1930, a generation after the end of the great German immigration and after the war had discouraged the study of German, only six to eight million spoke German.[10] Fewer students in the universities and fewer enthusiasts for the German language were reading German-language books and the German press, and even native-born Americans were studiously avoiding the German-language theaters and operas. America's recognition of Austria after World War II as a liberated – not an enemy – country, helped when Austrian art or music was imported. But the language remained the language of the unpopular Germans and, as such, its popularity suffered seriously.

Indeed, the voice of Austria has never been a clear and penetrating one – in America or in Europe. A half century ago Hugo von Hofmannsthal, one of Austria's finest voices, wrote that Austria's voice was far from being clear: "*Es ist etwas Stummes um Österreich*" – and he went on to declare that Austria seemed to be able to express itself in music but not in words. He advocated the founding of an "Austrian Library" that would bring out in German the things that Austria could be proud of.[11] His Austrian Library has been published but not all of it has reached the United States. Time has passed, a great deal of fine literature has been written by Austrians since Hofmannsthal's 1917 appeal for an Austrian library, and America has come to know something of dozens of the Austrians, especially of the turn-of-the-century generation, whom Hofmannsthal knew and admired: Schnitzler, Rilke, Kafka, Musil, Broch, and the others. It is a pity that Americans so often think of these fine writers as Germans and not as Austrians.

During the nineteenth century when Austrian letters were of no great consequence even in Central Europe,[12] it was chiefly, in the United States, the refugees of 1848 who aroused interest in the German language. Many Forty-eighters of some distinction engaged in journalism here or produced political tracts in such causes as those of anti-slavery and of the young Republican Party. And they supported the German-language theater and the music hall, the latter with notable *Lieder* and librettos that served to remind the German and Austrian-born of their native tongue and to interest many native Americans in German for the first time. To that period also belonged the *Ratgeber*, the guidebooks for immigrants, written more often by Germans than by German Austrians, that were fascinating commentaries on American life. A reprinting of interesting portions of these *Ratgeber*, translated into English, would be a genuine contribution to American history.

Most interesting in the mid-nineteenth century were the romantics from abroad who wrote libraries of literary sketches and novels about America. A few, like the Austrian Francis J. Grund,[13] whose "Aristocracy in America" has so recently found a publisher in this country, were serious, intelligent critics. Some were merely enthusiasts who idealized America's very name, its freedoms, its Niagara Falls, its escape from Europe's tyrannies, and its noble redskins. Their books helped to draw an ever-increasing stream of optimistic migrants to America.

The best known of them all was doubtless "our favorite Sealsfield," as Longfellow called him, the author of dozens of American frontier tales including the first novel celebrating the Texan war for independence.[14] He called himself a native of the Austrian empire but wanted to be remembered as a citizen of the United States. Born Karl Anton Postl (b. Poppitz, Moravia, 1793 – d. Switzerland, 1864), educated to be a priest, too independent in his ways for the old Austrian Empire and its church, he fled Vienna to come to New Orleans and, disliking slavery there, to settle in 1824 in western Pennsylvania. As a further escape from his past he called himself Charles Sealsfield.[15]

Realizing that Americans paid little attention to literature not already acclaimed in Europe, Sealsfield returned to Europe to have his "United States of North America" published in Stuttgart (1827) and London (1828) and his bitter farewell to his homeland, "Austria as It Is" (1828), published anonymously in England. The critics were so impressed with his superb English and the non-Germanic name on the American volume that they suspected the author of being English. "Austria as It Is" remains a fascinating but unhappy commentary on the empire of Kaiser Franz I.

Sealsfield was a kind of German-language James Fenimore Cooper. Beginning with "Tokeah, or the White Rose" in 1828 and during the same years when Cooper was writing, he produced dozens of novels on the American frontier and the American Indian. Yet he was far more important as an interpreter of America to the Europeans than as an American author. As Henry A. Pochmann, the expert on Germanic culture in America, has pointed out, it was America that influenced Sealsfield and not *vice versa*. Sealsfield became so American that even Longfellow could enjoy his descriptions of the southwestern frontier; he knew personally many figures in our public life; probably served us as an American diplomatic agent on his trips to Mexico and Europe,[16] and was received by President Jackson himself on his return from one of his European tours. Professor A. B. Faust thought that his books were well enough known here to be plagiarized by such American authors as Captain Mayne Reid and William Gilmore Simms.[17]

During those same years Austria's greatest, nineteenth-century, lyric poet, Nikolaus Lenau (1802–1850), discovered America for himself and heartily disliked it. Like Sealsfield he was inspired with a romantic instinct to seek liberty in America's primeval forests and among the free children of nature in the New World's young democracy. Unlike Sealsfield he was revolted by the materialism and the grossness of the land which he had idealized from afar.

This remarkable figure was born in a German-speaking corner of eastern Hungary[18] and educated in part at the University of Vienna and at Pressburg. A romantic, melancholy, youth he renounced medicine in favor of poetry. When he was thirty and unhappily in love he emigrated, bought a farm of 400 acres in Ohio, wielded his ax with gloves to save his sensitive hands, and achieved the distinction of being called "the crazy German." He was what our pioneers often called "a Latin farmer" because they were more adept at Latin than with the plow.

Only a few months later, in 1833, Lenau returned to his life in Vienna and Stuttgart. He had liked Niagara Falls but was otherwise utterly disillusioned. "My visit in the New World has cured me," Lenau told his brother-in-law, "of the fancies about freedom and independence which I cherished in my enthusiastic younger days. I convinced myself there that genuine freedom lies in one's own breast . . ."[19] America discovered Lenau, not when he was here, but in the late nineteenth century when he shared America's new interest in German literature and began to be represented in translation in German-American anthologies.[20]

Lenau's influence as a deterrent to German and Austrian emigration to America was doubtless more significant. For he inspired the German-language counterpart of Dickens' famous anti-American "American Notes." The book was a novel called "Der Amerikamüde" (Frankfurt am Main 1855) by Ferdinand Kürnberger (b. Vienna, 1821 – d. Munich, 1879). Kürnberger had been a member of the revolutionary Vienna Academic Legion during the revolution of 1848, had spent nine months behind bars as a consequence of it, escaped to Germany, and there achieved a considerable reputation for the novel that he based upon Lenau's unfortunate episodes in the United States. Its author had never visited this country but capitalized upon Lenau's disillusionment with American life. Those who were disillusioned with Europe had produced the expression *europamüde*. Kürnberger turned the expression about in Europe's favor and his book brought him a considerable reputation.[21] Fortunately or unfortunately it has remained untranslated and almost entirely unknown on this side of the Atlantic.

Adalbert Stifter (b. Oberplan, Bohemia, 1805 – d. Linz, 1868), one of the earliest in the mainstream of Austrian writing, the fine representative of undogmatic, conservative Catholicism, was almost completely unknown in the United States. Only in recent years have a few American readers discovered that his was one of the great names in mid-nineteenth-century prose.[22]

Far more significant than Stifter was his great contemporary, the dramatist Franz Grillparzer (b. Vienna, 1791 – d. Vienna, 1872), who despised Metternich and idealized America as the land of Freedom. He was doubtless the first genuine Austrian man-of-letters – out of the German line and ready to write as a lover of his Austria; "*sein Österreich liebte er . . .*" "*Man muss nach Nordamerika reisen,*" he wrote in the "conversation book" of his dear friend Beethoven, "*um seinen Ideen freien Lauf zu lassen . . .*"[23] Lord Byron who thought he had "a devil of a name," found his play "Sappho" "superb and sublime! And who is he? I know him not but (the) ages will."[24]

It is claimed that Grillparzer has the distinction of being the first Austrian man of letters to receive a whole series of lectures at an American university. The Austrian-born Professor Joseph A. von Bradish (b. 1883) lectured on him in 1963 at New York University.[25] The German theaters in New York and Baltimore had played his "Ahnfrau," and his "Sappho" was translated long ago (1876) into English.[26] All his plays have now appeared in an excellent English translation and his fine short story, "Der arme Spielmann," is being prepared for publication in translation. His name is not ignored by the more learned American journals. Yet he himself complained that "foreign literary men have a prejudice against anything that comes from Austria."[27] Since his death there has been more interest in the neglected dramatist and by 1960 Arthur Burkhard, his translator, was able to write that he had recently been the subject of research at over two dozen United States universities.[28] Hopefully, the Grillparzer theme will lead to a realization of the origin and development of Austrian literature.

The German theater here in America also played dramas by Ferdinand Raimund (b. Vienna, 1790 – d. Pottenstein, Lower Austria, 1836) and Johann Nepomuk Nestroy (b. Vienna, 1801 – d. Graz, 1862). Theirs were the two greatest names on the light Vienna stage during the earlier years of the last century. It was Nestroy's "Einen Jux will er sich machen" that served as a basis for Thornton Wilder's fine play "The Matchmaker."

One of "the very greatest writers in the whole history of German literature" and, besides Thomas Mann and Franz Kafka, the one "who among representatives of German letters has left the deepest impact on the English-speaking world," is typical of the comments of the critics upon Rainer Maria Rilke (b. Prague, 1875 – d. Val Mont near Montreux, Switzerland, 1926).[29] This sensitive poet imagined romantically that he came of the Carinthian nobility. He was, strangely enough for a poet, educated in the military academies at St. Pölten, Lower Austria, and Mährisch-Weisskirchen, Moravia, as well as at the *Handelsschule* in Linz and at the German University of Prague. He was a restless soul who wandered from Prague to Germany and from one distant town to another, including several years in Paris as sculptor Rodin's secretary, before he finally settled in his last years in the charming Swiss canton of Valais.

Rilke's reputation as one of the great poets of his time has grown steadily since his death. Most of his works have been translated into English. The comments of the critics of the translations, varying from "the art of translation has triumphed in the two Rilke volumes" to "hardly any of the (translations) catch Rilke's rythm," indicate that his translations have produced some good and some poor versions for the English reader. Poetry in any language is difficult to translate.[30]

Rilke is, however, receiving increasing attention in America. When Jethro Bithell, the historian of modern German literature, wrote in 1946, he could list a number of British books on Rilke but none published in the United States.[31] Since then the American professors have "found" the great Austrian and such reputable university presses as those of Princeton, the University of Minnesota, and the University of Washington have published serious biographies. The general American reader may yet discover this man who has been called "greatest Germanic poet of modern times."

Americans concerned with the main currents of world literature can scarcely be unfamiliar with the name of Hugo von Hofmannsthal (b. Vienna, 1874 – d. Rodaun near Vienna, 1929). He was more Viennese than his contemporary Rilke and he was, like Rilke and Schnitzler, one of the *Jung-Wien*, or Young Vienna, group that turned away from the dullness of nineteenth century naturalism to poetry and prose that was more imaginative and more lyrical. Americans know him as the libretto writer for Richard Strauss and collaborator with Reinhardt at the Salzburg Festivals. He was one of the few great librettists. His adaptation of "Jedermann" for Salzburg is internationally famous. His librettos for Strauss's "Rosenkavalier," "Ariadne auf Naxos," "Arabella," "Frau ohne Schatten," and the tragic "Elektra" were as fine as the composer's great music. Most of his prose and his poetry are, however, relatively unknown to the American reader. Only after his death, did his plays and libretti appear here in well-edited form.[32] Selections from his prose writings have even more recently appeared in the United States.

Hugo von Hofmannsthal loved his Austria and Austria has long loved her Hofmannsthal. He wrote of figures who represented the finest Austrian tradition – like

Walther von der Vogelweide, the Minnesinger, whose songs, he felt, ennobled the magnificent mountain landscape which had given him birth. He wrote regretfully of "*jene selten in der Welt gehörte Stimme: die Stimme Österreichs*" – the seldom-heard voice of his country. He established the "Österreichische Bibliothek" book series (Insel Verlag, Leipzig) "to make the voice of Austria heard among those who love her."[33] In the Habsburg era he was scarcely *kaisertreu:* he was fond of the land and its people, not of its government. With genuine perception, "He saw his country more receptive than France to foreign ideas and points of view," his biographer Hammelmann wrote, "less insular than Britain, less isolated than Spain, more human, more adaptable, less rigid than the Germans; with a balance and a lightness of its own . . ." And he and his contemporaries of *Jung-Wien* did much to rescue Vienna from *fin de siècle* decadence. Political decay might overtake the old monarchy but, despite America's occasional unawareness, there was still an amazing vitality in Austrian letters.[34]

Far better known in America, although he never came here, was Arthur Schnitzler (b. Vienna, 1862 – d. Vienna, 1931). Much more than Hofmannsthal, Schnitzler represented the pessimism and moral laxity of his time. His plays and tales were written against the background of a sad Vienna that was listlessly trying to be gay.

Schnitzler was born of a Jewish family, studied medicine at the University of Vienna and practiced it, turned to writing, and produced much that was Freudian long before Freud became famous. Moralists criticized him and lamented his world-wide popularity, his Anatols and his Casanovas. In America he was first played in the German-language theaters but he was discovered by the English-speaking stage long before World War I. Most of his works were translated – by so many translators that his works in English lack any single characteristic style. "The Green Cockatoo" was played here by the famous Mrs. Fiske and John Barrymore acted in his "Affairs of Anatol" just fifty years before it furnished the theme for "The Gay Life," with music by Arthur Schwartz, at New York's Shubert Theater. His stories like his plays have enjoyed a popularity equaled in America by few Continental writers.

To the Nazis Arthur Schnitzler was a decadent. His personal papers were, however, rescued, taken to England, and copied for the University of California at Los Angeles. His son Heinrich was also a fugitive from the Nazis who spent the war years in the United States before returning to liberated Austria.[35]

While comparatively few of the great Austrian literary figures came to America to live, there were many of some distinction. Joseph Erhardt Fischnaller (b. Innsbruck 1862), a now forgotten poet, came here from the Tyrol in 1884.[36] Arthur Kober, Ludwig Bemelmans, Alexander King, and Vicki Baum, all better known, came later but before the migration of 1938.

Arthur Kober (b. Brody, Galicia, 1900) came as a child to New York City, married the well-known dramatist Lillian Hellman, served as press agent for many of the country's biggest theatrical names, wrote scripts for "The Little Foxes" and other good films, and contributed to the New York daily press. Devotees of "The New Yorker" will not soon forget his charming "My Dear Bella" letters.[37]

Ludwig Bemelmans (b. Meran, 1898 – d. New York, 1962), born in what was then the Austrian Tyrol, schooled in Bavaria, apprenticed to his uncle's hotels in the Tyrol, and, it is said, given the choice between a reform school and America, chose America. He settled in New York, waited on table, enjoyed painting, and wrote dozens of bright, sophisticated articles for the magazines that smart Americans read. Like Kober he found how to apply European charm to writing and sketching for American audiences and his urbane, witty Hotel Splendide episodes and Madeline stories charmed readers by the tens of thousands. "His is one of the original talents of current American letters," wrote one of the critics.[38]

Like Bemelmans, Alexander King (b. Vienna, 1900 – d. New York, 1965) was born with genius as illustrator as well as raconteur. An immigrant of 1913 and a student of the Cooper Union, the Sorbonne, and the Vienna *Sezession*, he wielded the editorial pencil for "Stage," "Life," and "Vanity Fair," illustrated limited editions and satirical efforts like his own ill-fated "Americana" magazine of 1932, and wrote several best sellers such as "Mine Enemy Grows Older" (1958) and "May this House be Safe from Tigers" (1960). The television found King a genuine attraction.[39]

Vicki Baum (b. Vienna, 1888 – d. Hollywood, 1960) was another well known name in the adopted country. When she was playing the harp in Vienna's finest orchestra (her education was musical and not at all literary) she invited her composer friend Oscar Straus and his wife Clara to the proper Vienna Christmas dinner of carp. Straus never forgot that carp. Vicki bought it alive weeks early to take advantage of lower prices, kept it in the bathtub, fell in love with it, refused to produce it for Christmas, and the Strauses had to eat Vienna's favorite plebian dish, the goulash.[40]

Both Vicki Baum and the Strauses were later to settle in the United States. But while Oscar Straus went back to Austria, Vicki remained on in Hollywood until her death. She wrote film scripts and dozens of novels, and some of them like "Grand Hotel" (translation 1931) were best-sellers.

There were other best-sellers on the American book market that were written by the Austrian-born. There were Joy Adamson's stories of her African lioness and its cubs, "Born Free" and "Living Free."[41] She received an award from the American Wild Life Federation for her work for animal-kind in Kenya. And her African story was converted into one of America's most popular films of 1966. Far more Austrian was the autobiography of the fascinating wife of Mahler, Gropius and Werfel, whose friendship with the Austrian-born artist Kokoschka added significantly to her catch of the great in Central Europe. Her little autobiography, "And the Bridge is Love" (New York 1958), sold well in the United States (Alma Mahler-Werfel was living in

New York in her old age) and contributed much to America's understanding of art and music in recent-day Austria.

Frederic Morton's (b. Vienna, 1925) "The Rothschilds" was on the best-seller list for months following the early 1960's when it appeared. Morton was essentially a novelist, a refugee of 1938, who studied at New York's City College and New School, received a prize for his novel, "The Hound," and continued to write in America while keeping in touch with Europe.[42]

One of the great American book successes of 1958, a Book-of-the-Month Club selection and a recipient a few months later of the National Book Award, was "Mistress to an Age: A Life of Madam de Staël." Its author, J. Christopher Herold (b. Brünn, 1919), born in what is now Czechoslovakia of Austrian parents, who like so many German Austrians in that area knew but little Czech, studied or traveled all over Europe, and was persuaded by grandfather Artur Schnabel the fine pianist to come to America in 1939. Here he published novels, wrote for the "Columbia Encyclopedia" and became chief editor of the Stanford University Press.[43] His "Age of Napoleon," a best-seller of 1963, was a sensation. Austrians overseas wrote on everything except Austrian themes. And in America Herold doubtless encountered Felix Salten (b. as Siegmund Salzmann in Budapest, 1869 – d. Zurich, 1945), who had been courageous enough to attack the powerful, anti-Semitic Mayor Lueger of Vienna in the "Neue Freie Presse" (Vienna's best daily). His "Fünf Minuten Amerika," or "Five Minutes of America," attracted little attention compared with that pleasant story of Bambi, the wild deer, that he had written long before he came to the United States and that American children will long love.[44]

Vicki Baum might, the critics tell us, have done finer work had she written all her life in German. The Hitler era brought to America, as it brought to England, a large group of Austrian men of letters who had to leave their lingual homeland. Some learned to write in English; others like Werfel had no need for English as publishers were eager to have their books even in translation. Many simply continued writing and publishing in German. What this latter group wrote, *Emigrantenliteratur*, was not American literature but Austro-German. Much of it was escapist, nostalgic, or concerned with the unhappiness of the exile. A review of a book by the refugee Alfred Polgar pointed out that that fine Vienna *Feuilletonisten*, or cultural columnists, had in exile simply lost the Vienna atmosphere and had found nothing to substitute for it.[45] Whether or not this was generally true of the entire group, the emigrant authors were significant people whose names often became well known in many an American publishing house. Most of them found a welcome in America although dozens of them suffered from the enforced isolation from their homeland and Stefan Zweig was not the only suicide in the group.[46]

Oskar Jellinek (b. Brünn, 1886 – d. Los Angeles, 1949) was one of the tragic figures. A sorry exile from his beloved Vienna he reached New York in 1940 and

Los Angeles three years later. But he found no inspiration in America and died in his early sixties leaving, of all his good poetry and fascinating *Novellen*, only "Uproar in the Village" (N.Y. 1933) in English translation.[47]

Stefan Zweig (b. Vienna, 1881 – d. Petropolis, Brazil, 1942) was a victim of Nazism who never succeeded in finding a second home. He was a pacifist who sought refuge from the first World War in Switzerland, returned to Austria, lived in Salzburg until the Fascist time, sought refuge in London and became a British citizen, first visited the United States in 1938, moved on to Brazil and committed suicide there. He was a fine, sensitive person who had written notable verse and brilliant critical essays. His pacifist drama "Jeremias" (1917) was produced by New York's Theater Guild in 1939 and his version of Ben Jonson's "Volpone" was a later success on the American stage. Best known in America were his fine, much-read literary biographies, of Marie Antoinette, Mary Stuart, Balzac and others. Few Austrians have been so avidly read in this country and throughout the world as Stefan Zweig.[48]

Another outstanding figure in the Austrian literary world was Franz Werfel (b. Prague, 1890 – d. Hollywood, 1945). A pacifist like Zweig, disillusioned and iconoclastic like many other literary Austrians of his day, he had to serve in the Austrian army during the war, then settled in Vienna where he loved the music and the cultural life and the nearby mountains. He was somehow able to combine disbelief and denial with a Messianic sweetness of faith and confidence.

Called "the most noted of the poets of expressionism," Werfel has been much less well known here for his poetry than for his fine plays and novels.[49] Even before he came to America his dramas, "Goat Song" and "Juarez and Maximilian" and his novel "The Forty Days of Musa Dagh," had been brilliant successes in Vienna and in much of America, on stage and screen and in book form.

Werfel was not, when he and his wife Alma Schindler came to New York in 1940, the typical, unknown, penniless refugee. He had first found refuge and a real welcome in France. But the Nazis were marching west and America seemed the only oasis of safety and hope for a Jew who had been expelled seven years earlier from the Prussian Academy of Art. At the shrine of Lourdes Werfel, intrigued with the story of the saint, vowed that he would write a song in praise of St. Bernadette if he and his wife were permitted to find haven in the New World. A Portuguese consul who admired Werfel's writings helped with a visa and the fugitives crossed the Pyrenees, shipped to New York, and soon went on to Southern California. There in Beverly Hills they bought May Robson's "dear house," and made themselves at home.

Others, like the refugee poet Annette Kolb, might find themselves "grateful and unhappy" in the new home. The Werfels were only a bit homesick. Out there in Hollywood they found almost as many notable Europeans as they had met at their *Hohe Warte* and Semmering homes – Schönberg, Thomas Mann, Bruno Frank,

Remarque, Max Reinhardt, Bemelmans, and many others. They only regretted that America was so long indifferent to Hitlerism.[50]

In America, in response to the vows he had made at Lourdes, Franz Werfel wrote his "Song of Bernadette" which became one of his Book-of-the-Month Club triumphs. And it was a film success for Hollywood which, at a loss for themes, was turning to psychiatry and religion, and found in "Bernadette" what it needed. His charming "Jacobowsky and the Colonel" was an immediate stage success in New York,[51] and his "Embezzled Heaven" (1940), with an Old-World theme, like everything he did, enjoyed only lesser popularity. Few refugees from overseas despotism have made greater contributions here in a few years of exile than Franz Werfel.

Werfel reminds one in many ways of the German-born dramatist Carl Zuckmayer (b. Nackenheim, 1896) who came to Salzburg in 1925, became an Austrian citizen just in time to see Hitler march on Vienna, escaped by way of France in 1939 to Vermont, to dream in America of the lovely Salzburg home in which he had meant to live and die. Like Werfel he was an expressionist (a school that was more Germanic than American), he did some fine work in Hollywood as in writing the lines for the "Blue Angel" and dramatizing "Farewell to Arms," he remained European in his outlook, and he stayed here only a few years during the war.[52]

The author of the Literary Guild's selection of 1943, "Beneath Another Sun," was Ernst Lothar (b. Brünn, 1890), a University-of-Vienna-educated lawyer who had turned to the theater and to writing. In Vienna he directed classical drama at the *Burgtheater* and then Reinhardt's fine *Theater in der Josefstadt*, came to grips with the Nazis, and succeeded in reaching America in 1939 where he wrote and lectured on the theater in New York and Colorado. Lothar is an interesting example of the Thirty-eighter who took American citizenship yet returned to his homeland as early as 1946. He returned, indeed, as a very distinguished Music and Theater Officer for the U.S. Forces in Austria but his book, "Return to Vienna," revealed the conflict of loyalties between the native and adopted countries.[53] It is interesting that another and younger Thirty-eighter, Ernst Haeussermann, Lothar's son-in-law, also returned to do cultural work in Vienna for the United States occupation authorities, graduated to direct at the same time two fine state theaters, was like Lothar married to a charming Vienna actress, and never returned to his adopted country.[54] In these cases, and in some others, the refugee of 1938 found that a more satisfying career awaited him *in der Heimat* than in America.

Berthold Viertel (b. Vienna, 1885 – d. Vienna, 1953), one of those cultured Viennese who could turn their attention to good theater or to good writing or to films, as opportunity offered, deserted Hollywood for Austria in 1947. He was one of those who, even in America, continued to write partly in German.[55] And Friedrich Torberg (b. Vienna, 1908), poet, *Feuilletonist*, and novelist, returned soon after the end of the war to work with the American occupation authorities and begin anew his life in Vienna.

Joseph Wechsberg (b. Mährisch-Ostrau, 1907), the keen commentator upon Austria and all of Central Europe, whom we mention in our chapter on journalists, was another who returned home – in his case as a roving American journalist who continued to write for the "New Yorker" and "Holiday" and to list his office as in New York. Others who had mastered the English language included those authors of childrens's books, Father Franz Xavier Weiser who taught theology and philosophy in Boston, Charlotte Steiner, and Bessie Feistiner White whose "A Bear Named Grumms" (1950) received a "Herald Tribune" award of honor. Miss Steiner wrote about Kiki and Lulu, Peter and Lolly.[56] And John Kafka (b. Vienna, 1905), no relation to Franz Kafka but a disciple of Freud, was a Thirty-eighter among the immigrant novelists.[57]

Among those whose distinguished poetry and prose were in German was the Catholic Guido Zernatto (b. Treffen near Villach, 1903 – d. New York, 1943), conservative enough to have served in the Schuschnigg cabinet and in New York on the Military Committee of Otto Habsburg to help the Allied cause, who was nevertheless a refugee of 1938. He taught German at Fordham University.[58] Richard Beer-Hofmann (b. Vienna, 1866 – d. New York, 1945) was a fine poet, dramatist and novelist of *Jung-Wien* who was a representative of neo-romanticism at the turn of the century. Beer-Hofmann emigrated in 1938, settled in New York, and, unlike so many of the older émigrés who left their inspiration to create back in Vienna, continued to write and publish. A volume of his verse appeared in 1941 and a volume of sketches about Austria came out in 1944.[59] Raoul Auernheimer (b. Vienna, 1876 – d. Oakland, California, 1947), the fine story teller, *Feuilletonist*, and biographer of Metternich (1941), was a Thirty-eighter.

The novelist and critic and poet, Johannes Urzidil (b. Prague, 1896), who published his witty, lightly satirical novel on New England and Vermont, "Das grosse Halleluja," in Zurich in 1959, lives in New York while he publishes in German across the seas.[60]

A grand old man of the Austrian lyric poets has been, since 1939, the prolific cosmopolitan Max Roden (b. Vienna, 1881 – d. New York, 1968). His tremendous vitality enabled him to produce much fine poetry, totaling over twenty German-language volumes.[61] Also writing in German was Ernst Waldinger (b. Vienna, 1896) who has been called the poetic voice of the German-Austrian immigration here. He has taught since 1947 at Skidmore College.[62]

Far better known in the New World is Arthur Koestler (b. Budapest, 1905) who found no difficulty in changing his language: from German at home (his father was Hungarian, his mother Viennese), to Hungarian in elementary school, again to German in and around Vienna where he went to school and university, and German during his early journalistic career. He finally adopted English with British citizenship and made England his home. Meanwhile in the early Thirties he had joined the Communist Party, suffered all the pangs of ideological uncertainty, and renounced Communism. The British had had to save his life twice, when he fell into Franco's hands in Spain and into Fascist hands later in Paris. The novels that he wrote that dealt with the pains of mankind at the hands of Roman tyrants and Communists and Nazis have been read by millions in dozens of languages. His "Darkness at Noon," most popular in America, was a Book-of-the-Month Club choice and, in 1951, the basis of a Broadway drama with the same title. He visited the United States first in 1948, lived for a time in Pennsylvania, but returned to Europe despite an act of Congress in 1951 which granted him permanent residence here. He was doubtless more welcome as a former Communist who had retracted than he was as a great man of letters. For that was the McCarthy era.[63]

The future historian of American thought may conclude that Austria's most important contribution in the field of letters came, not from any of the figures mentioned above, but from the tortured souls of the recent era of Franz Kafka. Rilke and Zweig might almost have been German or Swiss. Many who wrote in Austria can be placed in the mainstream of Germanic letters. Kafka, on the other hand, was unique. And Kafka and his group, according to the editor of "Books Abroad," made their contribution thirty years before they were discovered and imitated. They represented, wrote editor Fleischmann, the second and more significant mainstream of Austrian letters.[64]

"Had one to name the author who comes nearest to bearing the same kind of relation to our age as Dante, Shakespeare and Goethe bore to theirs," wrote W. H. Auden, "Kafka is the first one would think of."[65] He has been ranked with the Austrian Rilke and the German Thomas Mann as one of the three German writers of our century who have had the greatest impact upon the western mind.[66] One can hardly disregard the significance of such a figure in America even though he never even visited America and remained almost completely unknown here for a generation after his death. Austria scarcely knew him even when his first work "Das Schloss" appeared in 1926; and then the Nazis saw to it that he was not read. America read that first work as "The Castle" in 1930 and also forgot him. His horribly pessimistic drama "The Trial" appeared here in 1937 but his was still a distant voice, and critic Edmund Wilson still resented the effort of his admirers to rank him with Dante and Joyce and Proust. It was only after 1945 that a weary Austria and the outside world seized upon the prophet of despair and Freudianism, expressionism and existentialism. By 1945 he fitted the mood of the bombed-out tragic world.

Franz Kafka (b. Prague, 1883 – d. Kierling near Vienna, 1924) was educated in Prague in the best German-language tradition.[67] He also studied Czech but wrote in German. And he wrote of the decadence of Austria-Hungary and of mankind in general. He was concerned with portraying hate and indifference and injustice in terms of symbolism and allegory. The melancholy climate produced by the *Jung-Wien*, Young Vienna, school sixty years ago was an essential part of his background.[68]

The disillusioned generation of 1945 discovered Kafka and read him wildly. He became, with Eliot and Proust and Rilke and Joyce, one of the untouchables.[69] The Swiss-born, now Austrian Gottfried von Einem, who for years made Vienna his home, composed music for Kafka's "Der Prozess," "The Trial." Kafka's has become a name of tremendous significance.

Kafka's Catholic counterpart in poetry, Georg Trakl (b. Salzburg, 1887 – d. Cracow, 1914), who died in a military hospital in Galicia, is almost unknown here. Like Kafka, he was long neglected even in his own country, became much-read only in 1945, and his fine, morbid, unhappy lyrics were published, for the most part, posthumously.[70]

It was Max Brod (b. Prague, 1884) who persuaded Kafka to publish, or to preserve, the many writings that Kafka considered experimental and fit only for the furnace. Brod has some fame in his own right as novelist and biographer but America knows him chiefly as Kafka's literary executor and friend at the German University of Prague who rescued what Kafka wanted to destroy and who wrote a useful, if too moral and roseate, biography of his hero.[71]

In this uniquely Austrian mainstream of letters was Robert Musil (b. Klagenfurt, 1880 – d. Geneva, Switzerland, 1942) whom the "London Times" called "the most important novelist writing in German in this half-century" but "one of the least known writers of the age." Our "Library Journal" gave very grudging recognition to Musil's masterpiece, his much discussed "Man without Qualities" (3 vols., London and N.Y. 1953): "His style and manner are likened to that of Joyce, Kafka, and Proust and in many instances are just plain ponderous."[72] At the same time "Books Abroad," with a better understanding of the world scene, could say that Musil "belongs to the half-dozen Austrian novelists who have brought about the somewhat belated Golden Age of the German novel."[73] America has discovered Kafka but Musil's "ruthless psychological insight"[74] in a long out-of-time and out-of-space novel seems to be almost too foreign for American taste. American critics who commented upon the English-language translation of Musil's "Five Women" in 1966, revealed their understanding of Musil's significance but refused nevertheless to enthuse about the book. It, however, is doubtful whether Musil's European critics enthused over those stories when they first appeared years ago.

Buried in a little churchyard in Killingsworth, Connecticut, is another of those very modern Austrian men of letters of the Kafka tradition, Hermann Broch (b. Vienna, 1886 – d. New Haven, 1951). He was also concerned with the disintegration of social values, with "mass-madness," with sleep-walking – his first successful novel was the trilogy, "The Sleepwalkers" (1931). His thinking was based on the three strands of philosophy (in the German sense, including literature), science, and politics.

From Vienna, where he worked in his father's textile business, he went to Styria and the Tyrol, was arrested by the Nazis in the lovely mountains of the Salzkammergut, released through the intercession of James Joyce and other English friends, and finally reached Princeton and then Yale where he became a notable professor of German literature and wrote his novel, "The Death of Virgil." The younger Broch was a bit more optimistic of the future than his predecessor Kafka.[75]

And the last of this group in the second mainstream of Austrian letters, Heimito von Doderer (b. Weidlingau near Vienna, 1896 – d. Vienna, 1966), often compared with Proust, is represented chiefly in American libraries in English by "The Demons" (2 vols., N.Y. 1961). His charming epic "Strudlhofstiege" which discovered many of the same slightly decadent, world-weary Viennese characters, before they appeared in "The Demons," may have helped to make him "the most formidable German-speaking novelist now living."[76] But many Europeans find it difficult and Americans have not published it here in English.

That America is reading what Austrians write is evidenced by the most popular anthology of "German Stories and Tales" (Robert Pick, ed., New York 1954). In this little volume eight of the eighteen stories were written by Austrians and one more, which could almost serve to give the Austrians credit for half of the book, by the much-read Jacob Wassermann. Wassermann, from his native Bavaria, found refuge in Vienna from an unhappy youth and left there only years later to retire in Austria's Styria. In brief, virtually half of the German stories in this much-read volume were written by authors who could be called Austrian.

What Austrians wrote, like what they have written in the past, may still be thought of in the United States as German, not Austrian, literature. Contemporary Austrians of considerable importance in the literary world, like Ilse Aichinger and Ingeborg Bachmann, are writing and publishing in Germany where the market for German literature is of course far greater than that in Austria.[77] But, whether known as Germans or Austrians, the more significant Austrians are becoming better known in the United States. The older names are appearing more and more frequently in good translation and the more recent ones are generally available in good translations of some, at least, of their more notable works.[78]

[1] Otto Basil *et al*, *Das grosse Erbe*, Graz 1962, is a most significant group of three essays on Austrian literature as a whole. Also very basic in any consideration of Austrian literature as a whole is Hugo von Hofmannsthal, *Gesammelte Werke*, *Prosa*, vol. III, Frankfurt/Main 1952, *passim*. There are several excellent histories of German literature that treat of most of the outstanding Austrian writers.

[2] Hofmannsthal, *op. cit.*, p. 320.

[3] Arthur Burkhard, *Franz Grillparzer in England and America*, Wien 1960.

[4] June-July 1961, pp. 3–4.

[5] Burkhard, *op. cit.*, p. 41.

[6] *Austrian Information*, 15 March 1965.

[7] February 1948, p. 56.

[8] See especially the essay by Ivask in Basil *et al*, *op. cit.*

[9] *Washington Post*, 26 April 1966, p. A18.

[10] Josef Nadler, *Literaturgeschichte des deutschen Volkes*, 4 vols., Berlin 1938–41, IV, p. 564.

[11] Hofmannsthal, *op. cit.*, pp. 281ff.

[12] *Cambridge History of American Literature*, 1960 ed., II, pp. 572ff.

[13] See index to this volume for a fuller treatment of Grund.

[14] *Das Kajütenbuch*, in English *The Cabin Book*.

[15] There is a considerable literature in English and German on Sealsfield. He was the subject of A. B. Faust's doctoral dissertation, Baltimore 1892. See also Henry A. Pochmann, *German Culture in America*, Madison 1957; Wilhelm Schlag's article in *Österreich und die angelsächsische Welt*, Wien 1961; K. J. R. Arndt, "Sealsfield's Early Reception in England and America," *Germanic Review*, Oct. 1943, pp. 176–81.

[16] J. T. Krumpelmann's review of Eduard Castle, *Der grosse Unbekannte*, Wien 1952, in *Germanic Review*, Dec. 1953, p. 304.

[17] *Charles Sealsfield, a dissertation*, Baltimore 1892, pp. 43–48.

[18] Near the junction of Transylvania, Jugoslavia and Hungary in Csatad. He died in Ober-Döbling now Vienna. His original name was Niembsch Edler von Strehlenau. Lenau will be found in virtually all histories of German literature. See also Pochmann, *op. cit.*, which indicates that Walt Whitman knew of him, and Karl J. R. Arndt, "Lenau's Lost Poem," *Germanic Review*, Oct. 1944, pp. 180ff.

[19] Translated from German as quoted in Arndt, *op. cit.*, p. 185.

[20] Pochmann, *op. cit.*, p. 344, states that he ranked tenth with respect to the number of poems appearing in such collections 1830–99. He has fourteen pages in *The Oxford Book of German Verse*, 1946 reprint.

[21] *Neue Österreichische Biographie 1915–1918*, vol. VI, Wien 1929, pp. 166–73; R. E. Spiller and others, *Literary History of the United States*, N.Y. 1948, p. 679.

[22] *Books Abroad*, Spring 1960, cites Publications of the Modern Language Assc., LXXIV, 1959, pp. 398ff., as indicating a revival of interest in Stifter, in Europe and America. He is, for instance, one of the ten authors selected for inclusion in Harry Steiner, ed., *German Stories*, 2nd printing, Bantam Books, 1961.

[23] *American-German Review*, June 1942, p. 6. For an evaluation of Grillparzer as an Austrian writer, see Hugo von Hofmannsthal, *op. cit.*, *passim.*

[24] Gustav Pollak, *Franz Grillparzer and the Austrian Drama*, N.Y. 1907, p. 71.

[25] *Austrian Information*, 31 Oct. 1962, p. 8, 15 Nov. 1963, p. 5.

[26] Pochmann, *op. cit.*, pp. 356–58; D. Kunz, *Maryland Germans*, 1948, p. 248.

[27] Quoted from Pollak, *op. cit.*, p. 32.

[28] Burkhard's *Franz Grillparzer in England and America*, Vienna 1960, is authoritative on this subject.

[29] Quoted from Jethro Bithell, *Modern German Literature*, London 1946, p. 159, and a review by F. M. Wassermann in *Books Abroad*, Winter 1960, p. 24. Bithell contains a whole chapter on Rilke. See *Der Grosse Brockhaus* for a condensed biography. Like so many German-Austrians in Bohemia, Rilke knew but little Czech.

[30] *Book Review Digest*, 1958, 1960, and 1961.

[31] Bithell, *op. cit.*, pp. 566–67.

[32] W. H. Perl in *Books Abroad*, Spring 1960, p. 148, calls him "one of the most important phenomena in German letters in the early 20th century. More than Hauptmann or Thomas Mann, Hofmannsthal

stands in the succession of Goethe." See also *German-American Review*, Aug.-Sept. 1956, p. 24; *Books Abroad*, Spring 1961, p. 165, and Winter 1961, "The Libretto as Literature;" Bithell, *op. cit., passim;* and Victor Lange, *Modern German Literature*, N.Y. 1945, pp. 6–50. Pantheon Books published the third volume of his *Selected Plays and Libretti* in 1963.

[33] Hofmannsthal, *op. cit.*, p. 289. See page 322 for the reference to Walther von der Vogelweide.

[34] H. A. Hammelmann, *Hugo von Hofmannsthal*, New Haven 1957.

[35] Herbert Foltinek, "Arthur Schnitzler in America," *Österreich und die angelsächsische Welt*, Wien 1961. See also Bithell, *op. cit., passim; Twentieth Century Authors*, N.Y. 1942; Richard Plant in *Germanic Review*, Feb. 1950, pp. 13ff. For the popularity of English translations of his works see B. Q. Morgan, *A Critical Bibliography of German Literature in English Translation*, 2nd ed., Stanford Univ. 1938.

[36] *Buch der Deutschen in Amerika*, Philadelphia 1909, p. 389.

[37] *Who's Who*, 1962–63.

[38] *Twentieth Century Authors*, N.Y. 1942, and Supp. I.

[39] *Who's Who*, 1962–63.

[40] Bernard Grun, *Prince of Vienna*, London 1955, p. 83; Bithell, *op. cit.*, pp. 333–34; L. Kronenberger, ed., *Best Plays 1960–61*, N.Y. 1961, p. 401. Vicki Baum came in 1931 to the U.S. In *Who's Who*, 1952–53, she gave 1896 as the date of her birth. *Who's Who in Austria,* 1954, gives 1888 as does Bithell.

[41] *Born Free* was 48 weeks on the best-seller list and its sequel 22 weeks or more. Mrs. Adamson lectured in the U.S. in 1962 and 1963. *Washington Post*, 13 Dec. 1962.

[42] Harry Warfel sketches him in *American Novelists of Today*, N.Y. 1951, p. 313, mentioning the influence of Schopenhauer and Nietzsche.

[43] *Book-of-the-Month-Club News*, Oct. 1958; *Who's Who*, 1962–63.

[44] Published in German 1923, in English 1928. Walt Disney made it even more famous in film. W. A. Jenks mentions the Lueger incident in *Vienna and the Young Hitler*, N.Y. 1960. *Wer ist Wer,* Wien 1937, has a sketch.

[45] Robert Rie's review in *Books Abroad*, Summer 1959, p. 327.

[46] For refugee authors see W. K. Pfeiler, *German Literature in Exile*, U. Neb. Press 1957; E. J. Görlich in *Österreich und die angelsächsische Welt*, pp. 197–98; *Books Abroad*, Apr. 1961, pp. 151–52.

[47] See Ginzkey's introduction to Jellinek, *Gesammelte Novellen*, Wien 1950.

[48] Bithell, *op. cit.*, p. 384; Lange, *op. cit.*, p. 111.

[49] H. W. Puckett, "Franz Werfel's Mission," *German Review*, Apr. 1947, pp. 117–24; Bithell, *op. cit., passim;* Alma Mahler Werfel, *And the Bridge is Love*, N.Y. 1958.

[50] *Ibid., passim;* Franz Werfel, *Das Lied von Bernadette*, Hamburg 1953, p. 8.

[51] Adapted by S. N. Behrman, 1944.

[52] Carl Zuckmayer, *Second Wind*, N.Y. 1940; *Who's Who*, 1952–53; *Twentieth Century Authors*, 1942, and Supp. 1955.

[53] *Twentieth Century Authors*, 1st Supp., p. 595.

[54] It was unfortunate that Haeussermann was a victim of the so-called McCarthy period when foreign-born and single men working for the U.S. Government were, like Haeussermann, so summarily dropped.

[55] *Wer ist Wer in Österreich*, Wien 1953; *Der Grosse Brockhaus*, 1952.

[56] *Who's Who of American Women*, 2nd ed., 1961.

[57] Warfel, *op. cit.*, p. 204.

[58] *Freiheit für Österreich*, N.Y., 1 Mar. 1943, p. 10; *Der Grosse Brockhaus*, 1952.

[59] *Ibid.;* Bithell, *op. cit.*, p. 229; *Columbia Dictionary of Modern European Literature*, N.Y. 1947, p. 63.

[60] *Books Abroad*, Winter 1959, p. 58; Spring 1961, p. 141.

[61] *Books Abroad*, Autumn 1962, review of Roden's *Amerika ist um mich her* (Wien 1961); article by Richard Flatter in *Wiener Zeitung*, 1951, Nr. 172.

[62] Quoted from Jacob Picard, "Ernst Waldinger," *Books Abroad*, Winter 1957. See also: *ibid*, Winter 1957, and Winter 1962, p. 36; Pfeiler, *op. cit.*, pp. 74f.; *American-German Review*, Aug.-Sept. 1961, p. 11; *Directory of American Scholars*, 3rd ed.

[63] *Who's Who*, 1952–53; Arthur Koestler, *Arrow in the Blue*, N.Y. 1961 (autobiographical); *Current Biography*, Jan. 1962, p. 18.

[64] W. B. Fleischmann, "New Look at Austrian Literature," *America*, CIII, 1960, pp. 644–47.

[65] A. Flores, ed., *Franz Kafka Today*, Madison 1958, p. 1.

[66] H. Steiner, ed., *German Stories*, p. 276.

[67] Johannes Urzidil, review of *Franz Kafka and Prague* by Eisner in *Germanic Review*, Apr. 1951, p. 164. See the various critical references to Kafka and his successors in Basil *et al*, *op. cit.*, which indicate that they belong in the mainstream of Austrian letters.

[68] Heinz Politzer, "Kafka's Letter," *Germanic Review*, Oct. 1953, p. 168.

[69] From Philip Rahv's introduction to *Selected Short Stories of Franz Kafka*, Modern Library, 1952, p. v i.

[70] *Columbia Dictionary of Modern European Literature*. See especially Fleischmann, *op. cit.*, p. 645, for Trakl's significance.

[71] Jethro Bithell, *Modern German Literature, 1880–1950*, London 1959, pp. 381, 452–53; *Book Review Digest*, 1947, p. 107, for comments on his biography of Kafka.

[72] Quoted in *Fiction Catalog 1960.*

[73] Summer 1958, p. 266.

[74] Bithell, *op. cit.*, pp. 502–03.

[75] Robert Breuer, "Hermann Broch," *American-German Review*, Dec.-Jan. 1956–57, pp. 12–13; *Twentieth Century Authors*, p. 197.

[76] *London Times Literary Supp.* 1957. Cf. *Die schönsten Erzählungen aus Österreich*, Wien 1958, p. 835; *New York Times Book Review*, 24 Sept. 1961, p. 4 ("von Doderer is the foremost novelist writing in German today"); *Saturday Review*, 23 Sept. 1961, which calls *The Demons* the most important translation from the German since Thomas Mann's *Felix Krull.*

[77] For a significant critique on Bachmann, Aichinger and a number of other young Austrian-born authors who are, for the most part, not writing in Austria and who are relatively unknown in America, see the article by Ernest S. Pisko, "Literary Voice of Austria," in *The Christian Science Monitor*, 20 April 1965, 2nd section. Aichinger's *Bound Man* and *Herod's Children* were published in English in 1956 and 1963, and Bachmann's *The Thirtieth Year* has appeared even more recently.

[78] It is interesting to note how many book titles by Austrian-born or Austrian-connected authors mentioned in this chapter were "in print" in English in the American book trade in 1965 (*Books in Print . . . 1965*, N.Y. 1965). These were presumably the books that were in 1965 being purchased upon the American market, that is, books that currently interested the American public. We give the names of the authors in order of birth, fully realizing that the date of birth, like the number of titles ascribed to each author, may have but little significance: Raimund, 1 title; Grillparzer, 10 titles; Sealsfield, 1 title; Grund, 1 title; Nestroy, no titles; Lenau, 1 title; Stifter, 1 title; Schnitzler, 1 title (several plays in anthologies); Broch, 2 titles; Salten, 2 titles; Hofmannsthal, 7 titles; Rilke, 21 titles; Musil, 2 titles; Zweig, 4 titles; Kafka, 14 titles; Brod, 2 titles; Trakl, 1 title; Baum, 1 title; Werfel, 2 titles; Zuckmayer, 7 titles; Doderer, 2 titles; Bemelmans, 16 titles; King, 7 titles; Kober, 1 title; Koestler, 12 titles; Wechsberg, 6 titles; Herold, 5 titles.

CHAPTER XX

AUSTRIANS IN MEDICINE

The American Medical Society of Vienna has, since its establishment in 1904, been one of America's unique footholds in the Old World. Closed by two world wars and reopened soon after each, it has enabled mature English-speaking medical men, chiefly but not solely from America, to take "busmen's holidays" at the famous old University of Vienna medical school. It organized university courses in the English language (even the Austrian professors who found it difficult to chat about politics in English found they could lecture in the medical English which they had read so long to keep up with their profession) and it gave certificates for as little as a month of medical work by the foreign visitors.

American doctors came not only to get a breathing spell away from the demands of years of practice at home, to drink Kremser wine with friends from home at the nearby Café Edison, and to revel in the ample supply of cadavers but, primarily, to get inspiration from the great teachers at one of Europe's finest medical schools.

From 1870 to 1914 when the war put an unhappy stop to it all, some two-thirds of all Americans who came to Central Europe to study medicine came to Vienna, a total of over ten thousand. The American Medical Society of Vienna assisted two or three hundred of them each year during the decade before 1914. Only Berlin, with less than a third as many American medical students, shared Vienna's lure.[1]

For Austria has probably contributed more to medicine than to any other science or art excepting only music. And its period of greatness in medicine has been the last century. Very few of the pioneers of medicine from early times known to Americans worked in the German Austrian lands. There was, to be sure, the great Paracelsus, born Theophrastus Bombastus von Hohenheim, in Switzerland about 1494, the son of Wilhelm Bombastus von Hohenheim, who was brought up in Villach in Carinthia and died in 1541 at his Salzburg home. He was an itinerant alchemist whose chemistry, colored by the weird chemical ideas of his time, led to the remarkably enlightened use of new medicines. He introduced the use of mercury, sulphur, opium, arsenic and iron as specific remedies and played down the old humoral theory of disease.[2]

The phrenology that the German Dr. Joseph Gall preached to receptive Vienna audiences about 1800[3] may have captured its American devotees but it also belongs to the era before Austrian medicine entered upon its period of greatness.

Typical of that new period was percussion-of-the-chest Johann Leopold Auenbrugger von Auenbrugg (b. Graz, 1722 – d. Vienna, 1809).[4] Auenbrugger belonged to what we call the Old Vienna School and will long be famous for his discovery, after tapping his innkeeper-father's wine barrels to discover from the sound how full they were, that tapping the human chest is also an invaluable method of diagnosis.

For decades American medicine had looked for leadership to Paris. Then, just before the middle of the nineteenth century that leadership shifted, especially in clinical medicine and in pathologic anatomy, to Vienna. It was the New Vienna School of Josef Skoda and of Carl Rokitansky, "the greatest pathological anatomist of his time,"[5] that brought scores of Americans to study, in the second half of the nineteenth century, at the Vienna medical school.

There they found a growing appreciation for the great martyr, Ignaz Philipp Semmelweis (b. Buda, Hungary, 1818 – d. Döbling near Vienna, 1865), whose introduction of hand-washing with chlorine solutions at childbirth was one of the world's greatest contributions to infant survival. Clendening surmises that Semmelweis died of disappointment because his Vienna colleagues were so slow to accept the discoveries for which he is now renowned throughout the world.[6] The Americans found there Max Nitze whose cystoscope was the basic instrument in the development of urology,[7] and Theodor Billroth (b. Bergen, Rügen, Germany, 1829 – d. Abbazia, 1894), Vienna's famous surgeon whose excision of the thyroid gland was violently debated by the American school,[8] and Holzknecht and Haudek who learned how to X-ray the stomach,[9] and the Viennese pediatrist Clemens Freiherr von Pirquet (b. Hirschstetten, Lower Austria, 1874 – d. Vienna, 1929) who discovered the science of allergy. Pirquet taught at the Johns Hopkins University from 1908 to 1910 and he was the first president, in 1926, of the Austro-American Institute of Education that has ever since worked quietly but effectively to introduce things American to Austrian young people.[10] Another visitor to America was the world-famous cardiologist Karel Frederik Wenckebach. Born in Holland, he spent the last twenty-six years of his life at the University of Vienna, endearing himself to his adopted country by his valiant work among Viennese children after the malnutrition of World War I had left them in desperate straits. Wenckebach was one of the half dozen Austrian physicians (with Koller, Landsteiner, Pirquet, Pichler, and Freud) listed as visitors to the United States among the four or five dozen Austrian medical immortals who received places in a recent official volume on Austrian physicians who served mankind.[11]

Those were only a few of the great Austrian names in medicine that contributed to medical science in America and helped make Vienna a Mecca for American medical men.

Of the Austrian and near-Austrian Nobel laureates in medicine, two never came to the United States: Robert Bárány (b. Vienna, 1876 – d. Uppsala, 1936), who received the 1914 prize through diplomatic channels while he was in 1915 a Russian prisoner of war, and Julius Wagner von Jauregg (b. Wels, 1857 – d. Vienna, 1940) the famous neurologist who taught from 1893 to 1928 at the University of Vienna and received his Nobel award in 1927.[12] The other Austrian Nobel laureates in medicine became Austro-Americans.

Karl Landsteiner (b. Vienna, 1868 – d. New York, 1943) who was over fifty before he left Vienna spent his American career with the Rockefeller Institute. While working there in 1930 he received the Nobel Prize for the best-known of his several significant achievements, the discovery of the blood types. That made blood transfusions safe for the first time in medical history.[13]

Six years later Otto Loewi and an Englishmen named Dale received the award for their "medical-physiological discoveries relating to the chemical transmission of nerve impulses." Loewi was German-born (1873) but he had come to Vienna as a young man, was still teaching in Austria some thirty years later, at Graz, when he received the Nobel award, was purged by the Nazis, and came to work as research professor at New York University.[14] And Karl and Gerty Cori, both born in Prague in 1896, took their joint award in 1947 for research in enzymes while they were at Washington University in St. Louis. They had met as young researchers at the German University of Prague and had spent a couple of years at work in Vienna before they came on, in the early twenties, to the United States.[15] The Cori award reaped a deal of publicity because the man-and-wife team was reminiscent of the Curie history.

That most exciting of all tiresome reference works, "American Men of Science," fairly bristles with dry-as-dust accounts of scientists born or educated in Vienna who have found their way to America. The explorer seeking for Austrian evidence stumbles upon it so often that, in sheer funk, he discards item after item, doubtless retaining as illustrative of his theme many of the lesser exhibits and overlooking those that, any competent scientist would tell him, should not be overlooked.

Fortunately or unfortunately, the student of Austrian medical impacts a century or more ago had relatively little to discuss. The learned medical men among the refugees of 1848 were chiefly from Germany. But some were Austrian or came by way of Austria. Judging by Dr. Joseph Goldmark's frank comments about the sad state of medicine in America they did not come because of anything like American leadership in the field. Goldmark, a Jewish veteran of the Vienna barricades of '48, found it only too easy to compete with the shoddy American physicians of the 1850's and to achieve quite a reputation as an inventor and creator of items that helped the Union to win the Civil War.[16] And Dr. Hermann Kiefer, a German student at the University of Vienna, became more than prominent in Detroit.[17]

There were a few other Forty-eighters: Dr. Ernst Krackowitzer, the pathologist who helped build the Bellevue Hospital Medical College and achieved a bit of fame in 1858 by using a laryngoscope to demonstrate the vocal cords,[18] and Dr. Hans Kudlich, the famous *Bauernbefreier*, or liberator of Austria's peasants from the final remnants of serfdom, whose flight from Habsburg tyranny finally led him, after an effort to stir up revolution in the Tyrol from the safety of Switzerland to refuge and to what was apparently a lucrative medical practice in German-infiltrated Hoboken, across the river from New York.[19]

Dr. Simon Pollak who founded in 1838 at St. Louis the first eye and ear clinic west of the Mississippi was Bohemian-born[20] but Dr. Eduard Schauffler (b. 1839) who helped found the Kansas City Medical College was Viennese by birth.[21]

There were other ground-breaking Austrian physicians in the United States before World War I. Karl Koller (b. Schüttenhofen, Bohemia, 1857 – d. New York, 1944) was the father of local anesthetics in medicine. As a young doctor in Vienna he became interested in Sigmund Freud's use of cocaine in cases of nervous disease. Koller, an ophthalmologist, found in 1884 that a few drops of cocaine in the eye made it insensitive to pain during operations. Other surgeons followed his example in working elsewhere on the body and mankind had taken a long step toward painless surgery. Koller emigrated to New York in 1888 and was for many years a successful surgeon at its Mt. Sinai and other hospitals.[22] Freud never forgave Koller for claiming so much credit for the new use of cocaine.

Another great name was that of Joseph Goldberger (1874–1929), an Austrian Jew who came to New York at the age of six with his grocer father, learned his medicine there, and went to work on tropical and other diseases for the U.S. Public Health Service. It was his later discovery of the cure for pellagra that was his epoch-making contribution. Long a menace in Latin Europe, pellagra had invaded the American South with tragic effect. Goldberger was assigned the pellagra problem, he experimented for years on its victims and, despite the indifference and scepticism of his fellows, finally drove home the truth that pellagra was the result of unbalanced diet. It could be prevented by nothing more subtle than fresh meat and fresh milk. He had only to observe that babies and nurses who ate plenty of fresh meat were not dying of pellagra like the poor folk who lived on corn and salt pork. The result was the practical elimination of the dreaded disease.[23]

Still another notable physician was Harry Cohen (b. Austria, 1885) who was brought to New York in infancy, received his M.D. at Cornell, took literally dozens of high foreign and American awards, and was known for several inventions, especially for the invention of the clamp tourniquet.[24] And there were others who came as children with their parents like Max Joseph Exner (b. Austria, 1871 – d. 1943) in public health and hygiene and Louis Israel Harris (b. 1882) who became in 1926–1928 New York City's Commissioner of Health.[25] Paul Klepper (b. Vienna, 1888 – d. New York, 1964), a student of Freud, migrated in 1921 and became the chief of pathology at New York's Mt. Sinai Hospital.

It is difficult to generalize about these medical new-comers in the early years before the German-Austrian invasion of the Nazi period reached its peak. It is obvious that the early outbreaks of anti-Semitism in the era of von Schönerer in Vienna brought many fine physicians, like the orthopedist Arthur Steindler (b. Vienna, 1878) to

America — in 1907 in Steindler's case.[26] There were dozens of others like Cohen and Harris and Goldberger who had Jewish blood in their veins as well as Catholics who came because of the opportunities that America had to offer. The prestige of Vienna medicine helped them find first-rate openings here.

Geographically they were attracted to New York but many were drawn to other cities all over the East and Middle West by calls to good positions. Steindler went to Iowa; the Catholic Carl Beck (b. near Prague, 1864) wrote "born Austria" in "Who's Who", 1938—39) went to the University of Illinois and to Chicago to practice and to found the St. Anthony Hospital.[27] The anatomist Eduard Uhlenhuth (b. Wolkersdorf, Lower Austria, 1885) who immigrated in 1914 found a fine long career in Baltimore[28] and Hiram Bernard Benjamin (b. Austria, 1901, and emigrated 1916) worked chiefly in and around Milwaukee.[29]

Virtually all of these Austro-American physicians took American citizenship, not as promptly as during the Hitler years but with ever increasing promptness. The dermatologist Ida Jessica Mintzer of New York, for instance, immigrated in 1900 and was naturalized in 1916, Eduard Uhlenhuth and Hiram Benjamin who arrived in 1914 took ten and eleven years to take citizenship, and William Maxwell Hitzig (b. Austria, 1904), the internist who practiced in New York and was cited for conspicuous service to Columbia University,[30] was naturalized in twelve years after his arrival. The closing gap was illustrated by the ophthalmologist Peter Clemens Kronfeld (b. Vienna, 1899) of Chicago, Peking, and the University of Illinois, and the Middle Westerner Emmerich von Haam (b. Vienna, 1903), recipient of the gold medal of the American Society of Chemical Pathologists, who took citizenship in the minimum five years just as the Brown Shirts were coming into their own across the German border.[31] American attitudes towards "hyphenated Americans" during World War I doubtless helped also to speed up the naturalization process.

The famous Schick test for determining susceptibility to diphtheria was the discovery of an Austro-Hungarian, Béla Schick (b. Boglár, Hungary, 1877—d. Mount Sinai Hospital, 1967). His parents lived in Austria and Béla took his medical work at the University of Graz, taught for over twenty years at the University of Vienna, and came to the United States in 1923 to work at Mt. Sinai Hospital and Columbia University. But it was at Vienna in 1913 that he developed his well-known test. Schick was a pediatrician and his 1933 book on child care became a standard authority in his adopted country.[32]

Always cosmopolitan in its outlook, Vienna was not only a veritable exchange center for medical genius — Germans who took professorships there and Austrians who made their reputations there and then went on to Germany or America — but Vienna was also a center for the unity-of-science movement. Its scientists, like its philosophers, with hardly a trace of the nationalism that plagued so much of the

Western world in the pre-Hitler years, were convinced that scientists should coordinate their work without regard to national boundaries. Berlin scientists joined them and the result, in the immediate pre-Hitler years, was the International Institute for the Unity of Science. It was founded in 1936 after numerous Vienna-Berlin conferences. And America, not always international in its cultural interests, welcomed the fifth congress of the Institute at Harvard in 1939.[33] It was doubtless unfortunate that there was by 1939 no internationalist Austria to further the good cause.

Austrian medical schools were among the first to welcome women to their profession. There was in consequence quite a group of Austrian-born women physicians in the United States before the second World War. There were, among the distinguished ones, Olga Knopf of New York in the area of women's problems, Bertha Anna Klein of Chicago who won a gold medal from the American Medical Association, Ella Langer of the Maine Department of Health and Welfare, and Margarethe W. Poe, the New York dentist.[34]

Most of these Austrian-born ladies turned to the more lady-like phases of their profession: pediatrics or women's ailments or nutrition or the like. Somewhat typical was Ann Williams-Heller (b. Vienna, 1904) of New York whose Vienna-Zurich-Columbia education led her into a fascinating career giving nutritional advice on radio and television, to the United States government and newspaper readers, and via the press with a whole series of books including "Soybeans from Soup to Nuts" (1944) and the "Reducer's Cook Book" (1950).[35] Sidonie Matsner Gruenberg (b. 1881), educated at Hamburg and New York rather than in her homeland and versed in the problems of children, became in 1947 chairman of the National Council on Parent Education.[36]

Even since the war we have had lady new-comers from Austria like Elisabeth Friedl Turnauer (b. Vienna, 1926) and Margarete Elizabeth Hanson (b. Austria, 1913) in pediatrics (Dr. Hanson became one of the rare Austrian Presbyterians), and Emma Irene Jacoby from the *Wilhelminen Spital* in Vienna and seven years in China, Evelyn Madeleine Strange (b. Vienna, 1927) the children's dentist of Portland, Oregon, and Else Pappenheim (b. Salzburg, 1911) who taught at Yale University and Hunter College.

During the Nazi period, however, the Austrian lady physicians had come in amazing numbers. Most of them had been born in the Habsburg capital and had taken their M.D.'s at its university even though they may later have studied elsewhere in Central Europe and here in the United States. Some, but a relatively small proportion, found their American refuge in Jewish hospitals. That was natural when American Jews were doing so much for the Jewish refugees. And a goodly proportion of them, in private practice as well as in hospital work and public service, made their homes beyond New York City. They were well scattered. There seemed to be no Austro-American enclaves to welcome them.[37]

It is doubtless a bit easier for the males in medicine than for the females to achieve fame. In the case of the Austrians, Dr. Adolf Lorenz, the "healer of crippled children" whose visits to New York in the 1930's "reminded us that Vienna was still the center of great medical minds,"[38] won more fame in this country than most American physicians. He was the "bloodless surgeon" whose correction of children's deformities, such as club foot, by manipulation aroused controversy but who was sought out, here and in Vienna, by scores of Americans who had faith in his cures. One of his disciples who has also been well known on both continents was Dr. Lorenz Böhler (b. Vorarlberg, 1885), the noted accident surgeon, who has worked at the Mayo Clinic at Rochester, Minnesota, and has served as director of Vienna's Emergency Hospital.[39]

Another quiet Austrian who had a bit of fame thrust upon him in 1962 was Dr. Hans Kraus (b. Trieste, 1905), President Kennedy's medical adviser from New York whose treatment of the President put an end to much of the talk about overweight and rocking chairs for the President's sensitive spine. Kraus, like so many Austrians, had built his practice in generous part upon skiing and mountain climbing. He had served as physician to some of Austria's fine ski teams in the Olympics. He was a Vienna product who had come to New York University during the Hitler period and had been persuaded in 1961 to visit Washington regularly to start a program of physical rehabilitation for the President.[40]

Like the women doctors among the fine crop of Thirty-eighters, the men found their opportunities principally in the Northeast and the Middle West. And the great majority of them were Viennese or products of the medical faculty of the University of Vienna. There were some, like Dr. Eugen Grabscheid of Baden bei Wien (b. Austrian Galicia, 1903) who had settled in New York's German colony of Yorkville and married an American, who was not only appointed to a significant professorial chair at the Harlem Eye and Ear Hospital but who also did extremely well in private practice. There were others like Ernst Loewenstein (b. Czechoslovakia; 1920–38 professor of pathology at the University of Vienna and director of the Vienna Serum Laboratory) who brought tremendous reputations for research with them when they immigrated. Dr. Loewenstein had in 1909 discovered chemical methods for rendering toxins non-toxic, for immunization against diphtheria and tuberculosis in childhood, and his work had practically eliminated tuberculosis in Vienna. He immigrated in 1938 and settled a little later in San Francisco,[41] too little known and too little recognized.

That so many of the Austrian-born were welcomed by scores of America's best hospitals and laboratories was evidence of their competence. Some doubtless found refuge in such institutions when they firsc arrived in this country and before they could qualify to practice. But many of them, even after they had acquired practices of their own, retained their positions as hospital physicians and consultants or as distinguished directors of research. The ophthalmologist Dr. Paul Muller, for instance, born (1899) and educated in Vienna, combined work at a Harlem Eye and Ear Hospital and at the Suffolk Hospital with a private practice. Dr. Max Wachstein (b. Vienna, 1905; immigrated 1939), a pathologist, directed laboratories in Passaic, New Jersey, and Brooklyn, New York. The obstetrician and gynecologist Dr. Bernard Berglas (M.D. Vienna, 1925) found a career at Mt. Sinai Hospital in New York. And Dr. Hans Kaunitz (b. Vienna, 1905) has served at Columbia University as resident associate in pathology since 1941.[42] Indeed, there are so many such names in the medical directories that one wonders why there was no shortage of medical men back in Austria.

There were a great many of the Austrian Thirty-eighters who came, not only to practice medicine as soon as they could qualify under American regulations, but to teach it. For instance, Joseph Warkany (b. Vienna, 1902), the pediatrician who came to the Cincinnati Children's Hospital back in 1934, taught for a long generation at the University of Cincinnatti.[43] Dr. Ernst Peter Pick (b. Bohemia, 1877), who had taught pharmacology at the University of Vienna for almost thirty-five years, came to Columbia in 1938 as Clinical Professor of Pharmacology,[44] Professor Leo Hess of the University of Vienna came to Massachusetts in 1939 to teach at Brandeis University's School of Medicine,[45] and the Vienna surgeon Joseph Pick (b. Vienna, 1908) came to New York University in 1938 to make there a distinguished career for himself.[46] Paul Liebesny, a veteran of almost sixty when he emigrated after years of distinguished work in physiotherapy at Vienna's Cottage Sanatorium (a most comfortable U.S. Army hotel during the occupation period to 1955), remained active for many more years at the Bronx Hospital.[47] Ludwig von Sallmann (b. Vienna, 1892) the ophthalmologist also worked in New York before he went to the National Institutes of Health in Washington,[48] and Emil Froeschels (b. Vienna), president of the New York Society for Speech and Voice Therapy, worked at Washington University in St. Louis before he came to New York's Mt. Sinai Hospital.[49]

Almost all of those men, refugees of the National Socialist era or later comers were teachers as well as researchers. There was Professor William Hans Bauer (b. Prague, 1889) long of the University of Innsbruck who taught for years at St. Louis, Kurt Stern (b. Vienna, 1909) who worked in New York and after 1949 at the Chicago Medical School, and Wilhelm Raab (b. Vienna, 1895), possessor of two Austrian medals for bravery in war, at the University of Vermont.[50] The pediatrician Richard Wagner (b. Vienna, 1887) taught for long years at Tufts University. The pathologist Dr. Paul Klemperer, who had turned from law to medicine in his student days in Vienna, taught at Columbia while he conducted Mt. Sinai Hospital's pathological section. Cornell, Columbia, and New York University all profited from the teaching of Dr. Frederick Reiss (b. Edelsthal, 1891), a tropical dermatologist who, long before National Socialism, had found a useful career in Shanghai.[51]

Columbia University seems to have had a lion's share of the useful Austrians – men like Professor Zacharias Dische (b. Sambor, Austrian Galicia, 1895; M.D. Vienna, 1921) in biochemistry, Professor Franz Altmann (b. Vienna, 1901) in the diseases of the ear, nose and throat, and Professor George W. Hindels (b. Austria, 1914) in dentistry. But other New York schools like the New York College of Medicine attracted a goodly number. The New York College of Medicine, for instance, had among others Professor Paul Freud (b. Vienna, 1894) in pediatrics, Dr. David Scherf (b. Austria, 1899), a professor for clinical medicine, who was a vice president of the American College of Cardiology, Dr. David Lehr (b. Bukowina, 1910), professor of physiology and pharmacology who was a product of the University of Vienna, and Dr. Werner Kornfeld (b. Vienna, 1892; M.D. Vienna, 1924) in pediatrics. There was far less concentration outside of New York although Austria has been rather well represented in Chicago and notable figures, like Professor Robert Tauber (b. Vienna, 1893), professor of obstetrics and gynecology at Pennsylvania's Graduate School of Medicine, have found significant positions in schools well scattered throughout the country.

There were scores of other Austrian men and women of medicine who, in spite of the restrictions upon medical practice in the United States, managed to work their way into the profession. And there were many medical students who came to study and serve as interns in American hospitals who found a way to stay on and make their careers here. Austria's medical schools were, as a matter of fact, producing more physicians than the country needed. American medical schools were producing too few. The resultant transfer of medical talent across the sea was a fortunate development for both countries. American doctors who generally resented the importation of foreigners were quick to observe that the Austrians were "good ones" and were always glad to see them come over.

The significance of Austrian medical emigration to one American university is underscored by a message to the New York Medical Circle from the Dean of Columbia University's College of Physicians and Surgeons in 1961. It is read in part:[52]

"The medical profession of New York and the College of Physicians and Surgeons, in particular, has been greatly enriched by the contributions of a large number of Austrian physicians who have elected to make this country their home. Among those who have served our University are Drs. David Adlersberg, formerly Assistant Clinical Professor of Medicine (deceased); Franz Altmann, Clinical Professor of Otolaryngology; Frederick Blodi, formerly Research Worker in the Department of Ophthalmology, Erwin Chargaff, Professor of Biochemistry, Bernhard Dattner, formerly Assistant Clinical Professor of Neurology (deceased); Zachorias (sic) Dische, Professor of Biochemistry, assigned to Ophthalmology, Gabriele Ehrlich, Research Worker in the Department of Ophthalmology; Marcel Goldenberg, formerly Assistant Professor of Medicine (deceased); Alexander B. Gutman, Professor of Medicine; Hans Hoff, formerly Assistant Professor of Neurology; Hans Kaunitz, Research Associate in Pathology; Hans Popper, Professor of Pathology; Ludwig von Sallmann, formerly Professor of Ophthalmology; Alfred Schick, Associate in Psychiatry; Gerhart S. Schwarz, Assistant Professor of Radiology; Maximilian Silbermann, Assistant Clinical Professor of Neurology; Ludwig V. Chiavacci, formerly Assistant Researcher in Neurology; Hans Smetana, formerly Assistant Professor of Pathology, Herbert C. Stoerk, formerly Instructor in Pathology, Paul Wermer, Assistant Clinical Professor of Medicine and Paul Loewy, Assistant Neurologist, Presbyterian Hospital (deceased).

"It would take a large volume to enumerate the contributions of these men to medicine, particularly during their years in this country. Many of their contributions have been of fundamental importance and have helped to elevate American medicine to its high level of excellence."

[1] L. H. Rogers, "Medical Memories of Berlin and Vienna," *American-German Review*, Oct.-Nov. 1959, explains how the Vienna experience in 1908 "enriched the life" of one American doctor. For recent announcements see *Austrian Information*, 18 March 1961 and 15 June 1962. Our statistics are taken from Thomas Neville Bonner, *American Doctors and German Universities*, U. Neb. Press, 1963.

[2] A. V. Howard, *Chambers' Dictionary of Scientists*, London 1961, pp. 346–47; Österreichische Akademie der Wissenschaften, *Österreichische Naturforscher, Ärzte und Techniker*, Wien 1957.

[3] George Godwin, *Criminal Man*, N.Y. 1957, pp. 4–5. Gall studied and worked in Vienna before objections by the authorities sent him on to Paris. Mesmer's experience was somewhat similar. Cf. our chapter on science.

[4] Constant v. Wurzbach, *Biographisches Lexikon des Kaiserthums Oesterreich*, 60 parts, Wien 1856–91, I, p. 85, gives the two possible dates of his death. Erwin H. Ackerknecht, *Short History of Medicine*, N.Y. 1955, gives 1809 as the date of death.

[5] Richard H. Shryock, *American Medical Research*, N.Y. 1947, p. 50; Ackerknecht, *op. cit.*, pp. 141–42.

[6] Logan Clendening, *Behind the Doctor*, N.Y. 1933, p. 331.

[7] Ackerknecht, *op. cit.*, p. 185.

[8] Jürgen Thorwald, *Triumph of Surgery*, N.Y. 1959, pp. 49ff. Thorwald states that Billroth taught Dr. J. B. Murphy of Chicago who became famous for his removals of the appendix. Billroth worked in Vienna from 1867 on.

[9] Clendening, *op. cit.*, p. 419.

[10] *Bulletin*, Austro-American Institute of Education, Oct. 1962; *Der Grosse Brockhaus*, vol. IX, Wiesbaden 1956.

[11] *Österreichische Ärzte als Helfer der Menschheit*, Wien 1957.

[12] L. G. Stevenson, *Nobel Prize Winners in Medicine and Physiology*, N.Y. 1953.

[13] *Ibid.*, pp. 143–44.

[14] *Ibid.*, p. 186; *Universal Jewish Encyclopedia*, N.Y. 1942.

[15] Stevenson, *op. cit.*, pp. 248–49; *American Men of Science*, 9th ed., vol. II, N.Y. 1955. Carl Cori's father was a biologist stationed in Trieste. The Coris shared the Nobel Prize with an Argentine.

[16] Carl Wittke, *We Who Built America*, N.Y. 1945, p. 346.

[17] Carl Wittke, *Refugees of Revolution*, Philadelphia 1952, ch. 21.

[18] *Ibid.*, p. 333; H. L. Golden, *Jews in American History*, Charlotte 1950, p. 398.

[19] Wurzbach, *op. cit.*, XIII, p. 301; W. Schlag's article in *Österreich und die angelsächsische Welt*, Wien 1961.

[20] Golden, *op. cit.*, p. 398.

[21] *Das Buch der Deutschen in Amerika*, Philadelphia 1907, pp. 336–37.

[22] Ackerknecht, *op. cit.*, p. 177; Thorwald, *op. cit.*, *passim.*; *Who's Who*, 1938–39.

[23] Paul de Kruif, *Hunger Fighters*, N.Y. 1928, pp. 335ff.; *Dictionary of American Biography*. Goldberger died in Washington.

[24] *Who's Who*, 1952–53.

[25] *Who's Who*, 1938–39.

[26] *Ibid.; American Men of Science*, 9th ed., II.

[27] *Who's Who*, 1938–39.

[28] *American Men of Science*, 9th ed., II.

[29] *Ibid.*

[30] *Who's Who*, 1962–63.

[31] *Ibid.*

[32] Emil Lengyel, *Americans from Hungary*, Philadelphia and N.Y., 1948, pp. 238–39, states that Schick did not regard himself as a Hungarian. See also *American Men of Science*, 10th ed., and Golden, *op. cit.*

[33] Shryock, *op. cit.*, p. 253.

[34] All are mentioned in *Who's Who of American Women*, 2nd ed., 1961.

[35] *Ibid.*

[36] *Who's Who*, 1962–63.

[37] *Who's Who of American Women*, 2nd ed., lists Hedwig Fischer, Viennese dermatologist in Syracuse; Marianne Wallis (b. 1899), radiologist with U.S.A.F. in North Dakota; Ann L. Pollock (b. 1901), owner of her own Medical Literary Service; Gusta Davidsohn (b. Tarnopol, 1902), a Vienna M.D. at Chicago's Mt. Sinai Hospital; Emma Nuschl Plank (b. 1905) in child development at Western Reserve University; Stella Kohn Saslow (b. Bukowina, 1909) who brought a Vienna M.D. to her practice in New Jersey; Renée K. Imberman (b. 1910) with the N.Y.C. school system; Helene D. Mayer (Ph. D. Vienna, M.D. Basel), in anesthesiology in New York; Gertrude Slater (b. 1911), pediatrician in Stamford, Conn.; Renée Zindwer (b. 1913) with the New Jersey Health Department; Katherine Herschmann (b. 1914), pediatrician in Philadelphia; Ernestine Rosner Rosenberg (b. Austria) in practice at Bridgeport, Conn.; and Maria Weissenberg Barrows (b. 1925), pathologist at San Francisco's St. Joseph's Hospital. All were born in Vienna unless otherwise noted. Vienna-trained women who did not give "Austria" as the place of birth have not been included in this listing.

[38] Rachael Du Bois, *Germans in American Life*, N.Y., 1936, p. 117. See also his obituaries in *N.Y. Times*, 18 Feb. 1946, p. 21; *Time*, 25 Feb. 1946, p. 66; *Newsweek*, 25 Feb. 1946, p. 58. Lorenz (1854–1946) was born in Austrian Silesia, died in Vienna.

[39] *Who's Who in Austria*, 1959–60.

[40] *Directory of Medical Specialists*, Chicago 1961, p. 1073; *Washington Post*, 19 July 1962, p. A2.

[41] *Universal Jewish Encyclopedia*, VII, p. 164.

[42] For short biographies of these and other Austro-American medical personalities see *American Men of Science*, 9th ed., II, the *Directory of Medical Specialists*, and *Who's Who in World Jewry*.

[43] *Who's Who*, 1962–63.

[44] *American Men of Science*, 9th ed., II.

[45] *Ibid.* Ackerknecht, *op. cit.*, p. 221, describes Hess's work of 1910 on endocrine glands.

[46] *Ibid.*

[47] Austrian American Federation, *Österreichische Nachrichten*, Dec. 1962. He died at Washington in 1962.

[48] *Who's Who*, 1962–63.

[49] *Austrian Information*, 30 June 1961.

[50] *American Men of Science*, 9th ed., II, for Bauer, Stern, and Raab.

[51] *Who's Who*, 1962–63; *Who's Who in Austria*, 1959–60.

[52] Quoted from *Austrian Information*, 18 March 1961.

CHAPTER XXI

MENTAL HEALERS

"The concepts which Sigmund Freud . . . built into a mighty ideological superstructure have placed him," according to an American writer on mental health, "in the category of Darwin, Mohammed, Marx and others who have changed the thinking of their times."[1] Although Freud made only one brief, unheralded visit to our shores, his influence here was, and remains, far more important than that of any other Austrian. Indeed, his depth psychology ranks with music as one of Austria's two tremendous contributions to the modern world.

The heavy impact of Freudianism has not been confined to the doctor's office. It has upset our thinking in dozens of fields such as medicine, literature, philosophy, psychology, the various branches of sociology, social work and even in anthropology. And it has revolutionized most of them.

The other Austrians who have been most significant to us in the long struggle to treat the mentally ill with compassion and not as incurable criminals and rogues have, like Freud, seldom visited this country. Unlike Freud's world-rocking concepts, their discoveries have been more narrowly confined to the field of mental therapy—care of the insane and the mentally ill. Only in 1938 did the Austrian-born practitioners of the mind begin to come to America.

The pioneer in psychotherapy whose advocates in America included Washington, Jefferson, Lafayette, and Mary Baker Eddy, was the German-born Viennese, Franz Anton Mesmer (b. Znang on Lake Constance, 1734—d. Meersburg, 1815). His "animal magnetism" with all the ritual that Mesmer employed in making his cures may well have been only the application of the power of suggestion. But from the time that he healed a young friend of Mozart's in Vienna in 1774 he achieved some remarkable successes.

A University of Vienna graduate with a rich wife and all the social graces, Mesmer was a popular figure until the Vienna medical profession discovered only quackery in his amazing cures. So he went on to Paris, achieved first fame there and then the same hostility he had encountered in Vienna. The committee that the French academies created to investigate him included Benjamin Franklin and, ominously, Dr. Guillotin. Franklin and his confederates pronounced him a godless quack and that sent him back to Vienna. But his ideas spread. Jefferson realized their importance and Lafayette, who had studied with him and had himself performed an astounding cure or two, converted his friend Washington to the cause. Mesmerism might lead to some follies in the years to come but it is now generally recognized as the true forerunner of psychology.[2]

It was years after Mesmer that the Vienna medical faculty achieved greatness. And it was seldom strong in mental therapy. Yet any American historian of the medical arts finds himself compelled to mention Richard Freiherr von Krafft-Ebing (b. Mannheim, 1840 – d. Graz, 1902) who came to Graz in his early thirties and became a world-famous neurologist. His "Psychopathia sexualis" and the much denounced attack upon the Fair Sex, "Geschlecht und Charakter" by the young Otto Weininger, were, according to Farau, the two epoch-making Austrian works on sex at the time that America and Britain were reading the sex studies of Havelock Ellis. Krafft-Ebing was for years associated with the University of Vienna.[3]

Thousands of America's victims of syphilis were still being cured in recent years by the methods of Austria's great neurologist, Julius von Wagner-Jauregg (b. Wels, Upper Austria, 1857 – d. Vienna, 1940). In 1887 he proposed the treatment of paresis (produced by venereal disease) with artificially induced diseases such as malaria, and years later in 1927 he received the Nobel Prize for his epoch-making work. His methods are now largely superceded by penicillin treatment but they were, for generations, of tremendous importance. His work on the prevention of goiter was revolutionary. Wagner-Jauregg, a graduate of the University of Vienna Medical Faculty, taught four years at Graz and then returned to Vienna. There he worked with Freud in the neurological section of the Vienna hospital.[4] His son Theodor (b. Vienna, 1903), who came in 1948 to the United States Army Medical Corps, was a chemist who worked especially on the chemotherapy of leprosy and tuberculosis.[5]

Julius von Wagner-Jauregg was one of the pioneers of neurology, a younger sister of psychiatry that flourished in Austria and produced men like Otto Marburg (b. Römerstadt, Moravia, 1874 – d. New York, 1948) and Paul Ferdinand Schilder (b. Vienna – d. New York, 1940) who worked in New York as well as in Vienna.[6] By comparison with Freudian psychoanalysis (*Tiefenpsychologie*, to use the best German term), neurology was in Freud's time a respectable art.

Freudianism, like so many of the accomplishments of talented Austrians, was scarcely respectable in Austria for many years after its formulation. Indeed, its tremendous concern with sex and its materialistic conception of the mind that seemed to detract from the dignity of mankind rendered it unpopular throughout the entire western world during much of Freud's own lifetime. It was first accepted and became extremely important in America rather than in its place of birth. Austria has long had a habit of proving that prophets are without honor in their own lands.

Freud's theory of the unconscious, wrote one American historian, was part of the "major shift in thought" between the nineteenth and twentieth centuries.[7] And an American critic,[8] in describing the revolutionary character of changes in man's thinking about himself, declared that: "Three such revolutions have occurred in

Western thought in the past five hundred years — the Copernican, the Darwinian, and the Freudian . . . Copernicus dethroned man from the center of the universe. Darwin challenged his sense of divinity . . . And Sigmund Freud, the first cartographer of the unconscious, . . . profoundly troubled the sleep of mankind!" "The impact of this revolution has been incalculably great in the United States."

The author of "The Interpretation of Dreams" was born in Freiberg, Moravia, just over the border of what is now Czechoslovakia, in 1856. He was brought to Vienna at the age of four, entered Vienna's University in his teens, and lectured there as a young man, on nervous diseases. His rise to fame, his development of psychoanalysis, his battles over the important place he ascribed to sex, and his collaboration with Joseph Breuer[9] and his even more famous disciples make a long and often pathetic story. Clark University at Worcester, Massachusetts, was ironically enough the only university on any continent that ever gave Sigmund Freud an honorary degree.[10]

For Freud had visited America in 1909 and had given a few lectures. William James, who attended Clark University's anniversary to see what this controversial foreigner was like said "Bah!" For Freud had criticized American religious therapy.[11] America had not impressed him and our food had made him more than uncomfortable. But the president of Clark, G. Stanley Hall, became the first president of the new American Psychopathologic Association and Freud was to watch with delight the growth of Freudianism in the United States. Even the entertainment world soon fell a victim to Freud. The first program of the Provincetown Players offered a Freudian piece called "Suppressed Desires" in 1915 and Eugene O'Neill's fine tragedies all showed Freud's intriguing influence.[12] That was only the beginning of America's Freudian revolution.

American physicians came to Vienna to listen to Freud in German or in his bad English. And long before the Hitler persecution brought so many of his followers to American shores, psychoanalysis had become a very significant phenomenon in the United States. Our concern for the aging Freud was reflected by President Roosevelt when he persuaded the Nazis to allow the Jewish author of so many doctrines that Hitler found degenerate to leave the Gestapo jail in Vienna and pass his final sad days in London.[13] He died in 1939.

Freud and his followers gave America a new vocabulary, terms like "complex," "mother fixation," "wishful thinking," and "suppressed desires," that came for the most part even before the great immigration of psychoanalysts in Hitler times.

There were, to be sure, Freudians in America before that immigration: Men like G. Stanley Hall of Clark University and Adolph Stern (b. Eger, 1878) who had come to New York in his youth and was long president of the New York Psychoanalytic Society.[14] A. A. Brill (Abraham Arden Brill, b. Austria, 1874 — d. New York, 1947)[15] was a Columbia professor who did more, perhaps, than any other American to interpret his friend Freud to America through writing, lecturing, and the translation of Freud's writings. The Austrian psychoanalyst Dorian Feigenbaum, another friend of the great master, founded here in 1932 the "Psychoanalytic Quarterly."[16] And Dr. Heinz Werner (b. Vienna, c. 1890 – d. Worcester, Mass., 1964) taught psychology for thirteen years at Clark which Freud had visited a long generation earlier and established there the university's Institute of Human Development.

Psychiatry in America was nothing before Freud in comparison with what it became later after Freud's disciples invaded America in platoons and companies and regiments. Those disciples – psychologists, psychiatrists, psychoanalysts – came by the hundreds in the Hitler years. They reinforced the weak, native, American movement toward psychoanalysis. They provided the stereotype for the bewhiskered, foreign-born, Freudian psychoanalyst. They encouraged the new Freudian interpretations in drama, biography, fiction, and almost every branch of literature. What they brought with them was, indeed, an intellectual revolution. They replaced behaviorism that had so dominated the American scene and they challenged Logical Positivism that America had imported from Vienna itself.

For instance, Paul Federn, who was called the Nestor of the Austrians of Freud's intimate circle, who died in New York in 1950, came to add his prestige to the movement.[17] Peter B. Neuberger, another psychoanalyst from Austria, settled in New York in 1941 and became director of its Child Development Center.[18]

Many of Freud's disciples were crusaders with a zeal for proselyting in America. Despite the language barrier they produced scores of scholarly and popular volumes for the American trade. Otto Rank (b. Vienna, 1884 – d. 1939), a University of Vienna product and one of the founders of Vienna's psychoanalytical journal "Imago," whose early devotion to Freud ceased with disagreement in 1925, had at least eight volumes in print in America 22 years after his death in New York in 1939.[19] Another refugee of '38 was the ever-faithful Freudian Theodor Reik (b. Vienna, 1888) who became an outstanding New York psychoanalyst and who produced literally dozens of sound volumes for the American book trade. Freud's famous daughter Anna came from her English home to Clark University in 1950 to receive an honorary degree. Some of her students also found careers in the United States. There was, for instance, Lilli E. Peller (b. Prague, 1898 – d. New York, 1966), biologist and psychoanalyst, who helped found one of the bold Montessori-type schools in Vienna, taught in Jerusalem, and came to America to teach and practice in Washington and New York.[20]

There were other honored names like Franz Alexander (b. Budapest, 1891 – d. Chicago, 1964), a ranking neo-Freudian who became director of Chicago's Institute for Psychoanalysis[21] and Rudolph Dreikurs (b. Vienna, 1897) who came to America in 1937 after years of distinguished practice in Vienna to contribute to work at the Abraham Lincoln Center in New York and Hull House, the Chicago and Northwestern university medical schools, and the Alfred Adler Institute in Chicago.[22]

Dreikurs had long been in Vienna a disciple of the second of the great Austrian psychoanalysts, Alfred Adler (b. Vienna, 1870 – d. Aberdeen, 1937). Adler's "individual psychiatry" is, next to Freud's technique, the most widely accepted method for the treatment of neuroses. The expression "inferiority complex" was his.

Adler was a disciple of Freud's who in later years broke with him. He began visiting the United States in 1926, lectured in his poor English at Harvard and Columbia, and accepted the new chair in medical psychology that Long Island University set up in 1932. The fact that he was both a Jew and a Social Democrat made him uncomfortable enough in Austria to bring him to America in 1934 for the last three years of his life. Here his relaxation was the film with emphasis, according to his biographer, upon Charlie Chaplin and the Marx Brothers. Hundreds of American psychoanalysts who rejected such phases of Freud's teaching as his emphasis upon sex, were proud to call themselves Adlerians.[23]

Two years before his death Adler's daughter Alexandra (b. Vienna, 1901) left the University of Vienna and came here to work, first at Harvard and in Boston, and then at Duke, New York University, and at the Alfred Adler Mental Hygiene Clinic in New York. Alfred Adler's son Kurt joined the New York group as did Sophie Lazarsfeld, Helene Papanek, and Danica Deutsch who founded the Alfred Adler Consultation Center in New York. With other fine Adlerians like Dreikurs in Chicago it became, indeed, a distinguished group.[24]

An unusually high percentage of Jews and dissenters against Nazism were to be found among the mental healers. The Thousand Year Reich consequently lost a tremendous proportion of its neurologists and psychologists and their kindred spirits.

We may surmise that dozens of competent neurologists and psychoanalysts from Nazi Austria sought refuge in America rather than in Britain or Switzerland because they wanted, if they had to leave the good white wines and intriguing theater of Vienna, to join the friends and acquaintances who had come before. Those had settled principally in the East. Dr. Moses Keschner (b. Dobromil, Austrian Galicia, 1876),[25] for instance, who was educated in Przemysl and at New York's best universities, studied at Columbia and won his professorship there; and Anna Wunsch Cowen (b. Vienna, 1905)[26] who was brought here as an infant to find her work as a chemical psychologist in Rhode Island; and the Viennese Wally Reichenberg[27] who came here in 1928 and achieved, much later, a professorial chair at Duke University; and Ernst Spiegel (b. Vienna, 1895) of Temple University, who had known the University of Vienna as both student and teacher and who wrote voluminously on neurology in America's learned journals. Such people had come to America even before the establishment of Austria's own authoritarian regime in 1934.

The new-comers of the Hitler period settled, like their friends who had come earlier, in the East. There were exceptions like Richard F. Sterba (b. Vienna, 1898), Clinical Professor of Psychiatry at Wayne University and author of popular books (e.g. "Beethoven and his Nephew," Pantheon 1954) as well as technical ones, who came to Detroit in 1939,[28] and Karl Harry Pribram (b. Vienna, 1919)[29] who studied at Chicago and settled later, in 1959, at Stanford University.

Exceptions in another sense were distinguished figures who came like Professor Hans Hoff (b. Vienna, 1897), the later chief of the University of Vienna's Neurological Clinic who taught briefly at Columbia, only to seek temporary refuge in America, and Viktor E. Frankl (b. Vienna, 1905), the Viennese founder of existential analysis, who has never lived here but whose books are read here and who taught at Harvard during the summer of 1961.[31] Most, however, of the Austrian psychiatrists settled in New York.

Typical of the more notable among the Austrians in New York City was Dr. Joseph Wilder (b. Drohobycz, Austrian Galicia, 1895), a product of Vienna's university and a key figure at that city's Rosenhügel clinic for diseases of the nerves, who is known for his Law of Initial Values, Wilder's Law. He has been, since 1955, clinical professor of neurology at the New York Medical College that has discovered and placed so many of the competent Austrian-born.[32]

And best known of all to the layman was the distinguished Jew, Manfred Sakel (b. Nadworna, Austrian Galicia, 1900 – d. New York, 1958), the father of insulin shock treatment. He was one of the many notable Austrians who studied in Brünn in what is now Czechoslovakia, he spent six years in Berlin, returned to work in Vienna where he had taken his medical degree, and emigrated to New York in 1936 to lecture and to found the Manfred Sakel Research Foundation for Emotional and Mental Disorders. He had already developed his shock treatment for mental cases, especially for the most important of them all, schizophrenics, which was one of the great medical achievements of his age.[33]

There were dozens of others like Felix Deutsch (b. Vienna, 1884) the psychoanalyst who found his home at Harvard and around Boston;[34] the dream specialist Emil Gutheil (b. Czerlany, Austrian Galicia, 1899), an M.D. from Vienna, who became a New Yorker and co-founder of the Institute for Research in Psychotherapy;[35] Bernard Dattner (b. Silesia, 1887), another University of Vienna product who distinguished himself in and around New York, especially at Columbia and especially for his work on neurosyphilis;[36] and Edmund Bergler (b. Austria, 1899) who took his M.D. in Vienna in 1926, came to America with the Thirty-eighters, and turned out a whole series of popular books on the psychiatry of marriage.[37] Fritz Redl (b. Klaus, 1902) was a Thirty-eighter who had, by 1953, become chief of child research in the National Institutes of Health.[38] Professor Frederick Redlich (b. Vienna, 1910), consultant to the National Institutes of Health and to the United States Air Force, was another outstanding one. In 1938, three years after taking his M.D. degree at the University of Vienna, he came to Iowa, and then, by way of Boston and Harvard, to Yale where, since 1950, he has served as head of that university's department of psychiatry.[39]

And Karl and Charlotte Buhler (originally Bühler) constituted an interesting man-and-wife team. Both were born in Germany. They both taught at the University of Vienna for the better part of two decades before the *Anschluss* and then found their way to the United States where they taught and practiced and settled in 1949 in Los Angeles.[40] The significant Karl Bühler (1879–1963) was the leader of the Vienna School of psychologists. He was thrown into a Vienna jail by the Nazis in 1938 and succeeded only in 1939 in coming with his wife to America. Charlotte turned with success to psychotherapy. Karl was unhappy in the United States. His books, written in German, were unknown to American scholars who could read no German, and Bühler remained an isolated immigrant – an unrecognized prophet of the Vienna School.[41]

We have only named some of the outstanding Austro-American psychologists, psychiatrists, neurologists and psychoanalysts. It would be interesting, and significant for our study of immigration, to look into their careers as individuals. Some, like Bruno Bettelheim (b. Vienna, 1903) who became principal of the University of Chicago's Orthogenic School and who was concerned largely with the application of psychoanalysis to social problems, had been concentration camp victims. Bettelheim suffered in both Buchenwald and Dachau.[42] Many in this particular group of Thirty-eighters were Jewish. A large proportion came to America with their families – others were fortunate to escape alone with almost nothing but the clothes on their backs. Some found refuge with relatives or friends in the United States; many others depended upon the help of the fine American help-the-refugee organizations that were so active in the later Nazi years after Americans had finally opened their eyes to the horrors perpetrated by the Hitler crowd.

The younger ones generally looked for scholarships in American medical schools and universities where they could qualify for an American practice. The older ones taught or practiced in fields like psychology where the American requirements were academic rather than medical. Some who knew no English worked in German-speaking communities like Yorkville in New York City but an amazingly large proportion of them knew enough English to teach or practice, and even to write, for the general public. An interesting success story was that of Ernest Dichter (b. Vienna, 1907) whose former Vienna teacher, Paul Lazarsfeld, helped him in New York to an advertising job with a soap manufacturer and who, eight years after his arrival, established his widely known Institute for Motivational Research up in the Hudson. He wrote voluminously in English and introduced "depth interviewing" which became so famous in the American advertising world.[43]

The Austrian women in the field of mental medicine who came during the Hitler period were legion.[44] Almost all had been born in Vienna and had taken their Ph.D.'s or M.D.'s at the University of Vienna. Some had worked in London before they came to America. Many worked in hospitals or did social work but an amazingly large number taught at our colleges and universities. The women had more specialties like child guidance and speech correction and mental hygiene than the men. More of them left New York for Boston, the Middle West and California than was the case with the men. Almost none went south of Maryland. A number were Jewish and went often into Jewish hospitals here. And the distinguished ones, whose American successes were more than routine, were generally young or middle-aged. Few of them came with international reputations but many of them rose to real distinction in their adopted country.

No one in America ever speaks of an Austrian School of mental hygiene. The Austrian-born practitioners here are divided between Freudians and Adlerians and neurologists who have no interest whatever in psychoanalysis and the disciples of other Vienna masters who would never for a moment admit they were anything but American in their orientation. Yet these experts, who studied with Wagner-Jauregg and all the other fine Austrian masters, have made a contribution to the solution in America of the problems of mental health such as we have inherited from no other land beyond the seas. And Freudianism has become more American than Austrian.

[1] Robin McKown, *Pioneers in Mental Health*, N.Y. 1961, pp. 152—53.

[2] Stefan Zweig, *Mental Healers*, N.Y. 1932; E. H. Ackerknecht, *Short History of Psychiatry*, N.Y. and London 1959; Helmut Hirsch, "Mesmerism and Revolutionary America," *American-German Review*, Oct. 1943.

[3] Alfred Farau, *Einfluss der österreichischen Tiefenpsychologie auf die amerikanische Psychotherapie der Gegenwart*, Wien 1953, p. 34. It was Krafft-Ebing, if we can believe the accounts, who read the works of the Galician novelist, Leopold von Sacher-Masoch (b. Austrian-Galicia, 1836 — d. Germany, 1895) whose novels dealt often with the sexual abnormality in which satisfaction is derived from personal subjection to physical maltreatment. Masochism, known all around the world, was the term that the Austrian Krafft-Ebing used in describing the abnormalities that Sacher-Masoch depicted in the novels that he wrote while he taught at the University of Graz and before he went to Germany in his final years. His counterpart, the Marquis de Sade, has received in the cause of sadism, far more publicity than Sacher-Masoch has ever received in the cause of masochism. But the French are always better known in America than the Austrians.

[4] L. G. Stevenson, *Nobel Prize Winners in Medicine and Physiology*, N.Y. 1953, p. 125; McKown, *op. cit.*, pp. 201—03; Ackerknecht, *op. cit.*, p. 219.

[5] *American Men of Science*, 9th ed., vol. II, N. Y. 1955.

[6] *Founders of Neurology: 133 Biographical Sketches*, Springfield Ill. 1953, lists twelve founders who appear to have been Austrian and who worked chiefly in Vienna. For Schilder see also Farau, *op. cit.*, p. 133.

[7] R. H. Gabriel, *Course of American Democratic Thought*, N.Y. 1956, p. 427.

[8] Charles J. Rolo in *The Atlantic*, July 1961, p. 62.

[9] E. H. Ackerknecht, *Short History of Medicine*, N.Y. 1955, p. 193. Breuer has become well known in America through the popular stage and screen dramatizations of the Freud story.

[10] According to Jones's standard biography of Freud, III, p. 206.

[11] E. Harwick, ed., *Selected Letters of William James*, N.Y. 1960, p. 256.

[12] Bernard Sobel, ed., *New Theater Handbook*, N.Y. 1959, p. 229.

[13] Ernest Jones's biography of Freud is the basic authority for any study of Freud. Works describing Freud's influence upon various phases of American life and culture are too numerous to mention here.

[14] *Who's Who*, 1952–53.

[15] *Who's Who*, 1938–39.

[16] American Psychiatric Assc., *One Hundred Years of American Psychiatry*, N.Y. 1944, p. 262.

[17] Farau, *op. cit.*, p. 135.

[18] *The Atlantic*, July 1961, p. 84.

[19] *Books in Print*, 1961. He has a biography in the *Universal Jewish Encyclopedia*, 1948.

[20] *Ibid.*; Farau, *op. cit.*, p. 115, for Reik. Most recently his *Curiosities of the Self* was published by Farrar, Straus, in New York. The Peller obituary in the *New York Times* appeared 1 Sept. 1966, p. 35.

[21] Farau, *op. cit.*, p. 107; *American Men of Science*, 9th ed., II.

[22] *Ibid.*; *Who's Who*, 1962–63.

[23] Phyllis Bottome, *Alfred Adler*, N.Y. 1957; D. D. Runes, *Pictorial History of Philosophy*, N.Y. 1959; Ackerknecht, *op. cit.*, p. 194. Adler's Russian-born widow died in N.Y. April 1962, *Washington Post*, 23 April 1962.

[24] Farau, *op. cit.*, p. 79; *Who's Who of American Women*, 2nd ed., 1961.

[25] *Who's Who*, 1938–39; *American Men of Science*, 9th ed., II.

[26] *Who's Who of American Women*, 2nd ed.

[27] *Ibid.*

[28] *Biographical Directory of the American Psychiatric Association*, 1963.

[29] *Who's Who*, 1962–63.

[30] Austrian American Federation, *Österreichische Nachrichten*, Feb. 1963.

[31] *Who's Who*, 1962–63; *Austrian Information*, 17 July 1961.

[32] *Who's Who in World Jewry*, 1965.

[33] *World Biography*, 5th ed., 1954; *American Jewish Yearbook*, N.Y. 1959; *Who's Who*, 1952–53; Ackerknecht, *op. cit.*, *passim*. The Sakel Foundation remained active long after Sakel's death as indicated in the *Washington Post*, 1 Nov. 1962, article by A. J. Snider.

[34] *American Men of Science*, 9th ed., II.

[35] Farau, *op. cit.*, p. 106; *Who's Who*, 1952–53.

[36] *Ibid.*; *Austrian Information*, 18 Mar. 1961. He had obtained a captaincy in the U.S. Army in 1944.

[37] *Who's Who*, 1962–63.

[38] *Who's Who*, 1952–53; *American Men of Science*, 9th ed., II.

[39] *America Men of Science*, 10th ed.

[40] *Ibid.*; *Who's Who in Austria*, 1955.

[41] Albert Wellek, "Der Einfluss der deutschen Emigration auf die Entwicklung der nordamerikanischen Psychologie," *Jahrbuch für Amerikastudien*, X, p. 48. This volume contains several fine articles on the German-Austrian immigrants of 1938.

[42] *Current Biography*, July 1961.

[43] *Current Biography*, Jan. 1961.

[44] *Who's Who of American Women*, 2nd ed., 1961, lists some thirty who were clearly German Austrians. Some have been mentioned in the text. All of the following were born in Vienna and received their medical, etc., education at the University of Vienna unless otherwise indicated: Grete Lehner Bibring (b. 1899), professor at Harvard Medical School; Ilse Vivien Colett, Fresno, California;

Gertrude Krai Felsenburg, Denver, Colorado; Liselotte Koestler Fischer (b. 1910), Children's Hospital, Buffalo; Marianne Frostig, own school in Los Angeles; Ann M. Hart (b. 1907), Bronx, N.Y.; Dora Hartmann (b. 1902), New York City; Irene Link Hitchman (b. Hohenems, Vorarlberg, 1908), University of Maryland; Lilli Hofstatter, University of Missouri; Hedwig Erna Frederika Jahoda, New York City; Anny Katan (b. 1898), to U.S. 1946 from Holland, Western Reserve University; Edith Klemperer, New York City, introduced insulin treatment of delirium tremens; Elizabeth Christine Kris (b. 1925), ed. U. London, Ill. Inst. Tech., U. Ill., U. Chi., research Harvard, home Cambridge, Mass.; Helene Papanek (b. 1901), New York City; Claire D'Ane Selzer (b. 1914), New York City; Lydia Sicher (b. 1890), Los Angeles Psychiatric Services and chief counsellor Alfred Adler Counseling Center; Alice Slater Stahl (b. 1913), Williamsport in Pa.; Bellevue Hospital, New York; Iowa; Glen Oaks, N.Y.; Anna Sternbach (b. Austria, 1912), Jewish, New York City; Emmy Sylvester (b. 1910), Chicago, San Francisco and Stanford; Olga M. von Tauber (b. 1907), Bronx Hospital; Jenny Waelder-Hall (b. Lemberg, Austrian Galicia, 1898), Boston, Baltimore, U. Md; Charlotte Frisch Walker (b. 1914), Yale, Conn. State Hospital, Sibley Hospital D.C., Duke U., U. Mich., practice – Los Angeles; Edith Weisskopf-Joelson, Indiana, Purdue U.; Gertrude Lasch Wyatt who trained voices for the Max Reinhardt School in Vienna, worked in London and Boston, and became director of speech correction for the Wellesley schools.

CHAPTER XXII

AUSTRIANS OF THE STAGE AND SCREEN

If statistics could be applied to the theater they would doubtless prove that no foreign-speaking people except the Germans have contributed more to the stage in America than the Austrians.[1] For the Austrian is born with a passion for the theater. His smallest cities have their theaters and Vienna spawns theatrical groups by the score. Professional actors are the Austrian's heroes – rivaled only by musicians – and every Austrian has a passionate desire to act. Little wonder that he wants to take his theater with him where he emigrates.[2]

The earliest Austrian contributions were to the German-language theaters. About mid-nineteenth century some few theaters in New York began producing German plays and the city's first permanent German theater opened there in 1854. The productions of Austrian playwrights like Grillparzer were played along with those of the Germans, by immigrant actors.[3]

There appeared more and more good German theaters during and after the Civil War, not only in New York, but in other towns where the German-speaking newcomers were numerous. The acting was often excellent and the productions were frequently the best that Vienna or Munich or Berlin had to offer. The fact that Shaw's "Pygmalion" reached Milwaukee in the twentieth century after its triumph in Vienna and Berlin underscores the fact that even English plays reached America's German stage, not directly, but via the Viennese and the great German stages.[4]

The German Austrians played in those early decades a much less prominent part in America's German theater than the North Germans. Yet there were a few enthusiasts from the old empire who ranked among the most important builders of the German theater here. Alexander Reinagle was second-generation Austrian, English born (1756), an immigrant of 1786, and primarily a musician. But his partnership with the actor Wignell in the 1790's gave Philadelphia its first significant theater, the Chesnut Street Theater that was called America's finest. The partnership did so well that, some time before Reinagle's death in 1809, they carried theater to Washington, Baltimore and Alexandria on a part-time basis and they even invaded New York. It was doubtless America's most important theatrical venture at the turn of the century.[5]

The Forty-eighter Heinrich Börnstein (b. Hamburg, 1805 – d. Vienna, 1892), who had grown up in the Habsburg monarchy and learned his theater by writing about it for the Vienna press and by directing the famous *Theater in der Josefstadt*, made St. Louis a German theater center of significance in the 1850's. He began with an amateur group, made the St. Louis Opera House the city's first successful professional theater, promoted playwriting in German, and produced disciples like Heinrich Lischer who established in 1855 Davenport, Iowa's first German theater.[6]

Another Forty-eighter, the free-thinking Friedrich Hassaurek (b. Vienna, 1831 – d. Paris, 1885), founded a German theater called *Das deutsche Institut* in Cincinnati in 1851 which employed professional actors and able old-world directors. Cincinnati was enough of a German community to support, not only its own theater but also guest performances from time to time by Börnstein's company from St. Louis.[7]

Still another Austrian director was Geza Berger (b. Preßburg, 1842) of New York's German *Stadttheater* whose Vienna theatrical education (including acting in the *Theater an der Wien*) doubtless contributed to his ability, not only to act and direct but also to write some sensational box-office successes before he departed in 1886 for a journalistic career as editor of the "Cincinnati Volksblatt."[8] That these German-speaking theater-builders were bringing over some of Vienna's best talent was evidenced by the arrival in New York, shortly before Berger went to Cincinnati, of a guest actress, Kathi Schratt, who was not only a famous name at Vienna's *Burgtheater* but was, for years, the warmest personal friend of Kaiser Franz Joseph. The Hofburg Theater's famous tragedian Mitterwurzer was imported by Gustav Amberg (b. Bohemia, 1844 – d. 1922) who directed New York's Thalia Theater and later established the Amberg Theater which was to become better known as the Irving Place Theater.[9]

In 1862 came New York's first season of German opera with Mozart and Beethoven represented. Italian opera had previously dominated the American scene and it was a squeeze for the German. Lang tells us that when the Anschütz company of New York moved on by way of Philadelphia to Washington, Ford's Theater there did its best to seduce the town into thinking it was to enjoy some opera from Italy. Strauss's immortal "Fledermaus" reached the Thalia Theater in New York in 1874 and another great Vienna composition, "Fidelio," was presented during the second season of the infant Metropolitan Opera (founded 1883). But the Metropolitan was dedicated to Italian opera and the German and Austrian pieces were ousted in the revolution of 1891 – 92.[10]

The man who brought Kathi Schratt to America, mentioned above in Chapter IX, was named Cohn, and he also brought us Farrar, Caruso, Chaliapin, and some other immortal names. He was known here as Heinrich Conried (b. Bielitz, Austrian Silesia, 1855 – d. Meran, 1909), a great figure at the Metropolitan as well as in New York's German theaters. After a taste of fame in Vienna's *Hof-Burgtheater* and in managing Bremen's Municipal Theater he came to New York to give distinction to its Germania, Thalia, and Irving Place theaters. His successes were tremendous. He worked to destroy the "star-system" and to build up, on the European basis, well-balanced companies of fine, resident actors. And as manager of the Metropolitan for five years, from 1903 as Grau's successor, he made history. He introduced "Fledermaus" and "Zigeunerbaron" to its conservative audiences and Wagner's "Parsifal" for its American première. Richard Strauss's "Salomé" was too much for his clientele, the storm of protest that followed was doubtless a cause of Conried's retirement and his death a year later in Meran.[11] But before his retirement he had arranged for the importation from the Vienna opera of one of the greatest of conductors, Gustav Mahler, to be the Metropolitan's principal conductor.

The Salomé fiasco at the Met was a sign of the appearance of realism in the American theater to which Freud and dozens of other Austrians were to contribute. Even Hofmannsthal was applying psycho-pathology to Greek drama while Freud was stirring up the indignation of conservative fellow-countrymen with his subversive notions that Austrians would not really accept until they accepted Kafka a full generation later. Meanwhile a few Austrian dramatists like Schnitzler were to introduce some stark realism into America.

A realist in another sense was Max Reinhardt (b. Baden near Vienna, 1873 – d. New York, 1943), perhaps the theater's greatest in his time. "The arrival of Max Reinhardt upon the American stage," said a critic in reviewing an early Reinhardt triumph here, "The Miracle," "has proved a far more astounding and staggering business than any of his admirers could have imagined."[12] Born Goldmann, Reinhardt was sound evidence that Austrian Jews of the pre-Hitler era could, despite the carping voices of politicos like Schönerer, create tremendous careers for themselves. And his influence was German and American as well as Austrian.

Max Reinhardt, although damned in later years for helping Hollywood with spectacles that sensitive Americans could hardly boast of, was a giant whose passion was to build a theater which, as theater and not as literature or variety or the exploitation of a few stars, should bring its own theater art to its public. Since, with Reinhardt, the theater and its effectiveness was the thing, he could produce at the Salzburg Festival a "Jedermann" that was so finely produced that it remains until this day a primary attraction at Europe's finest music festival. He used light and shade – any of the new mechanical devices of the modern age, to give spectacular effect. He gave new vigor to the theater, first in Salzburg, then in Berlin and Vienna, again in Berlin, and in his last years, in Hollywood.

The operetta "Rosalinda" which ran well in New York during World War II was Reinhardt's American version of "Die Fledermaus." For the Nazis had sent him almost penniless to America in 1933 and he had opened his Reinhardt Workshop in Hollywood. He did Hollywood's "Midsummer Night's Dream" in Reinhardt fashion and left his imprint upon dozens of the younger generation in America's film industry in its balmy days.[13]

Some years after Reinhardt Yale University found in the Thirty-eighter Alois Nagler (b. Graz, 1907) a distinguished teacher of dramatic history and criticism for its School of Drama.[14]

As a great master, Reinhardt produced a swarm of famous students. One was Joseph Schildkraut (b. Vienna, 1895 – d. New York, 1964), son of one of Vienna's Yiddish actors, Rudolf Schildkraut, who brought Joseph with him to New York in 1910. There young Joseph studied at the American Academy of Arts and played for New York's Irving Place Thater even before, in 1913–1917, he acted for Reinhardt in Berlin. Schildkraut then worked in Vienna, played Liliom in "Liliom" in New York in 1921, worked for De Mille who gave him his American film debut in "Orphans of the Storm," managed the Hollywood Playhouse for a time, and left a great reputation in both Hollywood and New York for his parts in such never-to-be-forgotten pieces as "Anatole," "The Cherry Orchard," "The Green Bay Tree," and "The Diary of Anne Frank." He had two Academy Awards and he was one of the most admired of the Theater Guild's best.[15]

Elisabeth Bergner (b. Vienna, 1900) became famous under the direction of Max Reinhardt in the great days of the German stage and screen during the Weimar Republic before she found refuge from the Brown Shirts in England. Bergner's New York debut a year or two later in "Escape Me Never" brought her the critics' best-actress-of-the-year award. She took British citizenship, came to the United States, and was long one of the great figures in motion pictures.[16]

Another Viennese who worked under Reinhardt in Germany in the twenties was the director and lyric poet Berthold Viertel (b. Vienna, 1884 – d. there, 1953) who came first to America in 1928, directed for Fox and Paramount, and did films like "The Magnificent Lie" and "The Wiser Sex."[17] John Reich (b. Vienna, 1906) who gave up his professorship at Columbia in 1957 to direct the Chicago Art Institute's Goodman Theater, had worked for Reinhardt in Vienna and Salzburg. Like the noted conductor Fritz Reiner, also a native of the old monarchy, he received the Illinois Governor's Immigrant Service League Award for his significant contribution to the arts in the Middle West.[18] And among the others who had worked with Reinhardt were the author and script writer Herta Pauli (b. Vienna, 1909) and the actor Kurt Kaszner (b. Vienna, 1913) who made his New York debut in "The Eternal Road" and played later in the popular Trapp Family musical, "The Sound of Music."[19]

There were some great Austro-American names on stage and screen years before the Hitler menace produced the great migration. Paul Muni, born Paul Weisenfreund in Lemberg on September 22, 1895, (d., Santa Barbara, Calif., 26. Aug., 1967), who made his American debut with a Yiddish stock company in New York when he was thirteen, named Austria as his place of birth. His tremendous career, from vaudeville as a child with his parents to the Yiddish Art Theater as a young man, and on to play "Scarface," the first of the famous American gangster films, to his fine roles in "Counselor-at-Law," and, as Clarence Darrow, in "Inherit the Wind" and his endless triumphs in Hollywood where he or Edward G. Robinson played so many of the biographical parts like Pasteur (for which he received the Best-of-the-

Year Award) and Zola, made his name a family word far beyond our own borders.[20] He was of course an academy award winner.

Much decorated (by France, Italy, and Belgium, the Academy Award in 1935 and the Laurel Award in 1948 as the leading musical composer for the films) was the lesser known Max Steiner (b. Vienna, 1888). He wrote his first operetta in Vienna at fourteen, was conducting musical shows in New York at twenty-six, and went later to Hollywood to write music for the films. It was his music for the fine film "The Informer" that brought Steiner his award from the French government.[21]

Jack Krantz (b. Vienna, 1899), who was far better known as Ricardo Cortez, came here in the era of the silent film, a matinee idol to charm the female audiences in early films like "The Private Life of Helen of Troy."

Jed Harris (b. Vienna, 1900), born Jacob Horowitz, was a Yale man who made one of America's greatest reputations in theatrical production. From 1925 when he broke into Broadway, did the box-office success "Love 'Em and Leave 'Em," and was proclaimed as the wonder boy of Times Square, his name was one to be conjured with. Disagreeable and difficult as he was, and taking pride in his reputation as such, he still remained for decades one of the greatest.[22] He was utterly unlike his genial and rotund *Landsmann*, Walter Slezak (b. Vienna, 1902), the son of the immortal Leo, who came to New York in 1930 and was quickly absorbed in an Austrian stage and film career. Slezak's little volume, "What Time's The Next Swan," is perhaps the most charming account of the career of an Austro-American that has ever been published.[23]

Austria has not only given America a notable abstract designer for the theater and stage in Friedrich Kiesler, who produced the "space stage" for America's contemporary theater,[24] but it provided us far earlier, in 1911, to design for Boston's new opera, the famous Joseph Urban (b. Vienna, 1872 – d. New York, 1933). He was one of those versatile artists who could make charming illustrations for Grimm or Anderson's fairy tales, or design New York's Ziegfeld Theater, or give the film "When Knighthood Was in Flower" some fine scenic sets, or turn from settings for lavish revues of the Ziegfeld type to modern design like his impressionistic sets for the Metropolitan's production of "Pelléas et Melisande." He brought Continental design to the American stage when he thought it was needed. Few of the Austrian immigrants in the arts were more useful in the New World than Joseph Urban.[25]

There came, nevertheless, during the Nazi era, a truly formidable group from the Austrian theater which contributed more than one can estimate to the American stage and film. Some of these Thirty-eighters whose English was insufficient or who did not relish always having to play the parts of despicable Nazis and of villains in general, found temporary roles in New York with The Players from Abroad, a German-language group that gave a distinguished revival to New York's German theater.[26] It was Felix Gerstmann's vision that created The Players, and Austrians like

Oskar Karlweis and Hans Jaray (long of the *Theater in der Josefstadt*, who was to return to Vienna after the war) helped with the project. And the participants constituted an honor roll that would have ensured the fame of any stage or film studio: Maria Jeritza (who was to be at home in New York among the Met's great stars for years to come), Elisabeth Bergner, Josef Schildkraut, Paul Henreid, Leopoldine Konstantin, Ferdinand Bruckner, Ernst Deutsch, Ida Roland, Ludwig Stoessel, Rita Georg, Gisela Werbezirk, Erika von Wagner and John Wengraf, and others who came and went. One of the finest of The Players was the superb actress Helene Thimig, Reinhardt's widow (b. Vienna, 1889) who had already taught drama in the Reinhardt school at Hollywood and who was soon to return to Vienna to distinguish its incomparable *Burg-* and *Akademie-Theaters*.[27]

And in that unique group of Players from Abroad were Helmut Dantine (b. Vienna, 1918) of the Pasadena Community Players and of films as famous as "Mrs. Miniver" and "Call Me Madame,"[28] and Francis Lederer (b. Prague, 1906) of "Golden Boy" who was perhaps more German and English than Austrian and American.[29] And there was the Austrian Fritz Kortner (b. Vienna, 1892), a luminary of Germany's brilliant twenties in film history who returned to Germany soon after the end of the war.[30]

Oskar Karlweis (b. Hinterbrühl near Vienna, 1894 – d. New York, 1956) of The Players from Abroad was one of the great names, in Europe and America. He will long be remembered as the baron in the original "Grand Hotel," Prince Orlofsky in Reinhardt's "Fledermaus," and in America especially as Jacobowsky in "Jacobowsky and the Colonel." He boasted of being a coward in war but he broadcasted anti-Nazi programs for Vienna before the *Anschluss* and, in consequence, arrived via Paris, Spain, and Portugal, in America, with two words of English, in 1940.[31] He was one of those dozens and dozens of Austrians whose story, could it be written, would make a best-seller. The impresario of The Players, Felix Gerstmann (b. Vienna, 1898 – d. New York, 1967) left Austria in 1939 and fought with the British at Dunkirk before he arrived in New York to create careers for so many German-speaking actors who had not yet found themselves in English. Later he achieved success in presenting such fine productions as Lotte Lenya's "Threepenny Opera" or in developing concerts by great names that may have had no connection with his native land. His was a very considerable name in theatrical New York.

The Austrian label has never been impressive in America. A play like "Playing with Love" ("Mit der Liebe spielen") did well here in 1920 because it was played by the Lunts. Ferdinand Bruckner's "Die Verbrecher" (1929) and his "Die Rassen" (1934) which dealt with the Nazi threat made no impact here because Americans were unconscious of the Nazi threat in those early days. Chlumberg's "Miracle at Verdun," an anti-war drama, was as unsuccessful in the early thirties as was Fritz Hochwälder's "The Strong are Lonely" ("Das heilige Experiment") a generation later.[32] Even

Werfel's charming "Embezzled Heaven" was no great success on stage or screen.[33]

The Viennese label has always been far more attractive in America than the Austrian. The Lunts' "Reunion in Vienna" was an epoch-making success; and Graham Greene's "The Third Man" on film was the most popular Vienna story of the twentieth century in this country. The Rodgers and Hammerstein musical of the Trapp family of Salzburg, "The Sound of Music," which came near to breaking all Broadway records, was a tremendous attraction, on the stage and in film, because of its charm and its music and not because it was Austrian. On film it did break every American box-office record and it brought more Americans to Salzburg than popular Salzburg had ever before seen.

The Austrian personalities who have worked or taught in America were certainly more significant than the chance involvements of the Vienna theme in American drama: men like Ernst Lothar (b. Ernst Müller, Brünn, 1890) whose whole career was Viennese except for the four years (1940–44) when he taught drama at the University of Colorado, another of the thousands in Austria who could not stomach Hitlerism;[34] and the Austrian Professor Walther R. Volback, a professor of theater arts at Texas Christian University, who in 1961 introduced for the first time in America the Austrian Max Mell's "Joan of Arc." Another significant figure is Professor Alois M. Nagler, a native of Graz, who distinguished himself in Vienna as a critic and literary editor before he came to America in 1938. Nagler was appointed in 1965 Henry McCormack Professor of Dramatic History and Criticism at Yale University.[35]

More exciting to most Americans were the big-name actresses, Hedy Lamarr, Elissa Landi, Luise Rainer, Vanessa Brown, and Romy Schneider. A fine character actress was Adrienne Gessner, wife of Ernst Lothar, the charming little lady who played in some American successes like "Claudia" and "I Remember Mama," and went back to Vienna to play on its finest stages.

Lamarr was involved in an unbelievably silly shop-lifting scandal in Los Angeles in 1966. She had apparently capitalized upon her fame to walk off with a very few dollars worth of trinkets without bothering to charge them. This lovely Hedy Lamarr, who was born Hedwig Kiesler in Vienna about when the Allies were cutting up the Habsburg monarchy, became notorious in her nude role in "Ecstasy" (1933), a really fine Czech film. MGM found her a huge box-office attraction in the United States (she came over in 1937) and she starred in role after role: "Algiers," "H. M. Pulham Esquire," "White Cargo" and other fine and sensational successes.[36] Elissa Landi whom rumor called the granddaughter of Empress Elisabeth, was a novelist of some reputation in her later days after years on stage and screen.[37] Luise Rainer (b. Vienna, 1912), one of the early-comers among the Thirty-eighters, was another Academy Award-winning actress who charmed the millions here. She had acted in Düsseldorf and in Vienna under Max Reinhardt. And like the Landi she was at home in Britain as she was in America.[38] Vanessa Brown, born Smylla Brind in Vienna only in 1929, was another of the fascinating stars from overseas. She fled from reaction to Paris with her family as a child, was brought to America, and here she gave vent to her Viennese energy, in painting, in Democratic politics, in TV, on Broadway, and in films, while she went to school at U.C.L.A. She was one of those amazingly precocious Viennese (radio loved her on the once-famous Quiz Kids program) that seemed to welcome every opportunity for making a name for herself in the show business of her adopted country.[39]

It is impossible to do justice here to all the fascinating figures that came in the thirties and forties: people like the inimitable comedian Karl Farkas (b. Vienna, 1893), Oscar Homolka (b. Vienna, 1898 or 1901) who played here on the stage in "Emperor Jones" and "The Power and the Glory" and on the screen in "Mission to Moscow" and "I Remember Mama," and in dozens of other American productions. "Look" magazine called him in 1956 the best supporting actor of the year.[40] Herbert Berghof (b. Vienna, 1909) made his New York debut in 1942 and appeared later in Werfel's "Jacobowsky and the Colonel" and "The Andersonville Trial."[41] And the product of Israeli and London schools, Theodore Bikel (b. Vienna, 1924), the folksinger, has appeared in America in concerts, TV, dozens of recordings and in some excellent plays including the Trapp family's "The Sound of Music."[42]

When Vienna's finest music critic, the refugee Max Graf, denounced New York's Metropolitan for its dependence upon the millionaire community, his almost- American son, Herbert, was embarrassed. But Herbert Graf (b. Vienna, 1903 – immigrated 1934) had had too fine a career, from his first American years in Philadelphia, including his work there for the opera and later for the Curtis Institute, to his long years as a stage director with the Met that began back in 1936, to be shaken by his father's "indiscretions." Herbert Graf remained with the Metropolitan and his fellow-countryman Rudolf Bing there, for many years – an Austrian power behind the operatic throne.[43]

There was also, in the American theater world, Henry (Heinrich) Schnitzler (b. Hinterbrühl near Vienna, 1902), son of Arthur Schnitzler, educated in Habsburg Vienna, a disciple of Reinhardt in Berlin, a figure in the Vienna theater world, and an émigré of 1938 to the U.S.A. He worked with the American film industry, taught at the University of California, and returned to his beloved Vienna to direct the *Theater in der Josefstadt*, Reinhardt's former theater. It is difficult to estimate how much such visitors contributed to America's theater.[44] Schnitzler was one of the Jews among the distinguished immigrants, but they were not, by any means, all Jewish.

In American films, the Austrians have almost never been recognized as Austrians. Paul Rotha's fine book, "The Film Till Now" (London, 1960), is full of Austrians but "Austria" is not in its index. As a matter of fact Austria has exported the film art. Films produced in Vienna have seldom been important to America. Even the Walt Disney films on the *Sängerknaben* and the Spanish Riding School, photographed over there, have had no impact here. America is simply not interested in nostalgic Austrian themes; the "Sissi" story which came to America as "Forever My Love" with the lovely Romy Schneider in 1962, and even the Freud theme, that appeared in this country on stage and screen in 1963, and made no great sensation.[45] "The Third Man," produced in Vienna but not by the Austrians, was the fascinating exception to the rule. The Austrians have always done, not Kafka or Trakl in their films but the frothy sentimental romance of the old Habsburg days and that has seldom appealed to American audiences. The Austrian film impact in America has been, not from Vienna, but here in Hollywood.

Reinhardt's influence in Hollywood was tremendous. Men like Ernst Lubitsch and Emil Jannings and William Dieterle whom he had trained in Europe or here in California[46] made their mark in the America film world. And Reinhardt encouraged the building of an Austrian colony where dozens of notables, fresh from the Old World, found companionship as well as opportunity. By 1957 there were some forty so-called Austrians in the "International Motion Picture Almanac," and literally dozens of them, like Ricardo Cortez and Erich von Stroheim and Muni and Slezak and Billy Wilder, Erich Korngold and Hedy Lamarr, were more than well-known — they were household words in their adopted country and most of the way around the world.

Austria itself has been an eager market for American films. It was importing twice as many American films as German films in 1954, and eight or ten times as many as it was importing from France or Britain.[47] But America has imported almost none of any significance from Austria. Austria's genius, insofar as it had a passion for the film industry, has generally emigrated. Other parts of the old empire furnished great names for export like Adolph Zukor, William Fox and Marcus Loew. The German Austrians furnished them by the dozens. Many of them felt uncomfortable amid all the lurid glare of Hollywood — it was perhaps the most un-Austrian corner of the entire United States — but they signed their contracts, watched the publicity boys build up their names, and some of them even found that they liked it.

There came actors like the bold anti-Nazi Paul Henreid (b. Trieste, 1908), educated in the *Gymnasien* and academies of Vienna with experience in Reinhardt's *Theater in der Josefstadt*. In England he starred on the stage and appeared in notable films like "Goodbye Mr. Chips," played first on the stage in New York and then went on to find more fame in Hollywood in such films as "Of Human Bondage" and "Casablanca."[48] Henreid was one of the few Lutherans among the Austrian Hollywooders.

On the Catholic side the peripatetic Schells were among the best. With a Viennese mother and a Swiss father the family fled Vienna to Zurich in the year of the *Anschluss*. Typically Austrian-international, the multilingual Maria took Swiss citizenship, became Germany's favorite and Venice's prize winner, visited Vienna and London, and, in America, achieved fame in "The Brothers Karamazov" and "Cimarron" and in other good and bad films and TV programs, and was blasted by "Time" for being self-centered and greedy.[49] Handsome brother Maximilian (b. Vienna, 1930), Academy Award winner of 1962 for best actor of the year (in the anti-Nazi "Judgement at Nuremberg," his second American film),[50] was as indifferent as his sister to American applause. No Academy Award winner was ever so little known, and remained so little known here as Max Schell. Both are generally known in America as Germans like Curd Jürgens, a star of Zanuck's "The Longest Day" in 1962, who is actually German by birth although he won his reputation at the *Burgtheater* in Vienna and made his home there.[51]

There was also the pulchritudinous Romy Schneider (b. Vienna, 1939) who was more European than Austrian or American but who made a fascinating cover girl for America's lighter press. Known here for her successes in "Boccaccio '70" and Kafka's "Trial," she was selected for a still more important role in "The Cardinal." Director Preminger made Schneider family history while "The Cardinal" was being filmed in Vienna by staging a reunion of Romy and her parents who had separated and left Vienna twenty long years earlier.[52]

And there were two other blonde and beautiful actresses who had seen the disasters of Nazism and the perils of Soviet occupation in Vienna. One was Maria Perschy (b. Eisenstadt, 1938) who was introduced in the United States in 1963 with Rock Hudson in "Man's Favorite Sport."[53] The other was Senta Berger, the Viennese who could turn brunette as well as blonde, and who, after her appearance in the film "The Victors," was referred to as the Austrian Marilyn Monroe.

An Academy Award winner of 1942 was George Froeschel (b. Vienna, 1891), a screen writer who worked on many fine pictures including "Mrs. Miniver" and "The White Cliffs of Dover."[54] And much later, in the middle 1950's when Austrians were finding fame in Germany rather than in distant America, Rudolf Stoiber (b. Steyr, 1925) came to New York to interpret the New World to the Old. He was a product of the University of Vienna and of the Vienna Conservatory who came first to Canada to develop programs for the Columbia Broadcasting network and for the Austrian radio and to establish the *Deutsche Kammerspiele* in Montreal. In New York he did novels in English and United Nations programs in German for Austria and he worked out plans for bringing a Negro ensemble to the 1965 Vienna Festival Weeks, that were unfortunately much less well known to Americans than a dozen other European festivals, and plans for producing a play by the American Negro, James Baldwin, at the Theater an der Wien.[55]

To return a bit in point of time, one can scarcely neglect Carl Mayer (b. Graz, 1894) who introduced a revolution in motion-picture technique, the moving camera. He was one of the great script writers of the Golden Age of the German film (his

"Cabinet of Dr. Caligari" in Berlin was a landmark). Mayer never came to America but his "Sunrise" was a model in Hollywood, and his "Last Laugh," done with the moving camera, "led to the ubiquitous use (in America) of the camera-dolly and the crane."[56]

Synchronization was the discovery of the Viennese Rudolf Bach (b. 1893) who came early as an actor to New York, was interned at Ft. Oglethorpe during the first war, directed New York's German theater, and was later intrigued by the new sound films. With his synchronization device he found that he could substitute English voices for American to make American films more palatable to English audiences and then, with the huge success of the film "Der verlorene Zeppelin" in Berlin, he and MGM saw that there were fortunes ahead in synchronizing American films in foreign tongues. He returned to Vienna after his Hollywood career.[57]

Another fascinating innovator was the father of "Betty-Boop" and "Popeye," the developer of the animated cartoon, Max Fleischer (b. Austria, 1885). An immigrant at the age of five and later a cartoonist in journalism, Fleischer joined with J. R. Bray to develop the first practical process for animated drawings. Their "Koko the Clown" (1915) was the first of all animated cartoons on film. Fleischer invented a number of devices for producing animated cartoons. His devices for changing speed were particularly effective in comics—to achieve the exaggeration that Americans loved in all of their film comedies. And "Popeye" was only the most famous of all of Fleischer's creations on screen and paper.[58]

The impresarios of the film in recent America have been almost, but not quite, as Austro-Hungarian as the impresarios of music have been Austrian. America has had, out of Austria alone and without credit to the non-Germanic elements in the old monarchy, a truly impressive group of directors and producers: von Stroheim, Sternberg, Billy Wilder (an interesting name for an Austrian!), Preminger, Zinnemann, and, to stretch the Austrian label a bit, Sam Spiegel. These men have not dominated American film production in recent years but they have come far closer to it than has any other foreign-born group.

It may well be the genius of the realist Erich von Stroheim (b. as Erich Oswald Stroheim in Vienna, 1885) that will be longest remembered. Americans will not soon forget the villain roles that he played as a German officer. Actually he had risen only to the rank of corporal and that in the Habsburg army. But his significance lay in his role as Hollywood director: a role that was crowned with a best-director award of the critics in 1926. His "Greed," that lost money, has been recorded as a triumph of America's film industry, and his "Merry Widow," which made money, has been deplored as a shoddy attempt to rival his more spectacular rival, De Mille. He loved melodramas but his art had integrity and significance. Erich von Stroheim was one of the giants of the silent film.[59]

A disciple of von Stroheim was the creator of "The Blue Angel" (Germany 1930) which made Marlene Dietrich famous. He was Josef von Sternberg (b. Vienna,

1894), who carried a camera for the American army during World War I, found a place in the silent films, and, beginning with "Underworld" for Paramount in 1927 made the gangster film an American institution. "Dragnet" and "Shanghai Express" were typical of the more sophisticated of the gangland films, distinguished by their fine pictorialism, that Sternberg based upon America's machine-age criminals.[60]

Fred Zinnemann (b. Vienna, 1907) will long be remembered for "High Noon," one of the best of the westerns, and the explosive "From Here to Eternity." He had studied law in Vienna and cinematography in Paris before he immigrated in 1929 to work under Berthold Viertel at the Fox Studios and to begin directing on his own in 1934. He was one more of the Austro-American Academy Award winners and one of the finest.[61]

The holder of half a dozen Academy Awards was another Vienna-educated director, Billy Wilder (b. Lemberg, 1906). That genial but productive little man who came to America in his twenties, was considered by some in his fifties to be "the greatest creative talent in the motion picture industry." He had produced "Emil and the Detectives" (now in the Museum of Modern Art's collection), he had won distinction directing the psychological thriller called "Double Indemnity," and had directed, or had a deft hand in, dozens of other great ones: "Ninotchka," "Lost Weekend," "Sunset Boulevard," "The Apartment," to name only a few. Like his fine compatriots he seldom turned to Austrian themes in his films and it seems unfortunate that when he did, as in "The Emperor Waltz," the critics were most critical. Von Stroheim had the same experience with "The Merry Widow"—doubtless indicative that Austrian taste and American taste are not always identical.[62]

Otto Preminger (b. Vienna, 1906) reached the apex of his fine career a bit later than did Billy Wilder, a boyhood friend of Vienna days. By 1961 when his film "Exodus" was running in almost every American theater, his "Anatomy of a Murder" was a triumph, and his work on "Advise and Consent" was bringing him headlines, there was no better-known director in America. And his comments about cleaning up the politicians a bit in "Advise and Consent" because foreigners just wouldn't understand their motives, showed that he hadn't entirely forgotten his European background.[63] Indeed, he introduced an important Vienna episode into "The Cardinal" that ranked high in 1964 despite the hostility of the best critics. A heavy-built, balding gentleman with a twinkle in his eye, Preminger was once called "the only absolute dictator who ever made a picture about democracy." He was one of the few who were eager to identify themselves as Austrian and not German.

Otto Preminger's first wife, incidentally, was a Hungarian with a doctorate from the University of Vienna. Her interest in social work, in Africa and in New York where she lived, had made her the founder of the Albert Schweitzer Hospital Fund, the owner of the Preminger Collection of African Art, and the recipient of the medal of the French Legion of Honor.[67]

The producer of the sensational Academy Award winner of 1963, "Lawrence of Arabia," was Samuel P. Spiegel (b. Jaroslav, Austrian Galicia, 1903) who studied at Vienna's University and called Austria his native land. Tough, vigorous and dictatorial like Preminger, Sam Spiegel clung to his Vienna accent. He grew rich on films in Berlin, assembled a gallery of modern painting, came here in 1939, and in less than a decade he and his Horizon Pictures were producing one triumph after the other. "The Bridge on the River Kwai," an Academy Award winner, was perhaps his greatest before "Lawrence of Arabia."[65]

It is impossible to mention here all the other Austro-Americans who, during the post-war period, have contributed so much to the American film. Without those scores who were born so far from Hollywood, and in an old world so unlike Hollywood, our film industry would obviously have been much the poorer.[66]

[1] See, e.g., the biographical listings in recent books like Daniel Blum, *Theater World 1960–61*, and Louis Kronenberger, *Best Plays 1960–61*.

[2] According to R. Gunther in the *American-German Review*, Aug.-Sept. 1962, Vienna had 150 drama groups and still more in most of Vienna's 180 Catholic parishes.

[3] Carl Wittke, *We Who Built America*, N.Y. 1945, p. 382; Glenn Hughes, *History of the American Theater*, N.Y. 1951, p. 181. German dramatists like Kotzebue had occasionally been played earlier but French plays and Italian operas had been more popular than the German.

[4] *American-German Review*, June 1942, pp. 17, 37.

[5] Hughes, *op. cit.*, pp. 70, 78–80, 110–12. Gilbert Chase stresses Reinagle's importance in *America's Music*, N.Y. 1955, p. 112. Cf. *Dictionary of American Biography*.

[6] Carl Wittke, *Refugees of Revolution*, Philadelphia 1952, pp. 289–90; Heinrich Börnstein, *Fünfundsiebzig Jahre*, 2 vols., Leipzig 1884, *passim*.

[7] Wittke, *op. cit.*, p. 289; A. E. Zucker, *Forty-eighters*, N.Y. 1950, p. 300.

[8] *Das Buch der Deutschen in Amerika*, Philadelphia 1909, pp. 439–40.

[9] *Ibid.*, p. 432; *Deutsches Theater-Lexikon*, Klagenfurt und Wien 1953.

[10] P. H. Lang, *One Hundred Years of Music in America*, N.Y. 1961, pp. 55–65.

[11] *Cambridge History of American Literature*, vol. II, N.Y. 1960; *Dictionary of American Biography; Das Buch der Deutschen in Amerika*, pp. 430f.

[12] *Theater Arts Anthology*, N.Y. 1950, p. 601.

[13] Herbert Graf, *The Opera*, N.Y. 1941, p. 181; Victor Lange, *Modern German Literature*, N.Y. 1945, pp. 26–27; P. Hartwell, ed., *Oxford Companion to the Theater*, Oxford 1951; Hughes, *op. cit.*, pp. 357–89.

[14] *Austrian Information*, 14 Feb. 1962.

[15] *Who's Who in the Theater*, London 1952; *Theater World 1960–61; Who's Who*, 1962–63.

[16] Paul Rotha, *The Film Till Now*, London 1960, *passim; Wer ist Wer*, Wien 1937; *Universal Jewish Encyclopedia.*

[17] *Ibid.;* Rotha, *op. cit.*, pp. 288f.

[18] *Austrian Information*, 6 May 1961; *Who's Who* 1962–63.

[19] *Who's Who of American Women*, 2nd ed., 1961; *Theater World 1960–61.*

[20] *Who's Who*, 1962–63; Rotha, *op. cit.*, p. 457. Muni was a Roosevelt New Dealer who liked to play humanitarian roles in the New Deal manner.

[21] *Ascap Biographical Dictionary.*

[22] Harris was brought to Newark as an infant. *International Celebrity Register*, N.Y. 1959, p. 325; *Who's Who*, 1962–63.

[23] Published N.Y. 1962. See also *Who's Who*, 1962–63 and *International Motion Picture Almanac*, 1960.

[24] G. Freedly and J. A. Reeves, *History of the Theater*, N.Y. 1955, p. 532. Kiesler is discussed elsewhere in this volume as an Austro-American architect.

[25] Bernard Sobel, *New Theater Handbook*, N.Y. 1959; Wittke, *We Who Built America*, p. 364; Herbert Graf, *The Opera*, N.Y. 1941, p. 151.

[26] Wilhelm Schlag, "A Survey of Austrian Emigration to the United States," *Österreich und die angelsächsische Welt*, Wien 1961, pp. 139–196; *American-German Review*, June 1950.

[27] *Wer ist Wer*, XIII.

[28] Schlag, *op. cit.; International Motion Picture Almanac*, 1960.

[29] *Who's Who in the Theater*, London 1957.

[30] Rotha, *op. cit.*, p. 587; *International Who's Who*, 1960, p. 525; Freedly and Reeves, *op. cit.*, pp. 500–530; *Bulletin*, German Press . . . Office, 15 May 1962, p. 6.

[31] *New York Times*, 25 Jan. 1956, p. 31; *Wer ist Wer*, Wien 1937.

[32] Freedley and Reeves, *op. cit.*, p. 644–46.

[33] Hughes, *op. cit.*, p. 460.

[34] *Wer ist Wer*, XIII.

[35] *Austrian Information*, Oct. 1961, and June 1965.

[36] *Who's Who of American Women*, 1958–59; Rotha, *op. cit.*, p. 475.

[37] *Newsweek* and *Time*, 1 Nov. 1948. She died in Kingston, N.Y., 21 Nov. 1948.

[38] *New Century Cyclopedia of Names.*

[39] Amy Porter, "Four Cinderellas," *Colliers*, 1 Feb. 1947; *Who's Who of American Women*, 2nd ed., 1961.

[40] *Who's Who*, 1962–63; *International Motion Picture Almanac*, 1957.

[41] *Theater World*, 1960–61, Philadelphia and N.Y. 1961, p. 230.

[42] *Ibid.*

[43] *Who's Who*, 1962–63; *Universal Jewish Encyclopedia*, N.Y. 1948; *Baker's Biographical Dictionary of Musicians*, p. 598.

[44] *Who's Who in Austria*, 1959–60; *Universal Jewish Encyclopedia.*

[45] *Austrian Information*, 31 March 1962; *Die Presse*, 25 March 1962. For Romy Schneider, well known on the American screen, see *Look*, 11 Sept. 1962, pp. 38ff.

[46] Paul Rotha, *op. cit.*, pp. 177, 292, 493.

[47] *International Motion Picture Almanac*, N.Y. 1957, p. 831. By 1960–61 the number of American films had been reduced to 110, compared with 214 in 1954, but American imports still led. *Austrian Information*, 15 Sept. 1961.

[48] *Who's Who*, 1952–53.

[49] See the *New Yorker* magazine "Portrait," 20 Oct. 1961, and *Current Biography*, June 1961.

[50] *Philadelphia Public Ledger*, 10 April 1962; *Time*, 19 Jan. 1962

[51] *International Celebrity Register*, U.S. ed. Jürgens is said to have received $ 150,000 in 1957 for his first American film.

[52] *Life*, 14 June 1963, p. 45.

[53] *Parade* magazine, 12 May 1963, p. 8.

[54] *International Motion Picture Almanac*, 1957.

[55] *Curriculum vitae* from the Austrian Institute, N.Y., 1964.

[56] Paul Rotha, *op. cit.*, pp. 710–15.

[57] *Die Presse*, Wien, 26 Nov. 1961, p. 7.

[58] J. Halas and R. Manwell, *Technique of Film Animation*, N.Y. 1959, pp. 14, 164, 335; *Universal Jewish Encyclopedia*, IV, p. 323.

[59] *Who's Who*, 1938–39; Lewis Jacobs, *Rise of the American Film*, N.Y. 1939, pp. 343ff. He came to America in 1909, was naturalized 1926. He was a Catholic.

[60] Jacobs, *op. cit.*, *passim;* Rotha, *op. cit.*, p. 433.

[61] *Who's Who*, 1962–63.

[62] Rotha, *op. cit.*, *passim; Parade* magazine, 3 Dec. 1961, p. 20; *New York Times Magazine*, 24 Jan. 1960, p. 30.

[63] *Washington Post*, 13 Sept. 1961, pp. C1 and C3, 26 Nov. 1961, p. G1; *Who's Who*, 1962–63.

[67] *Who's Who of American Women*, 2nd ed., 1961.

[65] *Who's Who*, 1962–63; *International Television Almanac 1961;* J. F. Fixx, "The Spiegel Touch," *Saturday Review*, 29 Dec. 1962, pp. 13–14. *Das kleine Lexikon des österr. Films*, Wien 1959, states that Spiegel was born in Vienna.

[66] See, e.g. the *New Yorker* sketch (5 May 1962, p. 35) of Amos Vogel (b. Vienna, 1921), founder of Cinema 16, America's largest private film society; *Who's Who*, 1962–63, for Erica Anderson (b. Vienna, 1914) who made documentary films on famous personalities and for Adolph Schimel, a New York lawyer long vice president of Universal Pictures. *The International Motion Picture Almanac*, 1957, lists others: Julia Arnall (b. Vienna, 1930) in advertising films; Nathan Jarau (b. Austria, 1907) who received an Academy Award for the art work in *How Green Was My Valley;* Arthur Kober (b. Austria-Hungary, 1900) the New York critic; Fritz Lang (b. Vienna, 1890) who directed *Liliom* and *Western Union;* Max Steiner (b. Vienna), music director and Academy Award winner; W. Lee Wilder; and numerous others including Lilli Palmer, the actress who denied she was Viennese and stated she had never even seen Vienna. Some of the Austrian-born notables in films appeared also in television and there were a few Austrians who devoted themselves entirely to TV, but they were apparently fewer and less prominent than the celebrities of the screen. Among the Vienna-born one could mention the scenario writer F. Hugh Herbert who wrote the *Meet Corless Archer* serials; Ernest D. Gluckman who wrote comedy shows for Colgate and Chevrolet; Fred Schiller the author of *Charlie Chan* and the Loretta Young Show; and the producer Max Liebman. None of these worked exclusively with television.

CHAPTER XXIII

THE PRESENT AND THE FUTURE

The year 1955 when America and her allies withdrew their occupation troops from Austria marked the end of an Austro-American era. The United States no longer had any special interest in Austria. Austria, well on its way to economic stability, no longer needed American aid. And Austria's people, as surprised as the rest of the world to find that they needed no help from anybody, no longer had to look to America as the land of escape and of opportunity. Most of the Austrian talent that had emigrated to America in the sad years remained here, but some few began to return to the homeland and those who came after 1955 came, not as refugees seeking any port in a storm, but as substantial immigrants and invited guests. They come now, not because they must, but because they have relatives and friends and colleagues here and because, as ever, cosmopolitan Austria is too small to offer satisfying opportunity to all of its gifted sons and daughters.

The census of 1960 indicated that America had over a million of Austrian stock. Of those more than 300,000 were foreign-born. And, true to form, well over half of them lived in America's largest metropolitan areas: nearly 100,000 in New York, 20,000 in Chicago, and over 12,000 in Los Angeles. There were still relatively few in the South (Florida led with nearly 8,000 and Texas had almost 3,000). New York State as always had the largest Austrian-born quota with some 107,000, Pennsylvania followed with nearly 37,000, and Illinois and California each had well over twenty thousand. In proportion to the German-born Americans of 1960 (989,815) the Census found the Austrian-born about equal in Missouri, less well represented in Wisconsin, and better represented in New York and Pennsylvania. The differences were, however, small enough to show some relationship between German and Austrian immigration goals. With the Swiss, who went first to California and only secondarily to New York, there was far less correlation than one might expect from two neighboring countries.

With an annual immigration quota of about 1400 – less than that of Switzerland and far less than that of Ireland and Czechoslovakia – Austria's emigrants will not in future years be able to make any quantitative impact upon the United States. And America will not be able to drain off any such impressive proportion of Austrian talent and man-power as she has attracted and profited by during recent decades. That may be fortunate, not only for Austria, but also for America. If the little republic can keep its talent at home, it may recover more quickly from the blight of the National Socialist years and regain much of its traditional creative spirit.

It has, indeed, been the American fashion to proclaim the decline of Austria and Vienna ever since the days of Charles Sealsfield. Austrian history has generally been approached by Americans in terms of the disintegration and fall of the old monarchy and the decadence of a once brilliant Vienna. No American in two hundred years has seen Vienna as anything but a city with a great past. We saw only regression there in the early years of the present century when we failed to understand its Freuds and its Mahlers, its Schönbergs and its Kafkas, its expressionism, its excitingly modern architects, and its sociological ventures that were then so un-American. We failed to realize that despite the old regime in the Hofburg, much was stirring in old Vienna that was to contribute to the new twentieth-century world. Culturally we lived in the orbit of Western Europe and were unwilling to look beyond it. The representatives in America of all the other former Austro-Hungarian nationalities have been unwilling to have us believe that Vienna was a focal point — cosmopolitan, without the usual taints of nationalism, and sophisticated — a strategic point in Central Europe of tremendous importance. Since 1919 we have been even more reluctant than before to admit the importance of the former *Kaiserstadt*. Politically it has, of course, lost the importance that it had for us in the age of Metternich. Culturally it has continued to breed men and women who have contributed generously to the life of the entire western world.

The thesis of the decadence of Vienna is as difficult to prove in the 1960's as it was in the century's early years. If, according to "Who's Who in America," there were more than twice as many distinguished Austrian-born Americans in the early 1950's as there were in the year of the *Anschluss*, and almost twice as many in the 1960's as there were ten years earlier, and if only four foreign lands, each of much greater population, have recently contributed more distinguished foreign-born to America's honor roll, the thesis of Austrian decadence will scarcely stand. And located as it is at a focal point in Central Europe, Vienna may well, with the relaxation of the Iron Curtain, regain its old prestige as a great cultural center. The Central Europe that was Balkanized in 1919 needs such a center now as desperately as it needed it in the days of the Habsburgs. The Czechs, Hungarians, Galicians, Croats, and Transylvanians, and even the Germans, made Vienna a cultural melting pot in those days, not because it was the capital of a properly centralized nationalistic state, which it was not, but because it was a charming, intelligent and cosmopolitan center which welcomed peoples of all nationalities. The new Vienna, located in an Austria of quiet, unobtrusive patriotism, may well maintain its old position as Central Europe's cultural melting pot.

If the young Austrian republic with its time-honored capital city can find such a strategic place in the heart of Europe, America will discover that its ties with the Austrian people will be as rewarding and as significant as they have been in the past. We may even discover that Austrians are not Germans, any more than Americans were Englishmen after 1776, but that they constitute a unique cultural crossroads in the modern world – as unique for Europe as America has been for the world at large. Such an Austria would be of importance to world-power America far out of proportion to her size.

INDEX OF PERSONS

H

N

O

P

T

U

V